Evolving Values for a Capitalist World

In most of the world today, the issue is not whether or how to embrace capitalism, but how to make the best of it. The currently dominant capitalist values include competitive individualism, instrumental rationality, and material success. The series will explore questions such as: Will these values suffice as a basis for social organizations that can meet human and environmental needs in the twenty-first century? What would it mean for capitalist systems to evolve toward an emphasis on other values, such as cooperation, altruism, responsibility, and concern for the future?

Titles in the series:

Neva R. Goodwin, Editor. *As if the Future Mattered: Translating Social and Economic Theory into Human Behavior*

As if the Future Mattered

As if the Future Mattered

Translating Social and Economic Theory into Human Behavior

Edited by Neva R. Goodwin

Ann Arbor

THE UNIVERSITY OF MICHIGAN PRESS

Copyright © by the University of Michigan 1996
All rights reserved
Published in the United States of America by
The University of Michigan Press
Manufactured in the United States of America
∞ Printed on acid-free paper

1999   1998   1997   1996   4   3   2   1

A CIP catalog record for this book is available from the British Library.

Library of Congress Cataloging-in-Publication Data

As if the future mattered : translating social and economic theory
   into human behavior / edited by Neva R. Goodwin.
        p.   cm. — (Evolving values for a capitalist world)
   Based on seminars held at Tufts University, spring semesters 1991
and 1992.
   Includes bibliographical references.
   ISBN 0-472-10640-6 (hardcover : alk. paper)
   1. Economics—Moral and ethical aspects.   2. Economics—
Environmental aspects.   3. Capitalism—United States.
4. Capitalism—Moral and ethical aspects.   5. Externalities
(Economics)   I. Goodwin, Neva R.   II. Series.
HB72.A769   1996
330—dc20   96-10247
                                                                      CIP

This book is dedicated to my parents, who have always acted as if the future matters

Series Introduction

Neva R. Goodwin

A capitalist system is but one way of organizing human societies; relative to other systems it is a newcomer that has not been around very long. Hunting and gathering, for example, was a socioeconomic system that is thought to have endured for about the first 99 percent of our species' occupation of this planet. Of the systems that have prevailed in the remaining recent 1 percent of human existence, various forms of feudalism, for example, have far longer histories than does capitalism.

For all that, capitalism appears to be on its way to world domination: its present trajectory (which inspired the article, "The End of History and the Last Man" by Francis Fukuyama)[1] is one that is commonly expected to make capitalism the organizing principle for all of human civilization by the early twenty-first century. Trend projections, of course, do not necessarily make accurate predictions. The new market economies of the former Soviet Union or huge parts of Asia (including China and Vietnam), the Muslim societies struggling to shape the forces of capitalism so as to enjoy its productivity without its values, the rural and poor urban communities all over the world that are experimenting with ways of bringing older, relationship-oriented ways of doing business into balance with the callous cash nexus of the market—any of these could significantly alter the trend of global capitalism.

However, global capitalism already exists. In the West, on whose experiences this series will focus, the issue is not whether or how to embrace capitalism, but how to make the best of it: how to carry the system forward in ways that build upon its strengths while shaping it to accommodate human needs and values within the realities of the physical and social contexts that define human well-being.

Capitalism, as a way of organizing production, exchange, and distribution, is most often regarded as an economic system. So it is; but because of

---

1. Francis Fukuyama. *The End of History:* New York, NY: The Free Press, 1992.

its effects on social relations and its implications for how social decisions get made (among other things), it is also a political and cultural system. And underlying the political, cultural, and economic aspects of capitalism there is also a system of values—one that appears to support individualism, instrumental rationality, and a materialist notion of success more than, for example, communitarianism, religious or spiritual idealism, or the less quantifiable, unmarketable aspects of human development.

This statement of capitalist values, while widely accepted, is a gross simplification. Also, it should not be read as a purely critical outline of "what's wrong in the world." The successes of capitalism, and the benefits conferred directly through its values as well as its material results, are ones that few people are ready to reject out of hand. The foregoing description of core capitalist values is intended to represent a set of tendencies that have accompanied the historical development of capitalism in the West during the roughly two centuries since it began on its path to world dominance. However, capitalism is no longer just a phenomenon of the Western world nor of the industrialism of the nineteenth or even the twentieth centuries. In the process of extending beyond the Anglo-European/North American cultures that nurtured its early phases, and in facing the new world of the twenty-first century, capitalism is experiencing challenges to its very nature. It has become possible—and, I believe, necessary—to ask: Is it inevitable that capitalism must give first place to the values of individualism, instrumental rationality, and a materialist notion of success? Is it possible that capitalism could be realigned to accommodate and/or support other values—even some that now appear irrelevant or antithetical to it?

Capitalism, as we now know it, both derives from and encourages certain values. Evolving Values for a Capitalist World will look at these in two aspects.

> The series will identify and examine values that are in vigorous force at this time, despite being tolerated only on the edges, as it were, of capitalist societies. It will pursue the possibility that the evolution of capitalism will continue in a more beneficial manner if some of these now peripheral values are brought into the foreground.
> The series will also consider the values that are now central to capitalism; the possibility will be discussed that some of these deserve to receive relatively *less* emphasis.

This examination will not be intended as a basis for attempting to do away with capitalism—to replace it with some wholly different system. Rather, the focus will be the need for continued efforts to mold the system to accommodate evolving human and ecological needs and possibilities. There is also an evolutionary pressure coming from the system's values themselves as they, too, change and evolve within their context, sometimes running out ahead of the rest of the system so as to cause, for a while, an uneasy fit.

By the word values, I mean, most generally the answer that people give when they ask themselves, "What matters?" An anthropologist responded to the question "What values are general to all human beings?" by saying that all people, whatever their culture and degree of material wealth, place high value on "secure survival; comfort; honor; fairness; and amusement." [2] (By honor he meant how an individual is regarded by others—the basis for his or her relationships with other people.) This list could be argued over; for example, should other aspects of relationships, such as love, be given equal place with honor? or, what about spiritual urges or self-development? Nevertheless, when we think about values it is useful to start with some such concept of what may be universal in human nature.

We may note that the values mentioned earlier as especially associated with capitalism—individualism, instrumental rationality, and a materialist conception of success—are not perfectly coincident with the suggested list of universal human values. The two lists can be made partially congruent by noting that instrumental rationality and materialism both support the amassing of wealth (in its broadest sense) and that wealth can, in turn, be vitally important to permit survival, comfort, and amusement. However, this congruence only underscores the fact that the values popularly associated with capitalism are best understood as only intermediate goals—that is, they are *means* to the *ends* represented by the more fundamental human values. If these means were found to conflict with some critical aspects of the desired ends (for example, if they endangered the health of the earth's ecosystem upon which our species' survival depends), or if there were a popular belief that other means would bring us more directly or reliably to the desired ends, then there would be strong pressure for the means, not the ends, to give way.

As examples, I will mention two of the criticisms that have already been most frequently laid against capitalism as a system of means for supporting basic human values.

First, the use of material wealth as a support for honor has come

---

2. Allan Hoben, at a conference on Reconceptualizing Development in the Context of Sustainability, sponsored by the Global Development And Environment Institute at Tufts University (November 1994); and in subsequent personal communication.

into question, as the work of Fred Hirsch, for example, has made it evident that invidious comparisons and keeping-up-with-the-Joneses are zero-sum games. That is to say, when an individual's honor (or, to use less anthropological terms, his or her sense of success or self-worth) is based on the possession of more than average material possessions, it is not possible for a whole society to feel successful or to enjoy "honor." Such satisfaction is by definition attainable only for the relatively more well-off and is achieved at the expense of the relatively less well-off (whatever the actual level of security or comfort enjoyed by the latter).

Second, in the capitalist economist's equity/efficiency trade-off it appears that fairness for all has lost out to materialist success for some. However, to understand this matter properly it is necessary to be careful about how we understand the terms we are using. "Fairness" is not synonymous with "equity." The latter is an objective judgment that can be imposed upon a society from outside, to consider whether the underlying structure of the society distributes resources, rewards, and costs in an excessively uneven manner. The "fairness" criterion more or less takes cultural norms as given and then (from within the culture) judges whether or not the norms are being observed. Thus, as Milton Friedman points out, people in the United States are often willing to accept large *actual* inequalities in wealth and income as long as they believe that everyone could, *potentially*, do as well as the lucky ones.[3] With this said, however, the well-known tendency of capitalist systems to foster unequal wealth and income continues to receive criticisms from the relatively populist "fairness" perspective as well as on the basis of more abstract notions of equity.

Within the framework of the rather general terms just set out, this series will identify some more pointed (though still abstract) issues that require reconsideration in the context of the evolution of capitalist societies. These include: trust, responsibility, altruism, achievement, rationality (by what definition?), modern concepts of science, a nexus of values including "belongingness" and status (the latter perhaps to be seen as one category of honor) that have become closely linked to consumerism, and another group of values (including "environmentalism" and "future-regardingness") that are increasingly aligned with an anticonsumerist ethic. All of these are themes that will weave through all of the books in the series Evolving Values for a Capitalist World. They are revealed along a spectrum extending from theory to application—from a concern

---

3. In Milton Friedman, *Free To Choose; A Personal Statement* (New York: Harcourt, Brace, Jovanovich, 1980).

with the values shaping, and shaped by, academic disciplines, to a concern with how values influence, and are influenced by, actions taken by individuals, groups, and institutions.

Each of the books in the series will have its distinct focus, but each will relate closely to all the others. Thus, this first volume explores the ways that values relating to the future manage to be preserved and nurtured in spite of contemporary capitalism's many pushes and pulls toward shortsighted selfishness. This focus repeatedly broadens to take account of the tensions between altruism and self-preservation, needs and wants, and individual and society that have marked recent debates among ecologists and sociobiologists, economists and practical business-people, bureaucrats and statesmen.

The second volume will take consumerism and anticonsumerism as its main themes. Upon these are hung again, in new ways, the issues of honor, rationality, success, and so on that force us to probe the direction in which capitalism is going and to ask: how closely can, or should, the future resemble the past and who will participate in defining the differences?

Volume 3 will focus on the group of social sciences—called, here, the neoclassical social sciences—which have most directly evolved out of the existing capitalist value-system as characterized above in the trinity of individualism, rationality, and materialism. The intellectual forces that play their part in shaping values are not, however, confined to the classroom. A society's dominant intellectual regime establishes probabilities, if not possibilities, in what is believed, talked about, accepted as goals, and acted upon. We are living through an interesting historical moment in which postmodernism has been pushed forward by some as the dominant intellectual regime for the foreseeable future. Volume 3 will propose that the same motive forces that are championing postmodernism could also become the basis for a more constructive alternative, both within the social sciences and in society at large. It is only by taking capitalism as the context that these possibilities can be perceived, evaluated, and—it is hoped—acted upon.

The projected fourth volume will focus upon how values are learned (an issue that differs importantly from how values are taught). How the future is to be shaped depends upon who is to shape it: that, in turn, depends upon the process of value learning. This process is only of interest in a context in which the need for new, or newly configured, values has been defined. In this series, it is defined in terms of the ways that capitalism is related to human welfare and ecological health. Questions to be addressed in Volume 4 include: Can values be generated teleologically, in response to the need of the times? Is there any way of shortening the time lag between the emergence of a need and the emergence of an appropriate value-response?

Finally, there is the question that must be considered in light of this series, but will not be directly addressed in it: How differently would a capitalist economic system actually operate if it were to be aligned with a somewhat altered value-system? A focused analysis of this question will have to await other work.[4] However, it is hoped that this critically important issue will receive illumination from many angles as this series reflects upon the values associated with capitalism that are due for a new emphasis.

---

4. This question is being taken up by the editor of this series in other work, more directly within the discipline of economics, which she is supervising through the Global Development and Environment Institute at Tufts University. This includes a series of basic economics textbooks for new market economies, such as the Newly Independent States and China (by Neva Goodwin, Thomas Weisskopf and Kelvin Lancaster); a U.S. textbook on *The Economic System and the Environment* (by Jonathan Harris); and a series of surveys of subfields on the "frontiers" of economics (series editor Neva Goodwin; vol. 1, *A Survey of Ecological Economics*, was published in October 1995; Vol. 2, *The Consumer Society*, is in process).

Preface

The study on which this book is based was sponsored by the Program for the Study of Sustainable Change and Development (SCD) in the Global Development And Environment Institute at Tufts University. SCD is an interdisciplinary program linking economics to the adjacent social sciences and founded on the premise that there is a need for new, more real-world–oriented approaches to social science theory and application, especially in economics, to address the tensions between *present and future, individual and social*, and *local and global* needs and goals.

Work on the project of this book was advanced by a series of faculty seminars on the Tufts campus in the spring semesters of 1991 and 1992. Most of the essays commissioned for the study were first presented in the seminars, where they were discussed and debated by an interdisciplinary group including both academics and environmental activists from the greater Boston area.

Four of the essays in the book—those by George M. Newcombe, David Dapice, Franklin Tugwell, and Zbigniew Bochniarz—treat issues that fall squarely within the area defined as "environmentalism." In fact, the logical convergence of *future-regardingness* and *environmentalism* is so strong that the whole book could have become a contribution to the environmental literature exclusively. However, we resisted going in that direction because there are a number of topics not uniquely associated with environmentalism (investment is an outstanding example) that are of great importance for the future of every aspect of human experience, including, but not limited to, our interactions with the natural world.

It seemed particularly important to investigate areas of future-regardingness that are not commonly addressed by environmentalists because there are times when people with social concerns find themselves in opposition to the environmentalists. This is especially true when protection of nature seems to conflict with the needs of the more vulnerable members of human societies. While the champions of the poor and the champions of the environment have sometimes been involved in similar attempts to resist the powerful forces driving, and benefiting from, shortsighted economic development, only recently has this common threat resulted in a common cause. The integration of these interests is emerging as a goal of the 1990s. It can be called *socially and environmentally just and sustainable development*.

That phrase contains within it all of the elements that will be related, in this volume, to the issue of future-regarding behavior. Development, of course, is a future-oriented concept: it is about taking actions *now* that are intended to result in improved circumstances *later*. One reason it has been necessary to attach so many modifiers to the word is that many activities initially proclaimed as development successes have turned out to be only short-term achievements. Another reason is that there have been numerous examples of development that have improved the lot of the people who possess political and economic power at the expense of those without such power.

The leading voices of protest against development-for-the-powerful used to be the advocates for the poor and disenfranchised. Certainly these voices were not entirely futile. However, their recent alignment with those who press to make development environmentally sustainable may have the fortunate effect of causing several groups to recognize some shared goals. As we project our concerns further into the future, the concepts of social and economic health become increasingly relevant to the powerful groups that are most likely to benefit from development— as well as to the human and natural elements that are immediately hurt by social and environmental injustice and unsustainability.

In recognition of the diverse issues that need to be addressed if we are to achieve the recently formulated goal of socially and environmentally just and sustainable development, the papers chosen for this volume represent the experience of individuals from an unusually wide range of intellectual traditions. A significant limitation is that all come from within the industrialized North. This limitation was accepted on the belief that the experiences and traditions of other parts of the world regarding the subject of this book might be sufficiently different that it would be too difficult to represent them in a single volume. A companion volume, initiated from the South, would be most welcome.

Concern for the future, cooperation, justice—these subjects lie at the intersection of many streams of thought, including theories of economics and of ethics as well as the interdisciplinary approaches being pioneered under the heading, "environmental studies." In the past, this messy intersection has often been abandoned by the social science disciplines and left to be worked out in the political process. That is not entirely bad; in many cases moral issues may be better understood or resolved through living them than through discussing them. However, reflection and analysis also have their place. It would be a sad retreat if the social sciences were to conclude that they had nothing to contribute to matters with a significant moral component.

Thus, one of the underlying concerns of this book is to locate the areas in society—including in the academic disciplines—where we might find sources of intellectual leadership to contribute solutions to the problem of shortsightedness. It is therefore appropriate, in the rest of this preface, to give the reader an idea of the disciplinary or other traditions that are closest to each of the contributors to the book, keeping in mind that each of them has crossed disciplinary boundaries at least as much as he or she has depended upon them. It will be evident that the contributions were selected in such a way as to present a mix of theoretical speculation with descriptions of actual behaviors and institutions.

The topic of part 1, "Investment as a Link between Present and Future," assumes that no one who is without concern for the future will bother to make investments. The salient questions here are: to what extent, and under what circumstances, do investment activities tend to bring individual and societal interests into consonance and which institutional frameworks encourage or inhibit the longer-range and/or more socially beneficial types of investment? These questions are addressed in part 1 in essays by the following individuals.

1. Michael E. Porter, a professor at the Harvard Business School, was the coordinator of the school's massive Time Horizons Study (presented to the U.S. Senate Banking Committee in June of 1992). He contributes an exceptionally detailed understanding of the institutional environment that has developed in relation to capital investment in the United States.

2. Neva R. Goodwin, an economist by training, is co-director of the Global Development And Environment Institute at Tufts University. A theorist who is especially concerned with the development of the social sciences in general and economics in particular, in this paper she uses the work of such business observers as Michael Porter as the basis for examining the intersection of ethics and economics, especially in capital markets.

3. Fred Block is an economic sociologist who currently chairs the sociology department of the University of California at Davis. He has written extensively on the measurement of savings in the United States. His book *Postindustrial Possibilities: A Critique of Economic Discourse* (Berkeley: University of California Press, 1990) explores problems of economic measurement and economic argument.

4. George M. Newcombe is a member of the New York law firm Simpson Thacher and Bartlett. He specializes in advising clients and arguing cases where the focus is on the environmental liability of corporations, especially banks.

5. David Seckler is Director General, International Irrigation Management Institute, Colombo, Sri Lanka. A development economist, he views investment broadly as an essential contributory factor to development.

Part 2: "Political and Activist Approaches to the Subject." While the essays in this section are oriented more toward the experience of practitioners, this section begins (as part 1 ended) with relatively theoretical papers.

6. David Dapice is a professor in the Tufts University Economics Department, Faculty Associate at the Harvard Institute for International Development, and a member of the United Nations ACC/Subcommittee on Nutrition.

7. Robert L. Paarlberg is a political scientist with appointments at Wellesley College and at the Harvard Center for International Affairs.

8. Alisa Gravitz is the executive director of Co-op America, a Washington, D.C.-based organization that publishes a magazine (the *Co-op America Quarterly*) and engages in other activities to give support to socially responsible businesses. She describes herself as an entrepreneur.

9. Franklin Tugwell is now president of the Heinz Trusts. He wrote the paper for this volume in his former position as president of the Environmental Enterprises Assistance Fund, an experimental nonprofit organization working to initiate and build commercially viable and environmentally responsible renewable energy companies in developing countries. A political scientist by training, for nearly two decades he has worked on problems of energy policy in developing countries.

10. Zbigniew Bochniarz, environmental activist, economist and policymaker, is a founding member of such catalytic institutions in Central and Eastern Europe as the Institute for Sustainable Development in Warsaw and the Institute for Environmental Policy in Prague. He is a senior fellow and visiting professor at the Hubert H. Humphrey Institute of Public Affairs, University of Minnesota, where he has directed studies for Poland, Czechoslovakia, Hungary, and Bulgaria. Each study has resulted in a

document to serve as a "blueprint" for that country's development of legal and other institutions as they move to redesign their political and economic systems in the wake of the end of the communist regime in Central and Eastern Europe.

11. Robert S. McNamara is a policymaker with a long record of service in the public and private sectors. His undergraduate degree was in economics and his graduate study was in business management. Among the positions he has held, that which is most relevant to the spirit of his essay on how the United States needs to realign its priorities to move toward a better world was his tenure as president of the World Bank (1968–81).

12. In her conclusion to this volume, Neva R. Goodwin discusses some of the social science assumptions that underlie both economics and political science in their modern disciplinary forms. She then imagines an optimistic scenario for the future, one in which there is increased concern for the impact of present acts upon others who may be distant from the actor in time, space, class, and culture or group identity. The essay speculates on the necessary and sufficient conditions under which such a scenario may emerge.

Acknowledgments

This volume would not have been possible without the generous, patient, and imaginative funding that was provided through an anonymous gift. Because we do not know whom, in particular, to thank, it seems all the more appropriate to recognize here the critical role of the third sector (including what are variously called nonprofits, nongovernmental organizations, private voluntary organizations, philanthropy, charity, etc.). There, outside of the strictures of government or the profit motive of business, resources are applied to promote activities intended, in one way or another, to make the world a better place. Government (as the representative of society) and business (which is involved over time in investment, credit, etc.) each has a stake in the future. But we often see these "first" and "second" sectors acting as though they had eyes only for the immediate present. The third sector is, among other things, our insurance that the long-run concerns of the world we live in will be remembered.

At critical points in the writing of this volume, Paul P. Streeten has provided wise, pointed, and extraordinarily helpful commentary and advice. His name is associated with a number of direct quotations; his spirit imbues much more than those.

Most of the essays included here were presented at seminars at Tufts. I thank the university for its support and am grateful to the many participants in the seminars whose thoughtful comments and discussions, during the formal meetings and over dinners afterward, are reflected in the papers.

Jessica Tobin Pisano, as research assistant for the final assembly of the volume, has worked with intelligence and diligence. The final preparation of the manuscript has required much attention to fine details of editing and reference verification. I am grateful to Nandana Mewanda, Christine Bishop, and especially to Leigh Stoecker for their painstaking work on this task.

Contents

Introduction

Neva R. Goodwin

We're All Living in Someone's Long Run

"In the long run we're all dead." That undeniably true remark, made by
John Maynard Keynes in his *Tract on Monetary Reform,* has been
quoted in support of many a shortsighted policy. Some additional points,
however, are needed to put Keynes's truism in perspective. If you and I,
for example, look at 100 years as our long run, it is very likely that
within that time span we *will* be dead, but (we assume) not everyone will
be. In our great-grandparents' "long run," they have died, but we are
still alive. In fact, we are all living in *someone's* long run.

We are urged into greater awareness of our own impacts upon the
future as we experience the long-run effects of those who came before
us. We are the beneficiaries of the eras of railroad and road building and
of investments in communications infrastructures and in science and
technology. Most of us who think about this are grateful for these inheri-
tances. Recently, however, our attention has shifted to a more ominous
kind of inheritance, epitomized by deteriorated public infrastructure
and a degraded natural resource base. Moreover, there is growing concern that efforts to rectify such past failures in future-regardingness are
being hamstrung by mounting national and international debts.

One way of looking at all this is in the economic terms of "externalities." Actions taken in the present with rewards to be reaped in the
future have "positive future externalities." "Negative future externalities" are created when we gain in the present by deferring costs to
the future. Wilfred Beckerman (1992) has argued that the size of positive future externalities so hugely outweighs the negative ones that the
latter should be ignored. If all human activities were still taking place in
the nineteenth-century context of a population of one billion, this argument would be more persuasive. As the world population grows, however, the effects of the negative future externalities seem to multiply
faster than the positive ones.

We may not think of the United States, with its current low (near replacement) birthrate as suffering from a population boom, but it is worth remembering that the circumstances under which we are now attempting to govern our society are markedly different, in quantity as well as quality, from those under which our political and economic systems were initially formed. In fact, since 1776 the U.S. population has grown approximately fiftyfold, so that the average state population now is approximately equal to the total number of U.S. citizens at the time of the nation's founding. While this may create institutional stresses, our natural resource endowment is so extensive that (except for a sense of crowding in cities and loss of private space even in the most rural areas) population growth in the United States has not yet created natural resource disasters with obviously severe consequences for human beings. Other parts of the world have not been so fortunate.

In the United States, the negative externalities that our generation leaves to the future (the costs generated by present actions that will be paid for in the future) include an increasing cadre of people who are growing up with inadequate care and education, crack babies and other disadvantaged infants, and a snowballing prison population. They include systems like social security and medical insurance that appear to be headed for collapse. They include polluted industrial and military sites whose consequences embrace a buildup of nuclear wastes that will require many generations of surveillance as well as chemicals whose long-term (estrogenic and other) effects on animals, including humans, are only beginning to be known. They include declining crop acreage, declining soil fertility, and a growing shortage of clean water for farm, household, and industrial uses. They include an irreversible decrease in biodiversity.

The positive externalities (benefits sown by the present generation that will spill over to the future) include new developments in communications such as computers, the Internet, and cable television. They include significant advances in biotechnology and medicine. They include a wealth of new knowledge and understanding coming out of scholarship in the natural and human sciences. They include movements, such as civil rights, environmentalism, and feminism, that aim to mitigate or roll back long traditions of abuse of power. While relative imbalances in power are nothing new, allowing some people to abuse or parasitically prey on others, there are reasons to hope (as will be argued in the conclusion to this volume) that we in the United States and in many other parts of the world are experiencing cumulative increases in awareness, empathy, and political protection for the weak that may constitute one of our most important gifts to the future.

Optimistic hopes such as these relate to the issue of relative power among individual human beings. A different issue is the absolute power of the human species to exert control over its total environment (including not only the social context but also the built world and the natural environment). As our control grows, so does our power to do harm—whether through weapons intended for mass destruction or through the side effects of production and consumption. Looking at this century through Plato's polarities of control versus chaos, it has seemed, up until now, that control—enabling us to do what we want and intend (without asking the deeper question of whether what we want and intend is good for us)—has at least kept up with chaos, with the negative, unintended side effects. The paradigm for this success is the green revolution, which has so far warded off the mass starvation that was predicted to accompany the several population doublings of this century.

Increasingly, however, the neck-and-neck race between control and chaos is posing some fundamental questions. Are there absolute limits to the potential reach of human power—for example, limits that will be imposed by the second law of thermodynamics, or by the absorptive capacity of the ecosystem, or by something inherent in human nature or the dynamics of human societies? Or do we, as affirmed by Herman Kahn and other technological optimists, face a world in which there are no limits to what human ingenuity can achieve? Along these lines, the development economist and philosopher of development Paul Streeten (in correspondence about the subject of this book) has posed some of the questions that lie at the heart of what it means to act "as if the future mattered."

> Since there will be (uncertain) technical progress (e.g., in discovering substitutes for exhaustible resources), how much reliance can be placed on it? Since future preferences will be different from ours, what do we have to do to provide the same opportunities? Since there is a lot of present deprivation, how do we deal with this if there are conflicts between removing it and removing future deprivation? Can the consumption and life styles of the now rich countries be preserved, while promoting both current and future social justice?[1]

These questions are in the background, but not the foreground, of this book. They are the concerns that we have to grapple with if we do accept that *the future matters*. The premise of this book is, of course, that

---

1. Paul P. Streeten, personal communication, July 1994.

the future does matter to us, both individually and collectively. It matters for reasons both moral (morality begins with the belief that others matter, whether they are separated from us in time or in space) and evolutionary (no species would long survive that did not act as though it had concern for its continuance). However, in between the assumption that the future matters and the effort to answer questions such as those (on what to do about our concern) that are posed by Streeten, there are two, somewhat subtler issues.

1. Is it desirable to work to enhance individual and social awareness of the future? This would include making people more aware of how present actions affect the future (the positive and negative future externalities we are creating) as well as, perhaps, emphasizing the importance of acting with this awareness.
2. If we believe that the answer to question 1 is affirmative, do we know of any means for achieving this? What institutional or other mechanisms are available to make future-regarding behavior easier or more likely?

As editor of this volume, I took for granted the affirmative answer to question 1 and addressed most of my attention to question 2. It turned out to be harder than I had expected to clarify how it is that we translate social and economic theory into human behavior around the idea that the future matters.

Some of the proposals put forth in this book attempt concrete answers to questions such as Streeten's. Others attempt, at a more abstract level, to relate social science theory to the core questions of the volume: *how concern for the future can be expressed and encouraged.* Our goal has been to use a mixture of practical experience and theoretical considerations to tease out the underlying issues, if not for immediate resolution then at least to clarify what those issues are and what questions we should be asking about them.

Private Rationality and Group Interests in the Context of Capitalism

Of particular interest for this book is the search for intellectual frameworks that can assist individuals to transcend the conflict between short-term, individual self-interest and broader, long-term societal welfare. There have been, of course, many attempts to design such frameworks. Intellectual history includes a variety of proposals for attaining a harmony of interests—from Hobbes's belief that a monarch who owned all the nation's property could represent all the nation's interests to Durkheim's concept of "organic solidarity" (wherein differences among people are seen as the source of interdependence) to utopian visions in which, through appropriate education, individuals simply shift the locus of their concern from self to some larger community. I do not dismiss the last of these—the utopian visions—as irrelevant. Quite the contrary, as an economist who had it dinned into my head in graduate school that "rationality is the maximization of perceived self-interest," I have frequently observed that the meaning of that statement depends upon how the *self* is defined: does it end at the skin or does it include family, peer group, community, nation, the human race, all living things, or even the whole of the biosphere?

The cynic asking "What has the future done for me?" assumes that the answer is "Nothing" and that a rational person will therefore have no interest in the future. In fact, however, people do not always behave on the basis of shortsighted self-interest. Human history is full of examples of behavior that can be characterized as "future-regarding." People save money and tend land or other property with an eye to leaving their heirs in as good a situation as possible. Field commanders dying in battle use their last breath to specify who should take the command, and how they should carry on. People work and sacrifice to create impersonal institutions that will embody their ideals and will outlive them. It is part of human nature to derive something important—a sense of meaning—from ideas (be they as concrete as family or as abstract as democracy) that are larger, in time as well as in space, than the narrowly defined, skin-bound self.

Such relatively altruistic motivations are a critical part of what makes any society possible. Capitalist societies may be somewhat less dependent upon noncommercial motives than were their Cold War opponents. But capitalism cannot survive in a healthy fashion—perhaps not at all—if it succeeds in creating the world that is described in neoclassical economic theory, that is, a world run only on pure principles of rational maximizing.

A number of the essays in this book discuss ideas for improving upon the socioeconomic system of capitalism, especially as it is manifested in the United States of America. American business is important not only for what it does—the goods and services it produces and the financial power it wields in the world—but also for what it represents. American business is widely considered to demonstrate the superiority of a particular form of capitalism, which is commonly identified with the name of Adam Smith but which, today, is defined, described, and justified by Smith's modern heirs, the neoclassical economists. However, there are growing problems in that system that may be traced to what must be regarded as the core of any cultural, political, and economic system: that is, the definitions of success that it holds out for individuals.

The existing ways for an individual to achieve what our society defines as personal success often conflict with what is good for society. Thus, we have industries exercising their legal right to profit by addicting children to nicotine, oversweetened foods, or TV and movie images of violence and debauchery; by encouraging the sale of guns to urban teenagers; by overgrazing fragile lands; or by siting polluting factories in the midst of minority communities. Where the captains of these industries are successful in the way that capitalism defines success—by amassing riches—they also receive the social rewards of acceptance and admiration. At the same time, as we live in yesterday's future, we experience the long-run effects of the assumption that all economic behavior is based on a self-interest whose definition was, by default, understood to be relatively narrow and short term.

Can the structure of incentives, on the micro level, be changed to resolve this conflict? If such a resolution is not feasible (or perhaps as a necessary complement to it) it may be that a deeper cultural shift is required: one that would redefine individual success.

It may be useful to consider a macro framework within which some options for socioeconomic organization can be related to conflicts of interest and the ways they are resolved. In his 1977 book *Politics and Markets,* Charles Lindblom describes how two socioeconomic systems—polarized as capitalism and communism—have presented the twentieth century's dominant answers to the question of how societies should manage conflicts of interest. He proposes two models as modal "visions of how society might be organized to benefit 'the people,' " saying:

> The key difference between the two visions . . . is in the role of intellect in social organization. Model 1 might be called an intellectually guided society. It derives from a buoyant or optimistic view of man's intellectual capacities. On a more pessimistic view of man's intellectual capacities, Model 2 postulates other forms of guidance for society. . . .
> Model 1 assumes a match between intellectual capacity and the complexity of the social world. Model 2 argues that there is a gross mismatch. (Lindblom 1977, 248–49)

Describing communist societies as of the Model 1 type, Lindblom says they are motivated by the belief that human beings can assemble enough information, and use scientific inquiry and theory to analyze it wisely enough, so that all human problems can be solved through correct application of correct principles. Communist systems deal with the issue of conflict of interest by assuming an underlying harmony such that "Given a correct economic policy, in a socialist society there are, and can be, no groups of workers whose material interest lie in contradiction to the objectively necessary planned management of the economy"[2]

Capitalism, by contrast, is based essentially upon an assumption of conflict and a mistrust of motives. Lindblom sees institutions in capitalist democracies as exemplifying the Model 2 skepticism that conscious planning can bring about acceptable social organization and notes how such systems focus upon consumer demand as an *impersonal* mechanism to substitute for *intentional* planning. The consumer "participates in an interaction that solves the problem of resource allocation as a by-product or epiphenomenon of his own private problem solving" (257).

Lindblom also remarks that, though modern capitalist democracy may be described as belonging to his relatively pessimistic Model 2 category, it can look to an historical tradition that in the eighteenth century, was more compatible with Model 1. Going back to that time when rationalism was expected to find a way to harmonize interests, we find, in the writings of Adam Smith, one of the most ingenious of all attempts to discover, if not a convergence of interests, then at least a benign convergence of the *results* of divergent interests. While allowing the butcher, the brewer, and the baker to retain selfish interests that were not assumed to be the same as those of the reader of *The Wealth of Nations,* Smith brilliantly proposed that there was an inhuman mechanism (given an almost deistic personification in the famous phrase "the invisible hand") that would serve, through the market forces of supply and demand, to combine the results of individually selfish decisions into a socially optimal outcome.

The degree of trust assumed by communists has often not been merited by those who made their society's decisions. Not only were they unable to live up to such an optimistic view of human intellectual capacities, they have also been widely revealed as having failed in their responsibility to put the public interest over private gain. However, when we contemplate the widespread failure of Model 1, we must also note some signs of degenerative failure in a market-oriented polyarchy such as the United States of America. The hope that impersonal interaction could wholly take the place of such ethical elements as responsibility or future-regardingness has not been well borne out.

---

2. From a publication of the planning commission in the USSR, quoted in Lindblom 1977, 251.

Free Riders and Suckers, Cooperators and Leaders

Lindblom's suggestion that the system of capitalism is based upon cultural norms that include a relatively pessimistic view of human nature has been reemphasized by the ways in which modern social sciences have employed evolutionary theory to "prove" that the neoclassical rationality postulate must be correct. The postulate of self-interested behavior has also been backed up by the observation that such behavior constitutes a "winning strategy"—one that can dominate any other with which it comes into contact—in spite of examples from cultures that suggest that capitalism may also be compatible with more cooperative behavior.

In the geopolitics of the end of the twentieth century, it has appeared that the pessimistic view of human nature will prevail, carried as it is by the group that has the winning strategy. This view, and its implications, has been explored by Paul Streeten writing as a development economist about the problems of getting nations to work together for the *common* good. Streeten's framework can also be applied to the problems of getting nations (or individuals or groups of any kind) to contribute their efforts for the sake of the *future* good. He comments on how individual nations might be expected to view a suggestion that they contribute toward the resolution of some problem that cannot be solved by any nation alone but where neither the participation nor the abstention of any one nation seems critical. Such situations are familiar on the individual level; voting is an example. They are becoming increasingly common on the global level as well in, for example, actions to prevent global warming. He suggests that we can expect nations to rank their preference in the following way:

1. My country does not contribute while others do. (Free rider)
2. My country contributes together with others. (Cooperation)
3. No country contributes. (Prisoner's dilemma outcome)
4. My country contributes while no other country does. (Sucker)

(Streeten 1991, 126)

This sequence points up a dilemma: the individually rational hope of free riding and the fear of being a "sucker" deter the achievement of the jointly most desirable outcome, cooperation. Each actor fears taking the cooperative step for fear of looking around and finding that it is the only one to have done so.

Behaviors that give rise to this dilemma are "rational" as that term has been defined and refined by the neoclassical social sciences, led by economics. Calling such behavior rational does not mean that it leads to desirable outcomes; it simply means that it is behavior in which each actor tries to maximize its own perceived self-interest. In fact, Streeten's list is intended to emphasize that such "rational" behavior does *not* always lead to optimum outcomes. Insofar as the self and its interests are defined narrowly, on a short-term, selfish basis, neoclassical rationalism will lead to universal efforts to find ways to "free ride," while getting others to be the "suckers" who contribute to the common or future weal. The outcome of such a situation must be the one predicted in the story of the "prisoner's dilemma": in the end everyone avoids the role of sucker, no one cooperates, and all are worse off than they would have been if they had possessed both the responsibility to pursue a mutually beneficial course and the trust to believe that others would also behave responsibly.

How can we improve on the outcomes implied in Streeten's list? It is interesting to consider Denmark, which has gone further than any other industrialized country to reduce the emissions that contribute to global warming by taking the hard steps necessary to decrease energy use, and so on. Clearly, its sacrifices will be meaningless in the global warming context if most other countries do not follow suit. There is something to be learned from inquiring why Denmark might be willing to risk being a "sucker." In discussions with Danish colleagues on this interesting point, it became clear that we need two more categories beyond Streeten's four.

The category of *Innovator* emerged in a discussion of the specific actions Denmark has taken to promote windmills. Programs of tax and other incentives have resulted in an industry that satisfies a small percentage of the domestic energy requirement but that has also created the incentive to research and develop the technology to the point where it has become an important export. Here, Danes do not necessarily see themselves as making a sacrifice. In leading the way to a better way of living, they expect to benefit not only from moving to that better way but also from the use and export of the technology they will develop for getting there.

Another category is that of *Leader*. Political debate in Denmark in the early 1990s included the premise that we don't really know what will be involved in changing to a lifestyle that significantly reduces emissions of greenhouse gases, and we won't know until someone tries it out. Denmark is operating on the premise that, although that small country alone cannot make a significant difference in the global climate, it can hope to improve the future for all parts of the world, including itself, if its example as a leader affects actions taken elsewhere.

The issue of leadership may be even more salient at the individual than at the national level. There is a good deal of evidence that many individuals who are ready and willing to make changes in their lifestyle to accommodate environmental needs are, in fact, inhibited by precisely the fear of being suckered that Streeten cites (cf. Thörgersen). Many such people are waiting for a leader who will say "these changes are needed—let us all move together." They know that not everyone will respond to such an exhortation but are willing to trust that enough will so that the individual's efforts will not be wasted—they will be a part of a movement.

The sense of being part of a movement is one of the things that can encourage and allow people to make individual changes that, in aggregate, add up to a cultural shift. This loop may appear difficult to break into. A cultural shift could be the cause of such a movement, but first people have to feel that there is a movement to be part of, and how is that to happen? Historians debate the influence of leaders. This may be a case where leaders can have an especially significant impact (cf. Bochniarz, this volume, chap. 10).

Even given the selfish attitude that Streeten assumed the nations would take, it seems likely that many would put the role of innovator high among their preferences—perhaps at the top of the list. And the role of leader will appeal to some, too, because in a world whose complexities of interdependence threaten to make all feel powerless, the role of leader suggests a possible way of affecting one's destiny.

"What has the future done for me?" asks the cynic. In fact, that is not an answerless question. One of the things we can be given by the future is a sense of meaning and purpose in our lives. Not all individuals or groups have the imagination to be innovators or the confidence to be leaders. However, most dislike feeling powerless in a world seemingly hurtling toward catastrophe. Moreover, while most people would shrink from looking foolish or being a sucker who has sacrificed self-interest for something that others don't choose to support, it is not necessarily built into human nature to prefer the role of free rider—the one who contributes nothing. Given leaders who point the way, those who cannot themselves contribute leadership may care enough for meaning, participation, and self-respect that they will join in a movement that renews cultural habits of concern for the common and future good.

The Role of the Social Sciences

What can the social sciences—especially social and economic theory—contribute to such a cultural shift? First, as shown in this collection in, for example, the essays by Seckler, Dapice, and Paarlberg, the social sciences can contribute to the theoretical context within which we understand definitions of progress, of development, of what it is that we want from the future.

Second, it is inevitable that social science theory will emphasize certain aspects of human nature, for example, through particular definitions of "rationality" or "utility" or "development." In choosing what to emphasize, the social sciences can inadvertently undermine the social structures that contribute to responsible, trustworthy, or future-regarding behavior. This possibility (realized at present in some ways within the neoclassical social sciences) and what might be done to mitigate against it, are explored in my essay (chap. 11) and the conclusion to this volume. This will also be the subject of volume 3 in the series Evolving Values for a Capitalist World.

As shown in the essays of Porter, Block, and Newcombe (as well as others in this collection), the social sciences have an important role to play in providing understanding of the institutional contexts that may actively support or discourage practical expression of concern for the future. An especially salient area for consideration of such institutional contexts is in relation to investment, one of the most obvious and important links between present and future.

Third, building upon the theoretical support and the understanding of institutions that the social sciences can provide, these same sciences can also go further to help create a vision of what is possible and what is desirable. As we will see, for example, in the essays of Tugwell, Gravitz, Bochniarz, and McNamara, the human capacity to imagine different or better circumstances—a different or better world—from what we now experience is critical to the project of the social sciences.

The social sciences respond to our need to understand how the world of human interactions works. We weave such an understanding on the warp of the generalizations that sum up to theory, with the woof being the more concrete descriptions of the institutions into and through which we organize ourselves. The pattern that emerges on this loom is not only a picture of *what is*; both the interpreters and some, at least, of the creators of the pattern infuse into it beliefs and hopes about *what might be*.

One of the lessons from the project that engendered this book was that the legacy from the present to the future is only in part a function of the *concern* felt in the present along with the *understanding* and the capabilities that determine the extent to which that concern can be expressed. Our impact on the future also depends upon our *visions* of what is possible and on the *values* that determine what we regard as a desirable future. The twelve essays that follow weave together several aspects of theory with institutional analysis as well as with visions and values. These are a sampling of what we regard as the essential elements in the translation of social and economic theory into future-regarding behavior.

BIBLIOGRAPHY

Beckerman, Wilfred. 1992. "Economic Growth and the Environment: Whose Growth? Whose Environment?" *World Development* 20, no 4: 481–96.
Lindblom, Charles. 1977. *Politics and Markets*. New York: Basic Books.
Smith, Adam. 1981. *An Inquiry into the Nature and Causes of the Wealth of Nations,* ed. R. H. Campbell and A. S. Skinner. Indianapolis: Liberty Classics.
Streeten, Paul P. 1991. "Global Prospects in an Interdependent World." *World Development,* special issue, January.
Thörgersen, John. 1994. "Recycling of Consumer Waste: A Behavioral Science Approach to Environmental Protection Policy." In *Economy, Environment and Technology: A Socioeconomic Approach,* ed. Beat Bürgenmeier. Armonk, NY: M. E. Sharpe.

Part 1:
Investment as a Link
between Present and Future

1

Capital Choices: National Systems of Investment

Michael E. Porter

This essay surveys in a short space the complex topic of national investment practices. It is particularly important to keep in mind the complexity of the topic because the proposals that emerge from this analysis emphasize the interdependence of all parts of the system. Readers who wish to see the arguments laid out at greater length are directed to *Capital Choices: Changing the Way America Invests in Industry,* a research report available from the Council on Competitiveness in Washington, DC.

Following this introductory section, the essay is divided into two parts. Part 1 describes how the U.S. investment system works, considering the global context and the external and internal capital markets within which it must operate, as well as the issues of positive (and negative) social externalities to private investment behavior. Some evidence is given in support of the widespread belief that there is a problem with U.S. investing, especially in failing to align private with social interests, and especially in comparison with Japan and Germany. The largest part of this section describes how investment decisions are determined in the United States.

Part 2 lays out the specific institutional, legal, and other factors that, taken together, are particularly important in creating the existing problems in the U.S. system of investment allocation. A number of concrete suggestions are then made for how the different actors in the system (e.g., policymakers, owners, managers, and institutional investors) can move to reform the system.

Investment intimately links the present with the future. It is crucial not only for maintaining an economy's current physical and human assets but also for upgrading those assets to new and more sophisticated

---

This essay synthesizes the work of a two-year research project on corporate investment sponsored by the Council on Competitiveness and the Harvard Business School. The project included 18 research papers by 25 scholars from a wide range of disciplines, each probing a different dimension of the issue.

future uses. Yet the U.S. system of allocating investment capital, as it now exists, threatens the long-term growth of the national economy. Although the U.S. system has many strengths, including efficiency, flexibility, responsiveness and high rates of corporate profit, it does not seem to be the most effective in directing capital to those firms that can deploy it most productively and, within firms, to the most productive investment projects. Many U.S. firms invest too little in those assets and capabilities most required for competitiveness, while others waste capital on investments with limited financial or social rewards.

Although critics frequently blame the shortcomings of U.S. industry on a short time horizon, ineffective corporate governance, or a high cost of capital, these concerns are just symptoms of a larger problem involving the entire system of allocating investment capital within and across companies.

The U.S. system of capital allocation creates a divergence of interests between owners and corporations, impeding the flow of capital to those corporate investments that offer the greatest payoffs. U.S. owners, investment managers, directors, managers, and employees are thus trapped in a system in which all are acting rationally, but none is satisfied. The U.S. system also has difficulty aligning the interests of private investors and corporations with those of society as a whole, including employees, suppliers, and local educational institutions.

The problems with the U.S. system are largely of our own making and have been building over a long period of time. Yet the investment problem has surfaced particularly in the last two decades. Through a series of regulatory decisions and other choices with unintended consequences, important changes have occurred in such areas as the pattern of corporate ownership, stock valuation methods, and capital budgeting practices that have fundamentally altered the way investment choices are made.

At the same time, the nature of competition shifted to make investment more important, particularly in the forms that are most penalized by the U.S. system. Also, globalization brought more U.S. firms into more frequent contact with firms based in nations with different capital allocation systems, further intensifying the impact of U.S. investment practices.

Reform is needed to address the weaknesses in the U.S. system while preserving its strengths. Meaningful change will be difficult because the U.S. investment problem is far more complex than conventional wisdom suggests. Many current proposals aimed at addressing America's investment problem fail to recognize the holistic nature of our capital allocation system. Proposals such as taxing transactions, eliminating quarterly financial reports, or increasing the number of outside directors address the symptoms of the investment problem rather than its underlying cause—the system itself—and could well be counterproductive. Other proposals seek to deal with the investment problem indirectly, through government support for investment in particular sectors and the encouragement of widespread collaboration among competitors. These, too, treat symptoms and risk unintended consequences.

As will be suggested in Part 2 of this essay, reform must address all aspects of the U.S. system, ideally all at once. Policymakers, institutional investors, and corporate managers must all play a role in instituting needed changes.

1. How the System Works

Competitiveness in the Global Context

The context within which we must understand the structure of investment allocations is a world in which the rules of international competition are quite different from the concepts taught to economists and businesspersons 20 years ago. Classical comparative advantages in factors of production, such as natural resources or pools of labor, have been superseded by the globalization of competition and companies, coupled with the power of technology to nullify factor disadvantages (see Porter 1990). Generalized skills and generic scientific knowledge now move rapidly around the world, and competitors rapidly assimilate them.

Competitive advantage no longer emerges from optimizing within fixed factor constraints. Instead, it depends upon the capacity of a nation's firms to innovate and upgrade their competitive advantages to more sophisticated types, a never ending process that requires sustained investment in a variety of forms. Firms must invest not only in highly specialized physical assets but also, increasingly, in specialized knowledge, skills, and organizational capabilities. Making some investments that fail is integral and indeed essential to the dynamic process of innovation because such investments provide learning or create capabilities that benefit future investments. An institutional structure that overly penalizes "bad" investments may undermine the competitive capability of firms, industries, and the national economy as a whole.

Similarly, parallel investments by diverse competitors create the most favorable conditions for rapid industry and firm improvement. An environment in which a number of competitors invest in pursuing a variety of strategies but closely observe and respond to each other's successes and failures seems to create the conditions for the fastest rate of progress. It also leads to beneficial segmentation and differentiation of firms' products and strategies which makes competitive advantages more sustainable. A structure in which investment is restricted to a dominant competitor, or made collectively by a group of rivals, may be efficient in a narrow sense but is not ultimately the most productive.

Private Investments, Social Returns

There are many forms of investment, ranging from traditional plant and equipment to investments in training or the losses required to enter a new geographic market. For purposes of simplification, we can divide the forms of investment into those in *physical assets*; those in *intangible assets* such as R&D, advertising, employee training and skills development, information systems, organizational development, or close supplier relationships; and those in *positional assets* such as access to new geographic or product markets. Investments in physical assets represent a declining portion of overall corporate investment. The other "softer" forms of investment are of growing importance to competition and are also the hardest to measure and evaluate using traditional approaches for evaluating investment alternatives.[1] Ironically, many forms of investment are not treated as such on corporate books, which has implications for investment behavior that we will return to later.

The appropriate rate of investment in one form often depends on making complementary and sequential investments in others. A physical asset such as a new factory, for example, may not reach its potential level of productivity unless there are parallel investments in intangible assets such as employee training and product redesign to improve its manufacturability using the new production technology. Investments are linked not only at one point in time but also intertemporally. An investment today, even if unsuccessful, can create option value for future investments. Today's R&D, for example, results not only in today's products and processes but the possibility of developing those of tomorrow. Finally, investments in one product area can create benefits for others. Because of all these types of "spillovers" of investments within the firm, the appropriateness of many discrete investment projects cannot be evaluated in isolation.[2]

The optimal rate of investment for society may differ from that for

---

1. A number of authors have recognized the growing importance of intangible investments. See, for example, Itami 1987, Curtis 1990, and Baldwin and Clark 1992.

2. For further discussion of these issues, see Ghemawat 1991; Baldwin and Clark 1992; and Seckler, in this volume, chap. 5.

an individual firm because of the presence of externalities or spillovers from private investment.[3] These spillovers create benefits for the economy as a whole (referred to as social returns) that exceed the private returns that accrue to a firm's shareholders. Social returns include such things as potentially higher wages of employees due to productivity-increasing technology investments; the greater capabilities (and higher future wages) of employees that result from investments in training; and the returns to suppliers, customers, and other local industries (and their employees) due to spillovers from a company's investments in technology, research or training programs at universities. None of these benefits is reflected in a company's current profits. Such spillovers are greater within regions and nations than across national borders.

The difference between private and social returns varies by form of investment. Investments in intangible assets such as R&D and training seem to involve the greatest difference between social and private returns, while investments in physical assets such as replacement plant and equipment or real estate normally involve fewer externalities. For example, the social returns from R&D have been documented as being 50 to 100 percent higher than private returns (see Bernstein and Nadiri 1989; Mansfield 1991). Note that the forms of investment with the greatest potential externalities are some of the very same ones that are expensed in accounting statements rather than counted as assets and that raise the most daunting challenges for conventional capital budgeting approaches.

Given the presence of externalities, a bias toward overinvestment seems to offer higher social returns and perhaps also higher long-term private returns. Private and social returns will tend to converge more in the long term than in the short term. This is because the externalities created by the firm's investments will feed back to benefit the firm. For example, the suppliers or customers who have enjoyed positive spillovers may in the future become more effective suppliers or larger, more sophisticated customers. Similarly, better-trained employees may allow entirely new strategies in the future that reinforce a company's competitive advantage. Note, however, that the diffusion of a new technology may lower private returns over time while social returns stay high. This is one reason why the spread between private and social returns to R&D is so great, and why special incentives for R&D investments (such as patents and R&D tax credits) are necessary.

---

3. The supporting literature is extensive. See, for example, Summers 1990 and Mansfield 1991.

Evidence of the Problem

A good deal of evidence supports the view that U.S. industry invests at a lower rate than German and Japanese industry in many forms of investment and has a shorter time horizon. The facts, observations, and anecdotal evidence relating to this view include the following.

> Aggregate rates of investment in property, plant and equipment, civilian R&D, and intangible assets such as corporate training and related forms of corporate human resource development is lower in the United States than in Japan and Germany (see Farb 1992).
>
> Anecdotal evidence suggests that U.S. firms invest at a lower rate than their German and Japanese counterparts in nontraditional forms such as human resource development, relationships with suppliers, and start-up losses to enter foreign markets. Kochan and Osterman (1992) and Blinder and Krueger (1992), for example, both document a significantly lower rate of investment by U.S. firms in human resources.[4] The magnitude of the difference appears greater in this area than in other investment areas.
>
> The R&D portfolios of U.S firms include a smaller share of long-term projects than those of Japanese and European firms. A survey of CEOs in the United States, Japan, and Europe by Poterba and Summers (1992) found that 21 percent of the projects of U.S. firms were considered long term compared with 47 percent in Japan and 61 percent in Europe.
>
> The average holding period of stocks has declined from over seven years in 1960 to about two years today (Duttweiler 1991). This decline implies a dramatic shift in the frequency with which investors buy and sell corporate equities. It is perhaps the most telling evidence of shortening investor horizons.

Although these findings present a broadly consistent picture of lagging U.S. investment, there are some puzzling and important complexities that seem to defy the overall pattern. These puzzles derail many simple explanations for why the United States invests less or has a shorter time horizon. For example, the U.S. investment (and competi-

---

4. The only area of human resources in which the United States may invest as much as or more than other leading nations is in public education, although here there are significant concerns about quality. In public education, however, the private sector is not making the investment choices.

tiveness) problem varies by industry and even by company: the United States is highly competitive and invests aggressively in industries such as chemicals, pharmaceuticals, software, and telecommunications network equipment. The United States does well in high-risk, long time horizon start-ups and invests heavily in emerging industries. Finally, many U.S. firms seem to have overinvested in unrelated acquisitions. Any useful understanding of the broad problems we are addressing must also take account of these apparent counterexamples.

The Determinants of Investment

The determinants of investment can be grouped into three broad categories: the macroeconomic environment in which all companies operate; the allocation mechanisms by which capital moves from its holders to investment projects (it is on this second category that our research focuses); and the conditions surrounding specific investment opportunities themselves. (These latter include characteristics of the particular projects, companies, industries, and the geographic locations where investments take place.)

Investment capital is allocated via two distinct but related markets: the external capital market through which holders of equity and debt provide capital to particular companies and the internal capital market in which companies allocate the internally and externally generated funds at their disposal to particular investment programs. There are strong parallels in how these dual markets function. The equity holder's task of selecting and monitoring companies in which to invest bears a strong resemblance to the corporation's task of selecting and monitoring investment programs. Both markets also share attributes that will prove crucial to investment behavior: highly incomplete information that is costly to gather; the existence of principal-agent relationships (in some cases, multitiered ones) that create agency costs; important spillovers or externalities in investment; and the potential to influence the results of a given investment through intervention.

The Nature of the External Capital Market

The external capital market includes a number of entities. The first is the holders of equity capital, whom we will term owners. The second is the agents who, in some instances, make investment choices on the owners' behalf. In the United States, investment decisions involving a large fraction of equity capital are made by institutional agents, whether they are pension funds, mutual funds, bank trust departments, or other money managers. Because owners have incomplete information about the performance of agents, they must use proxies in monitoring and evaluation. Agents can be expected to manage investments in a way that is aligned with how they are measured and compensated.

A third important entity in the external capital market is lenders of debt capital. The fourth entity is, of course, the corporation in which equity is invested or to which a loan is made. The final important entity is the board of directors, which is the formal link between the owners and the corporation.

The way in which the national system for capital allocation deals with the problem of imperfect information is crucial to understanding investment behavior. How owners/agents cope with imperfect information in dealing with each other and in valuing companies will influence the particular corporate attributes that influence stock prices. Management's perception of the ways in which the external market values their companies affects internal investment choices. The way in which managers cope with imperfect information internally will influence the particular types of investment projects selected. Finally, the approaches used by owners/agents to deal with incomplete information will influence those used by management.

Four characteristics of the external capital market are of principal importance for investment behavior. The first is the pattern of share ownership and agency relationships, which refers to the nature of the owners, the extent of their representation by agents, and the size of the stakes held in companies. The second is the goals of owners and agents, which influence their desired investment outcomes. The ability to jointly hold debt and equity is one important influence on goals, as is the existence of a principal-agent relationship. The third salient characteristic of the external market is the approach and information used by owners/agents to monitor (measure) and value companies. The final important characteristic is the ways in which owners/agents can influence management behavior in the companies whose shares they own.

These separate characteristics of the external capital market in an economy are interrelated and will tend over time to become internally consistent. If the dominant investors are principals who hold large stakes and are permanent, relationship-driven owners, the incentive will be present to invest in and accumulate fundamental knowledge on long-term corporate prospects. Owners will demand and achieve more influence on management behavior. Their orientation will be to work with management to improve performance and sell out only as a last resort. Conversely, if the pattern of share ownership/agency relationship is dominated by transaction-driven agents holding small company stakes who are measured on near-term appreciation and are dependent on public information, the incentive will be to employ information-lean index funds or simple value proxies in monitoring and valuation rather than to invest in costly fundamental research. Share holdings will tend to be more transient if agents can exert little influence on management.

The U.S. External Capital Market

In the United States, publicly traded companies increasingly have a transient ownership base comprised of institutional investors such as pension funds, mutual funds, or other money managers that act as agents for individual investors (see Edwards and Eisenbeis 1992). Such agents account for at least 55 percent of the public market and, combined with member firms trading on their own account, *over two-thirds of all trading*.

Due to legal constraints on concentrated ownership, fiduciary requirements that encourage extensive diversification, and a strong desire for liquidity, U.S. institutional agents hold portfolios involving small stakes in many, if not hundreds, of companies. For example, one of the largest U.S. pension funds, the California Public Employees Retirement System (CalPERS) reportedly held stock in over 2,000 U.S. companies in 1990, and its largest individual stake was 0.71 percent (see White 1991; Sailer 1991). Due to restrictions on bank ownership of corporate equity, U.S. banks do not normally hold debt and equity in the same company. Neither do U.S. insurance companies, although they are not restricted from doing so.

U.S. institutional agents such as pension funds and mutual funds, and the managers of such funds, are typically measured on quarterly or annual appreciation compared to stock indexes, and they thus seek near-term appreciation of their shares. Quarterly performance evaluation encourages the documented practices of "window dressing" (selling poorly performing stocks at the end of the year) and "lock-in" (well-performing portfolios are sold and the investment managers buy S&P 500 to lock in gains relative to other funds), although these practices have limited effect on returns to shareholders. Managers are readily changed if performance is unsatisfactory. Pension funds, whose capital gains are not taxed, make buy/sell choices without considering the trade-off of having to pay taxes on appreciated stocks sold, which would encourage longer-term holding. Mutual funds must distribute income and capital gains annually so that investors pay taxes each year. This only serves to heighten the attention of funds to quarterly or annual realized performance and hence to realizing gains. As a result of all these circumstances, mutual funds and actively managed pension funds (which represent 80 percent of pension assets) hold shares, on average, for just 1.9 years.[5]

The situation just described—in which institutional investors have fragmented stakes in numerous companies, short expected holding periods, and lack of access to "inside" information through disclosure or board membership—results in a strong tendency to base buy/sell choices on relatively limited information, based on those measurable company or industry attributes that affect near-term stock price movements.

Current earnings are an example of a proxy for corporate value. Their use is problematical, first, because accounting earnings do not accurately measure true earnings. Many investments must be expensed, and as a result current accounting earnings understate true earnings in companies where high rates of intangible investment are needed. Second, even true current earnings do not accurately measure corporate value because they fail to measure the firm's competitive position and its ability to sustain or improve that position and hence its future earning power. *Maximizing a series of short-term returns is not equivalent to maximizing long-term returns* because of the role of multiperiod investments. Investments needed to build skills, capabilities, and market positions, or to defend existing positions at the expense of current earnings are penalized by the use of current earnings as a value proxy.

Despite their large aggregate holdings, U.S. institutional agents have virtually no real influence on management behavior. For various legal and regulatory reasons that will be discussed later, agents rarely hold seats on the board of directors and have little clout with management. Index funds, which might be seen as long-term investors, cannot play this role effectively either. With their investment philosophy, extreme fragmentation of ownership, and lack of incentive to invest in information, index funds have little realistic prospects of credibly monitoring and influencing management behavior.

Institutional agents are left, then, with the proxy system as the only direct means of imposing their views on management. The proxy system, while cumbersome and ineffective, has been employed with growing frequency in recent years, with the number of shareholder proposals increasing from 33 in 1987 to 153 in 1990. The great majority (91 percent) of shareholder proposals regarding economic matters, however, have little to do with strategy or investment behavior but relate to corpo-

---

5. See table 1 in Froot, Perold, and Stein 1992, which is slightly higher than estimates by Lorsch and MacIver (1991) who find that 1983 holding periods were 1.6 years for pension funds and 1.3 years for mutual funds.

rate policies affecting the ease of control changes. Here, shareholder proposals invariably aim to make takeovers easier. Given the goals of institutional agents and their approach to monitoring and valuation, this is not surprising. Yet many institutions do not even bother to vote their shares, and there is growing debate about the responsibility of institutions in voting proxies as agents for investors.

The only real remedy available to U.S. institutional agents who are dissatisfied with management decisions is to sell their shares. The stock prices of out-of-favor companies are bid down by investors seeking to limit their losses who are unable to wait (because of their need for rapid appreciation) for a rebound due to earnings improvement or for a possible control change. Successive stock price declines may ultimately create the potential for acquisition or takeover to unlock the unrealized value. Arbitrageurs, a largely different group of investors from institutional agents, provide a countervailing force that holds up share prices of companies for which takeover seems likely.

Control changes and voluntary restructurings to forestall them, then, represent the only real discipline on management behavior in the U.S. system, given the limited power of owners and the limited impact of the proxy system. Unfortunately, this form of discipline occurs only after protracted decline in corporate performance. It also involves high transactions costs and carries with it some potential negatives for long-term corporate performance. While takeovers and buyouts can reduce static inefficiency through forced restructuring, they replace institutional agents with another financially oriented owner, the LBO firm (ironically, the funding for takeovers often comes from the very institutional agents who were the previous shareholders). While the new owner may have a longer horizon than the previous ones, most LBO firms are prone to being transaction-driven and seek to realize gains from selling out or taking the company public. In addition, the leverage required to complete the takeover forces asset sales that may in some cases diminish competitive capabilities and instill a financial stringency that can make it difficult to fund investments that do not generate cash quickly, particularly unexpected ones.

The Internal Capital Market

The internal capital market is the system by which corporations allocate the capital available from both internal and external sources among competing investment projects within and across business units. The system of internal capital allocation in an economy mirrors and is significantly influenced by the external capital allocation system. The external market sends signals that affect how companies are organized and managed. However, there are also independent influences on the internal capital allocation process that arise from laws, regulations, and prevailing management practices.

The most important influences on the internal capital market parallel those that shape the external market: the particular goals corporations set, the organizational principles that govern the relationship between senior management and units, the particular information and methods used to value and monitor internal investment options, and the nature of interventions by senior management into investment projects. The issue that will be emphasized here is that of corporate goals. (For fuller exposition of the other issues, see Porter 1993.)

Corporate goals are influenced from a number of directions. One is the legal framework in a nation that defines corporate purpose, as well as the extent to which particular corporate goals are codified in law as the duties and responsibilities of directors and managers. Particularly significant to corporate goal setting is the extent to which shareholders' goals are given explicit legal primacy and how such laws are interpreted by participants in corporate governance and by the courts. The way such laws are interpreted and the risk of lawsuits are as important as the laws themselves because this influences the sensitivities of managers and directors and the tests applied in judging their behavior.

Also significant in corporate goal setting is the board of directors. The composition of the board defines the interests that board members represent and the knowledge they have available. A board consisting of major owners, for example, is prone to have a different orientation than one consisting solely of management. Also important in understanding the influence of the board on corporate goals is the board's power, in practice, to influence management choices. Power is a function of the information available to directors, their independence from management, and the extent to which directors speak for significant owners.

A final major influence on corporate goal setting is the way in which senior management is rewarded, notably its basis for compensation and promotion. A management that is compensated heavily based on current period accounting earnings, for example, will set different goals than one compensated based on market share. Similarly, a management that expects to hold its position for a decade sets different goals than one hoping to be promoted quickly or moved to a position in another business unit or company.

American corporate goals are centered on earning high returns on investment or maximizing "shareholder value," measured by the highly imperfect indicator of current stock price. While the prevailing legal interpretation allows for long-term shareholder value to outweigh short-term stock price in evaluating corporate decisions, the burden of proof has seemed clearly to rest in the opposite direction. Managements (and directors) who sacrifice short-term stock price for long-term shareholder value still run the risk of lawsuits, while companies that maximize short-term stock price at the expense of long-term shareholder value normally remain unscathed.

In the United States, the board of directors holds ultimate responsibility for corporate performance but exerts relatively limited influence on corporate goals or management actions. Nominees are selected by the current board. The CEO is often the source of ideas for new candidates and often exerts a strong influence over the election process as well as the ongoing operation of the board. This is partly because most CEOs are also board chairmen (in 83 percent of corporations surveyed by Lorsch and MacIver 1991). Recent growth in the size of boards has also weakened the power of directors by making discussion and decision making in formal meetings extremely difficult (see Johnson 1990).

The composition of the board further enhances the relative power of the CEO. Boards have come to be dominated by outside directors who exert limited influence on corporate goals, while board representation by major owners, bankers, customers, and suppliers has diminished. An estimated 74 percent of the directors of Fortune 1000 companies are now outsiders with no direct ties to the corporation, and 70 to 80 percent are full-time CEOs of their own companies (Eaton 1990; and Lorsch and MacIver 1991). Because employees, customers, and suppliers are typically viewed as having interests that conflict with the corporation they are rarely represented on boards and thus have limited influence on corporate goals.

Employee pension funds, which could serve to align the interests of employees and owners or represent employee views to management, are limited to holding 10 percent of their assets in the sponsoring firm. Pension funds are also essentially prohibited from holding seats on the board of directors. It is ironic that employee pension funds have come to embody the pressures of the external market even though they could provide a valuable role in balancing stakeholder interests.

The move to outside directors arose out of calls for greater board objectivity. Yet lack of ties by the director to the corporation limits the ability of directors to absorb the vast amounts of information required to understand a firm's internal operations. Moreover, directors typically hold rather limited ownership stakes. While the median aggregate holdings of the board account for an estimated 3.6 percent of equity, most directors have no shares at all or only nominal holdings (Lorsch and

MacIver 1991; Morck, Shleifer, and Vishny 1988). In practice, then, neither owners, lenders, directors, employees, customers, nor suppliers exert direct influence on corporate goals.

Thus, the dominant influence on corporate goals is management, which interprets signals from the external capital market (perhaps incorrectly) and which is often subject to limited direct influence by either boards or owners. The goals set by U.S. managements are typically framed in terms of ROI (return on investment) or enhancing stock price. Managers care about stock prices because, among other things, they affect the corporation's ability to raise new equity and its vulnerability to control changes, which diminish their power or eliminate their position.

As we have seen, U.S. managements are oriented toward reporting high rates of return and responding to investor signals about how to maintain high stock price. Table 1.1, which reports the comparative ranking of goals in a sample of U.S. and Japanese companies, highlights the primacy of current rate of return and stock price among U.S. managements. In Japanese companies, earnings are significant because they are necessary to fund other priorities, but stock prices are essentially irrelevant.

The pressures imposed by corporate goals have been exacerbated by a historical trend toward decentralized management structures. These began to proliferate as early as the 1950s, as wartime planning and budgeting techniques were adopted by corporate management and U.S. companies first reached huge scale and complexity. These developments began distancing senior management from the details of the business.

TABLE 1.1. Comparisons of Japanese and U.S. Corporate Objectives: Mean Importance Rating

U.S.	Rating	Japan	Rating
Return on investment	2.43	Improving products and introducing	
Higher stock prices	1.14	new products	1.54
Market share	0.73	Market share	1.43
Improving products and introducing		Return on investment	1.24
new products	0.71	Streamlining production and	
Streamlining production and		distribution systems	0.71
distribution systems	0.46	Net worth ratio	0.59
Net worth ratio	0.38	Improvement of social image	0.20
Improvement of social image	0.05	Improvement of working conditions	0.09
Improvement of working conditions	0.04	Higher stock prices	0.02

Source: Data from Kagawa, Nonaka, Sakakibara, and Okumura 1981.
Note: 3 = most important, 0 = least important.

An explosion of unrelated or loosely related diversification, dating from the 1960s, both reflected and reinforced these tendencies.[6]

Over time, information flow and top management involvement in business unit management have fallen, and extreme forms of decentralization involving little cross-business unit interchange have spread. Corporate leadership positions have come increasingly to be filled by nontechnical executives, and tenure in senior management positions seems to have decreased. With these changes, the view has developed that general managers can run any business, regardless of product line or technology. These organizational changes have been supported by, and have contributed to, an increased reliance on financial budgeting and other management systems that use quantitative techniques to evaluate the performance of business units and to make investment decisions.

A Comparative Perspective on the U.S. Problem

The cumulative and combined effects of the system that has been described here are especially visible in the comparison between U.S. investment behavior and the behavior of our Japanese and German counterparts. We may summarize the contrasts in the following ways.

The U.S. system is less supportive of investment overall because of its greater sensitivity to current returns for most established companies, combined with corporate goals that stress current stock price over long-term corporate position.

The U.S. system favors those forms of investment for which returns are most readily measurable, due to the importance of financial returns and the limited information available to investors and managers.

The U.S. system favors discrete, stand-alone investments that generate leaps in position over ongoing investments required to build capabilities, those whose payoffs depend on complementary investments in other forms, or those that create an option value for the future.

The U.S. system heavily favors acquisitions, which involve assets that can be easily valued, over internal development projects that are more difficult to value and constitute a drag on current earnings.

The Japanese and German systems encourage aggressive investment in established businesses to upgrade capabilities and productivity. They also encourage investment in intangibles and internal diversifica-

---

6. Morck, Shleifer, and Vishny (1990) find that "The source of bust-up gains in the 1980s is the reversal of the unrelated diversification of the 1960s and the 1970s. Hostile bust-up takeovers simply undo past conglomeration" (47).

tion in order to redeploy personnel and secure the future of the enterprise. This comes at the cost, however, of a tendency to overinvest in
capacity, to proliferate products, and to maintain unprofitable businesses indefinitely.[7] Especially in Japan, managers have discretion to
make poor decisions as long as results are tolerable. Managers also have
less incentive for strong individual performance in some respects, and
these systems are prone to overemployment and greater difficulty in
weeding out poorly performing employees. There is also an inability to
rapidly enter emerging fields, especially via start-ups. However, unlike
the U.S. firms in mature industries that invest their excessive cash in the
wrong areas, Japanese firms benefit from the forces in the external and
internal markets that tend to direct excess capital into the areas more
aligned with long-term value. The benefits from overinvestment are thus
higher.

If the U.S. system comes closer to optimizing short-term private
returns, the Japanese and German systems appear to come closer to
optimizing long-term private and social returns. They appear better able
to address the investment spillovers within the firm. Goals that stress
market position and corporate perpetuity and management processes
involving greater top management information and cross-unit interchange seem better able to encourage complementary, shared, and option value-creating investments. Their greater focus on long-term corporate position, and an ownership structure and governance process that
incorporates the interests of employees, suppliers, customers, and the
local community allow the Japanese and German economies to better
capture the social benefits that can be created by private investment.

The U.S. system for allocating investment capital has potent disadvantages, yet the Japanese and German systems are not ideal in every
respect. There are important trade-offs among national systems. The
U.S. system is good at reallocating capital among sectors, funding emerging fields, shifting resources out of "unprofitable" industries, and achieving high private returns each period, as measured by the United States'
higher corporate returns on investment (Lawrence 1992).

This responsiveness and flexibility is achieved at the price of failing
to invest enough to secure competitive positions in existing businesses
and investing in the wrong forms. The U.S. system discourages investment in many companies and industries, particularly in intangible assets

---

7. Kester (1992) notes that the Japanese system of governance has faults in excess
human resources, excessive product proliferation, overinvestment in declining businesses,
unrelated diversification beyond organizational capabilities, and mismanagement of huge
corporate excess cash balances.

and in the linked and complementary investments that are needed to sustain and upgrade competitive capability. It is skewed toward acquisitions as opposed to building businesses internally, which leads to highly consolidated industries in which competitive rivalry is threatened. It also fosters overinvestment in profitable, mature sectors with few attractive investment opportunities.

2. The Case for Reform

Regulatory Influences on the U.S. System

To a considerable degree, the U.S. investment problem is our own creation. Many of the changes that have occurred and the trade-offs now present in the U.S. system have developed out of the regulatory regime established in the 1930s to deal with the perceived abuses occurring in financial markets at that time. In the intervening years, a long series of piecemeal regulatory choices have been made that have resulted in the U.S. investment system in its current form.

The great majority of the regulatory choices underlying the U.S. system were enacted to address goals that were often laudable but different from corporate investment behavior. The first principle, dating back to the 1930s or even before, was to avoid the concentration of economic power. The alleged abuses of large, dominant owners of companies were seen as an important cause of the Depression. U.S. regulators sought to limit the power of financial institutions, in particular, to affect stock prices or to manipulate corporate behavior.

A second and related principle was to separate the investment and control functions. The view emerged that there was a conflict of interest between the role of an investment manager and the role of a controlling owner. Controlling owners could take actions that could hurt individual shareholders such as dumping worthless shares into their managed investment portfolios. Similarly, exercising influence as an owner through such vehicles as a role on the board of directors was seen as compromising the objectivity of an investment manager.

A third guiding principle of U.S. regulation has been equal treatment of all investors, big and small, by providing for equal disclosure of material information and protection against abuses by insiders. Closely related to equal treatment was a fourth principle—to protect small investors, pension holders, insurance policyholders, and bank depositors.

The principles guiding U.S. regulation address some legitimate and commendable purposes and have achieved the goal of keeping abuses to a bare minimum. The result is public markets that are superior in some important respects to those in Japan and Germany. However, the cumulative pattern of regulation has had unintended consequences for investment behavior in the U.S. economy. A number of laws and regulations have directly or indirectly ensured that U.S. institutional agents hold small stakes in companies and that their holdings are widely diversified. Mutual funds, for example, are discouraged by tax incentives for diversification in the Internal Revenue Code and by reporting requirements under the Investment Company Act, from owning more than 10 percent of the stock of any firm. The fiduciary responsibility of pension fund and trust fund managers requires "prudent" diversification. In practice, this means that managers hold small stakes in dozens if not hundreds of companies. State law governing life insurance companies also requires significant diversification.

By stimulating excessive diversification and the holding of many small stakes in companies, the U.S. system has encouraged frequent trading and heightened the influence of accounting earnings on buy/sell choices. This, in turn, made timely disclosure of event information crucial and insider trading a major concern, compared to a system in which share ownership was more stable.

Disclosure rules prohibit significant owners from becoming knowledgeable "insiders," while limits on board membership bar them from direct access to in-depth company information. While there is a great deal of information that leads almost instantaneously to significant swings in share prices, the information is of the wrong type to match capital with those companies with the best long-term prospects. The ultimate absurdity is that U.S. institutions are driven to index funds, which are information free, or to simple value proxy investing involving little or no fundamental information or concern about long-term company prospects as the best available investment alternatives.

In most cases, the abuses that most concerned regulators occurred in situations where there was unequal power and goals that were not aligned. The more powerful interest then took advantage of the other. Rather than better align the goals, however, regulators sought to equalize the power in the system by simply eliminating powerful owners or severely restricting their activities. Ironically, the result was that corporate managers became relatively free from direct influence or oversight by major owners, while they were still reliant on capital from owners whose goals increasingly diverged from those of the corporation.

The record shows a near total failure by legislators from the 1930s to the 1980s to consider the effects of regulation on corporate performance. Moreover, each successive area of regulation often led to more regulation. Due to the tendency toward mutual consistency, regulations in one area can also shape other parts of the system. Similarly, inconsistent regulations of different parts of the system can produce conflicts and frustration. A common outcome of such conflicts is further regulation.

Moving to Reform the System

Improving the U.S. system for capital allocation will require complementary changes in public policy, in the behavior of institutional investors, and in the practices of management. To be most effective, an array of changes must be implemented simultaneously; changes in one part of the system that are not balanced with changes in other parts can be counterproductive.

The ideal system is one in which the goals of owners and the agents who represent them are aligned with those of corporations and of society as a whole. A better alignment of goals would be the most important step forward and would itself lead to beneficial changes elsewhere. We need a system in which more and different information is used to guide valuation and investment decisions. More aligned goals and better information must drive a process by which constructive intervention occurs at all levels when behavior departs from the long-term best interests of the corporation. Finally, the system must be modified to better align private shareholder returns and those of the economy as a whole. What is needed, in many respects, is a reexamination of our entire capital market paradigm.

A more supportive macroeconomic environment, which provides the context in which all corporate investment takes place, will provide a foundation for the other systemic changes needed. Increasing the stability of this environment and enlarging the pool of savings will reduce risk premiums and lower the cost of capital.

Beyond the macro environment, reform is needed in the broad areas of (1) ownership, (2) goals, and (3) information. In the following sections, we will translate these areas into specific directions with implications for policymakers, corporate management, and institutional investors.

The directions for *policy reform* rest on principles that differ markedly from those that have defined the regulatory framework of the traditional U.S. system of capital allocation. Rather than avoid abuses by restricting the activities of the largest capital providers and large corporate owners, corporate ownership can be broadened while the goals of capital providers, corporations, managers, employees, and society are better aligned. Capital providers become knowledgeable and constructive participants rather than adversaries. Abuses can be prevented by modifying incentives and eliminating unneeded regulatory guidelines rather than resorting to regulatory constraints that carry unintended consequences.

Stated most boldly, our research suggests the need to reexamine much of what constitutes the U.S. system of *management,* with its extreme approach to managing decentralization, its limited flow of information, its heavy use of certain types of incentive compensation systems, and its reliance on financial control and quantitative capital budgeting processes.

While the U.S. system is partly the result of regulation, there are positive steps that can be taken by *institutions* without the need for public policy changes. First and foremost, institutions must begin to understand why managements view them as adversaries. They must understand the subtle consequences of their monitoring and valuation practices on corporate investment behavior. They must also recognize that greater influence over management will come only at the price of less flexibility, less rapid trading, and the need for greater knowledge of and concern with company fundamentals.

1. Expand True Ownership throughout the System

The current concept of ownership in the U.S. system is too limited and restricted largely to outside shareholders. While outside owners should be encouraged to hold larger stakes and to take a more active and constructive role in companies, ownership should also be expanded to include directors, managers, employees, and even customers and suppliers. Expanded ownership will foster commonality of interest and help make investors and managers more aware of the value of investment spillovers that strengthen firms, benefit employees, and enhance the economy as a whole. A number of policy changes could shift the pattern of ownership to favor appropriate investment and better address externalities, for example:

Remove restrictions on share ownership. The regulations that artificially restrict the ability of investors to hold significant corporate stakes should be reexamined, as should restrictions on joint ownership of debt and equity. Limits on significant holdings should be eased, diversification rules relaxed, and fiduciary guidelines governing institutional investors modified to better reflect the true risk to owners (it can be shown, for example, that the value of diversification can be gained by holding relatively few stocks, certainly many fewer than the 100, 500, or 2,000 that are now common).[8]

---

8. It is important to note that encouraging greater concentration of ownership in individual corporations will not result in greater concentration of wealth in the economy as a whole.

Lower tax barriers to holding significant private ownership stakes. Estate tax laws need to be reexamined to strike a better balance between the need to equitably collect estate taxes and the ability of significant private owners to maintain their ownership stakes. Ways of structuring estate tax rules to allow their payment over some extended period, where illiquid or hard-to-value assets are involved, would be desirable.

Seek long-term owners and give them a direct voice in governance. Perhaps the most basic weakness in the U.S. system is transient ownership, in which institutional agents are drawn to current earnings, unwilling to invest in understanding the fundamental prospects of companies, and unable and unwilling to work with companies to build long-term earning power. The long-term interests of companies would be best served by having a smaller number of long-term or near permanent owners, whose goals are better aligned with those of the corporation. This does not necessarily mean taking the company private but could involve a hybrid structure of "private" and public ownership. Ideally, the controlling stake would be in the hands of a relatively few long-term owners, though shares were publicly traded to allow access to the public markets when conditions were favorable. Some owners might represent syndicates of other, smaller, long-term owners.

In return for a commitment to long-term ownership and to becoming fully informed about the company must come a restructuring of the role of owners in governance. Long-term owners must have insider status, full access to information, influence with management, and seats on the board. The board, consisting primarily of owners along with suppliers, customers, and others highly knowledgeable about the firm's business, should be both influential and informed.

Nominate significant owners, customers, suppliers, employees, and community representatives to the board of directors. As described earlier, such directors are more likely to have the company's long-term interest at heart and to encourage management to make the investments required to ensure long-term competitive position.

Encourage long-term employee ownership. Ownership by employees is desirable for a variety of reasons, provided that employee owners are long-term rather than transient owners. Employees' goals as owners will tend to be aligned with the long-term health of the corporation, and employee ownership is likely to internalize some of the externalities in investment choices by heightening the pressures for investment in human capital. Taxes and other regulations should facilitate and encourage employee stock ownership. Currently, companies can offer shares to employees at a discount of up to 15 percent of market price with no earnings impact, and such incentives should be maintained or increased.

Rules that allow low-cost issuance of new shares for employee ownership should be enacted. To qualify for such fiscal advantages, however, employee stock ownership plans should be required to restrict the sale of affected employee shares for five years except in cases of genuine hardship and to limit the proportion of holdings that can be sold in a given year.

2. Better Align the Goals of Capital Providers, Corporations, Directors, Managers, Employees, Customers, Suppliers, and Society

More ownership per se will not be sufficient if the goals of owners, corporations, and others are not aligned with each other and with the maximization of long-term corporate value. It is possible to create a system of incentives and to alter rules in a way that helps align the goals of all constituencies. Since the goals of agents will inevitably reflect those of owners, we must address owner goals directly.

The single most powerful and practical tool for modifying owner/agent goals is establishing a significant incentive for making long-term investments in corporate equity. The governing principle behind this proposal is to fundamentally change the system by changing the concept of ownership and the approach to valuing companies, while at the same time encouraging the form of investment where the externalities are greatest.

The current debate over capital gains, focused on encouraging investment and raising short-term tax revenue, misses the point. Currently, ordinary income and capital gains are treated as equivalent, and the debate over capital gains incentives is stalled. Our proposal is to restrict the incentive to equity investments in operating companies. The incentive would not apply to capital gains from bond appreciation or real estate appreciation, from investments in nonoperating companies holding real estate, or from other financial assets.[9]

The long-term equity investment incentive would require a minimum five-year holding period, with lower tax rates for even longer holdings. Ideally, capital gains would also be indexed for inflation. The equity investment incentive would be prospective, applying only to new investments and new gains.

Other mechanisms for affecting the goals of owners and lenders

---

9. The definition of operating companies would have to be carefully constructed to avoid gaming. For example, some minimum level of employment relative to sales or assets could be used as a qualification so as to exclude shell companies holding only financial assets.

include extension of the long-term equity investment incentive to currently untaxed investors such as pension funds and eliminating restrictions on joint ownership of debt and equity.[10] It would also be desirable to reduce the extent of explicit and implicit subsidies for investment in real estate. The positive externalities involved in real estate investment do not seem to justify the disproportionate level of incentives compared to investments in corporate equity, R&D, and training.

Shifts in corporate goals will need to accompany regulatory changes such as those just suggested if they are to be effective. Existing corporation law identifies long-term shareholder value as the appropriate corporate goal. Stakeholder laws, which explicitly provide for the interests of other parties such as employees or the local community in corporate goals, are a less-than-ideal solution to this problem. Stakeholder interests are hard to clearly define, prone to overemphasis, and subject to wide discretion. The granting of director discretion to consider stakeholders' interest (implicitly, at the expense of shareholders) without those stakeholders for corporate performance having responsibility serves to further isolate boards from owners.

A far better solution is to explicitly identify long-term shareholder value as the corporate goal and shift the burden of proof on directors and managers to explain to owners or other major constituents why decisions build long-term value. This would be accomplished by modification of corporation laws designed explicitly to reduce the threat of litigation. The interest of shareholders, employees, the local community, and other stakeholders is far closer, if not identical, in the long run than in the short run. Improved aligning of the interests of owners and corporations, combined with the other changes we have suggested, can go a long way toward properly addressing the problem that stakeholder laws reflect.

Improvements in the internal capital allocation and investment monitoring process must primarily be the responsibility of management. However, some incentives designed to better align private and social returns on selected forms of investment would be desirable. In particular, regulation can provide investment incentives for R&D and training. Such forms of investment are particularly subject to externalities that make the optimal private rate of spending less than for society. Making the existing R&D tax credit permanent and creating a parallel tax incentive for training investments should take on high priority.

---

10. It should also be noted that extending the long-term equity incentive to pension beneficiaries extends the tax benefit to ordinary working people, not just Americans with high incomes.

The need for traditional investment tax credits, on the other hand, is more problematic. Investment tax credits are expensive and are subject to political distortions. The U.S. system of capital allocation is less biased against investment in hard assets, and the externalities involved in such investments seem more limited. Public resources would seem better spent in funding the long-term equity incentive, which will shift the entire valuation system to encourage investment and the funding of permanent incentives for R&D and training.

U.S. compensation systems need to move in the direction of linking pay more closely with long-term company prosperity and to actions that improve it. Performance awards should be based not only on rate of return for the year but on the extent to which the company's competitive position has improved (or weakened) based on objective measures. Stock options should be modified to include long (more than five-year) vesting periods and constraints on the number of shares that can be liquidated at one time. Otherwise, even some well-meaning managers will manage the stock price rather than build the company.

Another way to align the goals of management with the long-term health of the corporation is to move away from unrelated diversification. Unrelated or loosely related diversification not only wastes capital but also exacerbates the management biases that we have described. Concentrating on one or a few core fields and investing heavily to achieve a unique position in each of them is the only way to build highly competitive companies.

Institutional investors are a special case in that, as we have seen, they control the major part of the external capital market in the United States. The U.S. system of capital allocation creates perverse outcomes for institutional investors, especially pension funds. Such institutions should be the ideal long-term investors. Instead, we have the paradoxical situation in which many institutions, especially pension funds, are entrusted with funds for extremely long periods, yet trade actively. Institutions incur substantial transactions costs, yet most underperform the market. Many have been driven to index funds. Because of the widespread holdings of institutional agents, a gain on the sale of one stock comes as a loss on another stock. Thus, the only way for institutions to improve their overall performance is to improve the earning power of U.S. companies, which will increase their aggregate value. Society also has a large stake in creating a system where the "winning" institutions are those that are better at rewarding and directing capital to companies with the best long-term prospects rather than those whose earnings will improve next year.

Institutions can take the lead in moving toward the following changes.

Increase the size of stakes

Reduce turnover and transactions costs

More carefully select companies based on fundamental earning power

Encourage changes in agent measurement and evaluation systems to reflect long-term investment performance

Transform interactions with management to productive, advisory discussions

Create special funds to test these new investment approaches

Support systemic public policy changes

Institutions might find it easier to make such changes if, as a first step, they were to consider creating special funds earmarked for long-term investing in significant stakes in companies who agree to give major owners a greater influence in management. Given existing rules, establishing such funds might require agreements modifying the funds' fiduciary responsibilities. Such funds would be structured to provide liquidity without the need to sell positions through mechanisms by which existing investors or new investors could buy (at the current market price) the holdings of those investors needing to generate funds.

There are positive changes underway in some of these areas that can be built upon. Even CalPERS, for example, is attempting to reduce its number of portfolio companies, from over 2,000 to between 700 and 800 (White 1991; Lorsch and MacIver 1991). The more institutions that modify their approach to investing, the more the fruits of a shift to committed long-term investing will become a self-fulfilling prophecy, because enough funds will seek out the most competitive companies to drive market prices. Current earnings will begin to have less and less of an impact on share prices. Stock prices could become less volatile. The transactions cost savings alone of this approach will provide a head start in registering better investment performance.

3. Improve the Information Used in Decision Making

Even if goals are better aligned, the quality of information used to allocate capital throughout the system will affect investment choices. We must expand access by both investors and managers to information that better reflects true corporate performance. While some of the needed changes in this area can be initiated via regulation, much of it will depend upon corporations recognizing and correcting counterproductive organizational structures. For example, the mode of managing decentralization in place in many U.S. companies must be overhauled to provide greater information flow and to better align it with the imperatives of competitive advantage. The problem is not that decentralization is bad per se but that it has been inappropriately managed, partly because of excessive corporate diversification.

What is needed instead is a system that recognizes strategically distinct businesses as the proper unit of management but manages them differently. Senior managers at the corporate level must have a substantive understanding of both the technology and the industry. Top management must be directly and personally involved in all significant decisions, especially investments. There must be extensive consultation and coordination with employees and among related business units. Information must be exchanged both vertically and horizontally. Opportunities to share functions and expertise among units should be pursued aggressively because they leverage tangible and intangible investments. Incentives must be changed to promote the internalization of such spillovers within the company.

Such a system would shift measurement and control away from solely financial results, raise senior management confidence in understanding complex investment choices, and better capture complementarities among discrete investment options. A new philosophy of management control must be instituted, based as much or more on the company's extended balance sheet as on its income statement. A company's extended balance sheet measures the assets that constitute its competitive position. Financial measures of investment returns should be combined with measures of competitive position such as market share, customer satisfaction, and technological capabilities. A more appropriate control system must include the following elements.

Broader definition of assets
Measurement of asset quality and productivity in addition to quantity
Relative instead of absolute measures.
Move to universal investment budgeting
Evaluation of investment programs instead of discrete projects
Unified treatment of all forms of investment
Separate the determination of required asset position from evaluation of the means of achieving it.

Other constructive changes in corporate behavior would include the following points.

Modify accounting rules so that earnings better reflect corporate performance. The accounting profession, led by the SEC if necessary, should create new standards for accounting for intangible assets. R&D and other long-term intangible investments should be capitalized under rules that require disclosed write-offs of worthless investments as part of the auditing process. While there will inevitably be some abuses, as there are under the current system, the benefits in terms of improved valuation and the resulting shifts in corporate behavior should outweigh them.

Expand public disclosure to reduce the cost of assessing true corporate value. Accounting earnings, even if modified to better account for investments in intangibles, still fail to provide a measure of true long-term corporate value. Value resides in a company's activities, its stock of scientific and technical knowledge, its skill base, its reputation with various constituencies, and its market position. Disclosure should be extended in these areas in order to improve the information available for investment choices and to lower its cost as well as to help offset the biases against intangible investments.

Move to universal investment budgeting. Capital budgeting systems were designed not to evaluate the strategic investments required to remain competitive in the business but to decide among discretionary investment options. Discounted cash flow methodology requires that the benefits and costs of investments be quantified as cash inflows or outflows. As Baldwin and Clark (1992) suggest, however, the option value of investments is ignored.

Allow disclosure of "inside" information to significant long-term owners under rules that bar trading on it. Beyond expanded public disclosure, institutions and other owners who have held a significant ownership stake (e.g., 1 percent or more) for a qualifying period (e.g., one year) should have access to more complete information about company prospects than that which is disclosed publicly, provided that such information is not disclosed to third parties.

The Promise of Reform

The U.S. system is already experiencing changes in several areas. Institutional investors have begun, in some cases, to shift from influencing management through indirect proxy proposals to raising important issues through formal discussions. Boards are also beginning to take a more active role in monitoring poorly performing managements. In the internal market, some firms are developing closer relationships with customers, suppliers, and employees, while others are encouraging greater information flow through increased cross-functional training. Yet the underlying causes of our investment problem, particularly the goals and information that guide the decisions of investors, directors, and managers, remain the same.

The changes that have been suggested here will work to increase true ownership in the economy; better align the goals of U.S. shareholders, corporations, managers, employees, and society; improve the information used in investment decisions; more effectively scrutinize managements based on criteria more appropriate to competitiveness; and make internal management processes more consistent with the true sources of competitive advantage. Changes in critical areas, such as ownership patterns and owner goals, will trigger constructive changes elsewhere in the system. The same changes will not only encourage investment in more appropriate forms in many U.S. companies but will also work to reduce wasted investment in those companies, and those forms, that are prone to it.

If progress can be made on these fronts, it will not only reduce the disadvantages of the U.S. system but can result in a system that is superior to that in Japan and Germany. A reformed U.S. system would be more flexible, more responsive, and even better informed in allocating capital than those in Japan and Germany. Investors in a reformed U.S. system would be long-term owners but not necessarily permanent ones. This would provide more flexibility than exists in Japan or Germany to withdraw capital if long-term prospects are genuinely unattractive. In a reformed U.S. system, the substantial number of sophisticated U.S. investors making independent choices would redirect their valuation methods and make investment choices that would arguably be better informed than those in Japan and Germany. A reformed U.S. system would also produce more careful monitoring of management, and more pressure on poorly performing managements, than exists in Japan or Germany. A reformed U.S. system, with its already higher levels of disclosure and transparency, would also be fairer to all shareholders than the Japanese and German systems.

Altering the U.S. system of capital allocation is complicated by the fact that systemic change will be necessary to make a real difference. It will also be complicated by the need for all the major constituencies to sacrifice some of their narrow self-interests in the pursuit of a more satisfying overall system. Yet we must avoid the tendency to tinker at the margin. The widespread concern and dissatisfaction with the status quo suggests that systemic reform may be possible. The gains will accrue not only to investors and firms but to the rate of long-term productivity growth, competitiveness, and the prosperity of the U.S. economy.

BIBLIOGRAPHY

Baldwin, C. Y., and K. B. Clark. 1992. "Capabilities and Capital Investment: New Perspectives on Capital Budgeting." In *Capital Choices: Changing the*

Way America Invests in Industry. Washington, D.C.: Council on Competitiveness, 1992.

Bernstein, J. I., and M. I. Nadiri. 1989. "Research and Development and Intra-Industry Spillovers: An Empirical Application of Dynamic Duality." *Review of Economic Studies* 56:249–69.

Blinder, A. S., and A. B. Krueger. 1992. "International Differences in Labor Turnover: A Comparative Study with Emphasis on the U.S. and Japan." In *Capital Choices: Changing the Way America Invests in Industry.* Washington, D.C.: Council on Competitiveness.

Curtis, D. A. 1990. *Management Rediscovered: How Companies Can Escape the Numbers Trap.* Homewood, IL: Dow-Jones Irwin.

Duttweiler, E., ed. 1991. *Factbook 1991.* New York Stock Exchange.

Eaton, L. 1991. "Corporate Couch Potatoes: The Awful Truth about Boards of Directors." *Barron's,* December 24, 22–24.

Edwards, F. R., and R. A. Eisenbeis. 1992. "Financial Institutions and Corporate Investment Horizons: An International Perspective." In *Capital Choices: Changing the Way America Invests in Industry.* Washington, D.C.: Council on Competitiveness.

Farb, W. E. 1992. "An International Comparison of Investment Behavior as a Key to the Time Horizons of American Industry." In *Capital Choices: Changing the Way America Invests in Industry.* Washington, D.C.: Council on Competitiveness.

Froot, K. A., A. F. Perold, and J. C. Stein. "Shareholder Trading Practices and Corporate Investment Horizons." in *Capital Choices: Changing the Way America Invests in Industry.* Washington, D.C.: Council on Competitiveness, 1992.

Ghemawat, P. 1991. *Commitment: The Dynamic of Strategy.* New York: The Free Press.

"Institutional Investors and Capital Markets: 1991 Update." 1991. In *Institutional Investor Project.* Columbia University Center for Law and Economic Studies, September.

"Institutional Concentration of Economic Power: A Study of Institutional Holdings and Voting Authority in U.S. Publicly Held Corporations." 1991. In *Institutional Investor Project.* Columbia University Center for Law and Economic Studies, October.

Itami, H., and T. W. Roehl. *Mobilizing Invisible Assets.* 1987. Cambridge, MA, and London: Harvard University Press.

Johnson, E. W. 1990. "An Insider's Call for Outside Direction." *Harvard Business Review,* March-April, 46–55.

Kester, W. C. 1992. "Governance, Contracting, and Investment Time Horizons." In *Capital Choices: Changing the Way America Invests in Industry.* Washington, D.C.: Council on Competitiveness.

Kochan, T. A., and P. Osterman. 1992. "Human Resource Development and Utilization: Is There Too Little in the U.S.?" In *Capital Choices: Changing the Way America Invests in Industry.* Washington, D.C.: Council on Competitiveness.

Lawrence, R. Z. 1992. "Time Horizons of American Management: The Role of Macroeconomic Factors." In *Capital Choices: Changing the Way America Invests in Industry*. Washington, D.C.: Council on Competitiveness.

Lorsch, J. W., and E. A. MacIver. 1991. "Corporate Governance and Investment Time Horizons." In *Capital Choices: Changing the Way America Invests in Industry*. Washington, D.C.: Council on Competitiveness.

Mansfield, E. 1991. "Social Returns from R&D: Findings, Methods and Limitations." *Research Technology Management* 34, No. 6, 24–27.

Morck, R., A. Shleifer, and R. W. Vishny. 1988. "Management Ownership and Market Valuation: An Empirical Analysis." *Journal of Financial Economics*, 20, 293–315.

Poterba, J. M., and L. H. Summers. 1992. "Time Horizons of American Firms: New Evidence from a Survey of CEOs." In *Capital Choices: Changing the Way America Invests in Industry*. Washington, D.C.: Council on Competitiveness.

Porter, M. E. 1990. *The Competitive Advantage of Nations*. New York: The Free Press.

Porter, M. E. 1992. *Capital Choices: Changing the Way America Invests in Industry*. Washington, D.C.: Council on Competitiveness.

Sailer, J. "California Public Employees Retirement System." Harvard Business School case no. 9-291-045, 1991.

Summers, L. H. 1990. "What Is the Social Return to Capital Investment?" In *Growth/Productivity/ Unemployment: Essays to Celebrate Bob Solow's Birthday*, ed. P. Diamond. Cambridge, MA: MIT Press.

White, J. A. 1991. "Pension Funds Think Less May Be More." *Wall Street Journal*, October 23, sec. C.

2

Economic Meanings of Trust and Responsibility

Neva R. Goodwin

> A great deal of economic life depends for its viability on a certain limited degree of ethical commitment. Purely selfish behavior of individuals is really incompatible with any kind of settled economic life. There is almost invariably some element of trust and confidence.
> —Kenneth J. Arrow, "Social Responsibility and Economic Efficiency"

The social sciences are expected to discover and analyze truths about various aspects of human experience. The motivation for such work is to contribute to human welfare. This paper will focus on the roles of trust and responsibility in economic life. The first section will consider the possibility that, if a social science theory undermines welfare by ridiculing a reliance on such important contributors as responsibility and trust, this should raise a question as to whether there is something wrong with the theory.

Section 2 explores particular areas of economic life where the importance of responsibility and trust are especially evident: for example, the experience of running a company; the relations among owners (stockholders), management, and other stakeholders; and the effect of distrust (e.g., an expectation of irresponsibility) upon the work experience.

Section 3 speculates on how concern for environmental values may assist in bringing the future home to the present. In section 4 the focus shifts to a consideration of how social conflicts of interest are handled in part by norms and in part by force (i.e., government intervention through the legal system, with good behavior enforced by the threat of punishment). Neither threats nor morality, nor both together, have ever succeeded in controlling all antisocial impulses. I will suggest that nonconvergent interests that are not effectively controlled by these two mechanisms may, nevertheless, be affected by the balance struck between them. In particular, I will put forward a tentative hypothesis that the more the balance tips toward regulation and away from norms, the larger the uncontrolled portion is likely to grow.

This possibility creates a dilemma that leaves us, it seems, to choose

I am especially indebted to Paul Streeten for helpful comments on this essay.

between, on the one hand, a laissez-faire prescription that is closely associated with the position of neoclassical rationalism, which (I will argue) has a corrosive effect upon the possibility of moral behavior, and, on the other hand, an emphasis on government intervention as the regulator and enforcer of moral behavior, which at best is not very effective and at worst may actually motivate people to get away with as much as they can.

The discovery of a resolution to this dilemma would be no small thing. It might, indeed, be the entry to the much sought-for "third way"—the alternative to capitalism and socialism that would have the virtues of each without their drawbacks. Whether such an El Dorado is achievable or whether our best hope is to move beyond the best of existing experience through a series of marginal improvements, it is reasonable to assume that the social sciences should contribute to this exploration. The final section of this paper will suggest some directions in which we need to shape the social sciences (with economics especially in mind) to make them more useful in conceptualizing our social goals and suggesting how to achieve them.

1. Moral Behavior, Economic Life and Neoclassical Theory

> [T]he more the capitalist technique grows up, the more complicated economic relationships become, the more people become concentrated in towns, the more each man's prosperity becomes bound up with that of others whom he may never have seen, the more necessary it is that each one's conduct of life should come up to certain minimum standards. . . . Social responsibility—the sense that "we are all members of one body"—becomes more important . . . and so we find following on the development of capitalism a paradoxical situation; the individualist idea destroys the old solidarity and makes for the growth of capitalism, and capitalism in turn, by increasing every individual's dependence on his neighbor, demands a return of that same solidarity. (Croone and Hammond 1947, 207)

In the nineteenth century, economics was regarded as a moral science; many of the seminal thinkers in the field (with Adam Smith the most outstanding of these) were moral philosophers. As the above quotation suggests, the need for an integration of moral and economic understanding has grown, not diminished, in modern societies. The point made by Croone and Hammond in 1947 could be buttressed in many ways. Just to take one: modern technology (after the convulsion of

Fordism) has progressively called for more responsibility on the part of workers. Supervision is appropriate for manual tasks—those that are increasingly being turned over to machines. It is difficult or impossible to supervise the mental work that is left for human agents. However, the intersection of the economic and moral spheres has become a largely neglected area.

There is a little more awareness of the problems arising from the neglect of the ecological/economic connection. Both of these inter-sections—economics and ethics, and economics and environment—are equally salient for the relationship between present actions and future outcomes. Indeed, it can be argued that to bridge the disjunction be-tween economics and ecology it is first necessary to make the appropri-ate connections between economics and morality. The environmental connection between future and present may serve as an objective correla-tive to, and even an enforcer of, the moral connection.

Rather than taking in one gulp all aspects of morality and their interrelation with capitalism, I will emphasize, in particular, the issues of trust and responsibility. It will be useful to distinguish between individ-ual trust and social trust. The former is based on a degree of personal familiarity at least sufficient such that, because of prior experience ("she has always done what she said she would") or intuition ("he has an honest face"), one concludes that the acquaintance can be counted on to behave in a manner that falls within some predefined limits.[1]

More central to this paper is the second issue, of social trust. By this I mean our general sense that people of a particular group (it might be residents of Sienna or Filipinos, people with a college education, or pharmacists or laborers) can be counted on to uphold the standards of good social interactions. In the context of market relations, these stan-dards usually refer to the degree to which persons can be expected to speak truthfully, keep promises, abide by social norms of fairness (e.g., in setting wages and prices vis-á-vis employees or customers) and make an effort to fulfill their side of any implicit or explicit bargain—in other words, to behave responsibly. Individual trust has an important role in many business dealings (see, for example, Mody 1992, Hart 1988, and Lorenz 1988). However, of the two types, social trust has, as I see it, a wider economic importance and contributes in important, perhaps un-derappreciated, ways to the well-being of individuals. Social trust im-

---

1. In the case of friendship, these limits usually include "not acting so as to know-ingly cause me harm." Other kinds of limits may define other kinds of trust relationships: for example, if you know that the leader of an enemy nation is, in his own terms, a patriot, you will trust him to do what he believes is good for his country.

plies being able to count on people to perform their roles responsibly, even when we do not know them personally and possess, at best, only a little, general information about them.[2]

Trust is as essential in the context of business as it is in other human relations; it is the grease that keeps the wheels turning. Responsibility, however, is an important part of what makes trust possible. In general, responsibility has to do with taking care to perform appropriately and well one's assigned functions. I will emphasize, in particular, that aspect of responsibility that has to do with fulfillment of duties in work, whether the worker is a government bureaucrat whose job is to facilitate citizens' use of government services, a CEO whose job is to serve the interest of the stakeholders of his or her firm (the definition of those stakeholders is an important issue to which we will return), or a production worker whose job is to stay alert in order to maintain high standards of quality in output.

One measure of the importance of these issues is the direct money costs that are incurred when trust and responsibility are absent: the firm's costs for monitoring employees, customers, and suppliers in order to avoid being robbed or cheated and its losses when the monitoring isn't sufficient; government's ever mounting costs for monitoring businesses and, increasingly, other parts of government, to see that they do not rob or cheat one another or the public; or the costs in time to individuals who feel the pinch of the extra minutes or hours or days spent monitoring those with whom they have dealings to see that the other side is performing its job responsibly. In regard to the costs of production: "When workers do not trust management, they demand rigid work rules, which raise labor costs. When owners do not trust management, they demand higher returns, which raise capital costs" (Jacobs 1991, 63).

This essay does not argue that responsibility should be assumed or trust offered blindly. Rather, given the high costs now being paid because of the atmosphere of (often well-earned) distrust in which we live, we need to take another look at the ways in which we encourage or discourage responsible economic behavior. Every suggestion for how to encourage a moral economic environment will be seen to have associated risks. These need to be considered in comparison to the risks of

---

2. In the short run, it appears that social and individual trust are often interrelated, so that a growth or diminution in either may affect the other in the same direction. In historical terms, however, it seems possible that some societies have evolved with an emphasis on one type of trust to compensate for a deficiency in the other. On the individual level, one can also imagine a negative correlation, as when a blow to one's sense of social trust may make one cling all the more fervently to trust in a few known individuals. See Putnam 1993.

continuing on a trajectory that may include a long-term trend of declining responsibility and trust.

For reasons that will become clear in the last section of this essay, I will give particular consideration to the possibility that the view of humanity that is promulgated by those neoclassical social theories where rationality is defined as the pursuit of self-interest has a corrosive effect upon responsibility and trust. How seriously one takes this possibility partly depends upon how much influence one expects a social science to have upon actual human behavior. Several studies have concluded that economists, at least, are affected by their own doctrine. As the *Economist* notes, in a review of this literature, "Economists are not merely dismal, it appears, but selfish and uncooperative as well."[3]

It is natural for people to avoid behavior that they have been told is irrational. This fact may provide part of the explanation for the way economics students, and economists, appear to have been affected by their discipline. As one instance of this effect, the *Economist* quotes a survey in which 1,245 randomly selected college professors were asked how much they gave to charity each year: "About 9% of the economics professors gave nothing; the proportion of professors in other disciplines giving nothing ranged between 1.1% and 4.2% (despite generally lower income than economists)" (ibid).

Another well-known study is that by Marwell and Ames (1981). It examined the tendency of individuals to contribute to the provision of a public good versus the tendency to "free ride" on the benevolence of others and enjoy the public good without contributing. Their conclusion was that

> over and over again, in replication after replication, regardless of changes in a score of situational variables or subject characteristics, the strong version of the free rider hypothesis is contradicted by the evidence. People voluntarily contribute substantial portions of their resources—usually an average of between 40 and 60 percent—to the provision of a public good. This despite the fact that the conditions of the experiment are expressly designed to maximize the probability of self-interested behavior. Free riding does exist—subjects do

3. "How Do You Mean, 'Fair'?" "Economic Focus" section in *Economist,* May 29, 1993, 71. This article concludes:

Perhaps, then, there is a public interest in curbing the study of economics. Or alternatively—a conclusion that this column would prefer to endorse—economics needs to take psychology more seriously. The fact is that people do co-operate more than the self-interest model (useful though it is) seems to predict.

not provide the optimum amount of the public good, and tend to reserve a meaningful fraction of their resources. The "weak" free rider hypothesis is supported. Nevertheless, the amount of contribution to the public good is not easily understood in terms of current theory. (Marwell and Ames 1981, 307–8.)

There was, however, one dramatic exception to this conclusion: "Economics graduate students contributed only an average of 20% of their resources to the public exchange. They were much more likely to free ride than any of our other groups of subjects" (306–7).

The most charitable explanation for this finding is that the economics graduate students were, in their way, being altruistic—that is, they were doing what they felt would bring pleasure to people who, they assumed, expected results in accord with the neoclassical theory. Another interpretation is that they had been exposed to, and had learned, the lesson that free riding is how rational people *should* behave. Recognizing that economics graduate students are a small and specialized group, there is nevertheless reason to be concerned that a larger and more influential group of young capitalists (those who attend business schools) are exposed to portions, at least, of the same neoclassical philosophy—with the danger that capitalist firms are being run by people who have been told that they "should" behave amorally, if not immorally.

This is not a new problem. In the early industrial revolution in England we find curious stories of factory owners who led a double life. They showed to the world the face of Dickens's Gradgrind, which they had been taught to believe was the face of rational economic man. But they retained private notions of honorable behavior, often influenced by Christianity, which led them to take pay cuts and make other sacrifices to avoid laying off workers in bad times. For example, it was said of an early industrialist (in 1868), that

> He was not indifferent to the teachings of political economy, but he should be very sorry if the rigid and abstract rules of political economy alone prevailed in his workshops. It would be impossible for him to buy the labour of his workpeople, and for the workpeople to sell him that labour the same as an ordinary commodity over the counter of a shopkeeper. He felt a deep interest in the welfare of his workpeople. . . . The bond which united them was not the cold bond of buyer and seller. (Quoted in Joyce 1980, 134).

Neoclassical economic theory begins with the premise that "rational economic man acts [only] so as to maximize his perceived self-interest."

The word, *only,* is not found in most versions of this statement but is a useful addition because it expresses what is, in fact, assumed as the basis for the large majority of neoclassical economic models. Starting from this premise, an historian of the period of the industrial revolution correctly notes that one of the logically derived deductions is a significant normative statement.

> [B]oth friends and foes of capitalism often read into technical analyses of wage and price movements a very simple message: since the laws of supply and demand automatically transmute each individual's self-interest into the greater good of the greater number, *no one need be concerned with the public interest.* (Haskell 1985b, 549, emphasis added)

The theory behind this conclusion is less often defended from actual experience than from two other areas of theory: a rather narrow (and, some would say, eccentric) branch of the theory of evolution and the modern contributions of game theory.

In their critical analysis of game theory (among other areas of modern economics), Kahneman, Knetsch, and Thaler have compared theoretical predictions with actual human behavior. They find two constraints upon purely self-interested motives in markets. One is a set of norms that prescribe behavior so that the lay public expects that "some firms apply fair policies even in situations that preclude enforcement." The other constraint is an implicit contract in which "[f]irms that behave unfairly are punished in the long run" (Kahneman et al. 1986, 729).

Bhide and Stevenson, of the Harvard Business School, are impressed with the importance of the first of these constraints and argue that economists have given much too much weight to the second—the "implicit contract" side of the motivation for moral behavior:

> Game theorists argue that retaliation sends a signal that you are not to be toyed with. This signal, we believe, has some value when harm is suffered outside a trusting relationship: in cases of patent infringement or software piracy, for example. But when a close trusting relationship exists, as it does, say, with an employee, the inevitable ambiguity about who was at fault often distorts the signal retaliation sends. (Bhide and Stevenson 1990, 126)

These authors insist that the rational reasons given for honest, principled behavior are generally impotent, and that such behavior is very widespread, but that its existence has little to do with the rationality of economic maximizing. They give scant credence to the idea that the benefits of trustworthiness "can be factored easily into a rational business analysis of whether to lie or keep a promise," and go on to discuss another rationalist idea: that businesspeople can or do assess the value of maintaining trust relationships that are redundant to what can be accomplished by economic power against the possible day when their economic power will have diminished.

> It is almost as difficult to anticipate the possibility of divine retribution as it is to assess the possibility that at some unknown time in the future your fortunes *may* turn, whereupon others *may* seek to cause you some unspecified harm. With all these unknowns and unknowables, surely the murky future costs don't stand a chance against the certain and immediate financial benefits from breaking an inconvenient promise. The net present values, at any reasonable discount rate, must work against honoring obligations.
>
> Given all this, we might expect breaches of trust to be rampant. In fact, although most businesspeople are not so principled as to boycott powerful trust breakers, they do try to keep their own word most of the time. . . .
>
> One reason treachery doesn't swamp us is that people rationalize constancy by exaggerating its economic value. . . .
>
> Just as those who trust find reasons for the risks they want to run, those who are called on to keep a difficult promise cast around for justification when the hard numbers point the other way. Trustworthiness has attained the status of "strategic focus" and "sustainable competitive advantage" in business folklore—a plausible (if undocumented) touchstone of long-term economic value.
>
> But why has it taken root? Why do business men and women want to believe that trustworthiness pays, disregarding considerable evidence to the contrary? The answer lies firmly in the realm of social and moral behavior, not in finance.
>
> The businesspeople we interviewed set great store on the regard of their family, friends, and the community at large. They valued their reputations, not for some nebulous financial gain but because they took pride in their good names. Even more important, since outsiders cannot easily judge trustworthiness, businesspeople seem guided by their inner voices, by their consciences. (Bhide and Stevenson 1990, 127)

It is interesting to compare this picture of businesspeople rationalizing their moral preferences by reference to "sustainable competitive advantage" with the tension expressed by early industrialists (see the quotation from Joyce above). In the intervening century and a half, the rationalist attempt to dictate norms that conflict with moral impulses has still not been quelled, but the modern businessperson has at least learned to counter neoclassical "expertise" with fancy terms of his or her own. The most telling point, however, is that something (I believe it is partly the neoclassical conception of rationality) has created a felt *need* to justify moral behavior and to pretend that moral behavior is really just another form of self-interest. This is not likely to deter those whose hearts are really set on responsible behavior; however, it cannot be expected to raise the moral standards of those who have not been so well socialized. Nevertheless, the U.S. capitalist system described by the various commentators quoted here continues to have a moral character that, though not as developed as might be wished (for the sake of efficiency, as well as for other reasons) is well beyond the predictions of neoclassical theory.

Kahneman et al. flesh out the Harvard Business School picture with particulars on the way that norms of fairness operate in wage and price setting.

> Conventional economic analyses assume as a matter of course that excess demand for a good creates an opportunity for suppliers to raise prices, and that such increases will indeed occur. The profit-seeking adjustments that clear the market are in this view as natural as water finding its level—and as ethically neutral. The lay public does not share this indifference. Community standards of fairness effectively require the firm to absorb an opportunity cost in the presence of excess demand, by charging less than the clearing price or paying more than the clearing wage.[4]
>
> [In general] The cardinal rule of fair behavior is surely that one person should not achieve a gain by simply imposing an equivalent loss on another.[5]

---

4. A reasonable economic response to this passage is that, if there is an excess of demand over supply, some people will have to do without the good. Raising prices is one way of choosing who gets and who goes without. Other ways include government rationing, queuing systems, bribes, or personal relationships ("favoritism"). Each of these has its problems. The lay public's standards of fairness do not necessarily take into account the practical or moral side effects of alternatives to profit-seeking behavior. As Paul Streeten notes, it is curious that economists, who usually take people's preferences as given, dismiss these preferences when they are against short-term price increases and for rationing (personal communication, 1994).

5. Kahneman et al., 735, 731. Interestingly, this rule may be seen as a prime requirement of Adam Smith's famous "impartial spectator" of conscience:

"Community standards" of fair behavior are data that can be inter-preted as either normative or positive. If the latter, they are "facts" about what people think should happen, not necessarily about what does happen. I am not claiming that morality in accord with community stan-dards is the only guide to business behavior—just that it is an important factor, that actual market transactions rely heavily upon it, and that it has been put under unnecessary and possibly harmful stress by the neo-classical definition of rational behavior. "[T]he rules of the marketplace as they were embodied in the Anglo-American law of contract at its zenith in the nineteenth century" were, evidently, more informed by the rationalist approach than by the community standards to which Kahneman et al. referred. These rules "assume that everyone will put his own interests first and withhold even customary or neighborly levels of concern for else. The seller charges what the market will bear, not what the buyer can afford to pay."[6]

Given these two visions of what market relations are or should be, should we anticipate that one vision will, over time, gain over the other? Or should we assume that the neoclassical view, on the one hand, and the popular/Adam Smith/Harvard Business School view, on the other, have reached some kind of equilibrium modus vivendi in which they will remain? The second assumption leads to a passive acceptance that it does not matter, for real-world outcomes, what theory we teach and learn. The other view is expressed by an economist and a philosopher who together wrote.

> Suppose that adherence to moral norms or values really does con-tribute significantly to Paretian social welfare, but economists fail to recognize this contribution. If this is true, then ignoring the role of social norms will lead to a failure to see and be concerned that this important "social capital" may be eroding over time.[7]

To disturb [another's] happiness merely because it stands in the way of our own; to take from him what is of real use to him, merely because it may be of equal or more use to us, or to indulge in this manner, at the expense of other people, the natural preference which every man has for his own happiness above that of other people, is what no impartial spectator can go along with. (Smith 1982, 137)

6. The quotations in this paragraph are from Thomas Haskell (part 2, 548). He is an historian who has written an intriguing account of some of the moral effects of capitalism, stressing its positive over its negative effects. Haskell's article will be discussed in some detail in the concluding chapter to this book.

7. Griffin and Goldfarb (1989), 20. See also, ibid., 9; Phelps 1975; Hirsch 1976; Bergsten 1985; Brunner 1987; Gauthier 1978; and Coleman 1987.

The danger described in the paper just quoted is that the assumption of universal selfishness can be a self-fulfilling prophecy. Our present system, based on distrust, may encourage irresponsible behavior that confirms the validity of distrust. It may also (as suggested in Michael Porter's essay in this volume) help to erect or strengthen barriers that prevent the convergence of interest among significant actors—that is, withholding the information and the responsibility that would permit them to express the motivations that, if unleashed, would be rationally oriented to long-term economic health.

What could, or should, economists do about issues like trust and responsibility? I would propose that, first, they should give serious attention to three matters: (1) the critical importance of such moral issues to economic life, (2) the possibility that these important elements are being undermined by economic theory, and (3) defining more precisely the economic sphere in which trust and responsibility are relevant. Then what? Should we change a theory because we dislike its side effects?

If our theory were the most accurate representation of truth we could achieve, one might be reluctant to prescribe any tampering with it. However, there is little pretense that modern economic theory is closely related to truth. Milton Friedman's dicta, in the 1953 essay, "Towards a Positive Theory of Economics," have been taken seriously by economists (even though they have been ridiculed by philosophers of science), so that economics has accepted a very narrow area in which it expects, or hopes, to find truth. Certainly not in its assumptions:

> the relation between the significance of a theory and the "realism" of its "assumptions" is almost the opposite of that suggested by the view under criticism. Truly important and significant hypotheses will be found to have "assumptions" that are wildly inaccurate descriptive representations of reality, and, in general, the more significant the theory, the more unrealistic the assumptions (in this sense). (Friedman, 14)[8]

---

8. It is possible to accept Friedman's (not fully explicit) argument that the complexity of the real world can never be fully expressed in any model and that a successful hypothesis " 'explains' much by little, that is, . . . it abstracts the common and crucial elements from the mass of complex and detailed circumstances surrounding the phenomena to be explained" (ibid.) while still striving to come closer to an ideal of accurate representation. Some simplifications do less violence to the reality they represent than others. The simplifications that are not just *less rich than* reality but that in some important way *contradict* it (more accurately called *falsifications* than *simplifications*) constitute hidden time bombs within a discipline. They are likely to be the basis of what later become "stories that blow up" into paradox or meaninglessness or highly inappropriate policy recommendations. See Goodwin 1991, chap. 11.

If we do not hope for "truth" in the *assumptions* of economics, neither should we expect to find it in economic *models*. One of the more sensible modern neoclassical economists recently wrote a paper describing the difficulty of development economics in adapting modeling techniques to the realities of "imperfect competition" that characterizes developing economies, given that "[t]here are, unfortunately, no general or even plausible tractable models of imperfect competition." His conclusion is that "[t]his means that in order to do development theory one must have the courage to be silly, writing down models that are implausible in the details in order to arrive at convincing higher-level insights" (Krugman 1992, 7). My opposing conclusion would be that we are deriving the wrong higher-level insights from wrongly applied models and that the courage we need is to continue the difficult search for alternative methods and techniques.

According to Friedman, economic theory stands or falls on the closeness of the match between its *predictions* and the state of the real world at the future time predicted. However, the record of economic predictions over the last few decades is a poor one: the predictive models work as long as circumstances stay about the same, with present rates and kinds of change continuing into the future. Just when life gets interesting is when the models cease to track the real world. If we accept the evidence of experience, that predictive truth is not a strength of economics, we are left with a discipline that has little *external consistency*—little correlation, that is, between elements of the theory (whether they be assumptions, models, or predictions) and elements of the real world. The discipline of economics builds its credibility entirely upon possession of a high degree of *internal consistency* in the manipulation of extremely "powerful," "rigorous," and impressive symbolic techniques.

Coming back to the question—should we change a theory because we dislike its side effects?—I am prepared to say that the effects upon the real world should take precedence over such a theory as I have just described. In other words, if a theory's major claim is internal consistency, while it does a relatively poor job of reflecting the real world *and* may have harmful effects upon it, then, yes, it is of interest to look for an alternative theory.

What would one look for in an alternative? Attempts to create one or more such alternatives are still in their infancy.[9] All agree, however,

---

9. Efforts in this field include Herman Daly and John Cobb, *For the Common Good* (Boston: Beacon Press, 1990) and the first publication in my series: *Social Economics; An Alternative Theory,* Vol. 1, *Building Anew on Marshall's Principles* (New York: St. Martin's and London: Macmillan, 1991). See also *A Survey of Ecological Economics* (Washington, D.C.: Island Press, 1995).

that there is an urgent societal *need for economic theory to be broadened so that the health of society, and of the ecosystem in which it is embedded, will be included within the theoretical (as well as the practical) definitions of the objectives of economic actors, especially firms*—keeping in mind that firms are chartered by society for social as well as self-seeking purposes (see Ralph Estes, quoted below).

2. Owners, Stakeholders, and Externalities

> The standards of the system say this: If you are faced with a question of closing a plant in Dodge City, Kansas that will put 5,000 people out of work and devastate a community, devastate a school system, devastate a police department, devastate the social fabric of that community, leaving many of these people never to work again, in order to move that plant to Juarez, Mexico to earn a .5 percent higher return on investment for the stockholders and a few pennies more in earnings per share, the system now says, "Hey, you've got to do it." You can feel sorry for Dodge City, but you've got to do it. And managers don't like to do that, but they do it. (Estes 1991, 21)

To suggest that economic theory should take account of moral behavior and goal definitions as they impact upon economic life is not mere wishful thinking. Most human beings would, on the whole, prefer to do good than to do harm, especially if they can make the choice without great personal sacrifice. Part of what makes a job meaningful is the sense that, in some way, it does good in the world. Firms do not, as abstract entities, generate their own objective functions. Although certain pressures are developed out of bureaucratic inertia or in response to market signals, firm goals are subject to at least some molding by human beings. Especially as the growing wealth of society creates a wider range of choice for more and more people, they are becoming increasingly dissatisfied with norms that box them in to what they feel to be morally inferior choices.

Several sources may be quoted in support of the foregoing statements. One is a former CEO who has written an account of his decision to leave a company. He begins, "Most CEOs grow to hate the treadmill of quarterly reporting. I certainly did, and I was the CEO of a company that boasted 29 consecutive quarters of sales and profit growth in excess of 50% and four stock splits. We were the first software company to reach $1 billion in valuations" (Cullinane 1991, 1). However, he concluded that "[f]rom a personal standpoint . . . running a publicly held company focused on quarterly reporting was not an enjoyable, long term career path" (11). His reasons for this conclusion included the following factors.

> In a publicly held company, the overwhelming need to produce good quarterly results shifts the focus from the customer to the bottom line. As much as 30% to 50% of executive managements' time can be consumed in the reporting process, particularly as the quarter comes to a close. There isn't much time or energy left to focus on customer needs, and management's decisions, despite claims to the contrary, are greatly influenced by the quarterly reporting cycle. . . .
> Examples are endless, but in every case the focus shifts away from the customer in a publicly held company to the bottom line as management tries to keep Wall Street, analysts, large investors, and the trade press happy with a rich stock, which also happens to be the best defense against an unfriendly takeover. Despite economic theories to the contrary, it's virtually impossible to keep the customer as the Number One concern in this environment. (7)

The voice of the CEO is joined by other voices stressing the issues of company ownership and the related questions: To whom is a company legally answerable? To whom should it be morally responsible? How can the moral and the legal relation be made more nearly unified?

> Originally a share of stock was more than an economic investment, it was an ownership interest in a company embodying both rights and responsibilities. Today, a share of stock is a financial commodity, little different from an ounce of silver or a pork-belly futures contract. The increasing legal and regulatory barriers that prevent stockholders from behaving as owners, coupled with new technologies that make it less expensive and easier to trade stocks, are transforming the stock market into less of a place to raise capital and exercise corporate oversight than a gambling casino. (Jacobs, 31)

Michael Porter's essay in this volume illustrates, with examples from the market for investment capital, concerns similar to those cited here. At the center of the problems in the capital market in the contemporary United States we find a loss of human relationships between borrowers and lenders.[10] Porter's essay describes a number of ways in

---

10. See also Jacobs for a strong emphasis on the destructive effects of the loss of relationships in business. For examples of businesses and industries benefiting from

which individuals and groups, including legislators, have hurt their long-run interests by pursuing strategies that, in a narrow context, appeared rational.

In this atmosphere of distrust, legislators and regulators have accepted the strategy thrust upon them by all parties: to attempt to replace *responsibility* with *accountability* (see section 4 below). In the process, the system has become ever more rigid and incapable of empowering the appropriate individuals and institutional representatives with the information that would permit the discharge of responsibility. The intangibles that get short shrift in this situation are often precisely those investments—such as the development of new technologies or of human skills—that have the greatest positive externalities to society at large and to its future economic health.

As long as the firm's interests are defined only in terms of the owners (stockholders), then any of its actions that affect the other stakeholders but not the owners are, by definition, externalities. Reflecting on private versus social returns to investment, Porter notes that firms generate positive externalities when they raise the skill level of the society by worker-training programs; when productivity-increasing investments in technology raise the productivity, hence the wages, of workers; or when they develop new technologies that accrue to the advantage of customers or of other industries and their employees. The presence of such externalities results, however, in a difference between the optimal rate of investment for society and the optimal rate for an individual firm—the latter being lower than the former.

Beyond its stockholders, the stakeholders in a firm include the employees, neighbors, customers, creditors and suppliers, as well as a catchall term, "society." That last includes all of those who may be affected, positively or negatively, by the firm's environmental impacts, as well as by the effects of its actions on stockholders, employees, neighbors, and the like, in the future as well as in the present. If it were possible, through some fair system of proportional representation, to represent all stakeholders in the decision making of firms, we might face a situation in which there would be no externalities left to internalize (see the concluding chapter to this volume). This is a tempting line of thought. There is growth in interest in Employee Stock Option Programs (ESOPs) and other ways of establishing employee ownership, as well in the idea of socially responsible investing and in such promising

---

the cultivation of relationships, see, for example, Sabel 1990, Mody 1992, and Lorenz 1988.

initiatives as the European experiments with designating ombudsmen for the future or for the environment.[11]

Unfortunately, it cannot be expected that all stakeholders will, in fact, be able to be represented, or indeed that, if they were, it would be possible to designate the fair and appropriate proportion of representation for each category. We have seen that Michael Porter, who assumes that this ideal can never be fully realized, recommends legislative changes to shift the legal definition of "good business judgment" now enjoined upon directors and managers toward a definition that will explicitly emphasize the objective of enhancing *long-term* shareholder value. Others go further, believing that shareholder value, even when viewed from a long perspective, does not adequately include all of the stakeholders who should be represented in defining a firm's objectives.

One of the ways to approach accountability is to look at accounting systems. Ralph Estes, a professor of this subject at American University in Washington, D.C., notes that

> there is no accounting above all for the major purpose for which the corporation exists. A corporation is not chartered by society to provide a return to stockholders. We allow that. But the reason we give corporations valuable charters is because we expect corporations to serve the public purpose, to do something good for society. (Estes, 18)

As we saw earlier, such an expectation is embedded in community norms, but it has not been adequately institutionalized in the norms of business practice. Estes's recommendation on how to begin to change the standards of the system is to enlarge the requirements of accounting income statements, to include goods, bads, and bottom lines for each of the stakeholders who are at present under- (or un-) represented: employees, consumers, local communities, and society at large. The CEO quoted earlier similarly suggests that "government could do much in its regulatory and tax practices to solve this problem, including requiring

---

11 See Edith Brown Weiss 1984. Her proposals include "establishment of a trust fund for future generations, which could be used to clean up damages inflicted by prior generations and to provide compensation to individuals in future generations who suffer particularized harm from the acts of those in prior generations" (Superfund, for all its inequities, operates like such a fund, for a particular kind of damage; see Newcombe, this volume) as well as "representation of future generations in international, regional, national, and local decisionmaking" through the actions of publicly financed "ombudsmen charged with ensuring compliance with the proposed trust principles once they are embodied in positive law" (Weiss, 564). See also, Block, this volume.

audited information on gain or loss in market share and customer-satisfaction levels in annual reports" (Cullinane 1991, 15).

At issue here is the critical subject of goal definition. Most groups, as well as individuals, accept a significant portion of their definition of success from societal norms rather than thinking it all out for themselves. When an individual's definition of success is oriented to a code of honor, it is hard to persuade that person to accept money for a deed that would tarnish his or her reputation or self-esteem. A person who has been taught that getting rich is the only game in town will find it equally hard to comprehend passing up a quick buck for a more intangible reward.

It is a mistake, for several reasons, to think that the concept of profit maximization adequately sums up the goal definition of firms. Empirical evidence against such a simple view has been produced by three groups: (*a*) theorists who emphasize the primacy of selfish individual goals over any firm goals (e.g., Oliver Williamson, James Buchanan, and the public choice school); (*b*) institutionalists and others emphasizing the "behavioral theory of the firm" who suggest alternative firm goals, such as firm size, total sales, or market share; and (*c*) theorists of "social responsibility" such as Ralph Estes or Alisa Gravitz who affirm the obligation of firms to respond to society's needs.

Neoclassical economic theory has been slow in adapting to these alternative possibilities because the primacy of the profit motive has been so strongly built in that it has taken on a normative force. What neoclassical economics most powerfully offers to social welfare is the promise that, if certain conditions are met, certain types of optima can be expected to be reached. Abandonment of the central assumption of profit as the chief motivator for firms undercuts some of the logic on which this promise is made.[12]

The role of profits in contributing to a well-functioning market can perhaps be better understood if we distinguish between the *profit motive* and *profit discipline*. The latter refers to the fact that, for survival, private firms normally do have to ensure that market-determined revenues exceed market-determined costs. Examples exist of firms that can avoid this requirement for long periods of time; for example, those that

---

12. The neoclassical promise has other problems, too—of inequity and lack of realism. Pareto optimality and the optimal allocation of resources to their "most socially desired uses" both depend heavily on an assumption that *the existing distribution of wealth is just*. The conditions required to achieve these optima are also unrealistic, including an absence of market-affecting power, perfect knowledge by all economic actors (including knowledge of the future) and other unlikely characteristics on which "perfect competition" depends. See section 4 of this chapter.

can fall back on government bailouts or that possess power to raise prices with little or no regard to costs (e.g., through monopoly power or through political price-setting mechanisms such as may be found in military suppliers). Such examples teach us that firms that do not have to heed profit discipline are likely to waste resources.

Looked at this way, profit discipline is a constraint—one of many under which most firms must operate. However, while goals are affected by constraints, they need not be *defined* by them. A firm can pursue some primary goal other than profit as long as it operates within the parameters established by its total set of binding constraints. This total set includes, beside profit discipline, the laws of the country in which it operates, the laws of nature (such as gravity and friction), the norms of social behavior that set at least the minimum standards required to attract and keep workers and customers, and so forth.

This line of reasoning suggests that there is more leeway in goal definition for firms than has been suggested by much economic theorizing. Pairing this conclusion with the normative position that has been developed in this essay—that society would be better off if firms and the individuals within them accepted some basic concepts of societal well-being as important goals—how, then, should we proceed?

In thinking about corporate goal definition, a spectrum exists, one end of which begins with *legislation that is under public control*. Public bodies can, for example, exert various kinds of legal controls on the media and can bring about the kinds of legal changes and legally mandated accounting changes suggested by Porter, Estes, and others. The other end of the spectrum is anchored in the *individual moral convictions* that come from internalized values. Here public roles may also be found, for example, in formal education or in the influence wielded by the media. However, this end of the spectrum is more obviously dependent upon such cultural issues as how children are raised and what examples are set for children by admired figures in their immediate environment. There is no sharp line dividing the two ends of the spectrum; they shade into one another.

Somewhere in the middle of the spectrum—located, if anything, closer to the cultural than to the legislative end—is the effect of theory. There is at least some likelihood that businesspeople, in particular, will behave the way they have learned, in school, that rational economic actors behave; while workers, who may not have taken an economics course, can nevertheless be expected to be influenced by the behavior of those above them. When the boss puts his paycheck, his stock options, and his golden parachute first, with scant emphasis on the quality of production or the firm's service to social welfare, it seems likely that the workers on the shop floor will feel their performance is of diminished importance in terms of its meaning as part of a positive social contribution.

What is it that people seek, and get, from work? First, of course, a livelihood. At least since the beginning of the agricultural revolution, most people have faced the truth of the dictum "you have to work to live." Going back longer in history, to the hunting-and-gathering way of life that has been the human experience during approximately 99 percent of our species' existence, the second thing people get out of work is the thrill of the chase. This can take a number of forms: for an entrepreneur it can be the excitement of closing on a business deal (sharpened, for some, when it is a competitive win in which someone else loses); for an intellectual it can be the satisfaction of coming up with the answer to an abstract problem.

The third thing that people hope to get out of work is a sense of meaning, or purpose, in their lives. The necessity that "you have to work to live" can provide a simple, direct purpose that provides sufficient meaning for some. Also, the thrill of the chase can shade off into the quieter satisfaction of overcoming all the little obstacles (from fatigue to uncertainty to issues of interpersonal relations) that can stand in the way of doing a good job. In this way, the second motive for work (the thrill of the chase) as well as the first (life support) can both support the third—the desire for meaning.

However, the question—"What's the point of it all?"—is increasingly likely to occur to people as several factors in modern societies weaken the connection between their daily work and their survival. The two most obvious of such factors are a general rise in affluence, allowing many people to retire early or to take periods of time off from work without hardship, and the welfare state, which holds out the possibility, even to those without capital assets, that survival is possible without a conventionally defined job.

Following Max Weber, we encounter pessimistic predictions that the inevitable drift of any bureaucracy is away from the larger goals and responsibilities of institutions in society toward the narrow interest of the bureaucrats in perpetuating and extending their own power and influence. There are many examples of the fulfillment of this prediction. But there are also examples of economic activities and economic actors whose prime motivation is neither the maximization of profit nor the perpetuation of a government bureaucracy but rather contributions to some broadly defined conception of human welfare. I would suggest that an important clue to the understanding of such responsible behavior is the desire to find meaning in one's work. That desire, strengthened and liberated by the forces mentioned above (modern affluence and the security offered by the welfare state) surely must be taken into account if we are to understand the picture of social responsibility drawn, for example, in Alisa Gravitz's essay in this volume.

3. The Role of Environmental Concern in Bringing the Future Home to the Present

This essay has argued that trust and responsibility are essential if markets are to operate even reasonably well. At the same time, evidence has been presented to suggest that people have a variety of strong motivations that encourage them to behave responsibly and to encourage and extend trust. All of this should add up to a comfortable closed loop: there is a need for trust and responsibility, and human nature urges behavior that will fill the need. What else needs to be said? The problem is that the neoclassical social sciences, led by economics, have proved, to the satisfaction of some, that altruistic business behavior—behavior, that is, that is not strictly oriented to profit maximization—is doomed if there are any profit maximizers around and if the market system is sufficiently competitive to permit the maximizers to triumph over the altruists. As in the case where, at one time, physics had "proven" that it was impossible for a bumblebee to fly, one response may be merely to shrug off theory. However, theory has a potentially useful role. If we are to devise new theory that can develop that potential, a good place to start is by explaining something that cannot be accommodated within existing theory.

We might begin this effort by looking at the two "ifs" upon which the doom of the business altruists was predicated: "*if* there are any profit maximizers around, and *if* the market system is sufficiently competitive." The first is hard to rule out completely but may give rise to the observation that profit maximization is not, at least, nearly as prevalent as neoclassical economists have long assumed. Human nature may contain strong enough urges impelling individuals to strive toward other goals so that profit maximization may, at least in some situations, be reduced to a minority position. If not all of the neoclassical requirements for perfect competition are present, so that the second condition is not fully satisfied, then the minority profit-maximizing position will likely not be able to wipe out the nonmaximizers.

The requirements for perfect competition include such unrealistic elements as perfect information and no uncertainty for all participants; perfect mobility for all factors; the existence of markets in all commodities (including contingent markets); and the absence of any kind of market power that could erect barriers to entry or permit the externalization of any costs (increasing returns to scale, collusion, or ability to influence government actions are all related to market power). Here, it would seem, is an explanation for why the world is as it is and not as predicted by neoclassical theory. However, such observations have not sufficed to alter the way the theory is taught. We need more concrete evidence of how the loop may be closed between what should be and what (sometimes) is.

That evidence is finally emerging in a new formulation in which we can quite clearly see *environmental problems* and *concerns for the future* as two intermediate links between *the needs of the future* and *market behavior in the present*. One of the best exponents of these relationships is Stephan Schmidheiny, chairman of the Business Council for Sustainable Development. In his words,

> tomorrow's winners will be those who make the most and the fastest progress in improving their *eco-efficiency*. Why? Because:
>
> > Customers are demanding cleaner products, as well as products and services which are in keeping with the development goals of poorer countries;
> > Insurance companies are more amenable to covering clean companies;
> > Employees, particularly the best and the brightest, prefer to work for environmentally responsible corporations;
> > Environmental regulations are getting tougher, and will continue to get tougher;
> > New economic instruments—traces, charges and tradeable permits—are rewarding clean companies, and;
> > Banks are more willing to lend to companies which prevent pollution rather than having to pay for expensive clean-ups. (Schmidheiny 1992, 57)

Environmental problems are relevant because consumers, banks, insurance companies, and governments—as well as environmental interest groups—are experiencing the fact that we are living in someone else's long run. *Environmental concerns* enter the picture when, by analogy, these actors recognize that business behavior today will have important determining effects on tomorrow's environment, and they care about this. Thus, the projected problems of tomorrow are inserted into the business environment of today (see fig. 2.1).

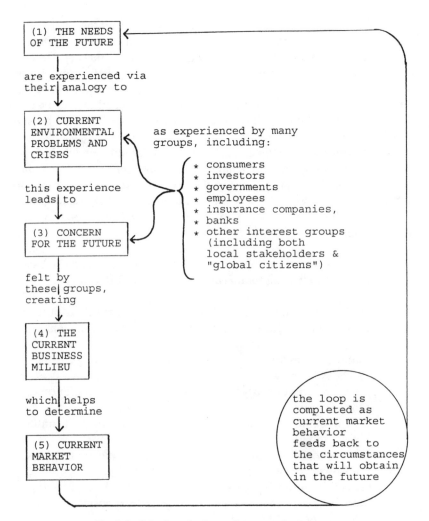

Fig. 2.1. Bringing the future home to the present.

This is a fairly straightforward chain of cause and effect. Starting at the end of the chain, current market behavior (link 5) emerges from link 4, the present business milieu, which is affected by link 3, people's concerns for the future, which are generated by link 2, existing environmental problems, which cause people to worry about link 1, future environmental problems. There is plenty of room in link 5 for neoclassical rationality to operate: self-interest could be a fully adequate explanation for corporations' responses to the demands of consumers and interest groups, to the need for insurance and credit and government regulations, and even to the need to attract high-minded employees. However, neoclassical economics failed to predict such a chain, and the reasons why it failed are probably to be found in the fact that "people's concerns for the future" (link 3) are social, not just individual, concerns. Moreover, the leap made by analogy from present to future problems is not at all predicted in neoclassical theory. This leap is the one that brings the future home to the present—it is the human tendency to say "if something is going to be important in the future, then we have to care about it in the present."

4. Convergence of Interests, Trust, and the Dirty Third Portion

> Lacking the confident self-discipline of the civic regions, people in less civic regions are forced to rely on what Italians call "the forces of order," that is, the police. . . . [They] have no other resort to solve the fundamental Hobbesian dilemma of public order, for they lack the horizontal bonds of collective reciprocity that work more efficiently in the civic regions. In the absence of solidarity and self-discipline, hierarchy and force provide the only alternative to anarchy. (Putnam, 112)

If all interests were perceived to be aligned together—or if all externalities were internalized—issues of trust and responsibility would be far less important than they are. It is when the interests of employers diverge from those of their employees—or of producers from those of their customers, or of upstream farmers from those of downstream water users—that the questions arise: "How far will you go to gain your ends? What code of conduct can I count on? What enforcement can ensure that you will not cheat me—or that you will not cheat me too much?" One point on which neoclassical rationalists and contextual economists like myself are likely to agree is the desirability of reducing the areas of conflict by finding ways to increase the convergence of interests as well as knowledge about such convergence.

The question may be raised whether there is not a logical contradiction in simultaneously promoting a convergence of interests, on the one hand, and trusting economic actors to behave responsibly, on the other: is not trust required when interests conflict and irrelevant when they converge? In fact, I will suggest that, while there is a contradiction here, the problem is not so much in the internal logic as in some practical realities.

The problem of internal logic vanishes when we consider two things. First, we know that the creation of a long-term perspective in which economic actors can perceive convergences of interest will not happen instantly. At best we can hope for an iterative process wherein there are changes in rules and expectations, then goals are redefined (as part of the cultural norms), followed by more practical changes and more goal redefinition. In order to set the sequence in train it is essential to recognize its different parts—especially the difference between the responsibility-related issue of goal definition and the other issues of institutional change related to convergence of interest.

The second point is that, of course, we will never achieve a world in which all interests will converge or will be seen to converge. Moreover, when a society has gone as far as is practical in fostering the convergence of perceived interests, the area that is left will be divided up not into two parts—where divergent interests are negotiated either through *legislation* or through *responsibility and trust*—but into three. Enforcement, together with the norms of trust and responsibility, cannot cover the whole area. There will always remain some loopholes where the flouters of norms will also be able to evade the law. To make this worse, there are some reasons to fear that, as enforcement expands to deal with such loopholes, the area covered by the cultural norms shrinks. In recent decades, this shrinkage appears to have been occurring more rapidly than the expansion of effective enforcement, so that the residual dirty portion, where neither norms nor enforcement are effective, is also growing.

An example of the dirty third portion is offered in Robert Putnam's book on Italy (1993) in which he observed a division of that country into "civic" and "uncivic" regions. In the uncivic regions, reliance upon hierarchy and force is accompanied by a society of free riders, defectors, and other sufferers from prisoner's dilemma-type outcomes:

Instead of recognizing that taxes had to be paid, the attitude was rather that if one group of people had discovered a profitable evasion, then other groups had better look to their own interests. Each province, each class, each industry thus endeavored to gain at the expense of the community. (Dennis Mack Smith, quoted in Putnam, 143)

The size of this third portion—where we find the unsatisfactory solutions engendered by criminals, free riders, and those who look for legal loopholes that allow them to pursue their own gain at an overall cost to society—and the cost of its burden on society as a whole may thus be related to the relative weight given to legal versus normative ways of dealing with the area of nonconvergence of interests: as our reliance on legal solutions grows, the dirty third portion may also grow. I suspect that there is some impossibility theorem to be derived here: the area covered by legal mandate pushes before it a broad leading edge in which responsible behavior has been ruled out but where law cannot enforce behavior for the social weal.

This conclusion accords with the belief of many neoclassical economists that the most important role for government is to free up the invisible hand of competition so that markets can perform their job of allocating resources to the uses most desired by society. This prescription has, however, generated its own problems and controversies. These may be considered under two broad headings.

The first is the practical question of how active a role this implies for governments. At the laissez-faire extreme, the prescription has been for government to do almost nothing and let the actors in the market fight it out among themselves. Others have pointed out that for markets to perform as the theory suggests there has to be perfect competition. Even if that ideal is unreachable (which it increasingly seems to be), government intervention is required (again, how much?) to preserve some degree of competition against the forces that would tend to concentrate market power in oligopolistic or, at the extreme, monopolistic configurations.

The second problem area relates to fairness, or equity. We can believe that markets actually do allocate resources to "the uses most desired by society" only if society is defined in a way that accepts the principle of "one dollar one vote" as appropriate and fair. A market system gives more weight to the wishes of a person with more money and less weight to a poor person. As far as the market is concerned, a person with no purchasing power (that is, with no money) simply does not exist.

Such equity problems have long been recognized and have often been brushed aside in the conclusion (a conclusion that, in fairness, has not been lightly reached) that we face an inevitable trade-off between equity and efficiency: if we want to equalize access to resources we must face the likelihood of less total product to be shared among the whole people. No one has shown a perfectly reliable way to escape this trade-off (though there are credible arguments suggesting that it is not as ubiquitous as suggested by neoclassical theory). Given the scale on which modern capitalism has believed it had to live, it has generally chosen to slide more toward one end (maximizing total output without regard for distribution) rather than the other (more equitable sharing of a smaller pie).[13]

Economists often suggest that equity questions would be better handled by some other group—philosophers, perhaps, or politicians. However, when politicians do step in to try to impose equitable outcomes upon a market system, economists like Milton Friedman are apt to protest that the resulting market distortions create unacceptable decreases in efficiency. The distortions might be more acceptable if they could be counted upon to produce an equitable result. But, too often, market interventions produce the undesired efficiency-harming distortions without the desired result of equity.

This discouraging observation does not mean that the laissez-faire extreme is the best social policy. Remember, again, that the theory of markets that has been the basis for government intervention within capitalist systems has started from an inadequate vision of a well-working market. A critical omission from the standard neoclassical theory is the meaning and importance, for markets, of the human issues of responsibility and trust. Modern commerce depends upon the presumption that contracts will be honored. Governments, so often castigated as inimical to "free" markets, are essential enforcers. But the whole system would come crashing down if it depended in each and every instance upon government enforcement.[14] Markets depend criti-

---

13. Streeten notes that this choice is made in spite of mounting evidence that

shows that providing poor people with education, health, credit, other resources, and jobs, utilizes the most important resource: human beings, and contributes to greater efficiency. Small farms are more efficient than large ones, and small farmers save at least as high a proportion as large ones. (personal communication, 1994)

14. Cf. Partha Dasgupta (1988), writing about the extent to which trust can be replaced with force, who notes that for the threat of punishment for errant behavior to be credible, "the enforcement agency itself must be *trustworthy*" (Dasgupta 1988, 50). He continues:

no contract, even if it is scrutinized by sharp lawyers, can detail every eventuality, if for no other reason than that no language can cope with unlimited refinement in distinguishing contingencies. Thus trust covers expectations about what others will

cally for their effective functioning on the existence of responsibility and trust as characteristics of the human actors within the markets. Failing to recognize this fact, we have so organized and regulated our markets that we have done nothing to enhance and protect the environment for responsibility and trust. We have also in many ways degraded that environment and turned these qualities into liabilities at the personal and even at the institutional level.

5. Business, Culture, and Social Science

How have we brought about these undesirable results? A broad statement of the problem is that fragmentation and depersonalization in the business culture have transformed *responsibility* (a personal commitment to doing what is right) into *accountability* (the requirement to meet externally set standards)—and the latter isn't working very well. A cultural devolution such as this is an enormously complex thing to trace. Drawing on characteristics of the American business scene, especially as described by Michael Porter (in this volume) and Michael Jacobs (1991), I will repeat here just a few aspects of what has happened:

Disintermediation. In a capitalist society, the relationship between borrowers and lenders is one of the focal points at which the interests of the future can be translated into present interests. When they are functioning at their best, banks, as important institutionalized borrowers, can be a powerful voice for long-run interests. The lender usually faces a relatively long payback period, and its concern for repayment creates an interest in the long-term health of the borrower (see also Newcombe, this volume). This interest can be expressed only if banks are allowed to share expertise with and give guidance to their borrowers, especially when the latter are in difficulties, but at other times as well. However, the American regulatory system has erected formidable barriers against such a flow of information and management assistance from lenders to borrowers. Borrowers, grabbing for the least expensive loan, and regulators, acting on a mistrust of banks that dates back to the Great Depression, have jointly removed from banks the information and the responsibility that, in other times or other places, allows lenders to give meaningful expression to their concern for the long-run health of borrowers.

The commoditization of corporate ownership. The market for capital is another of the places where the translation from future to present interests occurs. The mergers and acquisitions of the last two decades

---

do or have done (or what messages they will transmit) in circumstances that are not explicitly covered in the agreement. (52–53)

have affected the structure of the U.S. capital market in a number of
ways. One of these has been to obscure the original meaning of a stock
as representing a relationship with a particular activity. If, as has increasingly become the case, the entity to which the stock is attached is an
umbrella organization with no identity in terms of a specific productive
resource, then stocks represent nothing but money. This is the meaning
of Jacobs's reference to "the comoditized U.S. market where price is
virtually all that matters" (Jacobs, 153). Commoditization is the other
side of depersonalization: the breaking of what are essentially human
bonds and connections—of knowledge, concern, involvement, loyalty
and "voice."[15]

Principal/agent problems. In the world of American business, directors receive little guidance from owners (stockholders) who, when dissatisfied with a company, increasingly go by the "Wall Street Rule":
they exit rather than challenge management. Management has gotten a
bad name for inflating its own salaries within a vacuum of responsibility
that invites takeovers. At the same time, managers are suspicious of
owners whom they see as aligned on the side of hostile predators;
hence, managers' insistence on poison pills and golden parachutes and
their attempts to pass state legislation that makes it ever more difficult
for owners to exert control on management. Whom does this leave to
delve deeply into the company's business? The professional stock analysts whose job is to assess the value of companies should, ideally,
possess the best information. If they did, they would advise their clients
on the basis of good projections of the future health of companies.
Firms whose profits seemed likely to be on the rise would have such
predictions of future health translated into current value. That would
be the ideal antidote to short-termism in business. The reasons why this
does not happen, from information short circuits for fear of leaks to
competitors, to educational values elevating theory over reality, have
been outlined by Michael Porter in this volume and elsewhere.

This is a picture of a vicious cycle whose elements include:

Cultural norms, that is, commonly held beliefs about how people
should and *do* behave in various roles. I have cited economic
theory as a source of part of the belief system contributing to the
norms of behavior for workers, managers, owners, entrepreneurs, and so on.

Laws and regulations. Any law is, at best, an approximation, at-

15. Cf. Hirschman 1970. For a view of the broader historical context for this process,
see Mazlish 1989.

tempting to respond to the majority of the cases it covers with fairness and to minimize the unfairness of the outlying cases that get swept up in its general applications. In the logic of bureaucracy, regulations that fail to achieve their goal call forth more regulation. When they are based on an erroneous original analysis of the situation—of what is wrong or what is desired—successive regulations may simply add to the problem and to the perceived need for yet more legal solutions.

Particular institutional forms. Relevant examples include institutional investors, banks, boards of directors, unions, "quality circles," government bureaucracies, and institutions of learning such as universities and business schools.

On first considering the elements in this loop, there is little reason to expect that government (the force behind laws and regulations) could be effective in reinstituting trust among its business actors. Rules solidified as general application laws can never be nimble enough to follow the ability of humans to invent ways to circumvent them on a case-by-case basis. Only humans can follow humans as they swing through the jungles of inventiveness. But modern business theory and practice have, to an alarming extent, succeeded in removing humans and human relationships from the picture.

Once again, we seem to arrive at the neoclassical economists' conclusion: that governments do more harm than good when they attempt to meddle with markets beyond creating the basic institutions to enforce contracts and punish outright theft. If, for a moment, we accept that conclusion, we are still left with a motivation for change that comes from the fact that the situation we now experience is perceived as highly unsatisfactory, while the experience of other times, or other countries, suggests that it is possible to do better. If we despair of government as the agent of change, we must look again to the other two elements in the positive feedback loop that has brought us to this situation: cultural norms and institutions.

An examination of institutions will, I suspect, bring us to much the same conclusion as that regarding governments: whether we are looking at bureaucracies or businesses or third sector institutions such as educational institutions, it is the cultural norms that pervade the issues of trust and responsibility. Should we become so impoverished in our moral/economic culture that responsibility would depend entirely upon accountability, we would be in serious trouble indeed. However, it has continued to be true, at least up to the present, that *people often behave more responsibly than they are obliged to*. This is the fact that we must keep in mind and upon which we must build.

Albert Hirschman, the author of one of the few well-known articles (1970) by an economist dealing with these subjects, considers two different approaches to the "ingredient known variously as morality, civic spirit, trust, observance of elementary ethical norms, and so forth." Noting that "[t]he need of any functioning economic system for this 'input' is widely recognized," he goes on to examine two opposing models for how to use it. The traditional neoclassical one is exemplified in Hirschman's reference to Dennis Robertson's 1956 paper ("What Does the Economist Economize?"), which asserts that it is "the economist's job to create an institutional environment and pattern of motivation where as small a burden as possible would be placed, for the purposes of society's functioning, on this thing 'love,' a term [Robertson] used as a shortcut for morality and civic spirit." The alternative is to treat moral resources like skills, "whose supply may well increase rather than decrease through use," and to remember that "like the ability to speak a foreign language or to play the piano, these moral resources are likely to become depleted and to atrophy if *not* used" (Hirschman 1984, 93). Hirschman's conclusion, however, is that both of these models are wrong.

> Love, benevolence, and civic spirit are neither scarce factors in fixed supply, nor do they act like skills and abilities that improve and expand more or less indefinitely with practice. Rather, they exhibit a complex, composite behavior: they atrophy when not adequately practiced and appealed to by the ruling socioeconomic regime, yet will once again make themselves scarce when preached and relied on to excess.
>
> To make matters worse, the precise location of these two danger zones—which incidentally correspond roughly to the complementary ills of today's capitalist and centrally planned societies—is by no means known, nor are these zones ever stable. (94)

It is particularly illuminating to ponder Hirschman's comments about the correspondence of communism with the "ideological-institutional regime" that makes "*excessive* demands on civic behavior" and of capitalism with the danger of "atrophy of public feelings," which give rise to "anomie and the unwillingness ever to sacrifice private or group interest to the public weal" (94–95). Now, with the widespread collapse of communism, it appears that neither Castro's call for a "New Man" nor Mao's hopes for a "Great Leap Forward" based on individual willingness to sacrifice for the general good were within the reasonable range of the extent to which societies can depend upon economic morality. Unfortunately, however, the American capitalist system seems to have given up the search for that reasonable range. It contains within itself tendencies that, if allowed to go on determining the society's institutional and legal responses, will continue in the direction of "atrophy of public feelings."

As suggested earlier, there is another way of conceptualizing the balance that so urgently needs to be defined. At any given time in any society we face a certain amount of nonconvergence among perceived interests. We have two options for dealing with this: we can trust to the possibility of responsible behavior even when it may go against one or another individual's perceived self-interest or we can attempt to legislate accountability to replace responsibility.

Is it possible that the social sciences are capable of maturing to the point where they can be used to analyze, understand, describe, and ultimately prescribe a *balance* between different behavioral options? Among the social sciences, economics has led the way in the use of symbolic modeling techniques, relying on intimidating mathematical tools for a variety of powerful and sophisticated approaches to *optimization*. However, these approaches are more appropriately applied to clear-cut quantities than to vague behaviors, let alone moral tendencies. Yet there are social needs, not well addressed by such techniques, to which the social sciences should be able to make a useful response.[16]

The social needs may be stated in the following way:

Social trust and its foundation, responsibility, are eroded by an assumption (spread through the more highly educated members of society) that moral behavior is irrelevant. Far from being irrelevant, trust and responsibility are essential to economic as well as other kinds of well-being.

An economy can be undermined by behaviors, assumptions, cultural norms, institutions, and laws that reduce the scope for moral behavior.

We cannot, at a jump, assume a degree of trust that is far in excess of the actual exercise of responsibility. At the same time, we need to understand how to promote both responsibility and trust with-

---

16. There are other examples of the social sciences' need to shift from a maximizing to a "balancing" orientation. The environmental crisis makes it especially critical to support a shift away from the historically generated expectations that the prices of food, energy, and some other commodities will always decline as a relative portion of the average household budget or that the size of the human population and the gross amount of materials and energy processed through economic activity will always absolutely increase.

out resort to artificial programs that will merely produce hypocrisy and cynicism.

There is an acute need for social science to aid in understanding how to strike a good balance between responsibility and accountability, while keeping in mind that how that balance is struck may materially affect the size of the uncontrolled third portion of society that escapes the influence of either morality or law—the "dirty third portion" of free riding and other kinds of cheating.

There may be a special need to identify, clearly and publicly, the positions (especially, but not exclusively, in government) that are most critical to "the public trust" and to foster debate on the kinds of education and training appropriate for those who will fill these roles. The neoclassical economic conclusion, that governments should do as little as possible, has been arrived at without sufficient attention to ideas on how governments can be reformed from the inside, starting with individual civil servants.

An appropriate social science response to these needs must, first of all, come to grips with an overt *acceptance of the purposes of social science,* along with their implications. An admirable reason for the drive to positivism that has characterized the social sciences since early in this century was the recognition of potential conflicts between the goals of truth in science versus the commitment of science to human welfare and the conviction that, in order to give priority to truth, it was necessary to deny the other more value-laden goal of contributing to human welfare. If that had worked, it might still be an acceptable compromise. However, it has not worked: truth has not been especially well served, and the welfare goal has sneaked in the back door in the less savory guise of ideology (whether the ideology of the "free market"—a fiction—or of the "people's republic"—another fiction). The obvious thing to try next is conscious, honest admission of the role played by goals and purposes in each piece of social science work.

An overt social science response to social needs will look significantly different from the modeling and related techniques that now command the highest academic status. Such a reformed social science would include the following six characteristics.

First, it would *strive for a higher degree of realism*. There is some theoretical usefulness in hypothesizing a world of perfect competition, or perfect altruism, or perfect markets, or perfect governments, but most of the advantages from such exercises have probably already been derived, and those who still operate on these models are laboring against severely diminishing returns.

Perfect realism, of course, is also unobtainable. I am suggesting, however, that we reverse Milton Friedman's decision (see sec. 1) to abandon the attempt at being realistic. Instead, let us start with the modest goal of basing our social science theories upon *more* realistic images of the critical features of the world than neoclassical rationalism. To begin with, such realism requires a *willingness to accept complexity*. A common concern of all the social sciences is to understand human motivations. As causal agents, human motivations are as important to the social sciences as gravity, chemical bonds, and electromagnetism are in the natural sciences. Human behavior is, however, too complex to be sufficiently comprehended in the neoclassical simplification of "rational maximization."

Second, in contrast to the "heroic" simplifications of neoclassical theory, a more appropriate response to social needs would *identify the relevant actors* in ways that would not rule out, and might be more supportive of, responsible social behavior and its resulting trust. For example, in neoclassical economics individuals and families are modeled as providing labor for no reason but pay and as using their income in consumption behavior, which depends upon values that are diametrically opposed to the work ethic.[17] Attention to the continuity of goals between the roles of worker and consumer would be revealing on both sides. Attention to the need for meaning in work is likely to pay off in worker responsibility. A consumer whose goals also include the need for meaning would align more closely with social goals as distinct from the purely individualistic motivations of the neoclassical consumer.

A more complex awareness of differences among actors would highlight the divergences in their perceived interests while also recognizing varying needs, different sources of goal definition, varying institutional arrangements, and so on. It is also essential that the social sciences retain, or acquire, an acute sensitivity to issues of *relative power*, which "determines whose short-run interests are taken care of, at the expense of everyone else's collective long-term benefit" (Jacobs, 62).

Third, an overt purpose of such a social science would be to *find ways of bringing disparate interests into greater convergence*. For example, to encourage a convergence of interest among all economic actors it will be necessary to think about how to restructure the laws, institutions, training systems, and goals that affect the business climate. Theoretical as well as policy support will be needed, for example, in the following areas:

---

17. See Bell 1976; Sagoff 1988.

Supporting and increasing the value that is ascribed, in the present, to the well-being of the future. (Examples in the market for investment capital might include altering the capital gains taxes so that there is a relative penalty for rapid turnover of holdings or giving greater weight to the advantages of lower interest rates).

This recommendation rests on the assumption (subject to further empirical and theoretical testing) that there is a significantly greater likelihood of interests converging the longer is the time horizon perceived by the actors.

Including in the decision-making processes of business a wider group of stakeholders than only the stockholders.

Finding numerous ways of genuinely internalizing externalities (emphasizing bringing the costs of their activities home to the actors that generated the costs, as opposed to hypothesizing side payments to the losers).

Instituting accounting changes to support all the foregoing; for example, better ways of identifying both positive and negative externalities as well as ways of making it clear to all the stakeholders in a business enterprise how they are being affected by its activities.

Fourth, as we proceed with the effort to understand interests and motives, and to promote their true convergence, we also need to assess which of the remaining conflicts are likely to lead to abuses so intolerable that they must be legislated against. In making that assessment, we have to remember that we will never eliminate all abuses and that the size, incidence, and cost of the dirty third portion of unresolved conflict may be affected by *how we divide up the area of nonconvergence between mandated accountability, on the one hand, and trust and responsibility, on the other*.

Fifth, "society," as an entity, is more than just the sum of its parts. What use can theory make of the recognition that a healthy society requires more than just self-seeking behavior? Such a recognition suggests the application of a significant amount of intellectual resources to *understanding the forms and roles of morality* (including responsibility, justice, future-regardingness, etc.) in society's various sectors. It will be especially important to pay attention to the differences, in this respect, between the business (profit-disciplined) sector; government (theoretically dedicated to public service); the "third sector" (not-for-profit NGOs); and the household or family sector. The norms of each of these sectors is of great importance to societal welfare, including its economic health. Social sciences should seek to understand what influences these norms and how they are changed, maintained, or destroyed.

Sixth, it is also essential to adopt, as a central subject, a term that, it is hoped, will not become as desiccated and removed from human reality as "utility" and "self-interest" have become in neoclassical theory. This subject is *goals*—the things for which human beings strive and which are closely related to the *definitions of success* by which they measure themselves and to which their sense of well-being is closely tied.[18]

A subtext of this essay has been the question that is so often posed in modern times: for any given problem, is it the *market* or the *government* that is best able to provide a solution? Among the social sciences, economics is apt to reply, "the market," while political science looks to "the government." The point with which I wish to conclude is the following: in a society with a healthy moral context—one in which there is a high level of responsibility, supporting a high level of trust—*both* markets and governments will function well. If the moral context (or, in Seckler's terms, the moral regime) is lacking, then many problems will exist that cannot be solved either by markets or by governments. It is urgently important that the social sciences that are concerned with the effectiveness of markets or governments turn more of their attention to the moral context upon which both depend.

BIBLIOGRAPHY

Akerlof, G. 1983. "Loyalty Filters." *American Economic Review* 73, no. 1: 54–63.
Arrow, Kenneth J. 1972. "Gifts and Exchanges." *Philosophy and Public Affairs* 1:343–62.
———. 1973. "Social Responsibility and Economic Efficiency." *Public Policy,* summer, 303–17.
———. 1974. *The Limits of Organization.* New York: W. W. Norton.
Axelrod, Robert. 1984. *The Evolution of Cooperation.* New York: Basic Books.
Bell, Daniel. 1976. *The Cultural Contradictions of Capitalism.* New York: Basic Books.
Bergsten, Gordon. 1985. "On the Role of Social Norms in a Market Economy." *Public Choice* 45, no. 2: 113–37.
Bhide, Amar, and Howard H. Stevenson. 1990. "Why Be Honest if Honesty Doesn't Pay." *Harvard Business Review,* September-October, 121–29.
Bromley, Daniel W. 1990. "The Ideology of Efficiency: Searching for a Theory of Policy Analysis." *Journal of Environmental Economics and Management* 19: 86–107.

18. A social science that would have the characteristics just listed would come close to that which the philosophers of science Silvio Funtowicz and Jerome Ravetz have called "post-normal science." This option will be described in volume 3 of this series, being written by Neva R. Goodwin, Bruce Mazlish, Silvio Funtowicz, and Jerome Ravetz.

Brunner, Karl. 1987. "The Perception of Man and the Conception of Society: Two Approaches to Understanding Society." *Economic Inquiry* 25, no. 3: 367–89.

Colander, David C., ed. 1984. *Neoclassical Political Economy*. Cambridge, MA: Ballinger Publishing.

Coleman, James S. 1987. "Norms as Social Capital." In *Economic Imperialism*, ed. Gerald Radnitsky and Peter Bernholz. New York: Paragon House, 113–55.

Croome, H. M., and R. J. Hammond. 1947. Economic History of England. London:

Cullinane, John J. 1991. *Widows and Orphans*. Westborough, MA: Coalition of Information Technology Executives.

Dasgupta, Partha. 1988. "Trust as a Commodity." In *Trust: Making and Breaking Cooperative Relations,* ed. Diego Gambetta.

Doeringer, Peter B. 1986. "Internal Labor Markets and Noncompeting Groups." *AER Papers and Proceedings: Occupations and Labor Markets* 76, no. 2: 48–52.

Doeringer, Peter B., Phillip I. Moss, and David G. Terkla. 1986. "Capitalism and Kinship: Do Institutions Matter in the Labor Market?" *Industrial and Labor Relations Review* 40, no. 1: 48–60.

Estes, Ralph. 1991. Interview in *Corporate Crime Reporter* 5, no. 41 (October 28): 18–22.

Field, Alexander James. 1979. "On the Explanation of Rules Using Rational Choice Models." *Journal of Economics Issues,* March, 8, no. 1: 49–72.

Frank, Robert H. 1987. "If *Homo Economicus* Could Choose His Own Utility Function, Would He Want One with a Conscience?" *American Economic Review,* September, 593–604.

———. 1988. *Passions Within Reason—The Strategic Role of the Emotions*. New York and London: W. W. Norton.

Frank, Robert, Thomas Gilovich, and Dennis Regan. 1993. "Does Studying Economics Inhibit Co-operation?" *Journal of Economic Perspectives* 7, no. 2 (Spring): 159–71.

Friedman, Milton. 1953. *Essays in Positive Economics,* Chicago: University of Chicago Press.

Gambetta, Diego, ed. 1988. *Trust: Making and Breaking Cooperative Relations*. New York: Basil-Blackwell, Ltd.

Gauthier, David. 1978. "Economic Rationality and Moral Constraints." *Midwest Studies in Philosophy* 3: 75–96.

Goodwin, Neva R. 1991. *Social Economics: An Alternative Theory*. Vol. 1, *Building Anew on Marshall's Principles*. New York: St. Martin's Press, and London: Macmillan.

Griffin, William B., and Robert S. Goldfarb. 1989. "Amending the Economist's 'Rational Egoist' Model to Include Norms." Unpublished manuscript.

Hart, Keith. 1988. "Kinship, Contract, and Trust: The Economic Organization of Migrants in an African City Slum." In *Trust: Making and Breaking*

Cooperative Relations, ed. Diego Gambetta. New York: Basil-Blackwell, Ltd.

Haskell, Thomas L. 1985a. "Capitalism and the Origins of the Humanitarian Sensibility, Part 1." *American Historical Review* 90, no. 2 (April): 339–61.

———. 1985b. "Capitalism and the Origins of the Humanitarian Sensibility, Part 2." *American Historical Review* 90, no. 3: 547–66.

Hausman, Daniel M., and Michael S. McPherson. 1992. "Taking Ethics Seriously: Economics and Contemporary Moral Philosophy." *Journal of Economic Literature* 29, no. 1. This essay includes a detailed bibliography of writings relevant to the intersection of economics and ethics.

Hirsch, Fred. 1976. *Social Limits to Growth.* Cambridge, MA: Harvard University Press.

Hirschman, Albert. 1970. *Exit, Voice and Loyalty: Responses to Decline in Firms, Organizations, and States.* Cambridge, MA: Harvard University Press.

Hirschman, Albert O. 1984. "Against Parsimony: Three Easy Ways of Complicating Some Categories of Economic Discourse." *American Economic Review* 74, nos. 1–2: 89–96.

Jacobs, Michael T. 1991. *Short-Term America.* Boston, MA: Harvard Business School Press.

Joyce, Patrick. 1980. *Work, Society and Politics: The Culture of the Factory in Later Victorian England.* New Brunswick, NJ: Rutgers University Press.

van de Kragt, A. J. C., R. M. Dawes, and J. M. Orbell. 1986. "Doing Well and Doing Good as Ways of Resolving Social Dilemmas." In *Experimental Social Dilemmas,* ed. A. M. Henk, Dave M. Messick Wilke, and Christel G. Rutte. New York: Peter Lang.

Kahneman, Daniel, Jack L. Knetsch, and Richard Thaler. 1986. "Fairness as a Constraint on Profit Seeking: Entitlements in the Market." *American Economic Review* 76, no. 4 (September): 728–41.

Krugman, Paul. 1992. "Towards a Counter-Counter-Revolution in Development Theory." Paper presented at the World Bank Annual Conference, Washington, D.C., April 30 and May 1.

Leibenstein, Harvey. 1982. "The Prisoner's Dilemma in the Invisible Hand: An Analysis of Intrafirm Productivity," *Microeconomics Reconsidered* May, 92–97.

Lorenz, Edward H. 1988. "Neither Friends nor Strangers: Informal Networks of Subcontracting in French Industry." In *Trust: Making and Breaking Cooperative Relations,* ed. Diego Gambetta.

Mansbridge, Jane J. ed. 1990. *Beyond Self-Interest.* London: University of Chicago Press.

Marwell, Gerald, and Ruth E. Ames. 1981. "Economists Free Ride, Does Anyone Else?" *Journal of Public Economics* 15, no. 3: 295–310.

Mazlish, Bruce. 1989. *A New Science: The Breakdown of Connections and the Birth of Sociology.* New York: Oxford University Press.

Mody, Ashoka. 1992. "Making Institutional Choices." Unpublished manuscript.

Phelps, Edmund. 1975. Introduction to *Altruism, Morality, and Economic Theory*, ed. Edmund Phelps. New York: Russell Sage Foundation, 1–9.

Platteau, Jean-Philippe. 1991. *The Free Market Is Not Readily Transferable: Reflections on the Links Between Market, Social Relations, and Moral Norms*. Cahiers de la faculté des sciences economiques et sociales, Notre Dame de la Paix, Namur, Belgium, November.

Pomery, John. 1989. "Economists' Understanding and Understanding Economists: The Roles of Metabeliefs." Unpublished manuscript.

Putnam, Robert D. 1993. *Making Democracy Work: Civic Traditions in Modern Italy*. Princeton, NJ: Princeton University Press.

Roth, A. E. 1988. "Laboratory Experimentation in Economics: A Methodological Overview." *Economic Journal* 98, no. 393: 974–1031.

Runge, C. F. 1984. "Institutions and the Free Rider: The Assurance Problem in Collective Action." *Journal of Politics* 46, no. 1: 154–75.

Sabel, Charles F. 1990. "Studied Trust: Building New Forms of Co-Operation in a Volatile Economy." In *Industrial Districts and Local Economic Regeneration*, ed. Werner Sengenberger and Frank Pyke. Geneva: Institute for Labour Studies.

Sagoff, Mark. 1988. *The Economy of the Earth: Economy, Law and the Environment*. Cambridge: Cambridge University Press.

Sen, Amartya. 1984. "Adam Smith's Prudence." Unpublished manuscript.

Sen, Amartya. 1985. "Well-Being, Agency and Freedom: the Dewey Lectures 1984." *Journal of Philosophy* 82, no. 4: 169–221.

Schmidheiny, Stephan. 1992. "Business, Banking and Sustainable Development." *International Economic Insights*, September-October.

Smith, Adam. 1982. *The Theory of Moral Sentiments*, ed. D. D. Raphael and A. L. Macfie. Indianapolis: Liberty Classics.

Stigler, George. 1981. "Economics or Ethics?" In *The Tanner Lectures on Human Values II*, ed. Sterling M. McMurrin, 143–91. Salt Lake City: University of Utah Press.

Tendler, Judith. 1994. "Trust in a Rent-Seeking World: Health and Government Transformed in Northeast Brazil." *World Development* 22, no. 12 (December): 1771–91.

Tullock, Gordon. 1984. "How to Do Well While Doing Good!" In *Neoclassical Political Economy: Rent-Seeking and DUP Activities*, ed. David Colander. Cambridge, MA: Ballinger Publishing Company.

Vanberg, Viktor. 1986. "Spontaneous Market Order and Social Rules." *Economics and Philosophy* 2: 75–100.

Weiss, Edith Brown. 1984. "The Planetary Trust: Conservation and Intergenerational Equity." *Ecology Law Quarterly* 2, no. 4: 495–581.

Wright, Gavin. 1990. "The Origins of American Industrial Success, 1879–1940." *American Economic Review*, September, 651–68.

3

A Second Paradox of Thrift: Investment Strategies and the Future

Fred Block

Thus our argument leads towards the conclusion that in contemporary conditions the growth of wealth so far from being dependent on the abstinence of the rich, as is commonly supposed, is more likely to be impeded by it. (John Maynard Keynes, *The General Theory of Employment, Interest, and Money,* 373)

This statement in the final chapter of *The General Theory* succinctly states the first paradox of thrift. While orthodox economists had lauded the rich's willingness to save as the vital key to economic growth, Keynes offered a radically different perspective. He insisted that the decision to save by the rich does not automatically translate into an increased demand for investment goods. Too high a rate of saving can depress demand, and the economy could reach equilibrium with high unemployment and substantial unused capacity. The policy prescriptions were obvious. Income should be redistributed downward into the hands of people with a higher propensity to consume, and the government should take a more active role in bolstering aggregate demand.

This first paradox of thrift has now been largely forgotten. The pre-Keynesian view that the supply of saving is a fixed pool that constrains the level of investment spending has been restored, and we have heard constantly about the declining rate of household saving in the United States.[1] Nevertheless, Keynes's analysis is enormously relevant for understanding what happened in the U.S. economy during the 1980s (Block 1992a). A system of income and wealth distribution that was already skewed in favor of the rich became even more favorable toward them. Until the late 1980s, the economy was spared the consequences of which Keynes warned because of massive deficit spending for military purposes, which sustained aggregate demand. However, with the end of the Cold War and the exhaustion of the boom in commercial real estate

---

1. For decline of savings argument, see Bernheim 1991. For alternative views, see Blecker 1990 and Block and Heilbroner 1992.

development, the weakness of consumer demand has produced the longest economic slump since the Great Depression.

Here, however, my interest is in a second paradox of thrift that lies buried in the *General Theory* but that is also critically important for making sense of our contemporary economic problems. Keynes wrote, "If human nature felt no temptation to take a chance, no satisfaction (profit apart) in constructing a factory, a railway, a mine or a farm, there might not be much investment merely as a result of cold calculation" (150). His argument is that, given the inherent uncertainty of the future, purely rational calculation might veto virtually all long-term investment decisions as too risky. It is at this point that he invokes the "animal spirits"—the irrational side of human nature that accounts for entrepreneurial willingness to take risks.

Keynes's argument can be generalized: if the rational calculation of self-interest that is the hallmark of "economic man" is carried to its logical limits, market economies would collapse. This is precisely the argument that Karl Polanyi (1957) elaborated at length in *The Great Transformation*. Elsewhere (Block 1990), I have argued that when individuals recalculate their self-interest on an hourly basis, the result is a destruction of the ties of loyalty and trust that are fundamentally necessary for any kind of production. My point here is that, as individuals and institutions become more calculating and "rational" in the management of their financial portfolios, the result is an ever greater unwillingness to make funds available for the kinds of productive long-term investment on which the future health of the economy depends. In Keynes's language, an upward shift in the liquidity preference of investors can serve to discourage productive investment.

I will also argue that postindustrial changes in the nature of the production process exacerbate this problem. Increasingly, it is intangible forms of investment—on research and development, on employee training, on organizational and software development—that are the key factors in the productivity of the firm. This shift from tangible to intangible—or from more solid to less solid—types of investment capital intersects with rising liquidity preferences to further weaken the economy's capacity to provide for the future.

My argument will proceed in three steps. First, I will elaborate the idea of liquidity preference and provide some evidence that it has been rising. Second, I will discuss the "desolidification" of the firm—the shift toward more intangible forms of investment—under postindustrial conditions and point out the contradictions under which we now labor: investors' preferences have been shifting toward greater liquidity while the essential investments for the health of firms are shifting toward illiquid "desolidified" capital. The conclusion will suggest some institutional reforms that could reorient economic decision makers to act as though the future matters.

Capital and Portfolio Strategies

Keynes insisted that the rate of interest was the result of two factors— the supply of money capital and the liquidity preference of those who hold the money capital. Liquidity preference can be understood as the strength of the attraction to hold wealth simply in the form of money. The higher the liquidity preference, the higher the rate of interest that borrowers would have to pay to induce the owners of money capital to purchase a less liquid asset. Liquidity preference is a variable that is influenced by the overall rate of uncertainty, the rate of inflation, and other factors such as the transactions costs of converting assets to money.[2] But the key point is that if the liquidity preferences of investors are rising, even an increase in the supply of capital might not suffice to lower the critical long-term interest rates that have most influence on corporate investment decisions.

My argument is that changes over the past 25 years in the organization of financial markets have significantly increased the overall liquidity preference in the United States. Innovations in financial markets have produced secondary markets in a wide variety of financial obligations, and these have generally reduced the transactions costs of converting a particular asset to cash. Hence, investors can hold commercial paper or mortgage debt in their portfolios with confidence that those assets can be resold on a secondary market. However, such secondary markets usually involve significant variations in the price of assets as interest rates and other economic conditions change. Since the risk of price changes is likely to rise in inverse proportion to the reduction in transactions costs, the net effect of the emergence of secondary markets on the liquidity of a particular asset is difficult to predict.

In the period 1969 to 1979, the postwar stability of the U.S. economy came to an abrupt end, leading to significant shifts in the portfolio

---

2. Assets that fluctuate significantly in price are less liquid because the investor might face a significant loss when the asset is converted to cash. I am assuming that the transactions costs of converting an asset to cash, the length of time the asset must be held, and its volatility can be captured in a single metric that would rank the most commonly held assets in terms of their degree of liquidity.

strategies of investors. Inflation rates were high and the stock market experienced much greater volatility than earlier in the postwar period. Almost any particular long-term investment strategy that an investor might be pursuing was likely to produce terrible results in at least several of those years. Moreover, since uncertainty was very high, investors could not know if those terrible returns were a short-term aberration or were likely to continue in the future.

Increased uncertainty about investment returns stimulated two intersecting responses. First, there was an enormous increase in the provision of investment advice to consumers in the form of books, newspaper columns, radio and television shows, and people who made their living by selling investment advice directly to consumers. Second, there was a parallel increase in the range of investment instruments that were made available to investors. The key turning point was the birth of the money market funds in 1974, which placed strong competitive pressure on banks and led to a series of "reforms" that freed commercial banks and savings and loans (S&Ls) to offer depositors "market rates" of interest on certain types of deposits.[3] Before these reforms, bank and S&L interest rates on deposits had been subject to government-mandated ceilings.

It should be emphasized that the logic of the market for financial advice and for selling new financial instruments was quite different from the idea of increasing the public's macroeconomic sophistication. People were told that if they pursued X financial strategy or invested in Y instruments, they were likely to become rich beyond their wildest dreams. The idea that investors in the aggregate could not increase the value of their assets over the long term any faster than the rate of growth of the economy as a whole was rarely mentioned.[4] If workers are sometimes fooled by "money illusion" into believing that a nominal wage increase is worth more than it actually is, then investors were routinely fooled by the promise of high nominal rates of return.

At any rate, the profusion of advice and new instruments created a

---

3. The shift of resources into money market funds meant that investors were taking greater risks than those involved in federally insured bank deposits. However, the interest premium they received over bank rates meant that this shift could be consistent with a rising liquidity preference. For example, if the only way they could gain a comparable rate of interest at the bank was to commit the money for a five-year term, then the choice of the riskier—but more readily redeemable—money market would be the more liquid investment.

4. To be sure, sharp increases in asset prices can lead to returns that are substantially higher than the economy's rate of growth. However, over the long term, prices of assets such as corporate equities or real estate are supposed to correspond to the future flow of services they are expected to produce.

more "sophisticated" modal investor who generally recognized the futility of pursuing a stable long-term investment strategy and sought instead to rearrange his or her portfolio on a regular basis to assure high short-term returns. This approach to investing requires minimizing holdings of assets that cannot be transformed into cash relatively quickly. In particular, one has to reduce holdings of multiyear bank certificates that cannot be redeemed for cash without penalty.

Above all, this more sophisticated investor was ever alert to the possibilities of dramatic capital gains when prices in certain asset markets began to rise very quickly. In several recent years, for example, the combined return—dividends and appreciation of capital values—on the Standard and Poor's New York Stock Exchange index was more than 20 percent per year. Such returns reinforced the desirability of a portfolio management style in which one could quickly take funds out of assets with a lower rate of return in order to participate in the rapid appreciation of asset prices.

The consequence, of course, was that this more "sophisticated" investor chose investments with higher liquidity than his or her less sophisticated predecessor. He or she was less likely to hold any particular asset for the long term, and if the returns on the stock market or bank deposits turned down, sophisticated investors in the aggregate would shift billions of dollars to assets with higher returns.

At the same time that these changes occurred in the orientation of individual investors, there was also a dramatic shift in the role and importance of institutional investors. The pools of capital controlled by pension funds, insurance companies, money market funds, bank trust departments, and other institutional investors have grown spectacularly over the last 20 years. According to one analysis, institutional investors held 21 percent of corporate stocks in 1970, 29 percent in 1980, and 45 percent in 1990 (Useem 1993). Here again, the uncertainty and turmoil of the 1969–79 period disrupted older habits of money management. As the risks of any particular long-term strategy became evident, institutional investors were also forced to adopt more "sophisticated" strategies that meant greater diversification and continual reorganization of investment portfolios. These tendencies were intensified by the "professionalization" of money management. As these organizations became larger, individuals came to specialize in portfolio management, and they expected career opportunities and compensation to keep pace with the exercise of their skills. For purposes of evaluation, the relevant information was the rate of return earned by a portfolio manager for the most recent quarter or year. Had the "profession" not grown so rapidly, it might have been possible to also evaluate people on their rate of return over a five- or ten-year period, but since many practitioners had not been around that long the shorter time frame became the relevant one.

The result, of course, was that virtually all money managers had to compete to keep up with those with the best short-term results.[5] Here again, there was no choice but to abandon an orientation to high long-term returns in favor of an orientation to short-term returns. As with individual investors, the effective result was an increase in liquidity preference through the avoidance of strategies that tied up assets for long time periods.

To be sure, there are some additional twists and complexities to this story. In the 1980s, for example, some money managers at pension funds and insurance companies shifted a portion of their portfolios toward real estate through acquisition of land and participation in development projects, particularly for commercial real estate. At the time that these investments were made, they appeared to offer both high liquidity and very high short-term returns because of the rapid appreciation of real estate prices. Even joint participation in certain real estate development projects appeared to be an asset that could easily be resold to a third party. Of course, this appearance of liquidity was a mirage and when prices tumbled, these money managers found themselves locked into assets that could only be sold at huge discounts.

The key point is that the impact of the growing sophistication of individual and institutional investors was most profound in the stock market. The effect was greatest on established firms with moderate growth prospects. Small high-technology firms that held out the promise of extremely rapid growth—the Apple Computers of the future—had little difficulty attracting shareholders even when dividends were minimal or nonexistent. This was because the possibility of very rapid appreciation in share value made purchase of these stocks attractive to many investors looking for high short-term returns. It was a different story with those firms that might expect their sales or profits to grow 3 to 15 percent a year if everything went well. If a firm with that kind of growth potential decided to pay a relatively small dividend in order to reinvest profits in future growth, it found itself in a difficult situation in this new environment.

---

5. Keynes recognized this problem already in the 1930s. He wrote: "Finally it is the long-term investor, he who most promotes the public interest, who will in practice come in for most criticism, wherever investment funds are managed by committees or boards or banks. For it is in the essence of his behavior that he should be eccentric, unconventional and rash in the eyes of average opinion. If he is successful, that will only confirm the general belief in his rashness; and if in the short run he is unsuccessful, which is very likely, he will not receive much mercy" (157–58).

The problem is that for investors with a strong orientation toward short-term results, the combination of small current dividends and only moderate future growth prospects does not provide a sufficiently high rate of return. Such a firm finds its stock relatively undervalued, and it becomes a prime target for a hostile takeover. In order to avoid that fate, management has little choice but to increase dividends and rely more on debt issues to finance new investment. However, given the higher transactions costs involved with borrowing as compared to the use of retained earnings, the firm will be more cautious in its investment planning.[6] In short, the pursuit of higher short-term returns by stockholders will push this firm to curtail its rate of investment in productive capacity (Greenwald and Stiglitz 1987). As Stein (1989) has noted, this managerial myopia is most likely to mean cutting less visible forms of investment such as spending on human capital.

Another attractive option for these firms has been to attempt to grow at a faster rate through acquisitions.[7] This path is appealing to potential investors because growth through acquisitions can justify a rapid increase in the firm's stock price. However, the only reliable way to finance such acquisitions is through increased borrowing, so acquiring firms find themselves facing a heavier debt burden. Since many of these deals are motivated by growth for its own sake, they often do little to improve the efficiency with which resources are used in the acquired firms. Hence, in order to produce a large enough flow of profits to cover the debt obligations, such a firm also has no choice but to curtail its rate of productive investment both in its core businesses and its newly acquired subsidiaries. In sum, the orientation of shareholders toward high short-term returns has a major impact on the decision-making parameters of corporate managers.

Evidence of Liquidity Shifts

It is essential for this argument that the alleged shift toward short-term portfolio strategies be more than a useful assumption or "stylized fact."

---

6. For a powerful critique of these pressures on the firm by a corporate CEO, see Cullinane 1991. I am grateful to John Dunlop for bringing this piece to my attention. For a useful discussion of the extremely high hurdle rates for justifying new investments that firms adopted in response to these pressures from the financial markets, see Lowenstein 1991.

7. Another option is for management to engage in a leveraged buyout (LBO) so as to eliminate the threat of a hostile takeover. However, the heavy debt burdens in these LBOs also force many firms to curtail their productive investments (Kaplan and Stein 1991).

It is difficult to figure out a single composite measure that would allow us to compare portfolios systematically over time. Nevertheless, there are significant indicators that support the hypothesis of increasing liquidity preferences. One of the most important is the increasing spread between short-term and long-term interest rates. Assuming that the risk of default is held constant, it would seem that higher interest rates on long-term instruments are necessary to induce investors to hold a less liquid asset. An increase in the spread between short-term and long-term rates would indicate that investors' preference for more liquid assets are growing stronger.

Figure 3.1 compares the yields of three-month Treasury bills with 10-year Treasury bonds. For each instrument, the annual figures represent a five-year moving average to reduce the impact of cyclical changes. The yield figures for the long-term instruments are effective yields that reflect the shifts in bond prices. The upward trend of the spread became apparent in 1976, and it was only interrupted by the monetary squeeze of 1979–81. In that period, the Federal Reserve's tightening of credit pushed short-term interest rates to historic highs leading to three years during which short-term rates were actually higher than long-term.[8] However, as economic expansion resumed, the spread again became positive and by 1985 the gap exceeded three percentage points.

Another indicator is changes in the composition of household financial portfolios. The Federal Reserve estimates of the financial holdings of households indicate a dramatic shift away from ownership of equity in noncorporate businesses, a highly illiquid asset. In 1981, ownership of noncorporate businesses represented 32.1 percent of the total financial assets of households, but this figure dropped to 18.7 percent in 1990. It is not clear what factors fueled this shift, but the result was clearly a significant increase in the liquidity of household financial portfolios.

Another indication of the change of household financial behavior can be seen from the balance sheets of S&Ls. In 1970, 53 percent of federally insured S&Ls' liabilities—or $84.1 billion—were in the form of passbook savings deposits. By 1984, passbook savings accounted for only 6.7 percent of S&L liabilities (*Statistical Abstract 1988,* 486). Consumers fled the traditional low-interest-rate–passbook account in search of higher yields. The result has been a strong upward trend in the amount that these federally-insured S&Ls have had to pay for deposits. This

---

8. Long-term rates also reached unprecedented highs. Ten-year government bonds produced an effective yield of 13.91 percent in 1991 as compared to 7.42 percent in 1987. Increased purchases by foreign investors of long-term instruments might account for the failure of long-term rates to move even higher during this period.

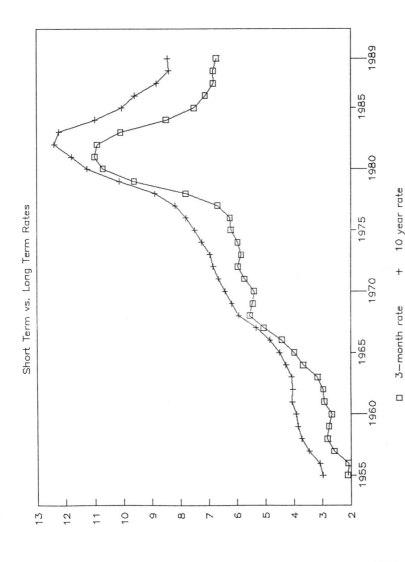

Short Term vs. Long Term Rates

Percentage Points

□ 3-month rate   + 10 year rate

Fig. 3.1. Short-term vs long-term rates. Data are five-year moving averages. (From: *Economic Report to the President 1992*.)

upward trend is indicated in figure 3.2, which shows the cost of deposits to S&Ls. At the same time, household investments in money market funds that are restricted to holding debt with an average maturity of four months or less, rose from $2.4 billion in 1974 to $438.6 billion in 1990 (Federal Reserve, *Balance Sheets for the U.S. Economy 1960–91*).

Institutional investors such as pension funds and insurance companies have been responsible for dramatic increases in stock turnover. Institutional investors account for almost all of the larger stock transactions, and as Useem (1993) reports:

> In 1965, only 3 percent of the shares traded on NYSE were exchanged in blocks of 10,000 or more. In 1980, the proportion had reached 29 percent. By the middle part of the decade, it soared to some 50 percent.

These large transactions are responsible for increasing the number of shares traded each year on the New York Stock Exchange by a factor of 10 between 1975 and 1987. While some large institutional investors might have been patiently holding on to corporate shares for the long haul, these aggregate patterns show that large institutional investors have become far more active as traders, turning over their stock portfolios at a rapid pace.

Desolidification and Liquidity Preferences

The awkward term *desolidification* is designed to express a fundamental shift in the nature of production in developed market societies. Implicit in the metaphor of liquidity is the idea that the plant and equipment of a firm are the opposite of liquid—they are solid. Yet it is increasingly clear that the capacity of firms to be profitable depends on factors that are not so solid—the skill and energy of their labor force, their ability to produce products of high quality, the effectiveness of the software that runs their computers, their ability to pursue technological innovation, the speed of their responses to changing markets, and their capacity to develop resource-conserving strategies as it becomes less feasible to impose environmental externalities on others. However one wants to categorize these different aspects of organizational effectiveness, the basic reality is that firms have to spend more resources on these less "solid" dimensions of production. Some analysts have made a distinction between tangible and intangible capital with intangible capital including expenditures on research and development, employee training, software, and improving organizational effectiveness. Such studies show that intangible capital

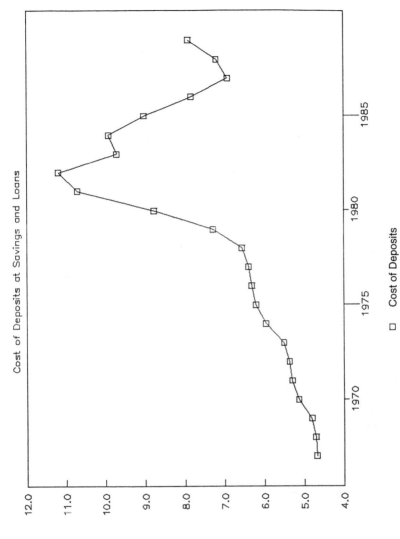

Cost of Deposits at Savings and Loans

Interest rate in Percent

□ Cost Of Deposits

Fig. 3.2. Costs of deposits at savings and loans. (From: U.S. Office of Thrift Supervision, *Savings & Home Financing Source Book*, 1989.)

expenditures have been rising as a percentage of all capital expenditures (Eisner 1989).

While it does not work in a strict sense, the analogy with solid, liquid, and gaseous states of matter is of some use here. As a firm's capital stock becomes less solid, it has more of the quality of a gas; it is not something one can touch nor is it easily contained. The purest case of this phenomenon is a firm that produces computer software. Its physical capital stock is quite limited; it consists of some buildings and some computers. The bulk of this firm's capital consists of two items. The first is the knowledge and experience of its programmers and of the people who manage the programmers. The second is the firm's reputation and the network of marketing agreements that help it to get its software to consumers.

As we know from examples such as Microsoft, this less solid type of firm can generate enormous profits, but it has marked differences from more traditional firms. Let us imagine the difference between this software firm and a firm producing consumer appliances in the 1950s if from one day to the next all their employees—below the highest management levels—simply walked away to take employment elsewhere.[9]

For the appliance firm, the impact of this departure would be serious but not catastrophic. We know, for example, that Ford survived a 67-day walkout by the UAW in 1967. It is probable that within three months, replacement workers could be hired and trained, and the plant would be running again at a reasonably high fraction of its previous output. Since highly skilled workers are needed for retooling, the firm would probably have to postpone model changes. However, its distribution network would probably be able to survive the three-month lull, and the firm would have a reasonable chance of regaining much of its earlier market share.

For the software firm, the consequences of this mass departure would be far more serious. The firm could not rely on local labor markets to find replacements. It would have to attempt to lure away skilled programmers from major competitors in other parts of the country. It would probably take years to reassemble a staff that was comparable to that which was lost. In the meantime, the firm would be able to continue to ship backlisted software, but it would not be able to upgrade existing programs or develop new products. Moreover, it might take as much as six months to reassemble competent teams to provide product support

9. The relevant comparison is with a consumer durable firm in a period when production and demand was relatively stable and standardized. As we move closer to the present, the production of consumer durables has also become less solid.

for customers, so that the firm's reputation for product support would collapse. Since the industry is highly competitive, with a rapid rate of innovation, the firm's market share would fall precipitously while it sought to reassemble a staff. Moreover, its partners in the industry would have strong incentives to cancel marketing agreements since such agreements assume both strong customer support and a continual flow of future products. In a word, the firm's prospects of surviving the mass departure are at best fifty-fifty, and its chances of regaining its former position are substantially lower.

The last step in this argument is to place oneself in the position of a bank that is a major creditor to these two firms. If the appliance firm were to go under and the bank were to foreclose on its physical assets, then the resale value of the physical plant would be considerable, provided that the facility was reasonably modern. One suspects that another appliance producer would be tempted to buy the plant and resume appliance production. In short, the solidity of the capital assets provides the bank with some significant degree of protection from default.

In the software firm example, once the firm has gone under and its employees have departed, the resale value of its buildings and its used computers would be quite limited. The millions of dollars that the firm spent on developing its human capital has no remaining physical embodiment that the bank can claim. It has simply evaporated.

To be sure, the software firm represents the extreme case, but there are other important segments of the economy that are quite similar in their level of desolidification—the entertainment industry, advertising, and publishing, for example. Moreover, many other industries that are increasingly dependent on innovation are moving toward the less solid end of the spectrum.

How then is this process of "desolidification" of capital linked to changes in liquidity preferences? The argument is that investments in "desolidified" capital are even more illiquid than investments in plant and equipment. The potential resale value of investments in research and development and human capital, for example, are unpredictable and indeterminate. Hence, we have a serious contradiction. Investors' preferences have been shifting toward greater liquidity whereas firms' needs have shifted toward increasingly illiquid assets.

This contradiction is likely to damage seriously the economy's potential for future growth. Even with increasing supplies of money capital, less of that capital is available for firms to spend on "desolidified" capital. Banks and bond issuers are reluctant to lend money for desolidified capital because the returns on such investments are uncertain and because creditors are far less protected from default. Moreover, paying higher interest rates to compensate for the higher risk will discourage many firms from making these investments. The stock market is equally unsupportive. Increased spending for "desolidified" capital will usually hurt the short-term bottom line, risking a fall in stock values and the increased danger of a takeover.

The key exception to this pattern is, of course, the eagerness of investors to finance start-up firms pursuing advanced technologies. Particularly in biotechnology and computer-related fields, new firms with reputable scientists have been able to raise large sums of money through venture capital and stock offerings long before they have any visible products. The problem, however, is that these investors are betting on the potential for huge increases in the firm's value if it develops a technological breakthrough. Once the breakthrough comes, however, the same sources of financing are not available to help the firm nurture the new technology into a successful product line (Florida and Kenney 1990). Even more importantly, these types of financing are not available for research work being done within established firms.

"Water, water everywhere, / Nor any drop to drink." The contemporary firm in the United States floats on a veritable sea of liquidity, but it faces major obstacles in drawing on those funds to finance the types of spending that would have the highest long-term returns. The most disturbing manifestation of this tendency is evidence that industrial expenditures by U.S. corporations on research and development peaked in the mid-1980s and began to fall in real terms after 1989 (Broad 1992). This is the second paradox of thrift.

Conclusion

This paradox is not rooted in human nature but in a particular set of institutional arrangements. For example, the Japanese system for providing corporations with financing has less of a bias toward the short term, and this has allowed many Japanese firms to cope more successfully with the transition to the more desolidified firm (Florida and Kenney 1990). Nor can these international differences in the time horizons of corporate managers be attributed simply to deeply rooted cultural differences. The latest scholarship on Japan, for example, suggests that many of the important features of its successful corporate model are of relatively recent vintage; they cannot be traced to some ancient Confucian past. In other words, it was only in the period after World War II that the Japanese developed a set of institutional arrangements that encouraged firms to plan for the long term. Similarly, the intense concerns about the short-term time horizons of U.S. managers are of relatively recent vintage. The distinguished business historian Alfred Chandler has recently emphasized the sharp discontinuity between this pattern and the previous history of the large U.S. corporations (Chandler 1990, 621–28). Hence, it makes more sense to attribute this shift to the institutional pressures of the financial markets described here than to some unchanging get-rich-quick strain in the American character.

If this failure of economic actors to act as though the future matters is rooted in institutional arrangements, then it is imperative to think of ways those institutions could be changed to reinforce longer-term time horizons. There are two basic reforms that could make a significant difference. Neither of these reforms are currently on the political agenda, but they should be widely discussed and debated.

The first is a reorganization of the system of corporate governance. Our present system for governing the corporation is a product of the nineteenth century, and it is badly in need of revision, particularly as the desolidification of the firm progresses. The core problem is that the power to choose the corporation's management is vested entirely in the shareholders. Other constituencies such as employees, lenders, and consumers are totally without representation unless they happen to also hold shares.

The sovereignty of the shareholders creates two severe problems. The first is the agency problem. Since the shareholders are a diffuse and ever changing group, they face severe difficulties in forcing the firm's management to act in their collective interest. The result is that top managers can easily become entrenched and pursue their own agendas. The second problem has been frequently suggested as the solution to the first. The diffusion of shareownership means that anybody who is able to borrow enough money to acquire more than 50 percent of the shares can replace the existing management. This is supposed to work to prevent entrenched managers from pursuing their own interests. The difficulty is that the new group that takes over the firm is totally unconstrained; its power to use the firm to pursue its own short-term interests is unlimited.

The deeper problem is that the "market for corporate control" as the means to solve the agency problem between shareholders and managers conflicts with the creation of a working environment that can maximize employee productivity. Employees are likely to be productive when they have developed a cooperative relationship with their supervisors that involves promises of future rewards such as employment security, promotional opportunities, and pay raises. These webs of reciprocal cooperation extend from the bottom levels of the organization to the top. However, they only work when there is a certain degree of stability and continuity of leadership in the organization or else the promises of one's immediate supervisor are worthless.

The possibility that the firm will be bought out tomorrow by a new group that will replace the existing top managers obviously conflicts with the desired level of stability and continuity. In such an environment, nobody can put any faith in anyone else's promises of future rewards, and the motivation of employees is likely to plummet. In short, "the market for corporate control" allegedly solves one problem but creates an even larger one.

The way out of these dilemmas is to reorganize the corporate board so that stockholders would choose only 35 percent of the board of directors.[10] Another 35 percent would be chosen by the firm's employees. The remaining 30 percent would represent other constituencies such as consumers, suppliers, lenders, and advocates for the interests of the environment. This arrangement would mean that the firm was not up for sale on a daily basis. On the contrary, one could own 100 percent of the shares and still not be able to dominate the board of directors. It would also be difficult for an existing management to become firmly entrenched in the pursuit of its own short-term interests. The possibilities of creating a winning coalition on the board to replace such managers would be high enough to discourage such behavior.

Most importantly, the substantial stake by employees in the firm would accurately reflect the realities of increasingly desolidified firms in which much of the productive capacity of the organization is embedded in its employees. The employees' legally mandated voice in the process of choosing the board of directors is designed to assure that top management of the firm pursues employment strategies that emphasize employment security and continual upgrading of employee skills.

The effectiveness with which employee interests are represented on boards of directors will vary with local conditions. Particularly in non-unionized firms, there will be a tendency for higher-level salaried employees to dominate the selection process. Moreover, some level of regulation will be necessary to prevent corruption of the process by which employee representatives are selected. In short, effective corporate democracy will not emerge overnight, but these reforms would

---

10. This could be done through legislative action. The first step would be to create federal incorporation of firms to overcome the irrationality of state incorporation laws. The new federal incorporation law would mandate these new procedures for choosing corporate boards that would apply both to "public" and privately held corporations above a certain threshold size.

begin a process of democratization that can be expected to unfold over many years.

Part of the logic of a board of directors on which no single constituency controls a majority is that key strategic decisions will have to balance the conflicting interests of different constituencies. For example, the tendency of shareholders to insist on high dividends in the present should be effectively balanced by other constituencies with a strong interest in the reinvestment of profits to assure the firm's growth.

Moreover, this set of arrangements should also avoid a problem that is often noted in the literature on employee ownership. Employees as a group tend to be risk-averse because their assets are relatively limited. When they own a firm, the individual ownership stake represents a very large share of each individual's assets. This creates the danger that employee-owned firms would be more risk-averse than traditional firms. Such aversion to risk might preclude reaching the levels of investment necessary to succeed over the long term in a competitive environment. However, in the proposed model of employees choosing 35 percent of the corporate board, the employees are not risking any of their own capital. The principal risk they face is that the firm's profitability will diminish, threatening their employment and wage levels. Hence, if they are properly represented on the board, they should support high levels of investment.

This is where the second institutional reform comes in. Particularly in the immediate aftermath of the first reform, firms would find it very difficult to raise new money through additional stock offerings. They would be dependent upon bank loans and bond offerings to finance those investments that could not be covered with retained earnings. Yet if the liquidity preferences of investors remain high, they will be forced to pay high interest rates that will force them to be quite selective in choosing which investment projects to pursue.

The reorganization of the corporate boards is intended to begin a shift toward top managers who are oriented toward long-term growth strategies for their firms. However, such strategies will require ample financing, and a means must be found to funnel savings to these firms at reasonable interest rates. The second institutional reform would create a series of semipublic commercial and investment banks that would provide a new channel to direct savings to productive investment.

The major purpose of these new banks would be to create a truly competitive banking environment in which existing financial institutions would be provided with a direct demonstration that long-term investment strategies are more profitable than short-term ones. The hope is that the existence of greater competition would also make it possible gradually to lower the long-term rates at which firms could borrow.

These new banks would be formally autonomous from direct political supervision, but their managers would be mandated by law to develop a long-term orientation to both commercial and investment banking. They would seek to emulate the practices of German and Japanese banks where bankers serve as important monitors of corporate strategies, and they would develop their organizational form and their career ladders to reward effective monitoring rather than high quarterly returns.

Initial capitalization would be provided by the federal government, but the firms would then raise money from investors in the form of deposits in the case of commercial banks or through the sale of securities in the case of investment banks. The idea is that these new banks would be up and running in advance of the change in the rules governing the selection of corporate boards.

If one extrapolates from the present behavior of capital markets, the proposed reorganization of the corporate form can be expected to lead to a sharp sell-off in the value of corporate stocks and bonds with a corresponding increase in long-term interest rates. One might also expect that in that climate existing bankers would be even more reluctant to help these reorganized firms raise the long-term capital that they need. However, in the face of competition from the newly created semipublic banks, this reluctance would mean a loss of business for the established banks. Moreover, one could expect that this competition to provide financing would gradually bring long-term rates down to a much smaller premium over short-term rates.

In this new economic environment, one would also expect that individual investors would gradually shift toward longer-term portfolio strategies. As they came to recognize that many of the new corporations with employee stakeholders had excellent prospects for long-term growth, they would be willing once again to see stock ownership as a way to participate in that long-term growth. Their willingness to hold on to portfolios despite cyclical ups and downs could be expected to increase.

To be sure, these two reforms alone will not be sufficient to establish a long-term orientation within the U.S. economy.[11] However, they represent important initial steps that could be taken to address the second paradox of thrift.

---

11. Some of the other necessary reforms are detailed in Block 1990 and 1992b.

BIBLIOGRAPHY

Bernheim, F. Douglas. 1991. *The Vanishing Nest Egg: Reflections on Saving in America*. New York: Priority Press.

Blecker, Robert. 1990. "The Myth of the Consumption Binge." *Challenge*, May, 22–30.

Block, Fred. 1990. *Postindustrial Possibilities: A Critique of Economic Discourse*. Berkeley: University of California Press.

———. 1992a. "The Keynes Mutiny." *Tikkun*, March-April, 17–20.

———. 1992b. "Capitalism Without Class Power." *Politics and Society*, September, 277–303.

———, and Robert Heilbroner. 1992. "The Myth of A Savings Shortage." *American Prospect*, Spring, 101–6.

Board of Governors of the Federal Reserve Board. 1992. *Balance Sheets for the U.S. Economy, 1945–1989*. Washington, DC: Board of Governors of the Federal Reserve System.

Broad, William J. 1992. "Ridden with Debt, U.S. Companies Cut Funds for Research." *New York Times*, June 30.

Chandler, Alfred. 1990. *Scale and Scope: The Dynamics of Industrial Capitalism*. Cambridge, MA: Harvard University Press.

Cullinane, John J. 1991. *Widows and Orphans*. Westborough, MA: Coalition of Information Technology Executives.

Eisner, Robert. 1989. *The Total Income System of Accounts*. Chicago and London: University of Chicago Press.

Florida, Richard, and Martin Kenney. 1990. *The Breakthrough Illusion: Corporate America's Failure to Move from Innovation to Mass Production*. New York: Basic Books.

Greenwald, B., and J. Stiglitz. 1987. "Keynesian, New Keynesian and New Classical Economics." *Oxford Economic Papers*, 39:119–32.

Kaplan, Steve, and Jeremy Stein. 1991. "The Evolution of Buyout Pricing and Financial Structure in the 1980s." *National Bureau of Economic Research Working Paper no. 3695*, May.

Keynes, John Maynard. 1936. *The General Theory of Employment, Interest, and Money*. Reprint, New York: Harcourt, Brace, and World, 1964.

Lowenstein, Louis. 1991. *Sense and Nonsense in Corporate Finance*. Reading, MA: Addison-Wesley.

Polanyi, Karl. 1944. *The Great Transformation*. Reprint, Boston: Beacon Press, 1957.

Stein, Jeremy C. 1989. "Efficient Capital Markets, Inefficient Firms: A Model of Myopic Corporate Behavior." *Quarterly Journal of Economics*, November, 655–69.

U.S. Council of Economic Advisers. 1991. *Economic Report to the President, 1991—Annual Report*. Washington, DC: U.S. Council of Economic Advisors.

U.S. Department of Commerce, Bureau of Census. 1987. *Statistical Abstracts of the United States, 1988: National Data Book and Guide to Sources,* 108th Edition. Washington, DC: U.S. Department of Commerce.

U.S. Office of Thrift Supervision. 1989. *Savings & Home Financing Source Book,* 1989. Washington, DC: U.S. Federal Home Loan Board.

Useem, Michael. 1993. *Alignment: Shareholder Power and the Transformation of Corporate Organization.* Cambridge, MA: Harvard University Press.

4

Factoring Environmental Issues into Investment and Loan Decisions

George M. Newcombe

The subject on which I was asked to write—motivating people to act as if the future mattered—is one of those wonderful topics that makes you pause and reflect on what should be obvious. Of course the future matters, right? However, our experience tells us it is not so obvious since people all too often ignore the future consequences of their actions. Why? Because at the time they act, the future consequences are either unknown to them, irrelevant to them, or just plain ignored by them. The simple fact is that you cannot get people to act as if the future mattered unless you can get them to believe that the future matters *for them today.* But how do we do that? It seems that several approaches have evolved to discount the future to present value, among them command and control strategies, compensatory schemes, and education. These approaches serve as a good framework for analyzing the issue of making our financial institutions act as if the future mattered by factoring environmental issues into their investment and loan decisions.

Command and control is, perhaps, the most effective and time-honored approach to making people act. A law is passed mandating or prohibiting certain conduct. If you violate the law, you get fined or go to jail. It does not matter whether you agree or disagree with the law or the values underlying its passage. Since most people find the process of prosecution and the prospects of fines and imprisonment to be less than pleasurable, this approach can be quite successful. It has its drawbacks, however. Its success depends upon the wisdom of the regulators and legislators to enact appropriate laws and regulations and on the ability of the enforcement structure to detect and prosecute violators. Since the resources allocated to the enforcement effort are necessarily limited and the process of enforcing the law expensive and time consuming, this is not the most efficient approach.

Compensatory schemes are also an effective means of affecting behavior. If your conduct causes injury or harm to someone to whom you have a duty, compensatory schemes, such as our strict product liability laws, provide a mechanism for the injured party to obtain damages from you. Such schemes internalize with the "wrongdoer" the costs to individuals and society resulting from the conduct giving rise to the claim for damages. This is an area where a stitch in time almost always saves nine. The amount of damages awarded to compensate for injury caused by defective products generally far exceeds the cost of design and production changes necessary to avoid or at least to minimize the likelihood of product defects. Thus, the presence of an effective compensatory system forces manufacturers, acting in their own economic self-interest, to produce safer products. Since there are powerful economic incentives for injured parties and their lawyers to prosecute claims for damages, the resources available to enforce compensatory schemes are quite large. Also, compensatory schemes do not require foresight on the part of regulators in specifying the particular conduct to be required or condemned. If any conduct causes injury that could have been avoided by designing or manufacturing a safer product or including better warnings for its use, the compensatory system is activated. Whatever steps are necessary to avoid whatever injury might be caused must be taken by manufacturers to avoid paying huge amounts in damages. The retroactive feature of our product liability laws, which makes manufacturers liable even if their conduct was reasonable at the time, may be unfair but it certainly is effective in causing manufacturers to carefully consider safety features in designing new products. This approach, however, is not without major flaws. The litigation process through which it is enforced is extremely costly and inefficient. Damage awards frequently far exceed the amount necessary to compensate the victim. The award of punitive damages, often on multiple occasions for the same conduct, can be excessive and can result in an inefficient allocation of resources.

Although education is initially the most difficult approach for getting people to "act as if the future mattered" it is the most effective in the long run. Once people accept and internalize a set of values, they will generally act in accordance with them even in the absence of external rules and regulations requiring them to do so. It becomes, if you will, a cultural norm—simply the way that things are done. This is clearly the most idealistic of the approaches, but it is also the most effective once the requisite level of awareness and acceptance is reached. This approach, in my view, is not sufficiently appreciated, perhaps because it does not yield good press, but it has had and continues to have a major impact on corporate behavior, especially in the environmental area. The drawbacks are obvious. There will always be cheaters. To the extent that there are no effective mechanisms to compel the cheater to tow the line, the cheater will achieve a competitive advantage.

All of these mechanisms for getting people to act as if the future mattered have been and continue to be used in the environmental arena. Indeed, it is the power of the combination of these approaches that underlies the thesis of this essay that investors and lenders should ensure that the projects in which they invest are put on a sound environmental footing at the outset.

Background

If you look back a mere 20 years, the environmental regulatory climate of the world bears no resemblance to that of today. The pace at which the developed nations in the Western world have enacted environmental legislation and implemented far-ranging and costly environmental regulations is breathtaking. The next 20 years will continue this process and extend its already substantial momentum to the developing world. So important have environmental concerns become that they recently served as the focus of the largest gathering of heads of state in history. Out of the Earth Summit, as it has been called, several legally binding and nonbinding agreements have emerged that will have significant impact on the way that economic development will progress in the future. As a result, investors and lenders who proceed with developmental projects anywhere without factoring into the cost structure the expense of complying with regulations comparable to those that now exist in the United States and most of Western Europe do so at their peril. Even if the efforts of already strong environmental movements do not result in enactment and enforcement of such legislation, international trade pressures may, over the next decade, play a substantial role in requiring the internalization of such environmental costs.

Because it is generally more efficient and cost effective to design environmental controls into a project at the outset rather than to retrofit them into an existing physical plant, investors and financing institutions should insist upon the integration of advanced environmental designs and controls into projects at the beginning, regardless of whether they are actually required under existing local law today. Indeed, many environmental modifications have cost advantages that in the long run pay for themselves, such as those relating to energy efficiency and waste minimization. If projects are financed without adequate environmental controls built in from the outset, the additional costs to the borrower of retrofitting plants and equipment may adversely affect the borrower's ability to repay the loan or alter the economic assumptions that underlie an investor's decision to commit capital to the venture. Moreover, the uncertainty over future compensatory schemes that may impose on the bank or investor liability for remediating contamination caused by such a borrower increases the risk to investors or banks financing a project that fails to provide for adequate environmental controls. The cost of preventing pollution is cheaper by orders of magnitude than the cost of cleaning up contamination. In addition, if the contamination causes bodily injury to persons coming in contact with it, the potential liability becomes staggering. For example, chemical companies that disposed of allegedly hazardous and toxic wastes at a Superfund site in Texas and the bank and builders that developed a housing subdivision adjacent to the waste site recently settled claims by residents of the subdivision for bodily injury and property damage for an amount in excess of $200 million.

Thus, I believe that as a result of all of the above factors it is in the investor's and financier's own self-interest to insist upon the incorporation of the best available environmental designs at the outset, even if they are not required by law. The trend in U.S. and European law strongly supports this premise, as does the increasing proliferation of environmental regulations throughout the world.

The U.S. Experience

As late as the 1960s, the command and control system regulating environmental matters in the United States was in its infancy. There were almost no environmental laws in the United States, save those enacted by local authorities and others adapted from statutes enacted for a different purpose (e.g., the Rivers and Harbors Act of 1899). One major factor that militated against individual state action to enact stronger environmental laws and against individual corporations instituting better environmental controls, was the fear that by doing so they would suffer a competitive disadvantage: companies would move to other states or risk becoming less cost competitive.

Comprehensive progress on protecting the environment in the United States did not really begin until the enactment over the next decade of a series of national environmental laws, such as the Clean Air Act Amendments of 1970, the Federal Water Pollution Control Act of 1972, the Solid Waste Disposal Act of 1980, and other federal laws. The U.S. Constitution makes federal law and regulations enacted thereunder binding on the states, preempting inconsistent state laws. Thus, these federal enactments resulted in high levels of environmental controls while maintaining a level playing field for companies operating across the country. In contrast to the long-standing external diseconomies of production whereby polluters passed along uncompensated cleanup costs to others, all companies operating within the United States were now required to internalize the cost of bringing their production methods into compliance with environmental regulations.

In the beginning of the 1980s, with the enactment of a broad compensation scheme in the Comprehensive Environmental Response, Compensation and Liability Act (known as CERCLA or the Superfund law), the process of internalizing environmental costs touched not only present operating processes but also reached out to the distant past to encompass unrealized costs of the legacy of waste disposal practices now decades old. Passage of the CERCLA legislation, along with refinements added during its reauthorization in 1986, reflected Congress's intent that polluters "bear the costs and responsibility for remedying the harmful conditions they created."[1] Responsible parties were broadly defined to include present owners and operators of a hazardous waste facility, owners or operators at the time of disposal of hazardous waste, those who arrange for disposal, and persons who transport hazardous waste to a given site.[2] The scope of the Superfund law was further expanded by its liability scheme, which because it is "strict" rather than "fault"-based, requires no showing of negligence or intent on the part of the person deemed responsible for the pollution. Liability arises under CERCLA solely on the basis of that person's (or entity's) status as an owner, operator, disposer, or transporter. Furthermore, because the majority of CERCLA cases involve sites where harm from the presence of hazardous waste in the environment is deemed to be indivisible, CERCLA essentially imposes joint and several liability on individual responsible parties. This result means that any single polluter can be sued by the government for *all* of the cleanup costs at a site, even if it disposed of only a minute quantity of waste at the site. Such a party is then entitled to bring a contribution action against any other person responsible for the pollution in order to recover a proportionate share of the cleanup costs it has

1. *Dedham Water Co. v. Cumberland Farms Dairy, Inc.*, 805 F.2d 1074, 1081 (1st Cir. 1986). *See generally* Senate Committee on Environment and Public Works, *A Legislative History of the Comprehensive Environmental Response, Compensation and Liability Act of 1980 (Superfund)*, 97th Cong., 2d Sess., Committee Print 1983; Senate Committee on Environment and Public Works, *A Legislative History of the Superfund Amendments and Reauthorization Act of 1986*, 101st Cong., 2d Sess. Committee Print 1990.

2. *See* 42 U.S.C. 9607(a); *see also* Chemical Waste Regulation Reporter, Outline of RCRA/CERCLA Enforcement Issues and Holdings, 206–39 (1991).

previously been forced to pay.[3] Finally, because CERCLA liability is retroactive and has been imposed with varying degrees of success on parent or successor corporations, subsidiaries, corporate officers, and shareholders, the statute significantly altered the conduct of corporations doing business in the United States.

As noted, CERCLA is retroactive, making persons liable for conduct that was perfectly legal and consistent with good engineering practice at the time, and it imposes strict, nonfault-based liability, making liable persons who had nothing to do with causing the pollution. For these reasons, CERCLA is anything but fair. Indeed, its joint and several liability provisions are nothing less than draconian. As a result, CERCLA has been challenged on every conceivable legal ground. However, because it is a remedial and not a criminal or punitive statutory scheme, CERCLA has survived all of these challenges. In enacting CERCLA, Congress elected to sacrifice fairness for perceived efficacy in attacking the legacy of decades of industrial development without regard to what we now realize to be necessary environmental safeguards and controls.

The burden of complying with the cleanup actions mandated by the government under CERCLA has impacted virtually every industrial company in the United States. Since companies in the same industry generally face the same type of legacy of the past, once again a relatively level playing field was achieved, although admittedly not as smooth as in the regulatory area.

The costs of complying with environmental regulations governing ongoing production processes and remediating environmental contamination caused by past production practices have become significant. As a result, they can no longer be ignored by financing institutions when assessing the creditworthiness of borrowers or by investors assessing the economic viability of a proposed venture. In addition, the broad definitions of who may be a liable party under CERCLA,[4] and judicial decisions construing them, exposed banks and in some instances parent corporations and shareholders to the risk of direct liability for the cost of cleaning up contamination caused by their borrowers or the corporations in which they hold stock.

Environmental Liability of Banks

Banks that participate in the management of companies in which they hold a security interest lose the so-called secured creditor exemption

---

3. 42 U.S.C. §9613(f) (1).
4. 42 U.S.C.A. §§9601 (20) (A) and 9607, Sections 101(20) (A) and 107.

contained in Section 101(20)(A) and become liable as an "owner or operator" of the facility. Likewise, banks that foreclose on contaminated property and, thus, become its "owner," also risk being held liable under CERCLA. Conflicting case law has muddied the potential liability of banks, adding additional uncertainty.[5] However, EPA recently promulgated a rule governing the liability of financial institutions under CERCLA,[6] that reduces this uncertainty insofar as liability to the government is concerned. Under the EPA rule, a lender who does not participate in the day-to-day management of its borrower's affairs or does not directly cause a release of hazardous substances will not be a liable party under CERCLA even if it forecloses on the contaminated property, provided it promptly attempts to sell it and otherwise abides by the terms of the regulation. Nevertheless, it is unclear whether banks and financial institutions may still remain liable to private parties for contributing toward the cost of remediating a site.[7] Accordingly, the promulgation of the rule does not mean that banks can ignore environmental matters when considering a new transaction. Moreover, as a practical matter, the value of property pledged as collateral for a loan will be reduced by the cost of cleaning it up since no one will purchase such property without discounting from the price the cost of remediation. Thus, even if a financial institution cannot be compelled to clean

---

5. Under *U.S. v. Mirabile*, No. 84–2280, 15 Envtl. L. Rep. 20994 (E.D. Pa. Sept. 6 1985), a bank that foreclosed and promptly sold its interest in the foreclosed property would not be liable under CERCLA. However, under the decisions in *U.S. v. Maryland Bank and Trust Co.*, 632 F. Supp. 573 (D. Md. 1986) and *Guidice v. BFG Electroplating and Mfg. Co., Inc.*, 732 F. Supp. 556 (W.D. Pa. 1989) banks that foreclosed on contaminated property would be liable as the "owner" of the property under CERCLA. Causing great uncertainty, the U.S. Court of Appeals for the Eleventh Circuit in *U.S. v. Fleet Factors*, 901 F.2d 1550 (11th Cir. 1990), *cert. denied*, 111 S. Ct. 752 (1991) held that a bank could be liable even without being an "operator" if its activities with the borrower were sufficient to support the inference that the bank could have affected hazardous waste disposal decisions if it chose to do so. The U.S. Court of Appeals for the Ninth Circuit in *In re Bergsoe Metal Corp.*, 912 F.2d 668 (9th Cir. 1990) disagreed with the *Fleet Factors* court, holding that the mere unexercised power to control the borrower was insufficient to impose liability under CERCLA. Actual participation in management was required. However, the *Bergsoe* court failed to define what actions constituted participation in the management of the borrower, leaving a significant area of uncertainty for banks.

6. See 57 Fed. Reg. 18344 (1992) (to be codified at 40 C.F.R. §300.1100)

7. One recent case has endorsed the EPA rule in the context of private party litigation, *Ashland Oil v. Sonford Products Corp.*, 810 F.Supp. 1057 (D. Minn. 1993). However, it is not certain that other courts will adopt this construction. *See Waterville Industries, Inc. v. Finance Authority of Maine*, 1993 WL 17058 (1st Cir., Feb. 3, 1993) in which the court did not reach the question of the effect of the EPA rule in construing the secured creditor exemption in a sales and leaseback arrangement, but relied solely on the language of CERCLA.

up property by the government under CERCLA, it will nevertheless experience an economic loss in the value of its collateral equal to the cost of cleanup. Notwithstanding the EPA rule on lender liability, financial institutions cannot ignore environmental issues in committing to new loans.

A study conducted prior to the promulgation of the EPA rule demonstrates that banks are not ignoring environmental issues. In a survey of 2,000 banks, the American Banking Association found that nearly 300 banks had abandoned collateral rather than foreclosing and risking environmental liability. Additionally, environmental cleanup costs for collateral were reportedly incurred by 220 banks. Not surprisingly, such liabilities have resulted in changes in bank lending decisions. The American Banking Association further reported that 63 percent of 2,000 surveyed banks had rejected loan applications on the basis of potential environmental liabilities. Additionally, 45 percent of the banks indicated that they had ceased all lending to certain businesses, such as gasoline stations, because of the potential environmental risks posed by such businesses.[8] In total, the American Banking Association stated that 88 percent of the surveyed banks had in some way altered their lending procedures in an effort to avoid environmental liability.[9]

The actual experience of banks in the United States demonstrates that there is good reason for such caution. Under CERCLA, it is not uncommon for banks to face environmental liabilities in excess of the value of their loans or collateral. For example, in *United States v Maryland Bank & Trust Co.* (632 F. Supp. 573 [D. Md. 1986]), the lender was threatened with cleanup liabilities in excess of $550,000. In that case, the relevant loan was for only $335,000.

Another example of substantial lender liability involves the remediation of the Silresim Chemical Corporation site in Lowell, Massachusetts. In October 1976, after several years of operating amid financial difficulties, the Silresim facility was closed. By the time of that closure, the five-acre site was grievously contaminated. Further, approximately 30,000 55-gallon drums of hazardous wastes were still stored at the site. Union National Bank, then a subsidiary of State Street Bank & Trust Company, held the mortgage on the facility. Union National Bank never foreclosed on the mortgage. However, it is alleged that Union National Bank aided Silresim Chemical Corporation in the management of the facility during that corporation's period of financial difficulties.

---

8. *See* World Insurance Report (July 19, 1991).
9. *See* BNA's Banking Report (Sept. 9, 1991).

That mortgage, and the assistance allegedly rendered to Silresim Chemical Corporation, was a sufficient basis for imposing environmental liability on State Street Bank. Specifically, the bank has paid over $500,000 in environmental remediation costs.[10] This payment was made in settlement of a claim by the United States Environmental Protection Agency (EPA) for the funds it expended in beginning the remediation of the site. However, that $500,000 could have been only the beginning of State Street Bank's liability.

The final cleanup of the Silresim site is expected to require the expenditure of up to an additional $400 million. That sum will eventually be obtained either from so-called potentially responsible parties which could include State Street Bank, or from other parties that allegedly sent hazardous waste to the Silresim site. Approximately 200 of these parties filed a $40 million lawsuit against the bank seeking to have it fund the completion of the site remediation.[11] In November 1992 the court in that action granted the Bank summary judgment on the grounds that it acted solely to protect its security interests and did not participate in the management of the site.[12] Even though the bank was successful in extricating itself from this lawsuit at the district court level, the transactions costs in defending the litigation and the potential for massive exposure to liability for site remediation in the context of the uncertainty inherent in any litigation will continue to serve as a strong deterrent to financial institutions becoming involved as a lender in projects that have significant potential for creating environmental problems.

Another notable instance of potential lender environmental liability involves an abandoned wood treatment facility near Butte, Montana.[13] The EPA spent approximately $2,800,000 in beginning the remediation of that site. Additional funds, however, will be needed to complete the cleanup. In 1991, the EPA sought these funds from a number of potentially responsible parties, including the Atlantic Richfield Company (ARCO), which owned the Anaconda Company. The Anaconda Company leased, and subsequently sold, the site to the wood preserving

---

10. State Street Bank sold Union National Bank in 1983, but agreed to indemnify the new owners for Union National Bank's liabilities.

11. *See Grantors to the Silresim Site Trust v. State Street Bank & Trust Co.*, No. 88-1324-K (D. Mass.).

12. *Grantors to the Silresim Site Trust v. State Street Bank & Trust Co.*, 1992 Lexis 20612 (D. Mass. Nov. 24, 1992). Plaintiffs have filed an appeal, which has not yet been ruled on by the First Circuit Court of Appeals.

13. *See United States v. Montana Pole & Treating Plant*, No. CV 91–82-BU-PGH (D. Mont.).

operation. The EPA, however, has taken the position that the bank that held the mortgage for the site, the Bank of Montana-Butte, would not be liable under CERCLA. This decision was based on what was then the EPA proposed rule on lender liability under CERCLA. Despite the EPA's decision, ARCO brought a lawsuit to impose CERCLA liability on the bank.[14] ARCO alleges that the Bank of Montana-Butte is liable under CERCLA because it at one point held the title to the site and participated in the operations of the facility. On June 1, 1992, the court denied the bank's attempt to dismiss those claims.[15] It is yet to be determined whether the bank will indeed be found liable.

Thus, lenders face environmental liabilities imposed both by governmental regulators and private parties. As demonstrated by the litigation regarding the Montana Pole & Treating Plant, governmental efforts to impose some additional limits on lender liability have not dissuaded private litigants.[16] Environmental liabilities are, and will remain in the future, a threat to lenders. Accordingly, lenders have adopted lending practices tailored to deal with that threat. As we will see, these practices not only reduce risks to the lender but also reduce risks to the environment itself. The inquiries of lenders serve to identify, and frequently prompt the expeditious remediation of, environmental problems that might otherwise not be discovered or remedied. The effect of the cost of compliance with environmental laws on the cash flow of borrowers, coupled with the possibility that the banks could be held liable for the cost of cleaning up waste at sites owned or operated by their borrowers, has catapulted environmental concerns to the forefront of the analysis of new and existing credit arrangements by financial institutions. This development has transformed the nation's banks and financial institutions into one of the most comprehensive environmental review and (because

---

14. *See Atlantic Richfield Co. v. Oaas,* Nos. CV-90–75-BU-PGH, CV-91-082-BV-PGH (D. Mont.).

15. *Id.,* 1992 U.S. Dist. Lexis 17574 (D. Mont. 1992).

16. A number of bills providing for the limitation of CERCLA lender liability have been introduced in Congress over the past several years. No such bill, however, has been enacted. Even if the scope of CERCLA lender liability is eventually circumscribed, plaintiffs will likely bring environmental lawsuits against banks pursuant to alternative bases for recovery. One example of such a successful action is *O'Neil v. QLCRI,* 750 F. Supp. 551 (D.R.I. 1990). In that case, the court held that a valid claim could be made against a lender for aiding and abetting a borrower's violations of the Clean Water Act. The court based its holding on the allegation that the lender knew of the borrower's violation and could have conditioned the grant of the loan on the borrower's compliance with the law. *See* John Vorhees and Robert M. Steele, *Birth of New Lender Liability Theory? Aiding and Abetting a Borrower's Violation of Environmental Laws,* 6 Toxics L. Rep. 950–55 (Jan. 8, 1992).

they generally insist upon attaining compliance) enforcement forces in the country.[17]

Environmental Liability of Investors

Under certain circumstances, shareholders also face risks of direct liability for environmental contamination caused by the corporation whose stock they own. There are two lines of cases that have carved an exception under CERCLA to the general principle of limited shareholder and employee liability for the acts of a corporation. Four federal courts of appeals have held that direct CERCLA liability may be imposed upon corporate shareholders, directors, and officers only when they have actively participated in the corporation's day-to-day operations, particularly in its hazardous waste management.[18] In contrast, a second line of cases has applied a prevention test that emphasizes the individual's authority to control the activities of the corporation and any efforts he or she may have taken to prevent or abate the environmental contamination.[19] Although the greater weight of authority lies behind the active participation test of direct shareholder and employee CERCLA liability, the majority of district courts addressing the issue have considered both direct participation and the capacity to control corporate waste disposal practices.[20] In general, however, if shareholders of a corporation act as shareholders, leave the management of the corporation to its duly elected board of directors, and otherwise respect the corporate formalities and separateness of the corporation in which they hold stock, no

17. *See Lender Liability Under Superfund: Hearing Before the Subcomm. on Transp. and Hazardous Materials of the House Comm. on Energy and Commerce,* 101st Cong., 2d sess., 136 *Congressional Record* D1017 (daily ed. Aug. 2, 1990).

18. *Riverside Mkt. Dev. Corp. v. International Bldg. Prods., Inc.,* 931 F.2d 327, 330 (5th Cir. 1991); *United States v. Kayser-Roth Corp., Inc.,* 910 F.2d 24, 26–27 (1st Cir. 1990); *Joslyn Mfg. Co. v. T.L. James & Co.,* 893 F.2d 80, 83–84 (5th Cir. 1990); *United States v. Northeastern Pharmaceutical & Chem. Co.,* 810 F.2d 726, 744 (8th Cir. 1986); *New York v. Shore Realty Corp.,* 759 F.2d 1032, 1052–53 (2d Cir. 1985). *See also United States v. Conservation Chem. Co.,* 619 F. Supp. 162, 190 (W.D. Mo. 1985).

19. *Kelley v. Thomas Solvent Co.,* 727 F. Supp. 1532, 1543–44 (W.D. Mich. 1989); *Kelley ex rel. Michigan Natural Resources Comm'n,* 723 F. Supp. 1214, 1219–20 (W.D. Mich. 1989). *See also Quadion Corp. v. Mache,* No. 89 C 3536, 1991 U.S. Dist. LEXIS 8222, at *11 n.5 (N.D. Ill. June 11, 1991) *(dictum).*

20. *See, e.g., Vermont v. Staco, Inc.,* 684 F. Supp. 822, 831 (D. Vt. 1988); *United States v. Medley,* 25 Env't Rep. Cas. (BNA) 1315, 1317–18 (D.S.C. 1986); *United States v. Carolawn Co.,* 14 Envtl. L. Rep. (Envtl. L. Inst.) 20699, 20700 (D.S.C. 1984); *NEPACCO,* 579 F. Supp. 823, 847–49 (W.D. Mo. 1984), *aff'd in part, rev'd in part,* 810 F.2d 726 (8th Cir. 1986).

liability under CERCLA should devolve upon them.[21] Nevertheless, unanticipated material environmental liabilities could very well undermine the economic assumptions upon which an investment was predicated, rendering it no longer viable. Thus, even where personal liability of the investor is not a concern, the significance of environmental liabilities can be so substantial that they cannot be ignored by a prudent investor in assessing the proposed investment.

The Effect of Concerns over Environmental Liability

As a result of these concerns, banks, financial institutions, and many investors are acting as if the future mattered with respect to environmental issues. Today, no major loans are extended and no significant mergers and acquisitions or purchases or sales of assets or real estate involving commercial property are transacted in the United States without the performance of an environmental assessment. The review extends not only to U.S. properties and operations but also to those abroad. Indeed, in most transactions involving property in countries without developed environmental law or with laws less stringent than those that exist in the United States, for the purpose of assessing potential future exposure, U.S. investors and financial institutions often assume that standards comparable to those that exist in the United States will ultimately apply. The nature and depth of environmental assessments varies depending upon the type of the transaction, the potential of the underlying property (including its past uses) or business to generate significant environmental liabilities and the results of preliminary investigations, which often reveal information that warrants further follow-up, including conducting soil and groundwater testing. The intent of the exercise is to identify and, to the extent feasible within the time and budget constraints imposed, to quantify any environmental liabilities found. The results of the assessment are factored into the economics of the transaction, and provisions in the transaction documentation are generally made for compliance to be achieved or remediation to be conducted. Escrow funds are sometimes set aside for this purpose. In those situations in which companies or assets are sold, the discovery of undisclosed environmental problems frequently results in a reduction in price. The lenders for the purchaser often insist upon this "discount" being applied to the cost of resolving the problems.

Banks and financial institutions have been extraordinarily successful at securing agreements such as these to remedy environmental problems.

---

21. *Joslyn Mfg. Co.,* 893 F.2dd 80.

Why? Because financing provides an unparalleled point of leverage. If the financing institution insists upon such undertakings as a condition for providing the required financing, the borrower has little choice. Either he agrees to remedy the environmental problems or the transaction does not go forward. A level playing field in the financial markets makes this result possible. The same environmental liability risks in the United States are faced by U.K., German, Japanese, and other foreign banks, all of which have become as sensitized to these problems as their U.S. counterparts. Thus, it is generally no longer possible for a company to say to a bank, "If you insist upon this environmental condition, I will go elsewhere for the loan."

It is unlikely that bank and investor concern over environmental liabilities will diminish in the foreseeable future. Despite criticism of the Superfund law by corporations, banks, and insurance companies, it is unclear whether any major revision of the legislation will occur. Although there have been efforts to lessen the potential exposure to lenders under CERCLA, they have not yet been successful. The United States E.P.A., responding to concerns raised about the consequences of imposing unlimited Superfund liability upon lenders, promulgated an administrative rule designed to clarify the existing exemption from liability for persons whose indicia of ownership exists primarily to protect a security interest. However, in 1994, a court struck this administrative rule on the grounds that the E.P.A. exceeded its legal authority in promulgating it.[22] In addition, lenders have supported passage of legislation that would significantly broaden the exemptions for financial institutions. These efforts have also been unsuccessful.[23] Even if these measures succeed, however, they will not eliminate the risk of lender environmental liability. Under the EPA rule on lender liability and the proposed amendments to CERCLA, lenders would still incur liability if their involvement with their borrower is sufficiently detailed on a day-to-day operational basis to support a finding of liability as an "operator." In addition, banks would still incur liability as an "owner" if they hold title to property after foreclosure for investment purposes rather than to merely satisfy the borrower's indebtedness and the bank's foreclosure costs. Likewise, shareholders who actively partici-

---

22. *Kelly v. E.P.A.,* 15 F.3d 1100 (D.D.C. 1994), cert. denied. *American Bankers Ass'n v. Kelly,* 115 S.Ct. 900 (1995).

23. Congressional efforts to amend specific portions of CERCLA dealing with lender liability have not succeeded. *See House Defeat of Broad Banking Bill May Imperil Lenders' Superfund Exemption,* 12 Inside E.P.A. 1, 9 (Nov. 8, 1991); *Despite Senate Approval, Banks' Superfund Exemption Appears Dead,* 12 Inside E.P.A. 11 (Nov. 21, 1991). It is likely that lenders will continue to press for an amendment to CERCLA. *See* 22 Envt'l Rep. at 333.

pate in the day-to-day management of corporations or who disregard corporate formalities and separateness will continue to incur environmental liability. Moreover, even without fear of personal liability for environmental damages, environmental matters will increasingly play an important role in the assessment of the economic risks and rewards of the loan or underlying investment in light of the cost of compliance. This will be accompanied by ever more complex environmental regulations and remediations of the remnants of past waste disposal practices.

In short, environmental costs have already been internalized to a very significant extent in the United States and, like any other significant cost, they cannot be and are not being ignored by investors or lenders. But the systematic identification and quantification of environmental costs has had another profound effect, namely, it has galvanized companies, investors, and managers to find ways to avoid or to minimize those costs in the first instance. More efficient designs at the outset, redesigning existing processes to avoid generating hazardous wastes, and developing more cost-effective ways to deal with existing wastes are all reactions to the internalization of these heretofore ignored costs.

The European Experience

The same general progression from local to common environmental regulation is occurring in the European Community (EC). Although initially conceived as primarily an arrangement to facilitate free trade among countries of Western Europe, the EC appears to be evolving into, among other things, one of the world's largest environmental agencies, issuing directives that impact all of its members. The driving force toward this result has essentially been the same as that which drove the United States to implement uniform federal standards. In a free trade environment, if major costs are not internalized on a consistent basis, competitive advantages arise for those not internalizing those costs. In the environmental arena, companies in countries with lax regulations or enforcement policies will have a lower cost structure than those in countries with more stringent controls. Thus, it is not surprising that in Germany, a country with relatively stringent environmental controls, the German Industry Association has advocated a harmonization of environmental standards throughout the EC and the centralization of regulatory power within the EC.[24] Since new plant and equipment generally include more efficient

---

24. *See* Gernot Klepper, *The Political Economy of Trade and the Environment in Western Europe,* Symposium on International Trade and the Environment, The World Bank (Nov. 21–22, 1991) at 12–13.

and environmentally sound designs, in expanding industries there will likewise be pressures to establish standards consistent with the new designs to enhance their profitability over old capital stock. In other words, once a country or segment of a market has already internalized certain environmental costs, it is to its advantage to require its competitors to do the same. This phenomenon will occur in each country and trading block, which should result over time in trade-based pressures for higher and consistent environmental standards—the cost for complying with which neither investors nor lenders can afford to ignore.

Of course, there is the risk of the converse happening. As demonstrated by intra-Community difficulties encountered by EC member states when conforming their individual environmental laws to the standards dictated by EC directives, disputes among trade agreement partners may engender de facto if not de jure differences.[25] These incidents, and others like them, point to a potentially negative consequence of imposing uniform environmental standards, which is that the overall quality of environmental regulation will deteriorate because the least stringent standards will predominate. According to this theory, analogous to the "race to the bottom" that occurs when one state enacts lax laws regulating businesses in order to entice companies to incorporate in that jurisdiction, even though EC member states are entitled to enact and enforce stricter standards than required by the EC directives, investments may flow toward those member states that impose the least regulation. This phenomenon is being resisted in the United States where constituencies such as environmental public interest groups have maintained pressure on the Congress not to degrade existing regulations when entering into bilateral trade agreements.[26]

One of the most important initiatives under consideration by the EC is the proposal for a directive on civil liability for damage caused by waste. If ultimately approved by the European Council of Ministers, all EC member states would be required to enact a strict liability regime, which, according to one commentator, would harmonize liability laws

---

25. *See Court of Justice Says Italian Government Failed to Implement Two Waste Directives,* 14 Int'l Envt. Rep. 680–81 [Current Reports] (BNA) (Dec. 18, 1991); *Dutch Ministry Accuses German Firm of Illegal Movement of Waste, Threatens Fine, id.* at 683–84.

26. *See Issues Relating to a Bilateral Free Trade Agreement with Mexico, Hearings Before the Subcomm. on Western Hemisphere and Peace Corps Affairs of the Senate Comm. on Foreign Relations,* 102d Cong., 1st Sess. 118 (1991) (statement of Michael McCloskey, Chairman, Sierra Club, Washington, D.C.) ("U.S. environmental standards and programs should not be harmonized downward. Our high standards must absolutely be maintained here and insulated from challenge").

among member states and thereby play "a crucial role in ensuring the efficient operation of the EEC internal market."[27] Although not as broad as CERCLA, the most recent version of a proposed draft EC directive on civil liability for damage from waste addresses the cleanup of contaminated sites through the establishment of a strict liability scheme pursuant to which "producers" of waste are liable for any damage caused by that waste.[28] As with CERCLA, the proposed directive provides (1) that liability is strict, (2) that liability is joint and several, and (3) that "waste" is defined broadly. Unlike CERCLA, the EC draft directive (1) does not impose retroactive liability, (2) permits a generator to absolve itself from future liability with regard to any wastes disposed of in a lawful manner, and (3) requires mandatory insurance or other financial security.

One aspect of the proposed directive that has rightly caused concern among lenders is the "deemed producer" provision. In the event that the producer of the waste is unknown or no longer available, liability shifts to the person or entity in control of the waste, who becomes the "deemed producer."[29] It remains to be seen how the "deemed producer" provision will be construed by the courts. Nevertheless, a bank in a foreclosure proceeding or a receiver in a bankruptcy proceeding that takes possession of a plant, a company, or a piece of property, thereby exercising actual control over it, cannot ignore the risk that it could become a "deemed producer" of the plant's wastes. In that event, it would incur liability for remediating environmental contamination if a triggering *incident* under the proposed waste directive—for example leaching of hazardous waste into groundwater—occurred during this period of control. Alarmed over the potential exposure of lenders for environmental liability, the British banking industry has already begun lobbying efforts for an explicit lender liability exemption from the directive. Thus, as in the United States, environmental liabilities should emerge as significant factors in future European financing transactions, assuming the draft directive is issued without a complete exemption for

27. Linda M. Sheehan, *The EEC's Proposed Directive on Civil Liability for Damage Caused by Waste: Taking Over When Prevention Fails,* 18 Ecology L.Q. 405–07 (1991); *see* Turner T. Smith Jr. and Roszell D. Hunter, *The Revised European Community Civil Liability for Damage from Waste Proposal,* 21 Envt'l L. Rep. 10718 (Dec. 1991).

28. *See* Amended proposal for a Directive on civil liability for damage caused by waste, 34 O.J. Eur. Comm. (No. C 192) 6 (1991); P. Luiki and D. Stephenson, *European Community Waste Policy: At the Brink of a New Era,* 14 Envt'l L. Rep. (BNA) 403, 405–6 (July 17, 1991).

29. *See* Directive Art. 2, ¶ 2; *See also* G. Freeman, Jr. and K. McSlarrow, *The Proposed European Community Directive on Civil Liability for Waste: The Implication for U.S. Superfund Reauthorization in 1991,* 46 Bus. Law. 1, 14–15 (1990).

lenders and investors. If the U.S. experience is any predictor, European banks and investors should greatly facilitate compliance with EC environmental directives to minimize the risk to themselves and to the venture of incurring substantial environmental liabilities.

The NAFTA Experience

The North American Free Trade Agreement (NAFTA), ratified in 1994, is expected to accomplish many of the same collective market benefits for Canada, the United States, and Mexico as the EC economic integration will have for its member states. Negotiations among the parties have included thorny environmental issues raised by the numerousness and relative stringency of U.S. federal and state environmental regulations compared with the differing standards of its neighbors, especially Mexico. Environmentalists and labor groups are concerned that Mexico's lax enforcement of its environmental laws will result in companies setting up operations in Mexico to avoid the cost of complying with U.S. environmental and labor regulations.[30] To prevent Mexican companies from achieving an unfair cost advantage over their American and Canadian counterparts, some mechanism will have to be devised to ensure that comparable environmental controls are enacted and enforced in all three participating countries.[31] Indeed, in an effort to take away this cost advantage, legislation has been proposed that seeks to protect domestic corporations saddled with the enormous costs imposed by comprehensive environmental regulations and strict liability schemes.[32] This bill, introduced by Senator Boren, would impose an import tariff in order "to compensate for the lax environmental requirements found in the originating country," thereby addressing what has been characterized as a "significant and unfair subsidy."

Thus, once again, trade pressures, along with pressures from tradi-

---

30. *See* Beatrice Prati, *A New Mexican Revolution?,* Int'l Corp. L. 25–28 (Sept. 1991); Stewart A. Baker and Jeffrey P. Bialos, *U.S.-Mexico Trade Talks: A Preview,* 20 Int'l L. News 1, 6–7 (ABA) (Winter 1991); D. Gonzalez and E. Rodriguez, *Environmental Aspects of Maquiladora Operations: A Note of Caution for U.S. Parent Corporations,* 22 St. Mary's L.J. 659 (1991); Michael Scott Feeley and Elizabeth Knier, *Environmental Considerations of the Emerging United States-Mexico Free Trade Agreement,* 2 Duke J. Comp. & Int'l L. 259 (1992); Diane M. Barber, *Bridging the Environmental Gap: The Application of NEPA to the Mexico-U.S. Bilateral Trade Agreement,* 5 Tul. Envtl. L. J. 429 (1992).

31. *See,* e.g., Draft Report, *Integrated Environmental Plan for the Mexico & U.S. Border Area* (Joint SEDUE/EPA Release) cited in 14 Int'l Envtl. Rep. 437–38 (Aug. 14, 1991).

32. *See,* e.g., S. 984, 102d Cong., 2d Sess. (1991) *("The International Pollution Deterrence Act of 1991");* 21 Envt'l L. Rep. at 10592, 10592 n.30.

tional environmental interests, are resulting in a process for harmonizing environmental controls among nations. This process should result in the imposition and enforcement of more stringent environmental controls—with their attendant costs—in Mexico, a country that previously either did not have or did not vigorously enforce such regulations. Loans or investments made without considering the impact of these environmental costs may not appear as attractive as initially anticipated.

Extrapolation from the U.S., EC, and NAFTA Experiences

As discussed above, a combination of environmental and trade-related pressures have caused and continue to cause a harmonization of environmental regulations within trading blocs. These same pressures, however, exist between trading blocs and countries not associated with any trading bloc. Outside of the trading bloc context, however, the mechanisms and instruments for bringing about harmonization remain relatively undeveloped. Among those mentioned as possible vehicles for harmonization is the General Agreement on Tariffs and Trade (the "GATT").

The recent tentative GATT decision to strike down restrictions imposed by the United States on tuna imported from countries that do not engage in fishing techniques that minimize the chance of catching dolphins illustrates that GATT prohibits the imposition of import restrictions on the basis of the method of production employed by the producing country.[33] It is not possible here to analyze in detail the limitations GATT may impose, either in theory or practice, upon environmental measures that are deemed to restrict free trade.[34] However, it is clear that the GATT, as currently drafted and construed, could not form the basis for imposing import restrictions or tariffs to offset the cost advantage achieved by companies operating in countries with lax environmen-

---

33. See *U.S. Embargo on Mexican Tuna Violates GATT Rules, Panel Finds,* Int'l Trade Daily (BNA) (Aug. 27, 1991); Matthew Hunter Hurleck, Note, *The GATT, U.S. Law and the Environment: A Proposal to Amend the GATT in Light of the Tuna/Dolphin Decision,* 92 Colum. L. Rev. 2098 (1992); *see generally* GATT, 61 Stat. A3, T.I.A.S. 1700, 51–61 U.N.T.S., arts. XI–XIII, Oct. 30, 1947, reprinted in II Bruce E. Clubb, United States Foreign Trade Law §7–3 (1991).

34. For an overview of these issues, *see* Eliza Patterson, *International Trade and the Environment: Institutional Solutions,* 21 Envt'l L. Rep. 10599–10604 (Oct. 1991); Kyle E. McSlarrow, *International Trade and the Environment: Building a Framework for Conflict Resolution, id.* at 10593–10595. *See also* Susan E. Holley, *Global Warming: Construction and Enforcement of an International Accord,* 10 Stan. J. Envtl. L. 44, 73–75 (1991) (discussing possible conflict between GATT and trade restrictions contained in Article 4 of the Montreal Protocol).

tal controls or enforcement policies. Nevertheless, the provisions of the GATT could be amended to transform it into a powerful international force in encouraging environmental controls and resource conservation. A particularly good discussion of the way in which the GATT could be so amended may be found in Charles Arden Clark, *The General Agreement on Tariffs and Trade, Environmental Protection and Sustainable Development* (World Wildlife Foundation Discussion Paper, June 1991). However, there is significant and heated debate over whether trade policy should be used to attain environmental objectives at all. It is interesting to compare Arden Clark with the excellent article by Patrick Low and Raed Safadi, "Trade Policy and Pollution," (Symposium on International Trade and the Environment, The World Bank, November 21–22, 1991). Nevertheless, it appears that steps have already been taken within the institutional structure of the GATT to address the issue.[35] Moreover, the director general of the GATT, Arthur Dunkel, recognized both the potential of GATT to deal with environmental issues and the fact that such issues are genuinely not protectionism by another name. Specifically, he said:

> Many trade disputes are already surfacing which owe their existence to differences between trade and environmental objectives. We are faced with the need to consider the extent to which the GATT as it is now, can adequately cover the requirements of governments to pursue environmental objectives using policies which sometimes may affect trade but which do not degenerate into protectionism with another name. One thing is clear, however; that the world's capacity to deal technically and financially with environmental challenges can only be helped by the reforms and potential for growth and development offered by a successful conclusion of the Uruguay Round. (162 BNA Executive Daily, August 21, 1991, A-4)

Thus, despite the tuna decision, there is reason to believe that the GATT may be modified to prevent cost advantages resulting from the failure to implement environmentally sound production methods or to encourage environmentally sound use of resources.[36] The developed industrial nations have the most advanced environmental controls. Their

---

35. *See* 21 Envtl. L. Rep. at 10603 n. 44 (discussing reactivation of GATT Working Group on Environmental Measures and International Trade [GATT Doc. L/3622REVI, C/M/74]).

36. *See* Hurlock, supra note 29, at 2145–2160; *see generally* Alan F. Holmer and Judith H. Bello, *U.S. Trade and the Environment: A Snapshot from Tuna/Dolphins to the NAFTA and Beyond,* 27 Int'l L. 169 (Spring 1993).

companies are already incurring the costs associated with advanced pollution controls. To the extent less developed countries permit environmentally reckless production methods at lower production costs, the domestic manufacturers in the developed countries are put at a competitive cost disadvantage.

Since the industrialized countries also have the most influence on the GATT, the experiences in the United States, the EC, and the NAFTA process suggest that trade pressures may result in an amended GATT being utilized in the future to level the international manufacturing playing field with respect to manufacturing environmental costs. Nonprocess environmental costs are much more difficult to harmonize. Nevertheless, disputes that have arisen during the GATT Uruguay Round talks suggest that it may be premature to place too much reliance upon the GATT as a realistic mechanism for integrating environmental change with global trade. Furthermore, the dispute settlement mechanism has been described as not only time consuming but ineffective, insofar as compliance is largely voluntary.[37] For example, despite the GATT panel decision that U.S. restrictions on the import of foreign tuna, based upon the Marine Mammal Protection Act, were invalid, a United States district court judge in San Francisco ordered the Commerce Department to enforce such a ban.[38]

Although the GATT has been the recipient of much attention as a vehicle for achieving international environmental objectives, it is by no means the only avenue available to accomplish this result. Multilateral agreements and treaties that directly address environmental concerns should be far more efficient instruments. (See, for example, the Montreal Protocol [to the Vienna Convention on the Protection of the Ozone Layer] on Substances that Deplete the Ozone Layer, September 16, 1987, 26 ILM 1550 [1987]). Concern over global warming has resulted in a framework convention for developing international agreements on the control of so-called greenhouse gases at the United Nations Conference on Environment and Development (UNCED).[39] International recognition of the serious problems posed by the shipments of hazardous wastes across national boundaries has resulted in widespread adoption of the

37. *See* Lisa Sue Klaiman, *Applying GATT Dispute Settlement Procedures To a Trade in Service Agreement: Proceed With Caution,* 11 U.Pa. J. Int'l Bus. L. 657, 66 (1990).

38. *See Earth Island Institute v. Mosbacher,* 785 F.Supp. 826 (N.D. Cal. 1992); *see also* Keith Schneider, *Balancing Nature's Claims and International Free Trade,* N.Y. Times, Jan. 19, 1992, at 5, sec. 4, Col. 1–4; Steven L. Kass and Michael B. Gerrard, *International Trade,* N.Y.L.J., Jan. 24, 1992 at 3, col. 3, 29, col. 1.

39. *See, Bush Signs Instrument of Ratification for UN Convention on Climate Change,* 15 Int'l Envt'l Rep. 676–77 (Oct. 21, 1992).

Basel Convention on the Transboundary Movements of Hazardous Wastes and Their Disposal *(supra* n. 9). The U.S. government has expressed its wishes to join in the Basel Convention, although significant changes to domestic law—in particular the Resource Conservation and Recovery Act, 42 U.S.C. §§9601–6992k—will be required.[40] Indeed, a survey of business leaders around the world conducted by McKinsey & Company revealed that 72 percent of senior executives of multinational corporations believe that within 10 years regional and global environmental regulations will be more important than national ones. Sixty-seven percent of the respondents also believed that international harmonization of standards would benefit their companies.[41]

Pressure from environmental interests, both nationally and internationally, coupled with multilateral trade pressures should result in an eventual leveling of the international environmental playing field. Thus, it is likely that environmental regulations comparable to those that exist in the United States and EC will be enacted in countries that currently do not have them. That likelihood cannot be ignored by investors and financial institutions. At a minimum, the creditworthiness of borrowers and the economic assumptions of investors in industrial projects in countries currently lacking strict environmental laws or enforcement policies will be affected by the cost of achieving compliance. At worst, the banks or the investors themselves may have potential liability should laws such as the EC Directive on Civil Liability for Waste or CERCLA be enacted in other countries.

The Challenge to the Financial Community

Demands on the banking industry and investors to fund development projects throughout the world will continue to grow over the next decade and beyond. If such development proceeds without regard to environmental concerns, the consequences for the entire world will be dire. If China alone were to develop its electrical power needs without using the most efficient and environmentally clean means, the output of greenhouse gases would overwhelm the efforts of the developed world to reduce these emissions. Because of the enormous leverage that financing institutions and investors have, they are in a unique position to influence how development proceeds.

---

40. *See* Thomas R. Mounteer, *Codifying Basel Convention Obligations Into U.S. Law: The Waste Export Control Act,* 21 Envt'l L. Rep. 10085, 10086 (1991).

41. McKinsey & Company, *The Corporate Response to the Environmental Challenge—Summary Report* (Aug. 1991), at 13.

The challenge to the banking and financing communities will be to exercise that leverage in a way that fosters if not compels environmentally sound developmental projects.[42] To do that, however, financial institutions have to institute procedures to identify at the outset environmental issues relevant to the proposed transaction. Such procedures have been implemented by most major banks in the United States as a means of quantifying the environmental risk to the bank under CERCLA and to determine whether environmental liabilities of the borrower may adversely affect its creditworthiness. These procedures generally include requiring the borrower to represent and warrant that it is in compliance with all existing environmental regulations and will maintain compliance with any future regulations. If the borrower cannot make that representation, it must describe all of the circumstances of noncompliance. In addition, most major banks on significant transactions conduct independent environmental assessments of the borrower's business to identify areas of noncompliance or potential liability.[43]

Once the problems are identified, the financing institution should insist upon undertakings by the borrower to ensure that it attains and maintains compliance with environmental laws and addresses any items that pose a significant environmental risk, such as contaminated groundwater that may spread further and affect other properties. Funds may even be set aside and dedicated to achieve these results.

Since implementing environmentally sound designs and controls is less expensive at the inception of a project than after it has been built, and since bank and investor liability for adverse environmental consequences of the project cannot be ruled out as a possibility in the future,

---

42. Multilateral development banks and development assistance agencies have already begun to study and implement mechanisms into their lending practices that reflect environmental concerns. *See*, e.g., *note, Avoiding Environmental Injury: The Case for Widespread Use of Environmental Impact Assessments in International Development Projects,* 30 Va. J. Int'l L. 517, 528–29 (1990): David Reed, *The Global Environmental Facility: Sharing Responsibility for the Biosphere,* Report Issued by the Multilateral Development Bank Program, WWF-International (1991); Main Report, *Report by the Chairman to the Participants' Meeting to Discuss the Global Environment Facility,* (UNDP, World Bank, UNEP) (April 1991); World Bank and the International Monetary Fund for the Development Committee, *Development Issues: Presentations to the Development Committee,* May 8, 1990; The Centre for International Environmental Law, *Environmental Protection and the European Bank for Reconstruction and Development: Proposal For a Two-Year Legal Policy and Advocacy Project,* (May 1990).

43. For example, the EC has already issued a directive mandating member states to adopt legislation or modify existing legislation that requires the performance of environmental assessments before certain types of development projects are undertaken. *See* European Community Directive on Environmental Assessment, 28 O.J. Eur. Comm (No. L 175) 40 (1985).

there are strong, purely economic reasons for banks and investors to take a more proactive role in ensuring that the projects they finance anywhere in the world are environmentally sound. Where the laws of a foreign jurisdiction are significantly more lax than those that exist in the United States and the EC, the banking and investor communities, for their own protection, should require the incorporation of environmental controls that are more consistent with those in the United States and the EC and monitor compliance on a periodic basis.

The financial community has to also be creative in devising ways to finance the incremental cost associated with the use of an environmentally sound design. Developing countries often simply do not have the capital resources to afford the additional investment. Where the additional environmentally dictated costs result in a net benefit to the borrower (for example, energy savings from the use of more efficient technology), that portion of the loan could be amortized over the time period necessary to pay back the loan from the savings realized by the more environmentally sound design, thus making the changes cost-neutral to the borrower. Where there is no direct cost savings associated with an environmentally sound design and where the project would not otherwise be economically viable, the additional costs may have to be amortized over a longer period than the rest of the loan and/or be subject to a more favorable interest rate to make these changes affordable to the borrower. Since the bank or other financial institution also benefits from an environmentally sound design, as discussed above, it is not unreasonable for it to grant concessions concerning the portion of the loan required to fund the marginal cost of such a design, especially where the economics of the project will not support these changes without such concessions. The international community will also have to consider ways to assist the developing world in defraying the marginal cost increases required by environmentally sound development. Side payments to such countries, technology sharing arrangements, payments for preserving biospheres or carbon sinks, among others, are all possibilities that will have to be explored.

Finally, until such time as the international playing field becomes environmentally level, the world's banking industry and investment community should internalize the responsibility to ensure that projects proceed on a sound environmental footing. For if that is not done, one bank's insistence upon the inclusion of environmental conditions in loan documentation will be easily defeated by the borrower simply taking his business to a less environmentally concerned bank. Since there are powerful economic reasons for banks and investors to insist upon environmentally sound projects at the outset of a transaction, it is in the banking and investment communities' interest to require such environmental conditions uniformly in all financing transactions. By doing so, they will not only benefit themselves but also contribute significantly to the process of making our world a better place to live.

BIBLIOGRAPHY

Baker, Stewart A., and Jeffrey P. Bialos. 1991. "U.S.-Mexico Trade Talks: A Preview." *Int'l L. News* 20, no. 1 (Winter): 6–7.

Bank of North America. 1991. *Banking Report,* September 9.

Barber, Diane M. 1992. "Bridging the Environmental Gap: The Application of NEPA to the Mexico-U.S. Bilateral Trade Agreement. *Tul. Envtl. L. J.* 5: 429.

Chemical Waste Regulation Reporter. 1991. "Outline of RCRA/CERCLA Enforcement Issues and Holdings." *Chemical Waste Regulation Reporter,* 206–39.

Congressional Record. 1990. "Lender Liability Under Superfund: Hearing Before the Subcommittee on Transportation and Hazardous Materials of the House Committee on Energy and Commerce." *Congressional Record* 136 (August 2): D1017.

Feeley, Michael Scott, and Elizabeth Knier. 1992. "Environmental Considerations of the Emerging United States-Mexico Free Trade Agreement." *Duke J. Comp. & Int'l Law* 2: 259.

Freeman, G., Jr., and K. McSlarrow. 1990. "The Proposed European Community Directive on Civil Liability for Waste—The Implication for U.S. Superfund Reauthorization in 1991." *Bus. Law* 46, no. 1: 14–15.

Gonzalez, D., and E. Rodriguez. 1991. "Environmental Aspects of Maquiladora Operations: A Note of Caution for U.S. Parent Corporations." *St. Mary's L.J.* 22: 659.

Holley, Susan E. 1991. "Global Warming: Construction and Enforcement of an International Accord." *Stan. J. Envt'l L.* 10, no. 44: 73–75.

Holmer, Alan F., and Judith H. Bello. 1993. "U.S. Trade and the Environment: A Snapshot from Tuna/Dolphins to the NAFTA and Beyond." *Int'l L.* 27 (Spring): 169.

Hurleck, Matthew Hunter. 1992. "The GATT, U.S. Law and the Environment: A Proposal to Amend the GATT in Light of the Tuna/Dolphin Decision." *Colum. L. Rev.* 92: 2098.

Inside E.P.A. 1991. "House Defeat of Broad Banking Bill May Imperil Lenders' Superfund Exemption." *Inside E.P.A.* 12 (November 8): 9.

———. 1991. "Despite Senate Approval, Banks' Superfund Exemption Appears Dead." *Inside E.P.A.* 12 (November 21): 11.

Int'l Envt'l L. Rep. 1991. "The International Pollution Deterrence Act of 1991." *Int'l Envt'l. L. Rep.* 21: 10592.

———. 1991. "Draft Report: Integrated Environmental Plan for the Mexico & U.S. Border Area (Joint SEDUE/EPA Release)." *Int'l Envt'l. Rep.* 14 (August 14): 437–38.

———. 1991. "Court of Justice Says Italian Government Failed to Implement Two Waste Directives." *Int'l Envt'l Rep.* 14 (December 18): 680–81.

———. 1991. "Dutch Ministry Accuses German Firm of Illegal Movement of Waste, Threatens Fine." *Int'l Envt'l Rep.* 14 (December 18): 683–84.

———. 1992. "Bush Signs Instrument of Ratification for UN Convention on Climate Change." *Int'l Envt'l Rep.* 15 (October 21): 676–77.

Int'l Trade Daily. 1991. "U.S. Embargo on Mexican Tuna Violates GATT Rules, Panel Finds." *Int'l Trade Daily,* August 27.

Kass, Steven L., and Micael B. Gerrard. 1992. "International Trade." *NY L. J.* 29 (January 24) col. 1.

Klaiman, Lisa Sue. 1990. "Applying GATT Dispute Settlement Procedures to a Trade in Services Agreement: Proceed with Caution." *U. Pa. J. Int'l Bus. L.* 11: 657, 666.

Klepper, Gernot. 1991. "The Political Economy of Trade and the Environment in Western Europe." In *Symposium on International Trade and the Environment,* November 21–22. Washington, D.C.: The World Bank.

Low, Patrick, and Raed Safadi. 1991. "Trade Policy and Pollution." In *Symposium on International Trade and the Environment,* November 21–22. Washington, D.C.: The World Bank.

Luiki, P., and D. Stephenson. 1991. "European Community Waste Policy: At the Brink of a New Era." *Envt'l. L. Rep.* 14 (July 17): 405–6.

McKinsey and Company. 1991. "The Corporate Response to the Environmental Challenge — Summary Report." August. Washington, D.C.: McKinsey and Company.

McSlarrow, Kyle E. 1991. "International Trade and the Environment: Building a Framework for Conflict Resolution." *Envt'l L. Rep.* 21 (October): 10593–95.

Mounteer, Thomas R. 1991. "Codifying Basel Convention Obligations Into U.S. Law: The Waste Export Control Act." *Envt'l L. Rep.* 21 (October): 10085–86.

Patterson, Eliza. 1991. "International Trade and the Environment: Institutional Solutions." *Envt'l L. Rep.* 21 (October): 10599–604.

Prati, Beatrice. 1991. "A New Mexical Revolution?" *Int'l Corp. L.* (September): 25–28.

Reed, David. 1991. *The Global Environment Facility: Sharing Responsibility for the Biosphere.* Washington, D.C.: Multilateral Development Bank Program Report, WWF-International.

Rothmyer, Karen. 1992. "Bush's Parting Gift: Clinton is Left to Deal with Free Trade Pact," *Newsday* (December 18): 57.

Schneider, Keith. 1992. "Balancing Nature's Claims and International Free Trade." *NY Times,* January 19, 5, sec. 4, cols. 1–4.

Senate Committee on Environment and Public Works, 97th Congress, 2d Session. 1983. *A Legislative History of the Comprehensive Environmental Response, Compensation and Liability Act of 1980 (Superfund)*. Washington, D.C.: Comm. Print.

Senate Committee on Environment and Public Works, 101st Congress, 2d Session. 1990. *A Legislative History of the Superfund Amendments and Reauthorization Act of 1986*. Washington, D.C.: Comm. Print.

Sheehan, Linda M. 1991. "The EEC's Proposed Directive on Civil Liability for Damage Caused by Waste: Taking Over When Prevention Fails." *Ecology* 18: 405–7.

Smith, Turner T., Jr., and Roszell D. Hunter. 1991. "The Revised European Community Civil Liability for Damage from Waste Proposal." *Envt'l L. Rep.* 21 (December): 10718.

Va. J. Int'l Law. 1990. "Avoiding Environmental Injury: The Case for Widespread Use of Environmental Impact Assessments in International Development Projects." *Va. J. Int'l L.* 30: 517, 528–29.

Vorhees, John, and Robert M. Steele. 1992. "Birth of New Lender Liability Theory? Aiding and Abetting a Borrower's Violation of Environmental Laws." *Toxics Law Report*, 6 (January 8): 950–55.

World Insurance Report, July 19, 1991.

5

Economic Regimes, Strategic Investments, and Entrepreneurial Enterprises: Notes toward a Theory of Economic Development

David Seckler

We make our vision, and hold it ready for any amendment that experience suggests. It is not a fixed picture, a row of shiny ideals which we can exhibit to mankind and say: Achieve these or be damned. All we can do is to search the world as we find it, extricate the forces that seem to move it, and surround them with criticism and suggestion . . . Too far ahead there is nothing but your dream; just behind, there is nothing but your memory. But in the unfolding present, man can be creative if his vision is gathered from the promise of actual things.

—Walter Lippman, *Drift and Mastery*

The theory of economic development typically is considered by economists, even by development economists, as simply the application of standard theories of economic efficiency and growth to the particular case of poor countries. This is vividly shown in economics texts where the microeconomic and macroeconomic sections are followed by a chapter on developing countries that contains little more than facts and figures showing how bad life can be. To paraphrase Wesley C. Mitchell's observation (1937, 24), the theoretical section and the development section of economic texts are held together by little more than the binding.[1]

---

1. Mitchell's comment was on the relationship between the theoretical and applied sections of economic texts. But it is remarkable how little integration there is even between micro- and macroeconomics. For example, in a recession firms may discharge workers to improve efficiency, but this action often is not related to its effects on aggregate employment and demand in exacerbating the recession. The opportunity cost of unemployed labor is zero, so aggregate efficiency decreases. Thus, the employment policy of many Japanese firms to keep workers employed in a recession is a more efficient macroeconomic policy, even though it appears to be inefficient from a microeconomic perspective. But the ultimate solution to this question must also involve the development dimension. Discharging workers can create important structural changes of opportunity sets in the future economy, as can retraining retained workers. All three dimensions of efficiency, growth, and development must be integrated to find a rational solution.

This essay presents a considerably different view of economic development. It contends that the theory of economic development is a field of its own, that it is one of the three fundamental dimensions of economic analysis, together with the theories of economic efficiency and growth. Real economic problems must be analyzed in terms of efficiency, growth, and development and proposed solutions must represent a rational synthesis of these three dimensions. Most economic analyses are based only on efficiency or growth dimensions without considering the development dimension, and they often produce false and counterproductive conclusions as a result.

The theory of economic development is concerned with the development of social and technical factors that ultimately determine the set of economic *opportunities* available to nations, regions, business firms, other organizations, and individuals. Theories of economic efficiency and growth relate to a *given* set of opportunities: that is, a particular state of development or, as it is called here, an "economic regime." The concern of economic development is how these opportunity sets, these economic regimes, *change*. Clearly, the three dimensions of efficiency, growth, and development are intimately interrelated since decisions taken in the present regime, within a given set of opportunities, largely will determine what the future regime of opportunities will be.

In emphasizing the importance of the theory of economic development, it is also important to emphasize how little is known about this subject. Compared to the theories of efficiency and growth, the theory of economic development is still in its infancy. Indeed, as shown in the section on Lord Robbins's problem below, some of the greatest minds in economics have considered this problem at length and concluded that, important as the theory of economic development obviously is, it is a subject completely outside the scope and range of expertise of economic science.

My discussion of the theory of economic development draws on standard economic analysis and decision theory. But some of the more promising leads are found in fields such as military science, in some of the more thoughtful works in management science, in philosophy, and even in studies of artificial intelligence. The major task of this paper, however, is to demonstrate some of the real and important limitations of economic analysis in economic development without purporting to have solved the problem. By understanding these limitations, it is hoped that better economic decisions will be made in the short run and that better economic theories will evolve in the long run.

The Limitations of Economic Analysis
in Economic Development

While the limitations of economic analysis are perhaps most severe in the field of policy analysis, this is a highly abstract field in which concrete examples are not easily expressed. For this reason, the discussion in this paper focuses on investment decisions in the context of benefit-cost analysis to provide a concrete setting for the general problem.

The World Bank, U.S. AID, and other donor agencies require that economic development projects satisfy the "investment criteria" of benefit-cost analysis. There is some disagreement among economists over which of the investment criteria should be used in evaluating the economic feasibility of projects. But it is generally agreed that as a minimum condition the benefit-cost ratio should exceed unity, the internal rate of return (IRR) should exceed the discount rate, and (or) the net present value (NPV) should be positive (Mishan 1976).

However, economists frequently lament that decision makers ignore the project evaluations upon which they have labored so carefully and long. As one economist elegantly observed (in an internal document of a major donor agency), "The imaginative search for acceptable rates of return, retroactive to the decision to transfer resources, has been the job of the project economist."

Neglect of economic evaluations is understandable in the case of policies and projects that have substantial effects on the distribution of income, health, environmental quality, the arts, or other so-called noneconomic values. In these cases, sensible economists are willing, and even happy, to content themselves with calculating costs and trade-off functions, leaving the final evaluations to be made on the basis of the subjective values of decision makers.[2] This is also true, or should be true, in some of the more ideologically intensive areas of policy analysis. As Theodore W. Schultz (1987, 2) rightly says in an important paper that addresses some of the issues discussed here, "The idea that there are pure economic policies ready-made for governments to adopt is a myth."

But decision makers sometimes ignore the investment criteria even in cases of purely economic investments. In the case of public sector

---

2. What if the Mogul emperor Shah Jehan said to his economic advisor: "I am considering a project to be called the Taj Mahal. Please let me know if this is a worthwhile project." While the advisor could help make this decision, he or she would want to explain carefully that the ultimate evaluation is completely beyond the range of economic science and must be left to the emperor.

investments, this problem is often dismissed by attributing it to the biases, vested interests, ignorance, or other deficiencies of decision makers. But when, as the following examples indicate, private sector decision makers sometimes also ignore the investment criteria, the problem is not so easily dismissed.

In the article "Japanese Technology," for example, the *Economist* (2 December 1989) reports that Japanese businesses are now investing more in research and development than they are in plant and equipment. However, the article says that "Japanese managers have ceased basing their investment decisions on such notions as rates of return. They say it is more like 'surf-riding,' with waves of innovations coming on one after another." As one Japanese authority says, either you invest or you get "wiped out."

Another example is the recent acquisition of the manufacturer of Jaguar automobiles by Ford Motor Company. Most investment analysts severely criticized this acquisition on the grounds that Ford paid so much for Jaguar that the expected return would be far below the opportunity cost of capital. This criticism was tempered, however, by the fact that the investment was made under the direction of Donald E. Petersen, the CEO of Ford who, in polls of his peers, is one of the most highly regarded executives in American business. Indeed, *Forbes* magazine (22 January 1990) applauded this decision. Petersen wrote to congratulate *Forbes* on its perspicacity:

> *Forbes* was one of the very few that understood the strategic implications that went into the Jaguar decision . . . and was not fooled by the immediate reaction of some to the short-term view of the initial cost.
>
> Inside the company, I was very pleased at the sense of long-term thinking that went into the decision-making process. . . . Perhaps we finally are learning that we must make many decisions knowing that it takes a long time for an acorn to become an oak. (*Forbes* magazine, 5 (March 1990): 16; also see the discussion of Ford's strategy in the appendix, section 2.

Similar issues arise in debates over economic policies. In discussing U.S. trade policy, for example, Clyde Prestowitz, formerly the chief U.S. negotiator for Japanese trade, criticizes economists who advocate the laissez-faire pursuit of comparative advantages under a regime of free trade. " 'Traditional economists,' he says, 'believe it doesn't matter if

America produces $100 worth of potato chips or $100 worth of computer chips. We think the composition of the American economy and American trade is important,' he adds, emphasizing that 'computer chips are a technology for the future while potato chips belong to the past' " (*Washington Post,* 5 June 1990). Prestowitz suggests, in other words, that the United States could be led "as though by an unseen hand" to the state of a "potato chip" republic.

In a later discussion of this issue, Michael Boskin, then chairman of the Council of Economic Advisors, "reportedly said there was no difference between computer chips and potato chips" (*Washington Post,* 22 January 1993, B3). In the same issue of the *Post,* there is an article on a major breakthrough in computer chips by Sematech, the joint business-U.S. government–supported research company, that "puts the U.S. in the lead in this technology."

To use a concept explained later in this essay (see "Economic Regimes") blind pursuit of comparative trade advantages in the present *economic regime,* which is determined by the social and technical conditions of society, can create comparative disadvantages in future economic regimes. To avoid this fate, firms and nations may have to invest in areas of comparative disadvantage in the present regime to *develop* comparative advantages in future economic regimes. While economists sometimes refer to this problem in terms of the difference between "static" and "dynamic" comparative advantages, it is a much more difficult problem than these words imply. It is a problem of structural change in economic systems, of *regime switches.*

Another example of these issues is the green revolution in India. Had benefit-cost analysis been rigorously applied and followed in India in the 1960s, it is likely that the green revolution would never have occurred. The reason, as explained below in the section "Strategic Analysis and Cost-Effectiveness Analysis," is that the green revolution depended on irrigation as "the lead input" to increased agricultural production. Yet few if any of the major irrigation projects undertaken by India over the last 40 years would have satisfied the investment criteria of benefit-cost analysis. Thus, the lead input of the green revolution would have been lacking, and the green revolution as a whole would have failed, as indeed it has failed in the unirrigated areas of India.

Most infrastructural investments in rural areas, both in developing and developed economies, fail to satisfy the investment criteria. This is one reason why donor agencies have been negligent in supporting such investments in Africa, and this, together with poor economic policies, is a major reason why African agricultural production is so low (Seckler,

Gollin, and Antoine 1992). As a recent study of agricultural growth in the Punjab of India (Bhalla et al. 1990) concludes:

> The first, most important lesson is that the basic requirement for a region to develop its agriculture and have a distinct comparative advantage in agricultural production is massive public investment in irrigation, power, research, extension, markets, roads, communications, and other rural infrastructure. From a policy point of view, infrastructural investment is the sine qua non of agricultural growth and specialization and is also important in other sectors of the economy in order to realize the benefits of that growth.

Last, an amusing perspective on these issues appears in a cartoon in the *New Yorker* (6 August 1990). It shows two archaeologists in a tomb, one translating hieroglyphics to the other. The caption reads, "And then, at the height of their power, they seem to have succumbed to a mysterious people known as 'the bottom-line types.'"

Granted that there is something worth considering in these examples, it is important not to throw the baby out with the bathwater. There is no question that benefit-cost analysis is an indispensable tool of analysis for making rational investments. For example, the manager of a bond portfolio who refused to consider rates of return on alternative investments would rightly be regarded as demented.

Benefit-cost analysis, in other words, is a necessary condition for making rational investments, but the degree to which it provides a *sufficient* basis for making such investments varies with the kind of investments being considered. This suggests that different kinds of investments may be arrayed along a continuum. At one end of the continuum are such decisions as the management of bond portfolios for which the investment criteria are virtually sufficient. At the other end are investments for which these criteria are only part of a much larger set of considerations.[3] At this end of the continuum, perhaps, "The heart [of the entrepreneur] knows things whereof the mind [of the economist] knows not."

Over 50 years ago, this problem was discussed by some of the greatest minds of economics. The review of that discussion in the next section provides the point of departure for the rest of this essay.

---

3. Of course, in the tautological sense of pure economic theory and under strict assumptions, all conceivable benefits and costs of any conceivable action are included—there can be no other considerations. The concern here is with problems that arise outside of this framework, when the assumptions (especially that of "perfect knowledge") are relaxed.

Lord Robbins's Problem

In his classic *Essay on the Nature and Significance of Economic Science* (1935), Lionel (later Lord) Robbins set out to define the scope and limitations of economic science. Such methodological discussions have fallen out of favor in contemporary economics, with most economists subscribing to Samuelson's declaration (or jest?) that "economics is what economists do." The problem with this position is that there is no assurance that "what economists do" is done well. That is why Robbins and other great economists worried about the scope and, especially, the limitations of their science.

First, Robbins reviews several of his eminent predecessors' definitions of economics. One is expressed in the grand title of Adam Smith's treatise *An Inquiry into the Nature and Causes of the Wealth of Nations*. Others are "the material means of life" (Marshall), the theory of "exchange" (Schumpeter), "prices" (Davenport), or whatever can be "directly or indirectly brought into relation with the measuring rod of money" (Pigou) (Robbins 1935, 4, 21).

Robbins contends that all these "classificatory" definitions are deficient and instead proposes an "analytical" definition. Economics does not study a kind of subject matter, he says, but rather a kind of *relationship*. "Economics is the science which studies human behavior in terms of the relationship between given ends and limited resources with alternative uses" (16). In short, economics is "the pure logic of choice."

Considering the universality of such choice relationships, Robbins could fairly claim to have seized the high ground for what since has been called "the imperial science." But Robbins then turns to the limitations of economics. He contends that the "theory of economic development" is *not* within the scope of economic science. The widespread belief to the contrary, he says, is but another manifestation of the confusion generated by classificatory definitions of the subject. The theory of economic development would be included under such classificatory definitions as "wealth," but it is excluded under the analytical definition of choice.

> The subject matter of Economics is essentially a series of relationships—relationships between ends conceived as the possible objectives of conduct, on the one hand, and the technical and social environment on the other. Ends as such do not form part of this subject-matter. Nor does the technical and social environment. It is the relationships between these things and not the things in themselves which are important for the economist. (38)

Developing the technical and social factors of a nation certainly is a central problem of economic development. But these factors are part of the environment of economic choice, they are not objects of economic choice. They enter the analysis as "given conditions," as "data." However, Robbins asks:

> Is it not possible for us to extend our generalizations so as to cover changes of the data? We have seen in what sense it is possible to conceive of economic dynamics—the analysis of the path through time of a system making adjustments consequential upon the existence of given conditions? Can we not extend our technique so as to enable us to predict changes of these given conditions? In short, can we not frame a complete theory of economic development? (131)

He answers:

> If the preceding analysis is correct the prospects are very doubtful. . . . We may forecast their effects when they have occurred. We may speculate with regard to the effects of hypothetical changes. We may consider alternative forms and enquire concerning their stability and change. But as regards actual capacity to foretell a process of change, with its manifest dependence on the heterogeneous elements of contingency, persuasion, and blind force, if we are humble, we shall be modest in our pretensions. (135)

And concludes:

> Thus in the last analysis the study of Economics, while it shows us a region of economic laws, of necessities to which human action is subject, shows us too, a region in which no such necessities operate. This is not to say that within that region there is no law, no necessity. Into that question we make no enquiry. It is only to say that from its point of view at least there are certain things which must be taken as ultimate data. (135)

Among the various criticisms of Robbins's position, one is particularly relevant to economists' participation in what is now called policy reform and structural adjustment. These are areas where ends, institutions, and technologies play a predominant role in decision making. Are economists according to Robbins to be silent about these important economic issues?

It has been held that because I attempted clearly to delimit the spheres of Economics and other social sciences, and Economics and moral philosophy, that therefore I advocated the abstention of the economist from all interest or activity outside his own subject. It has been held, in spite of activities which I feared had become notorious, I had urged that economists should play no part in shaping the conduct of affairs beyond giving a very prim and restrained diagnosis of the implications of all possible courses of action.

Robbins says (ix) that he holds only that the various fields of knowledge should be carefully sorted out "in order that we may know at each step exactly on what grounds we are deciding."

I quite agree with Mr. Fraser that an economist who is only an economist . . . is a pretty poor fish. . . . I agree, too that by itself Economics affords no solution to any of the important problems of life. I agree that for this reason an education which consists of Economics alone is a very imperfect education. I have taught so long in institutions where this is regarded as a pedagogic axiom that any omission on my part to emphasize it further is to be attributed to the fact that everybody would take it for granted. (ix)

F. H. Hayek (1955) put it even more strongly: "An economist who is only an economist is a nuisance, if not an outright menace." This is perhaps also the basis of Keynes' (1935) rather tart remark on overly formalized or "mathematical" economics. "Whereas, in ordinary discourse, where we are not blindly manipulating but know all the time what we are doing and what the words mean, we can keep 'at the back of our heads' the necessary reserves and qualifications and the adjustments which we shall have to make later on" (297).

Of course, no one contends that economists must recuse themselves from studies of the social and technical processes of economic development. It is only that these areas require knowledge beyond economists' particular scope of expertise. In these areas, economists must draw on the knowledge of other social and physical sciences, of history and philosophy, and on the practical knowledge of men and women of affairs.

Economists have grappled with this problem both before and after Robbins's discussion. Neglect of the social and technical conditions of economic systems is the platform of the institutionalist's critique of "neoclassical" or "mainstream" economics (Seckler 1975). Peter Wiles criticized Robbins's and other neoclassical economists for "wringing their hands" over marginal departures from economic efficiency in the static case, while the real economic problem is how to create the dynamic processes of structural change and economic growth. Albert O. Hirschman (1964) extended this position to the theory of "unbalanced growth" and other elements of his *The Strategy of Economic Development.* Kenneth Arrow has emphasized learning-by-doing processes, and Theodore W. Schultz (1987) investment in human capital. Hayami and Ruttan (1971) and their colleagues have developed a theory of economically induced institutional and technological innovations.

Yet it is fair to say that little of this thinking has become part of the formal apparatus of benefit-cost (or policy) analysis. These concepts escape the investment criteria. Thus, in many of the most important investments—those concerning the economic development of individuals, firms, regions, or nations—benefit-cost analysis is likely to exclude the very raison d'etre of the investment. As Robbins says, a science that is intrinsically based on the assumption of *given* social and technical conditions is not capable of dealing adequately with the problem of economic development, which is intrinsically concerned with the problem of how these conditions *change.*

Economic Regimes

The argument to this point may be reformulated in terms of the concept of an *economic regime.* In general, a regime is "a manner, method or system of rule or government, a system or institution having widespread influence." Thus, John Stuart Mill said, "Under the regime of competition, things are exchanged for each other at such values etc." Or to cite another usage of the word, "Under previous parliamentary regimes this evil was not patent."[4] An important characteristic of regimes is their widespread and diffuse influence. In agricultural development, for example, the agroclimatic regime affects all the input-output relations of the production system.

The regime concept is used precisely in econometrics in the context of structural changes, which are also called regime switches (e.g., Kennedy 1985), from whence the present usage. In this context, the behavior of an econometric model is determined by the parameters.[5]

---

4. Oxford English Dictionary, 1971, s.v. "regimes."

5. *Parameter* is itself one of the more difficult and misused words in the language, often confused with *perimeter.* Mathematically it means "any constant, with variable values, used as a referent for determining other values" (*Webster's Ninth New Collegiate Dictionary,* 1983). In regression analysis, the coefficients of the independent variables of the equation are called parameters. But the word also may be used to refer to both the coefficients and the variables, as when the variables themselves may change in a regime switch.

The parameters, in turn, are determined largely by the economic regime, that is, the basic social and technical conditions of the economy. So long as the economic regime is constant, the parameters will be stable and the behavior of the economic system will remain the same within a normal range of random variation. When the regime switches the parameters change, and the system behaves in a qualitatively different manner. Thus, in regression analysis, the regime may be left completely undefined, with a regime switch detected in cross-sectional or time series analysis only by statistically significant changes in the parameters. These regime switches are indicated by dummy, state, or qualitative variables, with values of either zero or one—hence, the "switch."

A regime switch may change any or all of the parameters of the system and create an entirely new complex of interactions—a new world, so to speak, with intrinsically uncertain outcomes. If it were not for regime switches, good econometric models would be able to predict the future within a known range of error, and the problems of choice would reduce to little more than simple arithmetic. As Goodhart's Law states, however, "All econometric models break down when used for policy" (quoted in Kennedy 1985, 6).

The concept of a regime is used, as in these examples, primarily to refer to the environment of activities. However, it implies not only the environment but also the pattern of *relationships* between the environment and the actor that produce particular kinds of activities. Thus, biologists frequently refer to "the interactions between the environment and the organism," but they do not have a name for this type of phenomenon. While the organism is clearly "in" an environment, the kind of environment it is in no less clearly depends on what the organism *is*.

Philosophically, such phenomena are "compositions," or as Hayek (1955) says, "complexes" or "wholes."[6] They consist of parts and the relations between parts, and as Bertrand Russell (1976) says, "the relations between the parts are 'real' in every sense that the parts are 'real.' " The word *regime* is used here in this general sense of patterns of relationships between actors and their environments.

In the specific context of decision theory, an economic regime refers to the set of opportunities available to a decision maker at any given point in time. The regime determines the decision space: the combined set of all of the production and indifference surfaces confronting the

---

6. Although most definitely not "holes," as in the philosophic sense of "holism," or irreducible entities. A whole can, in principle, be analyzed into parts and relations and synthesized from parts and relations. A "hole" is "just there," perhaps represented by only the most elementary, ultimate particles.

decision maker or, to use a less cumbersome word, "decider."[7] Clearly, the economic regime is unique to each decider.

As Robbins (1935) observes, a central task of economic analysis is to select the subset of opportunities within a given economic regime that achieves an optimal (the best under the circumstances) state of economic welfare. But certain kinds of decisions that are taken within an economic regime have social and technical effects that partly determine what the future economic regime will be and thus how the decider will be able to behave in the future regime.

Thus, there is a fundamental *dualism* in the theory of rational decisions. First, there is the short-run, or tactical, problem of optimizing opportunities within a given economic regime. Second, there is the long-run, or strategic, problem caused by the social and technical effects of present decisions on alternative future regimes (see app. sec. 1 and sec. 3). The next section introduces implications of this dualism in terms of the distinction between tactical decisions within a regime and strategic decisions between regimes.

Strategic Decisions

The distinction between tactical and strategic decisions is as important in military science as the distinction between the short run and the long run is in economics.[8] Both distinctions refer to roughly the same analytic conditions: the difference between the *present,* in which the resources at the disposal of the decision maker are fixed, and the *future,* in which resources are variable. In both cases, the period of analysis is determined by the variability of resources, not simply by time.

The word *strategy* (as distinguished from *tactics*) derives from the Greek *strategos,* or general, and pertains to "the science of planning and directing large-scale military operations, specifically of maneuvering forces into the most advantageous position prior to actual engagement

---

7. The use of the rather passive "decision maker," in the sense of "the decision is made" rather than the more active "decider" reflects more than simply preference for the passive voice in academic discourse. It reflects the philosophical issue of determinism versus volition (or free will) in the social sciences in which humans are indeed passive components, determined by, rather than determinants of, social systems.

8. Military science is probably the oldest branch of rational decision theory, as evidenced by the still widely read, 2,400-year-old classic by Sun Tzu, *The Art of War.* It is interesting to note that the ancient Chinese had as much trouble with these concepts as we have today. Thus, in the footnote (p. 85) to chapter 4 (entitled "Dispositions") the translator says, "The character *hsing* . . . means 'shape,' 'form,' or 'appearance' or in a more restricted sense, 'disposition' or 'formation.' Even the word 'appreciation' (of the situation) is used in military science as a way of expressing the artistic quality of these concepts."

with the enemy" (*Webster's Ninth New Collegiate Dictionary* 1983). The word also is used in biology to mean "an adaptation or complex of adaptations (as of behavior, metabolism or structure) that serves or appears to serve an important function in achieving evolutionary success."

Thus, in military science, tactical decisions relate to present events on the battlefield, while strategic decisions attempt to provide favorable opportunities for future tactical decisions. The task of the general, in other words, is to establish a favorable military regime that provides strategic advantages and avoids strategic disadvantages for tactical decisions. A paradoxical situation arises in which the entire rationale of strategic decisions lies in the results of tactical decisions, yet the tactical decisions cannot be known at the time the strategic decisions are made. This strategic paradox perhaps is what Dwight D. Eisenhower had in mind when he observed, "Planning is essential, plans are worthless." (Also see the discussion in sections 2 and 3 of the appendix.)

Investments in economic development have a similar strategic aspect. Improvements in social and technical conditions are intended to provide a favorable economic regime for future tactical (optimizing) decisions. Examples are investments in education and training, research and development, managerial improvements and institutional change, and in such infrastructural facilities as roads, power supplies, communications, and irrigation. As this list indicates, such investments tend to have the properties of public goods, which have been thoroughly analyzed in welfare economics. They create what J. M. Clarke aptly describes as "social overhead capital," which is one of the most important forms of capital, quite apart from the question of whether it is best provided by the private or public sector or some combination of them. But since investments in economic development are intended only to create *opportunities* that may or may not be transformed into future benefits by tactical decisions, they only create hypothetical and qualitative values that are not amenable to analysis in the essentially quantitative terms of benefit-cost analysis. The value of such investments is the strategic "position," the essentially qualitative set of opportunities they provide for the future.

This problem may be described as the "three-stage problem" of evaluating investments in economic development, in contrast to the two-stage problem of evaluating ordinary investments. Evaluations of ordinary investments essentially compare the economic costs of activities in the present stage with the economic benefits resulting from those activities in a future stage. But evaluations of investments in economic development must be based on a three-stage process. Activities in the present stage create an economic regime of opportunities in the first future stage. These opportunities may or may not then be transformed into economic benefits in a later, second future stage.

Decisions to proceed from the first future stage of opportunities to the second future stage of benefits are made on the basis of knowledge and information that is available only in or after the first future stage. But this knowledge and information is not available in the present stage in which the investment is made. Thus, while the value of the opportunities created by investments in development is derived from the value of the economic benefits obtained in the second future stage, it is impossible to know at the time the investment is made whether these opportunities will result in economic benefits or not.

For this reason, investments in economic development are made under conditions of true uncertainty, not simply of risk. They can only be rigorously evaluated ex post, during or after the second future stage, when the investment is already made. But it is often *necessary* to make such investments virtually "in the blind" because without the opportunities they create it is impossible to obtain their *potential* future benefits.

This three-stage problem is bad enough when the first-stage investor also makes the third-stage decision to utilize the opportunities of the second stage. But it becomes a particularly acute problem in the case of public sector investments in development that are intended to create favorable economic regimes for utilization by the private sector. Here there is even more uncertainty about whether the opportunities will be transformed into benefits and therefore about the justification of the investment.

For example, the public sector may build a road to a remote area, hoping that the private sector will use the road and thus make the investment worthwhile. But there is no *assurance* that the road will be used. Thus, investments in economic development are particularly prone to becoming those "white elephants" that some economists so delight in criticizing.

But much to the credit of public sector entrepreneurs, they often make such investments, understanding that they may become white elephants but also understanding that the alternative of doing nothing is worse. In the case of roads to remote regions, for example, there is a strong possibility that the road will be a white elephant. On the other hand, it is virtually *certain* that if a road is not built the region will *never* develop. But because the missed opportunity represented by the undeveloped region is invisible, it is much safer to reject such a project than to undertake it and risk creating an all-too-visible white elephant. Acts of omission are always safer than those of commission because nothing happens.

A related aspect of this problem is the common practice of assigning credit for successful developments to the private sector and blame for failures to the public sector. While this has become an especially popular pastime in recent years, it was fashionable even before Adam Smith. Thus, Jean Baptiste Colbert, the great seventeenth-century French minister of finance, who was an ardent supporter of private enterprise, voiced his exasperation with "these merchants, who . . . only understand their little commissions, and fail to understand the great forces that make commerce work" (quoted in Duignan 1990, 80).[9]

However, the question remains. If one is making investments in economic development, in new regimes, in qualitative opportunities for the future, how can these investments be evaluated? If benefit-cost analysis does not provide an adequate basis for evaluating these investments, is there any other kind of analysis, a "strategic" kind of analysis, that does? The remainder of this essay is devoted to this difficult question.

Sequential Decision Theory

Sequential decision theory represents the most extended attempt in economics to deal with the problems of strategic analysis. This theory has made fundamentally important contributions to describing the nature of the problem and to providing some important principles of strategic analysis. However, in this writer's opinion, sequential decision theory has also created a red herring by attempting to reduce the problem of true uncertainty to a problem merely of risk.

An exceptionally lucid application of sequential decision theory is the analysis of the California Water Plan by Rausser and Dean (1971). The basic problem in formulating the California Water Plan was to select among a large variety of investment options, ranging from water conservation to nuclear desalinization, a plan of action that economically would satisfy an equally large variety of projected water demands under changing social and technological conditions.

One of the many interesting aspects of this problem is that, like many other such investments, the gestation period of many of the alternatives is on the order of 20 years or more. In order to make rational

---

9. The same incident that provoked this comment may have stimulated the use of the phrase laissez-faire in economics. According to a familiar story, Colbert once assembled some of the leading burghers of Paris to a meeting and asked them, "What can we do for you?" They replied something like, "*vous pouvez nous laissez-faire*"—roughly, "you can leave us alone" (or more precisely, "allow us to do what we want to do"). This story may have been handed down by word of mouth for nearly a century when the "laissez-faire" philosophy was so named by the Physiocrats.

decisions, one must be able to see more than 20 years into the future, which of course is impossible. Is it possible to make rational decisions under such conditions, decisions that at least in principle are better than other decisions?

Figure 5.1 shows the hypothetical decision tree used in the study. Very briefly, beginning at the 1970 decision point there are two alternatives: "to build" or "to wait" for 1970–80 "chance events," including improved knowledge. Each of these decisions and all subsequent decisions have an outcome, indicated by the dollar signs, and a probability estimate of the outcome, indicated by the decimal signs. Multiplying the value of the outcome by the probability results in the mathematical expectation of the value of the outcome. Some of these outcomes have only a tactical significance in that their consequences end with the outcome, while others are of strategic significance in that they produce both an outcome and lead to future decisions. The strategic situation confronting decision makers is the *entire set of paths* originating from each decision point.

Rausser and Dean (1971) note several important aspects of sequential decision theory. "A principle result of formal sequential decision analysis under uncertainty is that there is no single 'best action' for all time, but rather a 'strategy' that is flexible in the sense that decisions in future periods depend on chance (or other unknown) events that occur in the interim."

Sequential decision processes also involve a kind of twofold way of thinking. First, there is the synthetic process of "looking forward" to establish a vision of the future. "Obviously, only the first step . . . must be taken immediately, but as figure 5.1 makes clear, that step depends on formulating the *entire* decision tree, not just stage 1 data, even though beyond stage 1 it is a 'paper plan.'" Second, the vision is then analyzed through a process of "working backward" to the current decision point, "that is we start from the 'tips' of the decision tree and work backward in time toward the initial decision point."

Sequential decision theory raises the exceptionally difficult problem of distinguishing between *risk,* where probabilities can legitimately be assigned to events, and *uncertainty,* where they cannot (Shackle 1949). This distinction has become almost hopelessly confused by the debates over classical, objective probability and Bayesian, subjective probability.

If one were certain about both the probabilities and the outcomes in figure 5.1, computation of the optimal economic path would be trivial. All that would be required is to multiply all the possible outcomes by their probabilities to obtain the optimum path. If this were possible, there would be no meaningful distinction between tactical and strategic

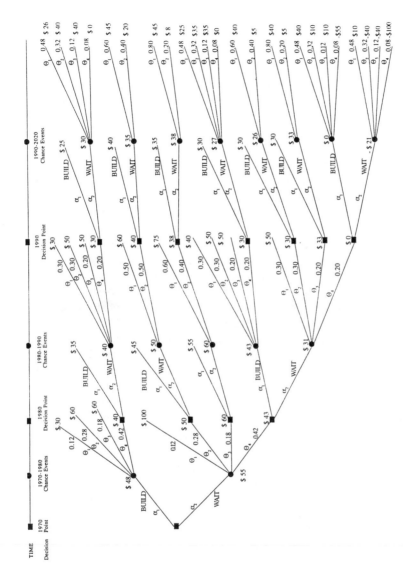

Fig. 5.1. Hypothetical decision tree illustrating framework for sequential decision making under uncertainty for the California Water Plan.

decisions. The fact that these are very difficult decisions whose validity is never known until the results are in is itself evidence that analysts and decision makers are truly *uncertain* about the probabilities, as well as the outcomes.

This is why analysts employ simulations, war games, and other kinds of mental experiments to test the robustness of the decision under wide ranges of probability estimates. These simulations provide information about possible losses and gains under various probability assumptions. In order to create such arithmetical scenarios, it is necessary to assign numerical indicators of expectations regarding the outcomes. But the arithmetic needed for such indicators should not be confused with real, objectively determined probabilities. This distinction is particularly important in regime switches. Virtually by definition, regime switches change the historic probability distributions in an unknown way.

Thus, while it is perhaps acceptable to move an objectively defined distribution curve about a bit in light of subjective knowledge and anticipation of future regimes, a purely subjective estimate of probability is at best no more than an expression of the sincerity of personal belief. A person may believe, as some no doubt do, that "the apocalypse is nigh" with a probability of 1.00, but whatever this indicates about the person's state of mind it has nothing to do with rational decisions. As Blyth says, "However meaningful and helpful such numbers are to the author, they are meaningless and irrelevant to his reader . . . what the reader wants to know from the author is 'Leaving your opinions out of this, what does your experimental evidence say?'" (quoted in Kennedy 1985, 174).

In any case, simulation exercises generate a wide variety of possible scenarios, ranging in consequences from triumph to catastrophe, from which entrepreneurs still must choose. The choice is based presumably on knowledge other than that contained in the analysis. Treating these fundamental problems of uncertainty as though they were only problems of risk creates a kind of "specious accuracy" (Morgenstern 1963) that is likely to be highly misleading to decision makers. They cannot obtain the qualitative feel for the situation, the "back of the head" conditionalities, and thus may be led astray.

In sum, sequential decision theory provides an elegant presentation of the problem of strategic decisions in the decision trees, and it provides fundamentally important propositions in strategic analysis, such as "looking forward" and "working backward." However, it fails to address adequately the essential problem of strategic decisions, that of true uncertainty. By attempting to transform uncertainty into risk, it indeed confuses the true nature of the problem and treats strategic decisions as though they were only tactical decisions.

Uncertainty and the Nature of Strategic Decisions

If there were no uncertainty, if there were only risk, there would be no substantial distinction between *tactical* and *strategic* decisions, and the words would be reduced to the mere cliches in which they are often used. It is therefore necessary to prove that true uncertainty exists, that is, that there are at least some outcomes of decisions to which probabilities cannot be assigned.

The philosopher of science Karl Popper has defined a large class of uncertain events in his famous "refutation of historicism" or what may be called "futurism" (Popper 1968, paraphrased in Seckler 1975, 81).

1. Knowledge influences the future.
2. It is impossible to predict future knowledge; otherwise it would be current knowledge.
3. Therefore it is impossible to predict the future.

Following this logic, risk is within the scope of present knowledge, while uncertainty depends on future knowledge.

An example of uncertainty in the field of technology is the recent confirmation of "quasi-crystals," a new form of matter, by Bell Laboratories. When one of the Bell scientists was asked about the technological implications of this discovery, he replied, "The possible applications are unimagined." If it is agreed that it is impossible to assign even a subjective probability to an *unimagined* event, the existence of true uncertainty is demonstrated.

Uncertainty pertains to the *uniqueness* of events of which new events or entire compositions of new events in regime switches are archetypal cases. This is in contrast to risk, which pertains to the quasi-repeatability of events or experience within a regime or in past regimes. That is why generals and other decision makers naturally tend to fight the last war. But even though future events may be uncertain, it may be possible to rationally evaluate *processes* in terms of their relative capacity or fecundity in producing opportunities for future events. This form of evaluation is similar to the process of scientific methodology: the process captured in the title of Popper's 1968 book, *Conjectures and Refutations*.

Strategic decisions thus can be interpreted as hypotheses derived from scientific theories of action. Like other scientific hypotheses, they are conditional propositions, of the "if . . . then" form. The validity of these decisions can only be known *ex post,* but *ex ante* errors in the decision can be reduced in the scientific process of objective criticism.[10]

In a managerial context, as Landau (1973, 533) says,

> Policies are reinterpreted as the equivalent of theories; plans as models; programs as experiments in the interest of displacing rationalization by verification, and establishing the spirit of criticism as the essential property of a scientifically managed organization.

This philosophy was systematically applied to the General Motors Corporation in its formative stages by its master strategist Alfred P. Sloan:

> Our decentralized organization and our tradition of selling ideas rather than simply giving orders impose the need upon all levels of management to make a good case for what they propose. The manager who would like to operate on a hunch will usually find it hard

---

10. As this essay was being completed, the writer read Bertrand Russell's (1948, 372–73) analysis of Keynes's (1921) theory of probability, which elegantly states the position I expressed, though not nearly so well, in the text:

Keynes's *Treatise on Probability* (1921) sets out a theory which is, in a sense, the antithesis of the frequency theory. He holds that the relation used in deduction, namely "p implies q," is the extreme form of a relation which might be called "p more or less implies q." "If a knowledge of h," he says, "justifies a rational belief in a of degree A', we say there is a *probability relation* of degree A' between a and h." We write this: "$a/h = $ A'." "Between two sets of propositions there exists a relation, in virtue of which, if we know the first, we can attach to the latter some degree of rational belief." Probability is essentially a relation: "It is as useless to say 'b is probable' as 'b is equal' or 'b is greater than.' " From "a" and "a implies b," we can conclude "b"; that is to say, we can drop all mention of the premise and simply assert the conclusion. But if a is so related to b that a knowledge of a renders a probable belief in b rational, we cannot conclude anything whatever about b which has not reference to a; there is nothing corresponding to the dropping of a true premise in demonstrative inference. . . .

Probabilities in general, according to Keynes, are not numerically measurable; those that are so form a very special class of probabilities. He holds that one probability may not be comparable with another; i.e., may be neither greater nor less than the other, nor yet equal to it.

I am also indebted to Professor Peter Rogers of Harvard University for sending me a copy of an interesting paper (Kunreuther and Hogarth 1990) that explicitly addresses the problem of uncertainty or, as they aptly say, "ambiguity" about both the outcomes and probabilities in actuarial analyses.

to sell his ideas to others on this basis. . . . In short, General Motors is not the appropriate organization for purely intuitive executives, but it provides a favorable environment for capable and rational men. (Sloan 1965, 432) [11]

An instructive example of the scientific nature of strategic decisions is the difference between two large U.S. programs: "getting a man on the moon" and the "War on Cancer" (Rubenstein, quoted in Ruttan 1989, 15). Both programs had a vision of the future, in the sense of a reasonably well-articulated goal; both involved development of an entire regime of new and complex technologies. But the lunar program was guided by the highly reliable theory of Newtonian mechanics, and therefore it was virtually certain that the mission could be accomplished. The war on cancer, on the other hand, was launched without the guidance of a reliable theory, and the mission has made only modest progress to date. However, as the experimental action proceeds, the theories become better formulated, and there is little doubt that eventually the war on cancer at least partly will be won.

Similarly, the Manhattan Project, which led to the development of the atomic bomb, was based on a "possibility theorem" in fundamental physics, just as attempts to discover a perpetual motion machine are excluded by an "impossibility theorem." Based on such scientific theories of opportunities, Erich Bloch, former director of the National Science Foundation, recommends establishing several national centers "devoted to what [he] calls 'generic, strategic technologies' that would focus on the development of new composite materials, biotechnology, electronics manufacturing and other such products" (*Washington Post,* 23 August 1990).

When strategic decisions are properly interpreted in terms of scientific theories of action, it is clear that many kinds of evidence and arguments, qualitative and quantitative, have appropriate roles in the process of objective, critical examination. As noted before, the most impressive aspect of sequential decision theory is not the arithmetic of subjective and objective probabilities, although they have an important tactical role, but the essentially qualitative character of the decision tree itself, the sequences of cause and effect relationships, the *theory of action* expressed in the decision tree.

As in science itself, the question of how theories are developed, the

---

11. However, Sloan also recognized the need for adapting the organization to accommodate "genius," as in the case of Charles F. Kettering, around whom Sloan created a large and autonomous research organization.

speculative leap into the unknown, remains a mystery. Some entrepreneurs, like some scientists and generals, seem to be better at creating valid strategic decisions than are others. Difficult though this subject is, appendix sections 2 and 3 provide a brief review of work in artificial intelligence that is relevant to the problem and speculates on some possible principles of strategic analysis.

Entrepreneurial Enterprises

As demonstrated in the "looking forward" component of sequential decision theory, one of the most important principles of strategic analysis may be stated as, "You cannot decide *what* to do until you decide *where* you want to go."[12] Tactical decisions are meaningless except in the context of a strategic analysis of the goals to be achieved and the resources to be allocated in the long-term development of a coordinated process of purposive action: an *entrepreneurial enterprise*. Once the entrepreneurial enterprise has been formulated and decided upon in strategic terms, the tactical components of the enterprise can be evaluated in terms of their contribution to the enterprise as a whole.

To put this principle in the more familiar terms of donor agency evaluation procedures, projects cannot be evaluated except in terms of their contribution to programs and programs in terms of strategies. Next only to strategic analysis, the program appraisal and identification stage is thus the most important stage of the evaluation process. But this is nearly the reverse of normal evaluation procedures: evaluations concentrate on projects, ignoring programs. Yet it is at the sectorial, program-

---

12. While this proposition may seem self-evident to noneconomists, it reflects a philosophic position that conflicts, in certain respects, with the philosophic basis of mainstream economics. As Jacob Viner (1958), himself one of the leading mainstream figures, observes, the economics of Adam Smith and his successors is premised on the idea of a natural order in which if the proper initial conditions are established the economic system will attain an *optimal* equilibrium position virtually on its own without further human interference—indeed, even without humans knowing what the optimal position is.

The concept of entrepreneurial enterprises reflects a contrary, teleological philosophy in human affairs in which there is no advance guarantee that the equilibrium that naturally occurs under any given set of initial conditions is desirable or optimal. The modern form of this teleological philosophy is due to Norbert Wiener's theory of cybernetics: "the theory of purposive behavior in man and machine" (see Seckler 1986, and Ashby 1964). In brief, the relationship between the actual outputs of the system and the desired outputs, the "results," controls the inputs to the system to produce optimal or satisfactory results.

The differences between these philosophic positions largely account for the differences between interventionists and noninterventionists in economic policy. This essay is obviously cast in the cybernetic mold.

matic level that evaluations should be focused because the value of projects is *derived from* the value of programs.

In formulating the strategy for entrepreneurial enterprises, two qualitatively different kinds of issues must be decided. These are *values* and *facts* (Landau 1986, 47). Values pertain to the ends of the enterprise, while facts pertain to the causal means of attaining the ends. Both can be the subject of intense debate in formulating an enterprise.

The green revolution in India provides an example of a highly successful entrepreneurial enterprise in which public sector investments and policies created a regime switch in much of rural India. The basic features of this process are briefly outlined below (Mellor 1976; Seckler and Sampath 1989).

The great droughts of 1965–66 and 1966–67 combined with the U.S. "food as a weapon" policy aimed at India caused agriculture to rise to the forefront of concern in Indian political circles. Government resources were reallocated from the industrial sector to the hitherto largely neglected agricultural sector. In the process of developing the strategy of agricultural development in India, public sector entrepreneurs engaged in a process very similar to that outlined in the discussion of sequential decision theory above.

In the "looking forward" stage of the strategy, there was the value decision to satisfy the basic food needs of the population at prices most of the people could afford to pay over the long-term. Since projections of food needs depend mainly on population growth, which is basically locked in by population momentum for about 50 years, this was not a difficult factual exercise. However, both values and facts were very much involved in and intensely debated in the determination issue of how self-reliant India was to be in food production. India decided on a policy of self-reliance in basic food grains in terms of the trend growth of food needs (not only economic demand).

Given these strategic goals, Indian decision makers worked backward to decide which social and technical paths would achieve them. Here is where genius and determination, and the trade-offs between values and facts, become most apparent. Two strategic decisions were made and implemented in the face of considerable criticism and controversy. First, it was decided that activities would be concentrated on the most agriculturally favorable areas, like the Punjab, with marginal areas left until later. This of course meant that better-off farmers would be made even better off while the poorest farmers would be neglected.

Second, it was explicitly recognized that developing agricultural production in India had to be an integrated enterprise, with all of the necessary inputs provided together. This was expressed by references to the "package" of inputs, ranging from high-yielding varieties, research, and extension, through fertilizers and market roads, to price support and credit systems with irrigation as the "lead input." It was decided to implement *all* the components of the enterprise simultaneously in a coordinated process of action to achieve synergism between the various components as a whole.

Thus, in making their decisions, the entrepreneurs of the green revolution paid very little attention to rates of return on irrigation projects, agricultural research, or fertilizer plants. Of course, economic analysis was used, in some cases quite decisively, to determine which investments would be made where and when. In other words, alternative tactical investments that contributed to the same goals were to some degree *ranked* according to investment criteria but little attention was paid to the absolute values of the investment criteria—that is, to whether the investments were economically feasible or not. The decision regarding the economic feasibility of the enterprise—and therefore of its necessary components—had already been made in the strategic design of the enterprise itself.

There are several lessons to be learned from this experience. First, the green revolution illustrates what may be called "the fallacy of misplaced incrementalism," or "piecemealism," in economic evaluations. By evaluating only the parts of the system, following the benefit-cost rule that all separable items must be separately evaluated, the integral value of the parts to the enterprise as a whole is likely to be lost. It is rather like evaluating the performance of an automobile with and without a carburetor. If one wants a running automobile one must have a carburetor and the evaluation must be at the level of the whole, not the part.

To put it another way, entrepreneurial enterprises are highly complex homeostatic systems that are stable within certain bounds of variation but are subject to abrupt changes and even collapse once these bounds are transgressed. Such systems are linear only within the homeostatic bounds of variation, beyond which they become nonlinear, "chaotic" systems, moving into regime switches. This is why hydraulic engineers do not fine-tune their dams. After precisely calculating the strength factors, they multiply by a factor of two or three. This is also why redundancy is an integral component of the design of managerial and other forms of social systems, no matter how wasteful it may appear if one assumes certainty or certainty about probabilities and risk (Landau, 1973).

In discussing the development strategy of General Motors, Sloan (1965, 261) refers to certain kinds of investment decisions, such as investments in research and development, as "end necessities." Given the ends of the enterprise, the investments are necessary; the investments can only be debated in terms of the ends, not the means, of the enterprise. Defining these end necessities is one of the essential functions of the "working backward" process of strategic analysis.

It was part of the genius of the decision-making process of the green revolution to recognize that, in all but the most favored agroclimatic areas, irrigation is indeed an end necessity that can be evaluated only in terms of the end of increased agricultural production. Fully 80 percent of the increased agricultural production of Asia since 1970 has been on irrigated land. It is regrettable and rather astonishing that only now is this fact becoming recognized in African agricultural development (Seckler 1990).

A second major lesson from the green revolution is that Indian decision makers wisely ignored economic advice to depend on food imports to capture the short-run, tactical benefits of comparative advantages and decided instead upon a long-run, strategic program of self-reliance in basic foods.

The consequences of this decision are somewhat as follows. In the mid-1960s, India was producing around 90 million metric tons (MT) of food grains. Today, it is producing around 170 million tons MT. Had the large investments of the green revolution under the strategy of self-reliance not been made, perhaps only 30 percent of the 80-million-ton increase in food grain production, or 24 million tons, would have been achieved. If so, India would now be importing about 56 MT of food grain per annum to reach present levels of consumption (which still is about 20 million MT too low to satisfy basic food needs [Seckler and Sampath 1989]). This would amount to 37 percent of the total world food grain trade of 150 million MT. Even at the present average price of about $150 (C.I.F.), it would cost India about $8.4 billion per annum. This may be compared to India's total imports of $17 billion, with current foreign reserves sufficient only for two months' imports. Considering the enormous additional benefits of employment and income from domestic food production, there can be little doubt that the self-reliance strategy was right for India.

Third and last, India decided to subsidize irrigation, fertilizers, and other inputs, most of which are used in food grain production, to keep basic food prices within the reach of most of the poor. While many economists object to such subsidies, they cannot legitimately quarrel with the goal of providing low-cost food to the poor, which is a value judgment, but they can argue with the means of attaining the goals, that is, the facts. But even when economists recognize that they cannot make value judgments, the evaluation procedure of benefit-cost analysis may, in effect, cause adverse value judgments to be made in practice. Thus, by achieving the value of lower food prices through increased production, the projected economic benefits of future investments in food production are decreased. This makes many of these investments economically infeasible. But if for this reason these investments are not made, food prices will rise and the goal of low food prices will be sacrificed.[13]

A similar effect also occurs in cases where governments support agricultural crop prices to encourage production and perhaps to conserve foreign exchange yet donor agencies insist on evaluating projects in terms of generally lower international prices, whether the country has sufficient foreign exchange to purchase the commodities or not. In such cases, benefit-cost analysis clearly subverts the strategy. Evaluations have to be carried out at the strategic and program levels—not, as it were, under the table, at the project level.

Strategic Analysis and Cost-Effectiveness Analysis

Strategic decisions are part of a general class of "intertemporal externalities" that are rather neglected in economic theory. Decisions made in the present economic regime (R_1) may determine which of a set of alternative future regimes (R_2), (R_3) . . . (R_n) the decider will be in. In considering this possibility, deciders must conduct a mental experiment to determine if in one of the future regimes, say R_2, they would be willing to pay, or "bribe," themselves in R_1 to make a different decision than they would make considering the conditions of R_1 alone. The present value of the bribe is the value of the strategic advantages or disadvantages of the decision.

Economic analysis recognizes an aspect of strategic decisions in the form of "option demands." Option demands are the amount people are willing to pay for a future option that may or may not be exercised. This can be interpreted as the willingness to pay for an expected strategic advantage or to avoid an expected strategic disadvantage.

Option demands provide a concrete example of intangible or purely qualitative phenomena in economic analysis. They can be quantified *ex post* in terms of demonstrated willingness to pay. But they are not formally included in *ex ante* evaluations because (with the partial exception

---

13. This problem can be corrected partly, at least in principle, by the use of consumers' and producers' surplus rather than the marginal values of price in economic evaluations. But then the true social demand curves should be corrected for the distribution of income, which unfortunately is never done and may be impossible to do in practice (Seckler 1966).

of sequential decision theory) there is no methodology, no strategic analysis, by which they can be objectively evaluated in a way similar to the tactical methodology of benefit-cost analysis. Option demands do point, however, to the way in which tactical and strategic considerations can be combined by incorporating benefit-cost analysis in the more general framework of cost-effectiveness analysis.

This methodology is best illustrated in terms of the benefit-cost ratio, although it can be extended to the other investment criteria. Assume, for example, that an evaluation of Ford's acquisition of Jaguar yielded a benefit-cost ratio of only 0.80. As the critics observed, it is, ipso facto, an economically infeasible project. But Ford made the acquisition. This situation may be interpreted as meaning that the expected tactical (within regime) benefits of the acquisition compensate for 80 percent of the total expected costs. Then the question for the entrepreneur to answer is whether or not the strategic (between regimes) advantages of the acquisition are worth the remaining 20 percent of the costs. If they are, then the project is strategically feasible even if it is tactically infeasible; and if not, not. Of course, the converse also may be true. A project may have a benefit-cost ratio of 1.20 yet create strategic disadvantages that are greater than 20 percent of its estimated benefits and therefore be strategically infeasible even if it is tactically feasible. Such issues are at the heart of environmental controversies.

In sum, in addition to tactical investments within the present regime for which benefit-cost analysis is suited, public and private sector entrepreneurs also have to make investments in development processes, in *paths of action,* that are intended to create or to enable them to achieve strategic advantages and avoid strategic disadvantages in future economic regimes. Investment in research and development and in education are but two of the most notable kinds of such investments. Others are in institutional change, whether at the level of the structural adjustment policies of nations or managerial reforms of corporations. In such cases, benefit-cost analysis is only the limiting case, the purely tactical case, of a more general strategic analysis. The specific value of the benefit-cost ratio may be regarded in these cases as a data reduction technique, a means of synthesizing all the quantifiable costs and benefits into a single number that provides information to, but is not a sufficient criterion for, the decision.

Summary

The evaluation of projects and policies in economic development requires recognition of the dualistic nature of rational choice. First there are tactical decisions, within a regime, for which benefit-cost and related forms of economic analysis are appropriate. But second, there are strategic investments in processes and paths of action that require consideration of the opportunities available in future regimes. There is no reason to believe that these two aspects of rational choice are complementary; in many cases they may be contradictory. The difficulty of making strategic decisions in the face of genuine uncertainty does not negate the fact that these decisions have to be made and that it is presumably better to make them consciously than otherwise. Once the necessity and problem of strategic decisions is consciously recognized, it may be possible to improve the decision-making process in economic development.

APPENDIX

The three sections that follow are working papers developed in the course of writing this essay. Some present background material to further explain concepts in the text; others are more speculative, extending beyond the text, as parts of a possible research program for the future. They are included here partly for the convenience of the author—to keep these materials together, and partly for the reader, to provide more detail and perhaps to stimulate further thought.

1. Economic Regimes

The Harrod-Domar growth model provides a good example of the relations between regimes and parameters. Given the growth of population and other conditions, the growth of an economy in this model depends on two basic parameters: (a) the average propensity to save and (b) the marginal output/capital ratio. If (a) has a value of 0.20 and (b) 0.25, the rate of economic growth in this model can be obtained by multiplying the two—that is, 5.0 percent per annum. Also, as Samuelson has shown, the roots of the Harrod-Domar equation determine the path the economy will follow over time (continuous growth or decay, increasing or dampening fluctuations around a trend, etc.). Given these parameters, both the growth rate and its path over time are determined. But if social and technical change causes a regime switch, these parameters and, hence, the dynamic behavior of the system change. It is interesting that Robbins's (1935) denial of the possibility of an economic theory of economic development rests precisely on the difference between economic dynamics within a regime and structural change between regimes.

One need not go to the level of an entire economy, however, to perceive economic regimes and the difficult kinds of decisions they pose. They indeed constitute some of the most important and difficult decisions of everyday life. Investment in education, for example, is not just a tactical expenditure of current resources for future returns. It is also an attempt to effect a regime switch into virtually a new world of resources, opportunities, values, and activities that, from the point of view of the period in which the investment is made—in the present regime of the investor—literally are unimaginable.

Similarly, when entrepreneurs invest in new regimes, in basic social and technical change, they confront an altogether higher order of uncertainty than the normal risk faced by managers investing in present, known regimes.

The problem of entrepreneurial decisions is illustrated in the simplified Venn diagram of figure 5.2. Here the entrepreneur is confronted with a set of opportunities in the present regime (*R*p). One subset of these opportunities, indicated by the inner circle of *R*p, represents an economically favorable subset of activities, while another subset, the outer ring of *R*p, presents an unfavorable subset of activities. At this point, the problem is simply the managerial task of selecting and implementing the favorable activities, within resource constraints, and avoiding unfavorable activities.

However, there is also a future regime (*R*f) with similar subsets of favorable and unfavorable opportunities, so far as the entrepreneur can see. The problem is somehow to select the most favorable activities appraised in terms of both regimes. As shown in the Venn diagram, there are nine subsets to consider, which may be grouped as follows:

Subsets *I* and *H* are unfavorable in both regimes, so the only problem here is to recognize and avoid them.

Subsets *A* and *B* represent the classic case of a managerial, or tactical, investment decision. They are unfavorable and favorable, respectively, in *R*p, but have no effect on *R*f.

Subset *C* represents a very difficult strategic investment because it is favorable in *R*p but has unfavorable consequences in *R*f. Many environmental issues are of this nature.

Subset *D* represents the best of both worlds.

Subset *E* is the classic strategic investment, unfavorable in *R*p but favorable in *R*f.

Subsets *F* and *G* are favorable and unfavorable, respectively, in *R*f. However, neither is affected by activities in *R*p. They are exogenously determined subsets that must be left to fate.

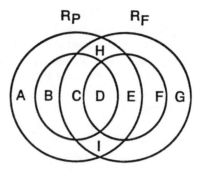

Fig. 5.2. Entrepreneurial decisions.

Of the nine subsets, two (*H* and *I*) are decisions to avoid mistakes; and two (*F* and *G*), whether for better or worse, are beyond control. Of the remaining five, three subsets (*A, B,* and *D*), represent easy decisions because they have only neutral or favorable consequences. The difficult entrepreneurial decisions thus reduce to (*C*), maximizing present benefits at the cost of future opportunities, and (*E*), forsaking present benefits to gain future opportunities.

Given that the benefits and costs in *R*p are risky and the opportunities in *R*f are uncertain, the challenge to the entrepreneur is clear. Also, it should be emphasized that this is the simplest case of entrepreneurial decision making. The problem becomes much richer when it is realized that there are many potential future regimes, all intersecting with the present regime.

The first task of the entrepreneur clearly must be to prune the decision tree to achieve a simpler, more understandable set of options than that of all the possible combinations and permutations. This pruning, simplifying function is accomplished in the same way as in other branches of knowledge, by creating a theory of the process—in this case, *a scientific theory of action*—that depends upon a limited number of controlling variables.

2. Strategic Decisions

In considering the problem of how people think strategically, much can be learned from the field of artificial intelligence, particularly that concerned with computer simulations in the well-defined situations of games. As John Maynard Smith (*New York Review of Books*, 15 March 1990) observes in a review of a book by Roger Penrose on the subject, it seems that much of strategic thinking depends on the ability to perceive integrated compositions of activities as a whole, or "all at once" (although, as he says, this impression may only be the conscious "print-out," so to speak, of detailed processing in the subconscious mode). These compositions seem to be like the "fields" of physics, but, for the nonphysicist, unable to comprehend a physical field, this hardly advances understanding. F. A. Hayek (1955, chap. 4) contends that the concept of compositions and the "compositive method" constitutes much of the difference between the social and the physical sciences.

Strategic compositions are expressed in such terms as "positioning." It is the "disposition," not just the "development," of forces in military studies that makes strategy, such as "commanding the high ground" in military operations or "capturing the center of the board" in chess. The composition of forces creates the qualitative, relational dimensions of strategic advantages and disadvantages.

The strategy behind Ford's acquisition of Jaguar may reflect this compositional quality. While Petersen did not explain the exact strategy, it may reflect the strategy developed by Sloan in the formative period of General Motors (Sloan 1965, chap. 9). The basic idea is that the corporation covers all the price niches of the market with specific models of automobiles. Then, as economies of scale permit, the price of a particular model can be reduced to crowd out the competition in the niche immediately below, with the vacated niche being filled with a new model. Pontiac, for example, was developed to replace Chevrolet, as Chevrolet descended from Ford's Model T. Clearly, in this strategy it is important to protect the top of the marketing structure. This is what Jaguar does for Ford. Even though Jaguar was perhaps not worth the price paid as a separate enterprise, its strategic value in the context of the Ford enterprise as a whole may have justified the cost. In mergers and acquisitions, the whole may indeed be worth more, or less, than the sum of the parts.

Similarly, one can actually see a composition in the disposition of balls on a pool table. An ordinary pool player simply tries to hit the balls into the pocket, one at a time. This is the tactical mode. A good pool player attempts to gain both this tactical objective and, with the same stroke, achieve "shape"—a strategically advantageous position of the cue ball in relation to future shots. Shape creates a future regime—a future set of opportunities for shooting balls. Good tactical players will succeed until the cue ball rolls into a position of poor shape. Good strategic players who can get shape, have an "edge," a strategic advantage, over tactical players even though the attempt to simultaneously get the ball in the pocket and achieve shape may cause more tactical errors.

A more complex example is provided in computer chess (as reported in the *Economist,* 23 December 1989). Computers make no effort to play games as people do. Subtleties of strategy, the suspense of tactical thrust and counterthrust, all these pass them by. Computers play games like somebody groping his way across a dark room. At each step, they feel about for obstacles, then move in the least cluttered direction. Unlike people, computers do not try to keep a mental map of where they are and where they are going. At each move they start afresh.

The reason for this "mini-max" search, according to the report, is that there are typically 36 moves from any position, and the computer has no way of discriminating between relevant and irrelevant positions. A good human chess player typically will consider only two moves at a time, 10 moves ahead, the other possible moves being considered irrelevant. To consider all 36 possible moves to this depth would take the fastest computer over two weeks.

> People pay attention only to those moves that are central to their strategy. The snag with teaching computers to be similarly discriminating is that they cannot make strategies because they cannot make plans. . . . Computers never try to break out of an inferior position. Because they cannot plan, they do not know how to take risks.

Also, the report notes, because computers cannot plan, they cannot play bridge since the bid depends on understanding the partner's plan. But for ordinary mortals, the visual imagery of pool may be more appropriate:

> On a cloth untrue
> With a twisted cue
> And an asymmetric billiard ball

Last, anyone interested in strategic analysis must find the thought processes in the formulation of military strategy fascinating, however disagreeable the subject itself may be. The quotation below justifies its length. In introducing a discussion of the battle of Gettysburg during the American Civil War, Bradford (1989, 366) summarizes General Lee's situation.

> After the Battle of Chancellorsville, General Lee had two immediate problems: finding, if possible, a successor to Jackson, and planning the future movements of the Army of Northern Virginia. It seemed to him that spring that any primarily defensive course could only result eventually in his being pushed back upon Richmond, and,

conversely, that there were persuasive reasons for his undertaking a second invasion of the North. His confidence in the fighting qualities of his men had never been higher. If he could threaten or capture Washington after a victorious march through Pennsylvania, perhaps England and surely France would recognize the Confederacy. Such a thrust might cause the people of the North to lose all confidence in their leaders and demand peace. It should make it necessary for the Union military planners to bring reinforcements from the mid-South, thus relieving the pressures on General Bragg in Tennessee and General Pemberton at Vicksburg. Finally Lee needed horses for his cavalry and food and shoes for his men, and they were all to be had in abundance north of the Potomac. All of Lee's officers favored the invasion (even the less sanguine Longstreet acquiescing when Lee agreed the campaign "should be offensive in strategy but defensive in tactics"); so early in June the new vast movement began.

The Union's General Meade, in the words of General Henry J. Hunt of the Army of the Potomac, seemed

to have determined not to advance until the movements or position of the enemy gave strong assurance of success, and if the enemy took the offensive, to withdraw his own army from its actual positions and form a line of battle behind Pipe Creek, between Middleburg and Manchester. The considerations probably moving him to this are not difficult to divine. Such a line would cover Baltimore and Washington in all directions from which Lee could advance, and Westminster, his base, would be immediately behind him, with short railroad communication to Baltimore. It would, moreover, save much hard marching, and restore to the ranks the thousands of stragglers who did not reach Gettysburg in time for the battle. From Westminster . . . good roads led in all directions, and gave the place the same strategic value for Meade that Gettysburg had for Lee. The new line could not be turned by Lee without imminent danger to his own army nor could he afford to advance upon Baltimore or Washington, leaving the Army of the Potomac intact behind and so near him—that would be to invite the fate of Burgoyne. Meade, then, could safely select a good "offensive-defensive line" behind Pipe Creek and establish himself there, with perfect liberty of action in all directions. Without magazines or assured communications, Lee would have to scatter his army more or less in order to subsist it, and so expose it to Meade; or else keep it united, and so starve it, a course which Meade could compel by simple demonstrations. There would then be but two courses for Lee—either to attack Meade in his chosen position or to retreat without a battle. The latter, neither the temper of his army nor that of his Government would probably permit. In case of a defeat Meade's line of retreat would be comparatively short, and easily covered, whilst Lee's would be for two marches through an open country before he could gain the mountain passes. As Meade believed Lee's army to be at least equal to his own, all the elements of the problem were in favor of the Pipe Creek line. . . . The battle of July 1st changed the situation. Overpowered by numbers the First and Eleventh corps had, after hard fighting and inflicting as well as incurring heavy losses, been forced back to their reserve on Cemetery Hill which they still held. To have withdrawn them now would have been a retreat, and might have discouraged the Federal, as it certainly would have elated the Confederate troops, especially as injurious reports unjust to both the corps named had been circulated. It would have been to acknowledge a defeat when there was no defeat. Meade therefore resolved to fight at Gettysburg. An ominous dispatch from General Halleck to Meade, that afternoon, suggesting that whilst his tactical arrangements were good, his strategy was at fault, that he was too far east, that Lee might attempt to turn his left, and that Frederick was preferable as a base to Westminster, may have confirmed Meade in this decision. (Hunt, in Bradford 1989, 368–69)

The consequence was that the Army of the Potomac now held the defensive position, and Lee, over General Longstreet's strong objections, moved to offensive tactics. The defeat of the Confederate army at Gettysburg, along with the capture of Vicksburg by Grant—remarkably, both virtually on Independence Day, 4 July 1863—made the eventual end of the war apparent. Economic evaluations would enormously benefit from similar kinds of strategic analysis in narrative form—if only we economists could think, and write, so well.

3. Principles of Strategic Analysis

Joan Robinson appropriately described economics as a "kit of tools" that can be used to help in the analysis of problems. The question is: Are there tools, or principles, that can help in making strategic decisions, or are these decisions so subjective and intuitive that nothing at all can be said? The answer is perhaps that there are certain rather common-sensical principles that provide at least a checklist of "things to look out for" in making strategic decisions. Figure 5.3 provides a picture of a

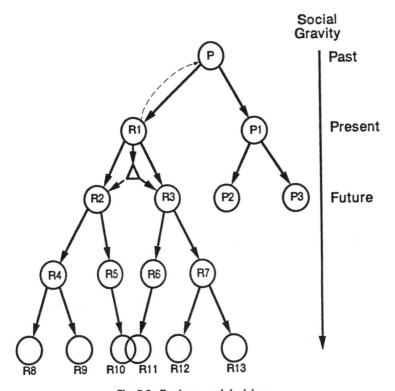

Fig. 5.3. Regimes and decisions.

simplified decision tree that illustrates some of these principles. It may be that there are less obvious principles to be discovered with further research.

The circles in the decision tree indicate regimes in which tactical decisions are made, in the same terms as figure 5.2. Each regime contains favorable and unfavorable activities, some of which may lead to a future regime, indicated by the arrows. The decision tree is rotated to present an image of what, for lack of a better term, may be called "social gravity"—the propensity of human affairs to change, no matter what anybody actually wants to have happen. Also, it is intended to indicate the partly random, partly deterministic, and partly volitional aspect of this process.

Following a metaphor developed by Waddington to illustrate his conception of genetic evolution, the decision tree may be pictured as on a slope with the paths consisting of round channels (like one half of a pipe). If a ball is dropped into this system at the top, it will roll down through the various channels to one or the other of the sinks at the bottom. However, the surface of the channels and circles is rough, causing each ball to roll in a somewhat different way and thus to a different sink. In this case, in addition to the deterministic structure of the system (the channels) and the random component (the roughness), the circles (regimes) through which the ball rolls are occupied by people who have volition: both preferences about where the ball rolls and the ability to affect its course (like "Maxwell's demon" in physics). Oddly enough, as this metaphor suggests, the old-fashioned pinball machine may be one of the better models of entrepreneurial decisions, if not of life itself.

The decision tree includes some of the past to emphasize the fact that the entire future decision tree confronting the entrepreneur is a product of past decisions. These past decisions therefore should have included consideration of the future decision trees they create to the extent possible, that is, to the limits imposed by uncertainty.

Some basic principles are briefly listed, in no particular order, as follows.

> *Reversibility.* The dashed arrows from R_1 back to P, the past, illustrate the property of reversibility. If R_1 is considered to have been a mistake, either in terms of its own results or the paths of future opportunities it creates, it may be possible to go back in time, as it were, to the old regime, P, and change the decision that created the present regime, R_1. This is an uphill battle against social gravity, but it is sometimes possible. Thus, in R_1 the possibility of P_1 may be perceived, and P_1 may have led to a superior regime, like P_2. But P_1, and therefore P_2, cannot be reached from R_1. Instead, to reach P_2 the decision has to be made to reverse direction, tear down the present regime, and effectively go back to P in order to reach P_1. This is a fair representation of the upheaval in Eastern Europe today. Of course, P_1 is not the same regime as would have been attained directly from P because the effect of R_1 cannot be wholly destroyed. Thus, in Eastern Europe the movement to capitalism is said to be inhibited by the egalitarian attitudes that have developed under the socialist regime. While reversibility is possible in many cases and always desirable from a risk/uncertainty-reducing point of view, it is not always possible and it is usually extremely costly. That is why irreversible decisions are willingly taken only by the young and other innocents.

> *Exploration.* Decision trees present an overly strict picture of entrepreneurial processes. They imply either "wait" (magnificent inactivity, as the British say) or decisively "commit." Between these

extremes is the possibility of "explore." Exploration reduces uncertainty, helps avoid the trap of irreversibility and reduces the costs of reversibility. The exploration regime is shown in the triangular regime indicating tentative changes out of R_1 to see what R_2 and R_3 might look or feel like.

Convergence. Alternative paths may converge to similar regimes, as shown in the intersecting regimes at the bottom of the chain. Where this is possible and acceptable, it makes the strategic decision much simpler because one can choose either R_2 or R_3, and subsequently either R_5 or R_6, and wind up at a reasonable place. This possibility, of course, vastly reduces the uncertainty of the process.

Compositions. As also illustrated in the convergence case, regimes are compositions produced by the interrelations between many different inputs. Effective regime switches usually cannot be accomplished on a piecemeal, marginal basis. They require large and simultaneous changes of many integrated inputs.

Sequential Processes. Regimes are typically sequential in nature, the orderly progression of one regime building another. It is very difficult to "leapfrog" over any of the logical steps in a development process.

End Necessities. Once it is decided that a particular end regime is the goal (say R_{12}) and a clear theory of action describing the path from the current regime to the end regime is defined (R_1, R_3, R_7, R_{12}), it is, so far as the entrepreneur knows, necessary (but not sufficient) to follow that path to achieve the goal. Once the goal is accepted the path is defined.

Theoretical Reliability. The scientific reliability of the theory of action is the ultimate determinant of the reliability of entrepreneurial decisions. Science is itself a high form of entrepreneurship, and much can be learned of practical importance to strategic analysis by studying its methodologies.

Tactical Control. Clearly, the confidence with which a strategic decision can be made increases as the major events following the decision are controlled by the decider. That is why, as in the example of road building in the text, the uncertainty of public sector investments designed to provide a favorable economic regime for the private sector is highly uncertain. It is possible to argue that in certain cases the public sector potentially has more control over the key variables of an enterprise than does the private sector (e.g., providing all the crucial inputs of the green revolution simultaneously) and that there is a kind of composition market failure in this respect. Thus, it may be rational for the public sector to develop certain kinds of enterprises and then turn them over to the private sector once they and their related infra-structure are up and running.

BIBLIOGRAPHY

Ashby, W. Ross. 1964. *Introduction to cybernetics*. New York: Rutledge, Chapman and Hall.

Bhalla, G. S., G. K. Chadha, S. P. Kashyap, and R. Sharma. 1990. Agricultural growth and structural changes in the Punjab economy: An input-output analysis. In *IFPRI abstract no. 82*. Washington, DC: International Food Policy Research Institute.

Bradford, Ned (ed.). 1989. *Battles and leaders of the Civil War*. Markham, Ontario, Canada: Penguin Books Canada, Ltd.

Duignan, Peter. 1990. *Colonialism in Africa 1870–1960*. Vol. 4. Stanford: Hoover Institution.

Hayami, Yujiro, and Vernon W. Ruttan. 1971. *Agricultural development: An international perspective*. Baltimore: Johns Hopkins University Press.

Hayek, F. A. 1955. *The counter-revolution of science: Studies on the abuse of reason*. London: Collier-Macmillan Ltd.

Hirschman, Albert O. 1958. *The strategy of economic development*. Reprint, New Haven: Yale University Press, 1964,

"Japanese Technology." 1989. *Economist*, December 2, 62.

Kennedy, Peter. 1985. *A guide to econometrics*. 2d ed. Cambridge, MA: MIT Press.

Keynes, John Maynard. 1935. *The general theory of employment, interest, and money*. New York: Harcourt, Brace, and World

———. 1921. *Treatise on probability: The collected writings of John Maynard Keynes*. Vol. 8. Reprint, London: MacMillan, 1988.

Kunreuther, Howard, and Robin Hogarth. 1990. How does ambiguity affect insurance decisions? In *Contributions to insurance economies*, ed. Georges Dionne. Boston: Kluwer.

Landau, Martin. 1973. On the concept of a self-correcting organization. *Public Administration Review*, November-December, 533–42.

———. 1986. On decision strategies and management structures: With special reference to experimentation. In *The contributions of management science and the management of irrigation systems*. Fort Collins, CO: International School of Agricultural and Resource Development, Colorado State University.

Mellor, John W. 1976. *The new economics of growth: A strategy for India and the developing world*. Ithaca: Cornell University Press.

Mishan, Ezra J. 1976. *Cost-benefit analysis*. Rev. and expanded ed. New York: Praeger.

Mitchell, Wesley C. 1937. The prospect of economics. In *The backward art of spending money and other essays,* ed. Joseph Dorfman. Sec. 7. New York: McGraw-Hill.

Morgenstern, Oskar. 1963. On the accuracy of economic observations. 2d rev. ed. Princeton: Princeton University Press.

Popper, Karl R. 1968. *Conjectures and refutations: The growth of scientific knowledge.* New York: Harper and Row.

Rausser, Gordon C., and Gerald W. Dean. 1971. The political economy of water resources. Appendix to *California water: A study in resource management,* ed. David Seckler. Berkeley: University of California Press.

Robbins, Lionel. 1935. *Essay on the nature and significance of economic science.* 2d ed. London: Macmillan.

Russell, Bertrand. 1948. *Human knowledge: Its scope and limits.* Reprint, New York: Simon and Schuster, 1976.

Ruttan, Vernon W. , ed. 1989. *Biological and technical constraints on crop and animal productivity: Report on a dialogue.* St. Paul, MN: Institute of Agriculture, Forestry, and Home Economics.

Schultz, Theodore W. 1987. *The long view in economic policy: The case of agriculture and food.* Occasional paper 1. Panama City: International Center for Economic Growth.

Seckler, David. 1966. On the uses and abuses of economic science in the evaluation of public outdoor recreation. *Land Economics,* 42 no. 4: 485–94.

———. 1975. *Thorstein Veblen and the institutionalists: A study in the philosophy of economics.* London and Boulder: Macmillan and Colorado Associated University Press.

———. 1986. *On the management of public organizations.* ISARD working paper. Fort Collins, CO: ISARD, Colorado State University.

———. 1990. Private sector irrigation in Africa. In *Irrigation in sub-Saharan Africa,* ed. Shawki Barghouti and Guy Le Moigne. Washington, DC: World Bank.

Seckler, David, and R. K. Sampath. 1989. Production and poverty in Indian agriculture. *Journal of Agricultural Issues,* 2:1–16.

Seckler, David, Doug Gollin, and Pierre Antoine. 1992. *Agricultural potential of mid-Africa: A technological assessment.* Discussion paper 5. Arlington, VA: Center for Economic Policy Studies, Winrock International.

Shackle, G. L. S. 1949. *Expectation in economics.* Cambridge: At the University Press.

Sloan, Alfred P., Jr. 1965. *My years with General Motors.* Edited by John McDonald with Catherine Stevens. New York: MacFadden Books.

Smith, John Maynard. 1990. What Can't the Computer Do? *New York Review of Books,* March 15, 21–25.

Sun Tzu. 1963. *The Art of War.* London: Oxford University Press.

Viner, Jacob. [1927] 1958. Adam Smith and laissez faire. In *The long view and the short,* ed. J. Viner. Glencoe, IL: The Free Press.

Wiles, Peter. June 1956. Growth versus Choice. *Economic Journal,* 244–55.

Part 2:
Political and Activist
Approaches to the Subject

6

Thinking about the Future: The Complementary Roles of Economists and Environmentalists

David Dapice

> [O]ur social institutions will not always choose the sustainable path. The economic system provides both positive and negative transfers to future generations. . . . The likelihood of negative transfers . . . has increased with the scale of activities.
> —Tom Teitenberg, *Environmental and Natural Resource Economics*

How different—and how inevitably different—are the positions of the economist and the environmentalist? Is the latter the sole guardian of the future and the economist, as sometimes caricatured, the despoiler concerned only with short-term gain? When faced with such a charge, economists indignantly claim that they are doing no more than showing people how to formalize and understand their behavior and their preferences. If a preference for the short run already exists in human nature, then it is not the economist's job, they argue, to mitigate against that preference.

This justification goes roughly as follows. Resources, including those emanating from our natural environment, are limited. If we are to get the highest output from what resources we do have, they must be used efficiently. The requirement that extra emissions of CO_2 be kept at zero is tantamount to putting output growth in the future at risk, even while the human population continues to grow. Who is it (the economist might ask) who tells people they cannot have more (or any) electricity, transport, or production? By what right does any group dictate to present and future generations? Our job (the economist might say) is not to tell people what they should want but to tell people how they can get what they want. Most people in the world today live in poor countries and want material living standards far higher than what they have. If their preferences put less weight on the future than on the present, then it is appropriate for us, as professional economists, to do so as well.

Perhaps the deepest difference between economists and environmentalists is on the question of whether such professionals should make moral judgments about, and take responsibility for, the preferences and values of economic decision makers (themselves excluded). It is almost a religion with economists that "you take preferences as given." Preferences, as revealed in spending behavior, are a primary—perhaps *the* primary—datum for economists. These are, of course, the preferences of people now alive; the people who are making economic decisions and being told "how they can get what they want" are the people of the present.

By contrast, members of the environmental community, seeing a deteriorating environment as an absolute moral wrong, and finding no other adequate spokesperson for the ecosystem's future, tend to believe that massive changes in social values, consumption and production patterns, technology, and demographics are needed to prevent the "cancer" of economic and even human population growth from overrunning and forever ruining the planet. They see humans as stewards, not owners, of the earth and refer to various religious and ethical beliefs to counteract the pernicious secular view that all nature exists to be used up and exploited for human ends.

Environmentalists maintain a skeptical attitude toward conventionally measured economic growth, while being in awe of the complexity, richness, diversity, and fragility of nature. Characterized as "Malthusian pessimists," they believe that human attempts to outsmart nature will end up being counterproductive. Economists, of course, are generally seen as falling into the opposite camp of "technological optimists" who believe that there is no problem in the physical world that cannot be solved by technology when human ingenuity is appropriately directed by freely competitive market forces. They believe that some combination of increased supply with new technology, lower demand driven by both technology and higher prices, and substitutes will solve most problems. Starting from such divergent positions, the practical recommendations made by these two groups are often very different.

Thus stated, the gap would seem to be utterly unbridgeable. Economists want nature to be used efficiently to satisfy existing human wants, while environmentalists want nature to be sacred and secure from human despoilment. Both have a vision of the future. However, one is impressed by the earth's fragility and need for caution and the other by the urgent needs of the present and the likelihood that new solutions will be found to the problems that arise as economic growth proceeds.

Are any of these caricatures true or relevant or useful? An interesting place to investigate this question is in a review of the green revolution and its aftermath. Here one can see the two different attitudes and their effects; but one can also see some possibilities for at least a partial convergence in recommendations and conclusions.

Let us start with a sketch of some of the relevant history. For many centuries Asian countries have largely depended on irrigated rice (or irrigated wheat in parts of the Indian subcontinent). Irrigated areas lend themselves to the green revolution solutions of "miracle" (dwarf or semidwarf) seeds, high fertilizer, and controlled water that have proven so successful in raising yields. These areas also lend themselves to double or triple cropping.

This combination of environmental and historical conditions with new seed varieties and attendant farming strategies is highly favorable to the growth of insect pests—especially if heavy pesticide applications destroy their natural enemies. Since pests develop resistance to pesticides before their predators do and since large stands of a single cultivar will speed up the pests' evolution to overcome the crop's natural genetic resistance, the "standard" practice of heavy pesticide use, nearly continuous monocropping, and high nitrogen application in a tropical environment has proved to be unstable. Pests evolve that can no longer be kept in balance with naturally resistant plants or chemically controlled except with an unending escalation of increasingly costly and toxic chemicals.

One scientific response is to create a more stable environment in which a multipronged approach is taken to control pests. Called "Integrated Pest Management" or IPM, it asks the farmer to manage rather than eradicate the pests. Increased rotation of crops will reduce the availability of a continuously hospitable habitat and cut the number of pest survivors, both in total and in those that might have the "right" genes to frustrate the inbred resistance of the plant host or be immune to the pesticides used. Highly restricted use of poisons will not kill so many predators, so they will keep the numbers of pests down to levels that do not cause major economic damage. Certain chemicals are highly pest specific, such as those that slow the development of a bug so that it does not attack a plant in its most critical growth phase. Others (such as BT) infect the pests with diseases or parasites of their own.

There have been some remarkable cases where IPM has not only worked but has rescued farmers from severe crisis. One of the most dramatic of these occurred in Indonesia. In this case, a growing inability to prevent leafhopper damage to rice crops in spite of heavy pesticide applications led to a presidential decision to reduce and then eliminate pesticide subsidies while teaching farmers how to control insect pests through IPM. The decision was spectacularly successful as farmers quickly learned how to adjust their own production practices. The IPM training helped them make their own decisions about when to spray, types of seeds to plant, and the like. This was quite different from past "top-down" instructions that tried to impose uniform practices on all farmers in a given region.

Taken together, IPM techniques appear to cost less while reducing the toxic burden to the environment. Sustainable yields appear to be higher with these practices than with the "standard" ones, and profits of farmers are also higher. This argument should not be construed to be unicausal. Of course, appropriate exchange rates, pricing policies, infrastructure investment, and other overhead spending are needed. But without an agricultural policy that recognizes that most technological change may need to be initiated in a manner somewhat different from the introduction of the green revolution—that the green revolution approach may now have been carried everywhere it can most usefully go— it will be much harder to make progress. Farmers will do better on their own if the other variables are in place. They will do very much better if they can take advantage of relevant research and are helped with access to relevant technology so that they can make their own decisions about the "best" investment mix.

Other things being equal, IPM can maintain high output while reducing some of the associated disruptions of natural biological processes. It is good for the present and (relatively) good for the future. It is a solution that should gladden the hearts of economists and environmentalists alike. We might expect to see it joyfully adopted throughout the world.

In fact, the Indonesian story, where IPM is the appropriate technology and is being used, is more the exception than the rule. We do not yet have enough evidence to be able to state how widely IPM should be employed (its most committed adherents believe it should be universal), but it does seem clear that there are other places where it is needed as badly as it was in Indonesia, yet where it is ignored. There are growing indications that the Mekong Delta, for example, may be facing similar problems as insect plagues visit even Ho Chi Minh City (Saigon) from time to time.

One could tell a host of similar stories concerning the competition between agriculture depending on "mostly material" (MM) inputs, of the type associated with the green revolution, and more information-intensive (II) systems (see Goodwin, "Lessons for the World from U.S. Agriculture: Unbundling Technology" in *World Development,* January 1991). Peter Kenmore of the UN Food Agriculture Organization (FAO) has also argued that IPM, in particular, represents the replacement of industrial-chemical technology with information technology. II technologies frequently have the social advantage of being more labor intensive—a plus in many parts of the developing world where large amounts of rural labor, made redundant by capital-intensive technologies, have not been reabsorbed elsewhere in the economy. They also require more skill and involve the farmer in a continuing learning process, thus potentially raising agricultural labor above the low-skill category that has traditionally helped to keep its wages depressed.

It will be useful to look at one other example of a competition between II and MM technologies. Whereas IPM may be considered more modern, even more scientific, than heavily insecticide-dependent approaches, this other comparison will be between a high-tech approach to tree crops where the most significant material input is the biological material itself (nursling trees created through cloning) and a more traditional approach that depends upon seedlings. The latter is appropriate to a more complex kind of farm, that is, the mixed system that is often compatible with a smallholder's risk-averse strategy of diversification. I will argue later that such systems may require more, not less, intelligent and information-intensive management than the monocrop systems wherein clonal trees can outperform all others. However, the kinds of intelligence and information needed in such traditional-appearing II systems are diverse, hard to predict, hard to control, and thus to some degree incompatible with modern, Western notions of science-based technology.

Many past treecrop investment schemes have tried to get smallholders to approach yields typically observed on (say) rubber plantations. Good clonal planting material, cared for over a number of years with adequate fertilizer, watering, weeding, and spraying and carefully harvested at the proper time, will yield much more than seedling rubber grown with only moderate care. The agronomists directing research on this subject have assumed that their job is done if they come up with a system that can produce more rubber (or even more rubber per hectare). However, the complex of methods and institutional arrangements required to support the clone-based plantations have relatively high unit costs and are inappropriate for many farmers. Seedlings are more robust than clones and are more appropriate for diversified holdings where farmers may choose to spread their labor over a number of plots and crops so that risk is reduced. The real farmer's attempt to maximize income, subject to a certain minimum level, may conflict with what agronomists perceive as the goal—to develop high-quality rubber stands.

Such divergences would be of only mild interest were it not for the fact that the World Bank and other aid agencies (and not a few agricultural ministries) have made available large loans to back the view of the agronomists. Resources are focused on relatively expensive block-planted clonal rubber projects, while support for less intensive seedling rubber is virtually ignored. (For a fuller discussion see Tom Tomich, "Smallholder Rubber Development in Indonesia.") The result is that few farmers have access to scientific progress in treecrops that is relevant to them, and thus there is less overall progress.

Note that this complaint is not standard World Bank bashing. The agronomic experts are acting in good faith. Their projects sometimes even show a reasonable rate of return. Often, the national bureaucracy is even more inclined than the Bank toward this style of project. The problem is that a more diversified, widespread, and (probably) more economically productive alternative is slighted. The distribution of income is also less equal than with a less intensive alternative. Less rubber is produced since few farmers are reached by World Bank loans, and the majority of the area spontaneously replanted benefits little from the intensive schemes.

Early on I cited the "technological optimists" belief that there is no problem in the physical world that cannot be solved by technology when human ingenuity is appropriately directed by freely competitive market forces. It is clear from the foregoing that such a simple position is inadequate. The examples that have been discussed here are interesting not because they represent problems for which there is no known solution but because they have to do with apparently good solutions that are blocked from application. They are also interesting because the solutions discussed here are ones that, in principle, should be appealing to both economists and environmentalists. They should, thus, provide a basis for the two groups to get their heads together and find out how to work in harmony toward win-win solutions.

Since I am an economist, I will take the problems posed here from the economics side and try to work toward a better understanding of why my discipline cannot come up with the whole solution. I will hope that environmentalists—and perhaps others, such as political scientists, historians, psychologists, and the like—will be inspired to work from their side to come up with what to me are the missing pieces.

The first thing we economists have to offer (and it is sometimes summarily rejected from the other side because the terminology is unappealing) is a set of concepts. Two particularly important ones are investment and "externalities."

Many societies seem to act as if they wanted their descendents to have at least as good a life as they have. At least in recent decades and even centuries, capital and technology have usually been accumulated so as to allow a slightly to greatly better future for children than that enjoyed or suffered by their parents. Wars or depressions may upset the outcome, but the rates of investment in "normal" times would seem to support this view. Economic theory would predict that what we know as normal investment rates, in the context of a free market, will result in growing incomes and material welfare—as long as there are no externalities. Many problems on the interface of environment and economics can be understood as stemming, in part or in whole, from the presence of externalities.

Economists explain externalities as what happens when you do something that has an unintended effect on somebody else and it is not captured within the market system. If you don't get a polio vaccination and get somebody else sick (who otherwise would have been well), that is an externality. If you are a dry cleaner and dump your fluids down the drain, the water supply downstream may either be unhealthy or more expensive to clean up. As long you don't have to pay for the downstream mess you caused, it too is an externality.

In a competitive market economy, the dry cleaner who dumps for free has lower costs than the dry cleaner who pays to have his fluids treated. This will allow the dumper to have lower prices and/or higher profits and ultimately puts the good citizen at a disadvantage and maybe even out of business. That is why most externalities require some type of collective intervention. Most cannot, in fact and theory, be solved by a freely competitive market with no rules or taxes or fees on pollution. (If a new technology cleans the dirty fluid and recycles it at lower cost than dumping dirty fluid and buying new, then the market would produce a "clean" outcome.)

Note that externalities can be of a positive or beneficial type, such as the help available in emergencies from ham radio operators or the pollination of fruit trees that goes on where beekeepers had intended nothing more than gathering honey. In general, within the narrow range of environmental impacts, there appear to be more cases of bad than of good externalities. However, our agricultural examples should remind us that one of the most important and common of all externalities is knowledge. Knowledge can be shared without reducing its availability. Its effects are often positive but can be negative—atomic bomb, terrorist, or chemical warfare technology have negative externalities. Because agricultural production knowledge is usually positive, agricultural extension services are normally paid for from the public purse: increased productivity among a country's individual farmers is sufficiently valuable for society at large that it is worthwhile paying for productivity-enhancing training that might not be justified by the individual farmer's own perception of his or her production function.

When externalities can be fully internalized—that is, their costs incorporated in market prices—it is likely that technological capability will be focused on the problem that created the costs. Thus, further impetus toward conserving or renewable technologies is likely to result from raising the cost to farmers of practices that will cause future pest or soil problems, from contaminated water running off fields heavily dosed with fertilizer and pesticides, or from lowering the cost of the training required for sustainable agricultural techniques.

There are other issues inherent in these examples that are not completely subsumed within the concept of externalities. A few additional economic concepts are relevant and should be mentioned before we return for a closer look at what is blocking the use of appropriate agricultural systems and what might be done to prevent these blockages.

Considering the detrimental effects of heavy pesticide use in the context of monoculture and other aspects of the green revolution package, a simple economic approach to analyzing the situation would be the statement that "the rate at which one should pollute is a cost-benefit problem." To pollute less today may mean that society incurs costs today that are balanced by certain benefits, such as better health or aesthetic conditions or eventually higher output, which would not have been felt if the costs had not been incurred. Typically, the costs and benefits both occur over time and have to be adjusted in order to be comparable. For this, a discount rate is used.

A discount rate—representing the rate at which the things in the present are preferred over things in the future—makes a benefit or cost of, say, $1 million in the distant future worth much less in today's value than $1 million received today, even with no inflation. To economists, this procedure seems natural and sensible; other approaches are viewed as irrational or extremist. (A small minority of economists argue for a zero discount rate, and some environmentalists support the use of economic analysis in looking at environmental policy. Neither group is dominant or representative of their own larger groups, hence, the summary caricatures of positions rather than scholarly dissections of minority views.) The economist resists taking the point of view of any preferences that have not already been revealed. Thus, the preferences of future generations, which obviously cannot yet have been revealed, are neglected unless they are reflected in the preferences of people here today. "Consumer sovereignty"—another phrase of economists—enthrones only the consumer of today. Economists would generally say that if a farmer can make a higher profit by "mining" the soil—farming so as to maximize present yields while exhausting its fertility—and investing the proceeds in some other productive asset with continuing yields, it would be economically rational to do so. Returns to land are only one source of income and a rather small one relative to others.

Environmentalists would ask, here, about the fallacy of composition: what if every farmer was so individually rational as to make future food production plummet? The economist would promptly point out that so long as the process happened gradually, falling supply would lead to higher prices and a reversal of behavior. Farmers would invest more in land and build up its fertility. However, the supply response may come most easily in richer countries, and the growth in population, if not effective demand for food, may come from the poorer ones. And what if the process happened quickly and was not easily reversible? There may be an argument for public policy to influence the choice of farmers regarding future soil fertility, as many soil conservation subsidies seem to acknowledge. Yet these programs are small relative to the worldwide nature of the problem.

One of the problems facing policy theorists is that of level of jurisdiction. One of the purposes of government is to eliminate the negative externalities caused by fallacies of composition, that is, situations where what is rational for each is not rational for all. However, a well-developed government mechanism does not always exist at the level required for handling a particular problem. Even a national-level mechanism is inadequate for handling issues such as rapid or irreversible change. Indeed, many countries are advised to solve their present or future food deficiencies through trade, a solution that may not work smoothly, or at all, for all those affected. Since economists often simply assume that institutions exist where needed, they might not be of much help in advising how to solve such an institutional vacuum. Environmentalists may be of more help, if mainly indirectly, by creating a climate of public support for creating bodies that can address such issues at the appropriate level.

Even when the appropriate institutions exist, they are always in danger of being pulled away from public goals toward special interests. This is most likely to happen where many people each suffer a little from a given situation, while a relatively small group stands to gain a lot. The big (per capita) winners organize and make their political weight felt: they are politically weighty both because, if they are in line for big gains, they are probably already rich, and also because they are organized. The majority is silent, unaware of or apathetic about a situation in which they face indirect, long-term, or uncertain effects. This is true even when the money value of the total losses to the public greatly exceeds the total gains of the "special interests."

It is most often the job of government to set the rules for correcting problems caused by either negative externalities (where individual interests produce a public bad) or positive ones (where, typically, there is underproduction of a public good). Thus, while we have been discussing situations requiring knowledgeable support from both economists and environmentalists, the process by which this resolution will occur is, ultimately, a political one.

Having laid out some of the general issues facing economists and environmentalists, let us now look at an issue that is more specifically relevant to the two agricultural examples sketched earlier. This is the matter of styles of development.

There is something fundamentally different about the modern practices of IPM when contrasted with the top-down approach of development as conceived in the 1960s and 1970s. In the older, top-down approach, the major inputs (water, fertilizer, seeds, pesticides) were provided by international or national groups to local farmers with a fairly set recipe. In the "top-and-bottom" approach used in IPM, the farmers are taught to use their own analytical skills to assess the situation and apply a number of different solutions, some of which may be very local or homegrown. While farmers have been managing their affairs for centuries, the change that has occurred is that now there is a possibility of a partnership between scientists and farmers. A lecture is turned into something more like a seminar. Farmers are more than employees following directions from their scientific betters; they have become managers who have the basic information they need to run their "firm."

This change in style is also relevant to an approach that will be needed in many nonirrigated agricultural systems or in systems that involve higher value crops. Treecrops are a a particularly good example. Most of Africa and large parts of peasant agriculture in Latin America and upland Asia lack irrigation. Farmers typically employ intercropping or relay cropping or have complicated farming systems involving staples, vegetables, fruits, livestock, and treecrops. These systems lend themselves to the top-and-bottom approach of IPM much more than to the typical green revolution approach developed for irrigated rice.

Critics will say that the difference is overblown. Not all irrigation is central—some is rainfed or pump. Farmers who were part of the green revolution have routinely made decisions about cropping patterns, fertilizer doses, and pesticide applications. Yet there is a fundamental difference between a more or less universal solution proposed by extension agents (even if not always followed by farmers) and a program designed to provide analytical training and alternative strategies to farmers. In the latter approach, it is the individual or group that makes the final decision—they become the local experts. The extension agent becomes more of a consultant or bridge to new or additional information. This is a significant change.

In order to "solve" the problem of agricultural growth for macro-economic purposes, or to alleviate poverty in rural areas, this partnership approach will probably need to be developed further. It is useful to understand why it is so hard to do well and why many institutions that work for irrigated agriculture don't work well for this more complicated style.

By using pest counts, multiple control strategies, and a more complicated analytical framework, IPM manages to produce greater economic, agronomic, and environmental benefits than the "standard" strategy in spite of the huge imbalance between spending on R&D for IPM versus spending on pesticides (the former is a small fraction of the latter). However, as suggested earlier, it takes rather sophisticated management at the farm level to make IPM work. Practices such as pest counts, unscheduled spraying, crop rotation, seed selection, cultural practices that minimize pest problems, and the like are not entirely obvious.

The Indonesian experience is noteworthy because it has worked. Similar efforts undertaken in Vietnam and China were viewed as failures. It is easy to fail using IPM techniques if the execution is less than excellent. Success requires both a high level of scientific and administrative effort and an interested and cooperative peasantry. The essential appeal of IPM is simply that the alternatives are less promising in the long run. This advantage may, however, be lost on a peasant who is risk-averse or who is faced with short-run crises that seem more readily solved by an MM approach. Without the requisite research and information, his or her solution will reflect the "bounded rationality" of heavy pesticide doses.

Why is cropping systems research so difficult to do and to utilize at the farm level? Shouldn't private sector actors perform some of the R&D that would result in more usable systems? Why do donors and national bureaucracies generally prefer funding MM over II alternatives? Clearly, there are a lot of questions that need to be sorted out. It may be productive to focus on national ministries of agriculture first, then aid agencies, and finally private sector actors. Each group has its own institutional imperatives and interests as well as its own capabilities.

With respect to ministries of agriculture and related national institutions, there are two concerns. One is that they will not have the resources to undertake the types of investments required for IPM or for cropping systems. Another is that, whatever their level of resources, they will not be interested in carrying them out. These two problems could overlap: an investment that looks difficult to implement success-fully (even if possible) may not appeal to a rational administrator, espe-cially if it is judged negatively on other grounds.

With respect to the first issue, many third-world nations are both poor and small. Thirty-four of the poorest fifty nations had under 20 million people in 1988, according to a recent World Development Re-port. These nations have low GDP per capita, few trained specialists, and very limited budgets. Agriculture has often been viewed as unprom-ising and backward in the past, and there is often little research infra-structure, reflecting a long period of underinvestment in the sector. Such resources as are available are typically focused on irrigated agriculture or a few cash crops, almost always grown in pure stands. It would be very difficult for most of these nations to originate the knowledge needed to sustain IPM or cropping systems research—even if resources could be used effectively. Even where significant agricultural R&D spending has been undertaken, as in Nigeria, the results have often been meager. Calling upon less developed countries' (LDC) governments to undertake demanding IPM-style work when even the "normal" R&D work has not gone well is not likely to lead to success.

Beyond this, there are some fairly basic questions about the general orientation of bureaucracies. There is a good deal of resistance to the notion that farmers know as much or more about their own situation as "experts" do. In Indonesia, the IPM project had to be put through the Planning Ministry rather than the Ministry of Agriculture. Even now, the gains are fragile and could be lost if jurisdiction were to be switched. Large projects offer more prestige as well as both legal and illegal pay-ments. A seemingly low-key extension program may have little to offer the upwardly mobile bureaucrat. In addition, the cropping systems or IPM work often involves farmers of small- to medium-sized holdings, while irrigated agriculture or block planting can involve larger holdings or be targeted to specific regions. To the extent that ministries are more responsive to larger farmers, favored regions, or to input providers (such as pesticide companies), they will be less enthusiastic about ignor-ing or slighting these clients and addressing those with less influence.

The whole notion of a "project" may in itself be part of the prob-lem. IPM and cropping systems approaches often lack the clear "pack-age" of inputs that creates a rationale for a project. Many donor agencies—who supply almost all of the development budgets in many poor nations—think primarily in project terms. They need to move large amounts of money in blocks and do not easily combine that with massive amounts of local technical expertise. It could take many years and not much money, but a lot of expert assistance, to build up the right kind of research and extension apparatus. Funding horizons rarely exceed three to five years for most donors, and supervision may switch even during that time. A long-term, low-cost, technically demanding program is not the most preferred activity. This has been true in the treecrop investment sphere, where disappointing economic results from the "standard" approach have not led to alternate approaches so much as to minor revisions of past efforts.

In short, an employee of a donor agency that is considering IPM or cropping systems funding would see many pitfalls. Lots of effort, little money moved, and delayed results—in addition to resistance from the national ministry—would add up to little prospect of success from his or her point of view.

If the national bureaucracy or donor agency finds it difficult to undertake these activities, the private sector must find it pointless. Much of what is gathered is knowledge, and this is as hard to sell profitably as it is easy to share. Private companies want to develop inputs that they can sell, often repeatedly, for a profit. Hybrid seeds are preferred to synthetic ones because their offspring do not reproduce copies of the parent seed—thus ensuring continuing sales. Simple bug traps, cropping rotations, and other expedients are not products in the normal sense that pesticides or herbicides are. It is no fault of the private sector that it does not produce goods that embody externalities.

If it is so hard to get organizations to support IPM or cropping systems, no matter how preferable they are to the alternatives, they may simply not be achievable. Is this an example of a good idea that simply can't fit into the real world? Are the successes attributable to lucky cases where the right people happen to be in the right positions? Can any group of actors be identified that is likely to make these alternatives work when so many others seem hostile or indifferent?

Thus far there has been no mention of international research institutes, national academic or technical institutions, nongovernmental organizations, or a handful of private firms that have developed IPM-friendly products for sale. Each of these, as well as other examples, may be cited to suggest that it is "simply" a matter of assembling the proper inputs and treating these alternative approaches much like others that have already been undertaken. I believe, however, that even the inclusion of many other organizations will not create any easy answers. It will increase the degrees of freedom, but considerable creativity, flexibility, and institutional imagination will still be needed to avoid the pitfalls that have prevented many successful examples from developing.

The problem can be posed as one of technological generation and propagation. Who will generate the technology needed for IPM or cropping systems used by peasants? How can the knowledge be efficiently transferred? Is there any realistic prospect of matching the R&D budgets of agribusiness firms, or is there simply so much momentum being generated by their huge sales and flow of new products that any alternative is doomed? Peter Kenmore, an FAO expert on IPM, recently cited figures that annual worldwide pesticide sales were $20 billion, while pesticide company R&D was $1.7 billion annually. Annual advertising on rice pesticides in LDCs exceeds FAO field education and R&D on IPM. After a decade, about half a million out of 120 million rice farmers have been reached with IPM messages. The most critical question of all is, what institutions can be counted on to take responsibility for creating public goods for the future when these are external to present markets?

Because the IPM approach is a top-and-bottom approach, perhaps a two-pronged attack will be needed. In a perceptive book on American agriculture in the nineteenth century, Clarence Danhof shows that until well after the 1860s, much progress in the field was accomplished simply by having farmers write in to agricultural magazines and newsletters, telling what had worked or not worked for them. It may be that investing more in this sort of international information exchange and its local dissemination would have favorable results. Danhof notes that some farmers would always be more experimental and progressive than others. Perhaps offering a few farmers in each county or province of selected LDCs cheap crop insurance or some other type of compensation if they report on their experiments would be one way to nourish the sources of such an information exchange. Research grants to agricultural stations or local agricultural universities to collate this information and try out some of the more promising ideas before recommending them might act as a sort of filter. Much of this funding could be handled through scientific or environmental ministries if it appeared that the ministry of agriculture was unsympathetic. It need not be overly expensive, especially if tried out on an initial sample basis.

Such an approach does not rule out contributions from the international research organizations, several of whom are already engaged in work on IPM and cropping systems. The issue is, what do they know and how can it be transferred to those who might use it? Through what other organizations does the information need to flow, and will it have to be augmented or modified significantly? Can links be fashioned among the international experts, the national experts, and the extension agents and experimental farmers? Obviously, some sorts of links already exist. The question is whether they can be improved and whether two-way communication is likely.

The issue of funding will inevitably arise. A few comments may suggest that this problem is less serious in some respects than many may believe. In the mid-1990s FAO is increasing its funding in this area and could play a major role in disseminating information. It has a budget that is large relative to the costs of communicating and may be a logical group to play this role. The entire annual cost of the IPM program in Indonesia was less than 5 percent of the $120 million annual pesticide subsidy it displaced. Many nations provide economically unproductive subsidies to credit, pesticides, water, and fertilizer. If even a fraction of these subsidies could be cut back, there would be adequate resources from existing budgets.

The economic benefits of this change are clear. The more difficult hurdles are the bureaucratic and political ones. Nonetheless, if a few success stories can create a presumption that these alternatives should be tried, it is comforting to know at least that funding should not be the problem.

With all this said, the prognosis is not especially bright. It is not easy to get the kind of cooperation needed to make IPM-type investments work. It would probably require a major ideological-scientific decision in a number of donor agencies, long-term investments in local capacity, and an unusual degree of superior management to pull off successful institution building. Unless the third world manages to create a lobbying group for these kinds of investments, and undertakes a good deal of the R&D itself, it will probably be left to the Rodale Foundations and tinkerers to compete with the juggernaut of agribusiness and project-oriented agricultural ministries. In such contests there will be few victories for those with so little money or power.

Unfortunately, national-level politics is beset by narrow interest-group pressures and a public that is concerned about many other issues. At the same time, the two major voices on the environment often seem to be at war, and the level of uncertainty surrounding any specific prediction is quite high. If there is a way out, it will require the efforts of both environmentalists and economists.

Economists argue from the low but solid ground of common interest. At best, they are seeking things we can do that benefit the environment and economic growth or else things that are only a bit more expensive at first but clearly pay off in the longer run. Economists are well equipped to search and argue for these fixes. Above all, they can argue persuasively that any particular type of growth in consumption or the economy should fully pay for any negative externalities. Congestion should be taxed. Higher-efficiency appliances should be subsidized. There are even serious suggestions that a "carbon tax" should replace the income tax. All of these suggestions more or less assume the kind of life people now know but work toward making it more sustainable and equitable. (For example, fancy packaging should be paid for by those who purchase it, not the general taxpayer.) Economists are also well placed to implement environmental measures in least-cost ways. Their favorite solution, taxing pollution, encourages the most flexible and cheapest steps to reduce it. Without this analysis and the actions it can spark, there is likely to be little understanding of or progress in many environmental problems.

On the other hand, economists assume that "preferences are given," and they have no adequate theory of institutional creation. While preferences may well be taken as given in the short run, they are clearly variable in the longer run. Environmentalists, even if they are in a worldwide minority just now, are right to preach a gospel that will change the way people think of themselves and their relations with nature. Much of what is now happening is unsustainable and, if continued, could create real disasters. To avoid these problems, changes in both preferences and institutions will be required.

While economists will probably, as a group, remain suspicious that environmentalists would trade not just a questionable dam but the entire GNP for the snail darter, this is an irritation both groups can live with. For the foreseeable future, the environmentalists will have to persuade the public that a certain type of house should be built, while the economists will act as good plumbers. Given the differences in eloquence, this is not an altogether bad division of labor.

BIBLIOGRAPHY

Danhoff, Clarence H. 1969. *Change in Agriculture: The Northern United States, 1820–1870.* Cambridge, MA: Harvard University Press.
Goodwin, Neva R. 1991. "Lessons for the World from U.S. Agriculture: Unbundling Technology." *World Development* Special Issue, January.
Tietenberg, Thomas H. 1992. *Environmental and Natural Resource Economics.* New York: Harper-Collins Publishers.
Tomich, Thomas. 1991. "Smallholder Rubber Development in Indonesia." In *Reforming Economic Systems in Developing Countries,* ed. Dwight H. Perkins and Michael Roemer. Cambridge, MA: Harvard University Press.

7

Caring for the Future: Minimizing Change or Maximizing Choice?

Robert L. Paarlberg

Good faith efforts to "care for the future" can take either of two quite different forms: *minimizing change* across generations or *maximizing choice*. In this essay, I will argue that thought about the future, until now, has erred by stressing the reduction of change rather than the expansion of choice. I will argue for more "pro-choice" thinking about the future and less "change-averse" thinking. This not only protects the choice privileges of future generations, it also avoids freezing into place the extreme inequalities that exist within current generations. I will then examine some of the changes that must be undertaken now, especially in the developing countries of Asia, Africa, and Latin America, if choice is to be expanded and extended to future generations.

Caring for the Future by Minimizing Change?

What obligation does one generation have to the next? Some of our legal and philosophical instincts tell us that we are obliged to preserve what Edith Brown Weiss has called "intergenerational equity."[1] The presumption here is that both present and future generations have an "equitable right of access" to the natural and cultural resources of the planet, a right that could be jeopardized by any change in the condition of those resources. The duties of the present generation are thus implicitly conservative: "conserve resources," "avoid adverse impacts," or "prevent disasters and mitigate damage." When not conservative, these duties are at best compensatory: "compensate future generations for environmental harm."

More explicitly conservative are the economists who define "sustain-

---

1. Edith Brown Weiss, *In Fairness to Future Generations: International Law, Common Patrimony, and Intergenerational Equity* (Dobbs Ferry, NY: Transnational Publishers, 1989).

able development" in terms of preserving and passing on to the next generation a constant "stock" of natural environmental assets ("natural capital"). Degrading this stock through the destruction of resources is viewed by such economists as the equivalent of "living off capital." The result is criticized as a kind of intergenerational "market failure"—the production of a negative "intergenerational externality."[2]

A still more extreme example of this kind of minimum-change thinking is Herman Daly's program for "steady-state" economics. Daly envisions stationary levels of population, capital stock, and consumption, secured by a central government issuing birth licenses and tradable depletion quotas for natural resources.[3]

There are several serious drawbacks to such minimum-change notions of what one generation owes the next. The most important of these is a persistent insensitivity to the problem of inequity *within* generations. It is no accident that those who promote this conservative vision of the future come, with few exceptions, from the privileged minority of our earth's citizens who live in Western industrial societies, where relative social equity and material comfort have already been achieved. It is much too easy for those few who are now living in such comfort to begin advocating steady-state economics for the many who are not. It reminds one of the cynic's definition of an environmentalist: someone who just *finished* building his summer house.

Perhaps comfortable, upper-middle-class North Americans and Europeans should formulate for themselves some "minimum-change" obligation toward the next generation. But, for the majority of Asians, Africans, and Latin Americans who are still living in relative poverty and deprivation, such an obligation toward the future would be an unjust denial, both to them and to the future, of equitable opportunity.

Some minimum-change thinkers are remarkably explicit about how little they value equity within generations. Dana Meadows, for example, ranks social goals such as material welfare, equity, and even freedom below what she describes as "survival of the total social and ecological

---

2. R. Solow, "On the Intergenerational Allocation of Natural Resources," *Scandinavian Journal of Economics* 88, no. 1 (1986): 141–54; T. Page, *Conservation and Economic Efficiency* (Baltimore: Johns Hopkins University Press, 1977); J. Hartwick, "Intergenerational Equity and the Investing of Rents from Exhaustible Resources," *American Economic Review* 66 (1977): 972–74.

3. Herman E. Daly, *Economics, Ecology, Ethics: Essays Toward a Steady-State Economy* (San Francisco: W. H. Freeman, 1980).

system."[4] This is bad news for those who are less comfortable than she within the current system.

Equally explicit is William Ophuls, who (borrowing from Edmund Burke) advocates entrusting the future to a "natural aristocracy" of "ecological mandarins."[5] The reference to Burke is appropriate but telling. Among political philosophers, Burke was one of the first concerned with "intergenerational" obligations (the nation, he says, "extends in time as well as in numbers and in space"). But his practical conclusions (that England's parliamentary reformers had the good sense to reject) were relentlessly and dangerously conservative. Burke pioneered the notion that the "natural aristocracy" of one generation, out of an alleged obligation to future generations, should assume the privileged role of "trustee" and in that role should *exercise greater authority than would otherwise be permitted over current generations.*[6]

Minimum-change thinkers may not fully appreciate the extent to which they are embracing such undesirable concepts of "conservative authority." Only a few, like Garrett Hardin and Robert Heilbroner, have been candid enough, or thorough enough, to acknowledge the need—given their views—for an authoritarian central government.[7] Others try to deny that this would be a "conservative" form of authoritarianism. Daly, for example, sees "wealth redistribution" as one of the necessary functions of central authority in his otherwise "steady-state" society. Redistribution would be needed, he argues, because the poor could no longer be pacified through economic growth. Still others (including "postindustrialists" like Milbrath) have argued that a "vanguard" of environmental "prophets" would act not as conservative trustees but as agents of social revolution toward a less wasteful kind of society.[8] It is an irony that this highly fashionable minimum-change school of thinking about the future should require, in the end, such a utopian—and unfashionable—vision of central political authority.

---

4. Dana Meadows, "Making Value Sets Explicit," in *Making it Happen,* ed. John M. Richardson (Washington, DC: U.S. Association for the Club of Rome, 1975), 28–29.

5. William Ophuls, *Ecology and the Politics of Scarcity* (San Francisco: W. H. Freeman, 1977), 163.

6. See "The Representative as Trustee," in *Representation,* ed. Hanna F. Pitkin (New York: Atherton Press, 1969), 157–76. Weiss, without explicitly embracing Burke, also suggests placing the "rights" of future generations in the hands of such a "trustee."

7. See G. Hardin, "The Tragedy of the Commons," *Science* 162 (1968): 1243–48; Robert L. Heilbroner, *An Inquiry Into the Human Prospect: Updated and Reconsidered for the 1980s* (New York: W. W. Norton, 1980).

8. Lester Milbrath, *Environmentalists: Vanguard for a New Society* (Albany: State University of New York Press, 1984).

An even larger drawback to the minimum-change school is its revolutionary presumption of beginning the process by shrinking opportunities and choices for generations not yet born. Current generations should count themselves fortunate that their own forbearers did not subscribe to this limiting view. For example, what if past generations in the United States, fearing the wanton destruction of indigenous peoples and natural habitat, had decided to prevent the colonization of the Western frontier? We have already noted that the United States would have needed an authoritarian political system to enforce this minimum-change decision on its own citizens. Consider, also, that millions of foreign citizens, seeking freedom and opportunity, would not have been permitted to emigrate to this kind of United States. It is important to ask what role this alternative United States (smaller, less democratic, less innovative, less wealthy) would have been able to play in a variety of twentieth-century struggles, for example, against fascism and Stalinism. How many of us, in the current generation, would now be thanking our "farsighted" forbearers for embracing this minimum-change approach to *their* future (i.e., *our present*)? I suspect most of us would wish to blame them for taking opportunities away from us.

Caring for the Future by Maximizing Choice

Knowing how jealously we in the current generation guard our own right to make choices, perhaps we should presume to make fewer such choices for future generations. Perhaps we should consider a pro-choice standard for judging the obligations we have to generations not yet born. Maximizing choice (or as Rawls would say, "liberties and opportunities") is, after all, the foundation of all liberal political philosophy.[9] The concept can be extended across time as well as space. And when extended across time, the concept of choice becomes one that *protects,* rather than threatens, those features of the natural environment that are valued by society.

The deepest concern of the modern environmental movement—a concern that we avoid *irreversible* damage to the planet—can be easily restated in this language of choice. Irreversible damage can be understood as damage that future generations will have "no choice" to restore or repair at an acceptable cost.

Maximizing future choice is not the same thing as maximizing what

---

9. Rawls constrains liberty and opportunity with concern for equality, and for protection of the weakest or worst off in society. See John Rawls, *A Theory of Justice* (Cambridge, MA: Harvard University Press, 1971).

economists call "welfare." Advocating choice is not the same thing as advocating "growth." Neoclassical economists, motivated by their own fascination with efficient resource use, often make the simplifying assumption that material wealth will be pursued (by what used to be called "Economic Man") ahead of all other goals. This traditional emphasis on wealth (originally, the "wealth of nations") is a limited and distorted view of what individuals actually use their freedom to pursue. Wealth is valued in free societies but so too is entertainment, education, affection, altruism, travel, and—increasingly, it seems—the protection of nature. The emphasis here on "choice" is intended to evoke this more inclusive, more realistic, and less economistic view of liberalism.

But how would it be possible to "maximize choice over time"? Every time we make a choice today, don't we necessarily *limit* the range of choice that remains available to future generations? This, again, is a prejudiced view of choice. Some choices that individuals make today may indeed be destructive of their future choices (for example, a decision to drop out of school before graduation). But other choices may actually be "choice-creating" (for example, a decision to leave home or to change careers).

What is true for individuals may also be true for societies. Decisions made at one moment may either expand or contract the range of decisions that will be available in the future. And here it must be said that the fear of many environmentalists—that current choices will foreclose future choices—is to be taken seriously. Consider, for example, the decision of the United States government, in 1956, to begin building a massive interstate highway system. The public construction of 44,849 miles of multilane, high-speed interstate highways immediately lowered the cost to American society of its large and growing dependence upon private automobile and truck transportation. As a result, that dependence grew even faster.[10] By 1970, there were 89 million registered cars on the road. By 1990, that number had increased to 144 million. As the cost of depending on private automobiles (plus trucks) went down, new investments in comfortable, efficient high-speed public transportation also went down. And new investments in automobile-dependent national lifestyles (e.g., suburban sprawl, exurban or beltway industries, shopping malls) became artificially more attractive. With every year that went by, these investments then moved American society further away from ever being able to revitalize its urban areas or switch back to public transportation. This is all the more the case

---

10. Fred Hirsch, *Social Limits to Growth* (Cambridge, MA: Harvard University Press, 1976), 109.

given that the public funds that might go into such projects will end-lessly be soaked up by the interstate highway system itself, which now will continuously need expensive repair.[11] The highways themselves have meanwhile become a new source of economic inefficiency. Americans now lose more than 2 billion hours a year in traffic delays, costing the economy $34 billion.

To some extent, then, a costly and *irreversible* choice has been made. If future generations might someday wish to lessen our national dependence on automobiles (perhaps in response to higher fuel costs, or more likely in an effort to reduce CO_2 emissions), they will find their economic and political options limited. A transportation choice made by one generation will have effectively *reduced* the range of transportation choices available to the next generation.

Fortunately, however, some choices made in the present can clearly *expand* the range of choices that will be available to generations in the future. The same United States society that was in the process of destroy-ing choices through costly highway construction in the 1950s was simulta-neously in the process of expanding the future range of social choice through its embrace of new information technologies such as television. For some individuals, perhaps, television dependence has become as constraining as automobile dependence. But most individuals are still able to "choose" their exposure to television (more than to automo-biles), and our national "stock" of television sets does not have to be maintained or replenished out of public funds.

Choice-expanding decisions often take the form of embracing, rather than resisting, new technologies. A dramatic example would be the courageous decision by the government of India, in 1964–65, to begin using highly responsive green revolution varieties of wheat. This decision was resisted at the time (and is sometimes still criticized) by those fearful of choice and change. But change of one kind or another was inevitable, because Indian wheat production had begun to stagnate early in the 1960s, despite good weather, to the point that steadily larger quantities of unreliable international food assistance (mostly from the United States) were required. In 1964–65, accordingly, the government of India decided to begin promoting the use of these newly developed "green revolution" seed varieties, despite criticism that this was a danger-ous and socially disruptive new technology that would only enrich large

---

11. The costs of these repairs were never borne, of course, by the politicians who launched the system. The Interstate Highway Trust Fund did not begin budgeting money for repairs until 1976. See John Sedgwick, "Strong But Sensitive," *Atlantic Monthly,* April 1991, 70–82.

commercial farmers, displace rural laborers, and increase India's dependence on seed and fertilizer imports.[12]

The Indian government stuck to this difficult decision, despite two years of severe drought in 1965 and 1966. In 1966, in the middle of this drought, India imported 18,000 tons of seed from Mexico, a record-breaking quantity at the time. Soon thereafter, with the return of an adequate monsoon, wheat yields began a dramatic increase. By 1971, total Indian wheat production had *doubled,* food-grain stocks rose to a record level of 8.1 million tons, and reliance on foreign food assistance could be terminated. Income levels for farmers also went up, for small farmers as well as large (the new varieties were more sensitive to water availability than to farm size).[13] Real agricultural wages in India, which had been constant or declining between 1956 and 1964, rose sufficiently during the period 1965–71 to offset the prior decline. Small farmers and rural laborers both shared in these income gains.

Some environmental damage resulted from the new technology, including groundwater and surface water contamination from the heavier chemical use that the new seeds required. However, this damage was arguably *less* than the damage that would have occurred if Indian farmers had been forced to invade fragile, sub-marginal lands in a struggle to meet their rapidly growing food needs using their own traditional, lower-yielding seed varieties. If India had attempted, in the 1960s, to use its traditional low-yield farming techniques to produce as much wheat as it did between 1964 and 1993, it would have had to plow an additional 36 million hectares of cropland.[14] Moreover, temporary environmental damage from farm chemical use can to some extent be ameliorated, in the short run through the development and adaptation of "integrated pest management" techniques and in the long run through the bioengineering of new pest-resistant crop varieties that will require fewer chemical applications.[15]

The net result of the green revolution in India was a fortunate expansion of choice across *both* space and time. For the generation that adopted this new technology, income expanded, employment rose, access to food increased, and dependence on foreign charity decreased. In

---

12. C. Subramanian, *The New Strategy in Indian Agriculture* (New Delhi: Vikas, 1979).

13. In fact, by increasing yields, the new seed varieties actually lowered the threshold of potentially viable farm size.

14. M. S. Swaminathan, "Sustainable Agriculture," commentary in *Environment,* April 1994, 3–4.

15. Paul S. Teng, "Integrated Pest Management in Rice," University of Hawaii, Department of Plant Pathology, Honolulu. January 1990.

fact, even dependence on foreign seed varieties soon decreased. As early as 1967, India's own scientists were developing their own high-yielding varieties for use not only in India but for export to other countries in South Asia.[16] All this gave India's next generation a more favorable starting point in its own struggle toward choice expansion. India's vast rural problems—poverty, illiteracy, and social inequity—were not by any means solved as a result of the green revolution of the 1960s, but at least some time was purchased to permit future generations to confront those problems anew and to do so without the constraints that food aid dependence and the immediate threat of famine earlier implied.

The Indian example should give special pause to those who prefer a minimal-change approach to caring for the future. It was actually fashionable, among a number of "future-oriented" thinkers in the 1960s and 1970s, to judge that India's vast and growing food needs could never be met. Instead of looking for ways to extend the choice of survival to future generations in India, some of these thinkers actually suggested that a choice of nonsurvival be made for them. The Paddocks, writing in 1967, advocated that assistance to India should be terminated because the continuation of aid would only prolong breeding and increase numbers in a society that (in their view) would never be able to support itself.[17]

If our preoccupation is passing on to future generations the same sort of world that we ourselves inherited (for example, a world using *low*-yielding seed varieties), we will open ourselves to just this sort of error. We will make choices in our time that restrict rather than expand the range of choice of future generations. The result will not be "intergenerational equity" or "sustainable development" but instead a form of "intergenerational imperialism," with one generation making poorly informed choices for the next and most likely retarding both equity and sustainability in the process.

In this sense, caring about the future does *not* mean trying to control the future, or even trying to predict the future. As David Seckler has pointed out, our ignorance of "future knowledge" makes prediction impossible in any case.[18] Caring for the future means giving to the future the same expanded range of choice that we would have wanted our forbearers to have given to us.

Obviously, in practical terms, none of the choices we make can be

---

16. Dana Dalrymple, *Development and Spread of High Yielding Wheat Varieties* (Washington, DC: U.S. AID, 1986), 35–36.

17. W. Paddock and P. Paddock, *Famine 1975* (London: Weidenfeld, 1967).

18. David Seckler, "Economic Regimes, Strategic Investments, and Entrepreneurial Decisions," in this volume.

either *purely* choice-creating or *purely* choice-destroying. The decision to colonize the western frontier, while creating choices for the vast majority of United States citizens, was of course a decision that destroyed choices for most of the less technologically advanced indigenous peoples that stood in the way. The pursuit of industrial development likewise creates new wealth and new choices for a vast majority of producers and consumers in society, while destroying choices for some others, including traditional craftsmen or low-skill farmers (it was Joseph Schumpeter who most succinctly described the process of rapid industrial development as one of "creative destruction"). And conversely, the United States decision to build interstate highways, while perhaps overall a destroyer of choice, was certainly a valued creator of choices for some significant segments of United States society, including both the housing and auto industries.

The best we can say of our choices, then, is that they will be either *net* creators or *net* destroyers of future choice. And the calculation of this balance will in all cases be highly imprecise (just as imprecise as calculations made by conventional utilitarians seeking "the greatest good for the greatest number"). It is an impossible task, especially before the fact, to assign specific value to the future choices that may be created or destroyed by the actions we are choosing to take today. The further our calculations move into the future, the more they must be discounted for the cascading effects of uncertainty. Even in the present, we might find it impossible to agree on exactly *which* choices (individual versus social or governmental) should be maximized or on which individuals (philosophers, illiterates, felons, the unborn) would deserve choice-making priority.

Let us concede that we cannot provide a fully operational means for confidently measuring the choice-expanding or choice-destroying tendencies of our current actions. Some cases are clear (a cure for AIDS would provide some net choice expansion in the future; a destruction of the stratospheric ozone layer or a nuclear war would do the opposite). But other cases are not so clear, and if the choice-expanding consequences of an action are uncertain, as they will be especially for the more distant future, then we owe it to ourselves to look for a less fallible means of promoting choice expansion.

Maximizing Range of Choice by Strengthening the Agents of Choice

Many of our current actions could have an uncertain impact on the future range of choice. If this uncertainty bothers us, why not concentrate our current activities in areas where we *know* that the impact on future choice will be beneficial? Once such area is investment in "capacity" for choice, by strengthening the (present and future) agents of choice.

It is not just the physical or technological environment that constrains choice. It is also the internal capacity of the (individual or institutional) agent of choice. Where individuals and institutions (such as governments) are knowledgeable of their physical and technological environment and strong enough to make autonomous decisions about the use of that environment, the effective range of choice is automatically expanded. Where the agents of choice are weak, choice will automatically be constrained. If we concentrate more of our actions today on strengthening the agents of choice (strengthening the knowledge and autonomy of individuals and strengthening the accountability of institutions to those individuals), we will be certain of making a contribution to both present and future choice expansion.

The imperatives that grow out of this abstract formulation become obvious as soon as we consider the dramatic differences that still exist between the rich and poor segments of our global society. In today's wealthy industrial countries, the internal choice-making capacity of both individuals and institutions is already quite strong, so the practical urgency of building still more capacity is relatively low. In today's poor developing countries, however, choice-making capacity remains extremely weak, and the urgency of building more capacity is extremely high. If we take this capacity-building approach, caring about the future therefore means working to bring the choice-making capacity of poor people in poor countries at least up to the standard that has been attained in today's rich countries. If we have concluded that caring for the future means passing on to the next generation as many choices as possible, it is to the choice-deprived non-industrial world that we owe our greatest attention.

The Industrial West: Agents of Choice Growing Stronger

Throughout most of the industrial world, both the agents and the agencies of future choice are strong and growing stronger. Most individuals in the industrial West now possess all the personal assets needed to participate in a choice-oriented society: health, literacy, education, and exchangeable wealth. And they are for the most part aided by the social, economic, and political institutions around them. Most live in societies that are increasingly tolerant of a variety of cultures and beliefs. Most have access to markets for the exchange of goods, services, and labor (markets that are increasingly open, extensive across borders, and competitive), and most participate in political systems that are accountable by virtue of being democratic.

By any absolute standard, of course, there are still glaring deficiencies in most of these Western industrial societies. Knowledge and tolerance among different racial, religious, and ethnic groupings is still far from adequate or complete. Wealth is not sufficiently well distributed so as to permit all to take comparable advantage of open markets. And democratic political systems too often provide choice with less than full accountability (in the United States system, for example, the *shared* responsibility for the federal budget deficit between Democrats in Congress and Republicans in the White House in the 1980s made it impossible for concerned voters to hold either party to account). But in most of the Western industrial world a "culture of choice" has been widely implanted and embraced, and the various individual and collective agencies of choice have been strengthened accordingly.

There is every reason to believe that this culture will survive into the future. This is because the personal assets necessary for a wide range of choice (health, education, wealth) are continually being passed on to future generations through durable institutions such as the family. The family is in some ways a paradoxical guarantor of intergenerational choice creation because it is the one institution into which each generation is born *without* any choice. Still, once a choice-oriented culture has been established, the powerful institution of the family (which tends to pass the culture of the parent on to the child) automatically begins to function in the service of future choice. Parents who are choice-oriented will stress health and education for their children over hard physical labor or religious instruction. They will see their children as the future recipients of a choice-creating inheritance and will burden them less with choice-destroying duties or obligations. They will take pleasure from knowing that they have passed on to their children not the same world they inherited, or even a "better world" (by their own generationally myopic standard), but instead a world of *greater choice* for the next generation, which will then be free to set its own standards.

From what we know about such pro-choice cultures, how have they performed in practice? One important asset they bring to the future is their greater capacity to keep the peace.[19] Military aggression is an activity almost never seen among democratic societies. The more appro-

---

19. Michael Doyle, "Liberal Institutions and International Ethics," in *Political Realism and International Reality,* ed. Kenneth Kipnis and Diana T. Meyers (Boulder, CO: Westview Press, 1987), 192–94.

priate question here, though, concerns environmental performance. The judgment on environmental questions must be positive as well.

The pro-choice societies of the industrial West are now doing a better job of controlling environmental destruction than either of the two "low-choice" regions beyond the West—namely the former Soviet bloc countries to the east, and the developing countries to the south. The environmental performance of the West is not yet adequate by any means. But, as the U.S. record demonstrates, it is marked by some significant recent achievements. Since the passage of the landmark 1970 Clean Air Act, urban air pollution in the United States has been significantly reduced. Between 1978 and 1987, atmospheric lead levels in the United States were reduced by 88 percent (thanks mostly to the removal of lead from gasoline), sulfur dioxide by more than 35 percent, carbon monoxide by 32 percent, and particulates by 21 percent.[20] Drinking water quality has improved, and lakes are generally cleaner.[21] Forest resources (measured as growing stock) have increased.[22] The Western industrial countries have shown that, at a high enough level of technology, goals such as choice-driven economic growth and environmental protection need not always clash. As industrial production processes become more information intensive, they tend to use up fewer (and more often recycled) natural raw materials.[23] And as the societies that house these modern industries become more sensitive to environmental questions, the protection of nature itself becomes a key industry.[24]

An earlier fear in the industrial world, that environmental protection concerns would clash with competitiveness, is now less persuasive. Today's leading global industrial competitors—Germany and Japan— also have some of the toughest environmental protection standards, and, in the United States, some of the industrial sectors subject to the

20. Office of Air Quality Planning and Standards, Environmental Protection Agency, *National Air Quality Emissions Trends Report,* 1987 (Research Triangle Park, NC: March 1989).

21. A. Myrick Freeman III, "Water Pollution Policy," in *Public Policies for Environmental Protection,* ed. Paul R. Portney (Washington, DC: Resources for the Future, 1990), 120.

22. Julian L. Simon and Herman Kahn, *The Resourceful Earth: A Response to Global 2000* (New York: Basil Blackwell, 1984), 9–20.

23. Raymond F. Mikesell, "The Changing Demand for Industrial Raw Materials," in *Growth, Exports, & Jobs in a Changing World Economy,* ed. John W. Sewell and Stewart K. Tucker (New Brunswick, NJ: Transaction Books, 1988), 139–66.

24. The global market for environmental products and services is now a $200 billion industry. The United States, stimulated by its own strict domestic environmental regulations, is now among the world's industrial leaders in water and air protection, treatment of sewerage, and solid waste disposal. *Journal of Commerce,* May 7, 1991, 4A.

highest internal environmental costs—such as chemicals, plastics, and paints—have actually improved their trade performance in recent years. Especially where government regulations have stressed pollution prevention rather than abatement or cleanup, the competitive private market has been provided with a commercial incentive to innovate, and the needed technical improvements have often been quick to appear.[25]

The industrial West still faces massive environmental problems, including many untreated forms of air pollution, toxic waste disposal, and of course both greenhouse gas and continued CFC emissions problems. Still, the environmental record of the industrial West has an undeniable number of positives. There are few such environmental positives yet visible among the low-choice societies of the South and the East.

The South and the East: Deficient Capacities for Choice

In much of the developing world, as well as Eastern Europe and the former Soviet Union, local environmental conditions have deteriorated badly. This deterioration will continue so long as local individuals and institutions lack the capacity to make autonomous, accountable choices.

In the poorest parts of the developing world, local natural resources that remain essential for a decent life—wood, soil, and water—are rapidly being destroyed or degraded. The UN Food and Agriculture Organization (FAO) estimates that nearly a quarter of a billion people, from the dry zones of Africa to the Himalayan and Andean regions, are suffering from acute shortages of fuelwood due to forest destruction. Almost half of all irrigated land in the developing world is suffering from salinity or poor drainage. Soil erosion and infertility are degrading 30 percent of rainfed cropland in Central America, 17 percent in Africa, 20 percent in Southwest Asia, and 36 percent in Southeast Asia.[26] Species loss, the most irreversible of all environmental losses, is a problem centered most heavily in the developing world.

In the more "industrial" of the developing countries, environmental problems are sometimes even worse. All five rivers in the city of Manila, for example, have been pronounced biologically dead. Chemical waste has rendered shellfish inedible in Hong Kong. Because of sulphurous coal smoke, entire cities in China are no longer visible on satellite photo-

---

25. See Michael E. Porter, *The Competitive Advantage of Nations* (New York: Free Press and London: MacMillan, 1990).

26. H. Jeffrey Leonard, *The Environment and the Poor: Development Strategies for a Common Agenda* (New Brunswick, NJ: Transaction Books, 1989) 25–27.

graphs.[27] Air pollution in Tehran and Calcutta has recently been measured as 10 times worse than in Tokyo or New York.[28]

In Eastern Europe and the former Soviet Union, meanwhile, more advanced forms of low-choice industrial development have produced even more advanced pollution problems. Among most of the centrally planned economies, dirty production technologies and the underpricing of energy encouraged decades of severe environmental abuse. Soils have been poisoned, river water is too dirty even for industrial use, and life expectancy has actually been in decline.

What explains these third-world and second-world environmental calamities? A conspicuous weakness among both the agents and the agencies of choice is at least one part of the problem. In many developing countries of the third world, a majority of the individual agents of choice continue to be weakened by illiteracy, poor health, and poverty. They live and work in societies that give them no legal, commercial, or political protection from the disruption that often accompanies technological change. For example, when a technological change in Central America (such as a new rural transportation network or a breakthrough in chemical pest control) suddenly makes a remote rural area attractive for commercial agricultural use, the poorest local residents will find they have "no choice" over how to respond. They will be obliged, because of their lack of legal and political protection, to make way for commercial farmers and give up their semifeudal squatting rights and their subsistence farming activities. As they are progressively evicted from good lands, these landless poor will have "no choice" but to cut down more trees, plow up more hillsides, and invade more fragile lands.[29]

Secure title to land or secure common property ownership would give peasant cultivators everywhere the incentive as well as the choice to take better care of rural resources. Insecurity of land ownership reduces interest in the long-term investments that enhance land productivity, such as irrigation and drainage structures, land terracing, livestock pastures, and tree crops.[30]

A lack of pro-choice social institutions also helps to explain some of the rapid population growth currently threatening the environment

---

27. "Pollution in Asia," *Economist*, October 6, 1990, 19–22.

28. Paul R. Portney, "Air Pollution Policy," in *Public Policies for Environmental Protection*, ed. Paul R. Portney (Washington, DC: Resources for the Future, 1990), 46.

29. Robert G. Williams, *Export Agriculture and the Crisis in Central America* (Chapel Hill: University of North Carolina Press, 1986.)

30. Theodore Panayotou, "Natural Resource Management: Strategies for Sustainable Asian Agriculture in the 1990s," Harvard Institute for International Development, August 1988, 16–17.

throughout much of the developing world. Declining mortality rates, caused by the import of modern medical and public health technologies, has yet to be matched by a rapid decline in fertility rates. Fertility would decline more quickly and destructive rates of population growth would be slowed if cultures in these developing countries could only offer—to women in particular—a greater range of personal and social choice. If women had a greater range of educational and occupational choices, the average marriage age would go up, the financial cost of keeping women at home bearing children would increase, and family size would come down. Cultures that deny education, employment, and social status to women are cultures that give women "no choice" but to continue in a role of endless childbearing. If choice were provided, fewer children would be born.[31]

In low-choice cultures, unfortunately, the institution of the family can thus be a part of the problem rather than part of the solution. In such cultures, family structures function to constrain rather than liberate the next generation. Strengthening traditional family institutions, which may be an appropriate strategy for those who care about the future in pro-choice societies, can actually be a problematic strategy in low-choice societies.

In many developing societies, however, it will be the public authority of government, in addition to the private authority of family or culture, that most perpetuates the existing maldistribution (or total lack) of individual choice. The developing countries still do quite poorly in any survey of political freedoms offered to ordinary citizens (e.g., voting in competitive elections, political access and participation, and civil liberties). One such survey has been prepared annually (since 1972) by Freedom House in New York. Of the 31 countries surveyed that Freedom House labeled "free," all but 8 were Western industrial democracies. Of the remaining 100 countries (labeled as either "partly free" or "not free") all but 2 were either nonindustrial developing countries or centrally planned industrial economies.[32] Governments in developing countries also tend to restrict economic freedoms by monopolizing or seeking to control markets for food, shelter, and labor. In many African countries, more than half of all jobs are provided directly through the ministries or parastatal agencies of the central government.

---

31. So-called KAP surveys (Knowledge, Attitude, Practice) conducted throughout the third world have revealed a preference on the part of parents, especially women, for fewer children. See Parker G. Marden, et al., *Population in the Global Arena* (New York: Holt, Rinehart and Winston, 1982), 71.

32. Roy L. Prosterman and Jeffrey M. Riedinger, *Land Reform and Democratic Development* (Baltimore: Johns Hopkins University Press, 1987).

The policies of such low-choice governments are frequently a contributing factor in the widespread environmental damage currently being done in the developing world. In Brazil, for example, virgin forests were heavily cut during the decade of the 1980s, largely in response to a combination of artificial incentive policies set in place by the Brazilian government. These included resettlement policies designed to relieve pressure for land reform in other parts of Brazil (where 1 percent of farmers occupied 50 percent of the land area being farmed), laws that virtually exempted cattle ranches from taxation (while fully taxing forests), generously subsidized credits to those intending to clear trees in preparation for ranching, and a land titling procedure that *required* land to be cleared before it could be titled.[33] The obvious beneficiaries of such policies have been large-scale cattle ranchers as well as other politically privileged Brazilian agriculturalists. The victims have been the unprotected indigenous forest dwellers, who are left with no choice but to give up their traditional habits of sustainable forest use. Other victims have been the landless Brazilian citizens who are now (for lack of employment prospects elsewhere) doing most of the hard physical labor associated with the Amazon settlement effort, without capturing an equitable share of the associated profits or property rights.

The less-than-democratic governments of Eastern Europe and the former Soviet Union have an even more dubious record on matters such as natural resource protection. It once was fashionable to argue that the "unplanned" economies of the West would be more likely to despoil environments than the "planned" economies of the East. Planned economies, it was said, would be more likely to take "externalities" (both positive and negative) into account, including externalities over time. Wasteful current consumption would be discouraged in favor of socially desirable future growth. The unplanned economies of the West, meanwhile, would only continue producing what Galbraith once described colorfully as "private affluence alongside public squalor."[34]

The centrally planned economies of the East could scarcely have done more, over the postwar period, to invalidate such generalizations. They not only failed to grow rapidly, they also failed to protect the natural environment. Levels of air, water, and soil pollution that would never have been tolerated in democratic market economies became com-

---

33. Hans P. Binswanger, "Brazilian Policies That Encourage Deforestation of the Amazon," The World Bank, mimeograph, March 31, 1989.

34. John Kenneth Galbraith, *The Affluent Society* (London: Hamish Hamilton, 1958), 196–97.

monplace. Rather than protecting the future, these nonaccountable cen-trally planned systems did the opposite.

Public policy analysts often complain about the difficulty govern-ment regulators encounter in pro-choice democratic societies such as the United States, where private citizens have so many means for resisting central authority. Yet it is precisely this widespread capacity to resist cen-tral authority—through individual or community access to independent court systems and to the independent private media—that enables many local environmental causes to succeed. The often criticized "NIMBY" syndrome ("I'm all for toxic waste disposal, but *not in my back yard*") deserves more appreciation as a powerful protection against actions (by the government or the private sector) that are insensitive to adverse spatial or temporal externalities. If individuals or small groups in the United States were not empowered, through local government, the legal system, and the independent media, to prevent more distant authorities from dumping the waste products of their activities into local lakes and streams, the United States environment today might more nearly re-semble that of Poland or Russia.

For those who care about the future, then, a government that gives choices to individuals is preferable to a government that tries to control the future by giving power to central planners. Those who liken our current environmental crisis to a new form of "national security" crisis, and who advocate the equivalent of an all-powerful "national security council" for environmental policy, are undervaluing the choice-making record and capacity of individuals and are overvaluing the choice-making record and capacity of national public authorities.

Conclusion

Our collective future is most imperiled today not by the "overdevelop-ment" of the affluent West, but by the continuing underdevelopment of the South (and the misshapen development of the East). What the South and the East most require is not a further infusion of Western technology so much as the emergence of Western-style pro-choice social and govern-mental institutions.

Precisely because of the high mobility of Western science and tech-nology, the alternative of holding on to the social institutions of the past no longer exists in any case. A safe equilibrium will never be restored so long as these highly mobile and profoundly powerful Western ideas and technologies continue to be imported into societies where adaptability is weakened by illiteracy, low levels of technical knowledge and compe-tence, rigid hierarchies of social and political status, explosive feelings of religious or tribal intolerance, and stifling nondemocratic governmental control over everything from the flow of public information to the conduct of private commercial exchange. The introduction of powerful new technologies (bulldozers, heavy industries, public health) into such societies will turn loose activities that rigid, choice-stifling institutions will be poorly suited to control. Only when the choice-making capacity of individuals and institutions is enhanced will such activities (cutting down trees, burning underpriced fossil fuels, conceiving additional children) become moderated out of self-interest, and become part of a sustainable pattern once again.

The implied remedy for this threatening "choice deficit" in the South (and the East) is relatively straightforward. Individuals in these societies who are currently weak and vulnerable must be strengthened and empowered: through improved access to health services, education, legal protection, political information and participation, technical training, and freely exchangeable wealth. The institutions in the South (and the East) that can facilitate such empowerment will include, most of all, community-level human service organizations, educational and training institutions, cooperative grassroots economic enterprises, competitive political parties, and independent news media. All must be strengthened. The institutions that tend to block or resist such empowerment will include noncompetitive one-party governments, illiberal and intolerant religious institutions, traditionally privileged or politically privileged economic groups or classes, and authoritarian social and family structures. All should be weakened. These authoritarian institutions not only threaten our collective future by virtue of being non-adaptive, their choice-stifling character means they are also a source of large-scale current social injustice.

So it is that we need not worry so much, in the developing countries, about "sacrificing the present" in order to protect the future. What the developing countries need at the present time—a larger capacity to make autonomous individual choice and accountable public choice—is also what they will need to protect their future, and by extension our own. If citizens in wealthy, developed countries are serious about their own frequently expressed concern for the future of our global society, they will need to turn more of their attention and devote more of their resources to these conspicuous needs in the South.

BIBLIOGRAPHY

Binswanger, H. P. 1989. "Brazilian Policies that Encourage Deforestation of the Amazon." The World Bank, mimeograph.

Dalrymple, Dana. 1986. *Development and Spread of High Yielding Wheat Varieties in Developing Countries.* Washington, DC: Agency for International Development, Bureau for Science and Technology.

Daly, H. E. 1980. *Economics, Ecology, Ethics: Essays Towards a Steady State Economy.* San Francisco: W. H. Freeman.

Doyle, Michael. 1987. "Liberal Institutions and International Ethics." In *Political Realism and International Reality,* ed. Kenneth Kipnis and Diana T. Meyers. Boulder, CO: Westview Press.

Economist. 1990. "Pollution in Asia." *Economist,* October 6, 19–22.

Freeman, Myrick A. III. 1990. "Water Pollution Policy." In *Public Policies for Environmental Protection,* ed. Paul R. Portney. Washington, DC: Resources for the Future.

Galbraith, J. K. 1958. *The Affluent Society.* London: Hamish Hamilton.

Hardin, G. 1968. "The Tragedy of the Commons." *Science,* no. 162: 1243–48.

Hartwick, J. 1977. "Intergenerational Equity and the Investing of Rents from Exhaustive Resources." *American Economic Review,* 66, 972–74.

Heilbroner, Robert. L. 1980. *An Inquiry Into the Human Prospect: Updated and Reconsidered for the 1980s.* New York: W. W. Norton.

Hirsch, Fred. 1976. *Social Limits to Growth.* Cambridge, MA: Harvard University Press.

Journal of Commerce. 1991. May, 4A.

Leonard, Jeffery H. 1989. *The Environment and the Poor: Development Strategies for a Common Agenda.* New Brunswick: Transaction Books.

Marden, Parker G., et al. 1982. *Population in the Global Arena.* New York: Holt, Rinehart and Winston.

Meadows, Dana. 1975. "Making Value Sets Explicit." In *Making it Happen,* ed. J. M. Richardson. Washington, DC: U.S. Association for the Club of Rome.

Mikesell, R. F. 1988. "The Changing Demand for Industrial Raw Materials." In *Growth, Exports, and Jobs in a Changing World Economy,* ed. John W. Sewell and Stewart K. Tucker. New Brunswick: Transaction Books.

Milbrath, Lester. 1984. *Environmentalists: Vanguard for a New Society.* Albany: State University of New York Press.

Office of Air Quality Planning and Standards, Environmental Protection Agency. March 1989. *National Air Quality Emissions Trends Report—1987.* Research Triangle Park, NC: Office of Air Quality Planning and Standards, Environmental Protection Agency.

Ophuls, Williams. 1977. *Ecology and the Politics of Scarcity.* San Francisco: W. H. Freeman.

Paddock, W. and P. Paddock. 1975. *Famine 1975.* London: Weidenfeld, 1967.

Page, T. 1977. *Conservation and Economic Efficiency.* Baltimore, Johns Hopkins University Press.

Panayotou, Theodore. 1988. *Natural Resources Management: Strategies for Sustainable Asian Agriculture in the 1990s.* Cambridge, MA: Harvard Institute of International Development.

Pitkin, Hanna F. 1969. "The Representative as Trustee." In *Representation,* ed. J. Roland Pennock. New York: Atherton Press.

Porter, Michael E. 1990. *The Competitive Advantage of Nations.* New York: Free Press and London: Macmillan.

Portney, Paul R. 1990. "Air Pollution Policy." In *Public Policies for Environmental Protection,* ed. P. R. Portney. Washington, DC: Resources for the Future.

Prosterman, Roy L., and Jeffery M. Reidinger. 1987. *Land Reform and Democratic Development.* Baltimore: Johns Hopkins University Press.

Rawls, John. 1971. *A Theory of Justice.* Cambridge MA: Harvard University Press.

Seckler, David. 1996. "Economic Regimes, Strategic Investments, and Entrepreneurial Decisions." In this volume.

Sedgwick, John. April 1991. "Strong But Sensitive." *The Atlantic Monthly.* 70–82.

Simon, Julian and Herman Kahn. 1984. *The Resourceful Earth: A Response to Global 2000.* New York: Basil Blackwell.

Solow, R. 1986. "On the Intergenerational Allocation of Natural Resources." *Scandanavian Journal of Economics,* 88, no. 1: 141–54.

Subramanian, C. 1979. *The New Strategy in Indian Agriculture.* New Delhi: Vikas.

Swaminathan, M. S. 1994. "Sustainable Agriculture." *Environment,* April, 3–4.

Teng, Paul S. 1990. *Integrated Pest Management in Rice.* Honolulu: University of Hawaii, Department of Plant Pathology.

Weiss, Edith B. 1989. *In Fairness to Future Generations: International Law, Common Patrimony, and Intergenerational Equity.* Dobbs Ferry, NY: Transnational Publishers.

Williams, Robert G. 1986. *Export Agriculture and the Crisis in Central America.* Chapel Hill: University of North Carolina Press.

8

Rewriting the Rules: Creating New Structures

Alisa Gravitz

"Never doubt that a small group of thoughtful, committed citizens can change the world. Indeed, it's the only thing that ever has." This belief, so eloquently stated by Margaret Mead, keeps untold thousands of people struggling through the uncharted, unheralded territory of sustainable change and development. These people are modern day pioneers who are rewriting the rules for society's businesses and institutions so that ordinary everyday actions of society will help sustain the planet and its people.

Though the going is tough and they often go unrecognized, or are even disparaged at times by their contemporaries, these pioneers are asking difficult questions, beginning the research and discussions that will lead to answers, and experimenting with new ways of organizing their own lives and perhaps society itself. They are sowing the seeds for a new vision, new kinds of interactions, and a new set of institutions that will make possible the just, sustainable world based on peace, cooperation, and environmental health we all long for.

In short, these pioneers are people who act as if the future matters. What follows is a report from the field on some of their work, organized to reflect the different strategies they use to motivate change: revitalizing existing institutions, creating new institutions, changing the rules of the game and persuading existing institutions to make changes, and building an infrastructure to support and further the changes.

This "field report" is by no means comprehensive, but I hope the examples are illuminating. I also hope this review of the work in progress will complement the cutting-edge research and theories presented throughout this book series on what can be—and is being—done to change perceptions, practices, and institutional arrangements to reflect concern for the future.

Revitalizing Existing Institutions

Many of the people pioneering in the realm of sustainable change and development use the strategy of changing existing institutions from within to realize their vision. Banking and business institutions are two arenas where one can see the results of future-oriented policies and practices when people with the vision and values of a sustainable society are at the helm.

Development Banking

"Development banking" is the name for an approach that puts an economic development and empowerment agenda together with the business of banking to create a powerful force to revitalize urban neighborhoods and depressed rural areas. This creates a future for these areas and unleashes the energy of people to participate in building a future for themselves and their communities—people who might otherwise be ignored or cast aside by society. This also creates economic and social justice today—bringing new jobs, affordable housing, and empowerment to economically disadvantaged areas.

There are at least five development banks operating in the United States, all of them modeled on Chicago's Shore Bank Corporation, the holding company that is the parent of the South Shore Bank. South Shore got its start in 1973 and since then has been successful and profitable. When you walk through Chicago's south side, you can literally see South Shore's work: in sharp contrast to the declining neighborhoods outside its boundaries, South Shore's neighborhood sports renovated buildings, lots of trees and grass, a new urban mall—and most importantly, children playing and people visiting out on the streets.

Shore Bank runs its banking operations on radical values and conservative banking principles with the goals of economic development and restoration of community self-confidence.[1] Its achievements are impressive: over 10,000 units of rental housing rehabilitated; profitable every year since 1975; 7,500 neighborhood borrowers with a cumulative repayment rate of over 98 percent (compared to a national average of 95 to 97 percent); the creation of a local rehab and rental industry; and the mentoring of similar programs in places as diverse as Brooklyn, New York; rural Arkansas; and Poland.[2] Shore Bank's strategy includes:

Targeting development so that individual loans and projects support one another. This improves the general economic environment and the quality of all the loans in the area—and makes the devel-

---

1. Ronald Grzywinski, "The New Old-Fashioned Banking," *Harvard Business Review,* May-June 1991, 87–89.
2. Ibid.

opment work highly visible in order to give residents hope and inspiration. Shore Bank created its structure to include a real estate development company to help spur this rebuilding.

Mobilizing the community. Shore Bank also created a not-for-profit subsidiary to advocate for the least advantaged, to provide education and technical assistance, and to assure that the neighborhood revitalization does not displace any residents. The not-for-profit subsidiary also allows Shore Bank to tap into government and foundation grants to support community education, development, and technical assistance that its for-profit subsidiaries can't utilize. Indeed, Shore Bank excels at piecing together dozens of different kinds of financing to assure affordable housing for the neighborhood. At a typical bank holding company, you'll find credit card and finance subsidiaries. In contrast, Shore Bank's subsidiaries are community development and not-for-profit subsidiaries that support its overall development banking agenda.

Raising deposits from outside its lending area. Over half of Shore Bank's deposits come from customers around the country. They choose to put their money in a bank in Chicago because they care deeply about the way their money is used—for renovating neglected apartment buildings, starting small businesses, helping young people get an education, empowering a community. This reverses the usual urban banking scenario in which banks use deposits from low-income–area customers to invest in lucrative downtown and suburban areas—or other states and overseas. (See the section "Building Infrastructure" for more about how people from outside South Shore's lending area are getting involved.)

Applying tough credit standards and closely monitoring its projects and businesses. Shore Bank's cautious qualification of borrowers, close oversight, and technical assistance help provide confidence to the community and assure that its activities are self-sustaining. Shore Bank believes that the presence of a commercial bank making disciplined, ordinary loans to private citizens sends the message that this is a good neighborhood—the bank believes in it; the people should too. Shore Bank finds that its work yields four or five units of unsubsidized renovated housing for every unit of subsidized rehab.[3]

Shore Bank's work successfully combines banking discipline with a vision of the future—in a structure that has proven to be replicable. It

---

3. Shore Bank Corporation 1990 Annual Report.

empowers and reenfranchises the people who participate in the redevelopment of their neighborhoods. Ronald Grzywinski, Shore Bank's chairman, describes the importance of Shore Bank's work this way:

> Wellsprings of entrepreneurialism exist in thousands of disinvested neighborhoods and rural areas all over the country . . . they represent an opportunity that most bankers and other members of the middle class have a hard time seeing. . . . Deliberate disciplined development banking . . . can revive a local economy, rekindle the imagination of its people, and restore market forces to their normal health and interdependency.[4]

New Vision Businesses

A new species of business is emerging that seeks to capture the ideas and values of a just and sustainable society. More than "green capitalists," the women and men who start and run these companies believe that every act of conducting business should move us closer to sustainability. Here are some of the changes the new vision business owners are institutionalizing:

They organize with purposes other than the sole pursuit of profit maximization. They often have bylaws or charters that lay out the social and environmental objectives they hope to achieve—and measure themselves against.

They choose to deliver products and services that reflect their social and environmental concerns.

They work to include all the stakeholders in their decision-making process—their workers, customers, community, and Mother Nature herself, along with the capital providers. Sometimes you'll see the different stakeholders on the board of directors or in special working groups within the companies.

They address economic justice issues specifically within their business. Some put caps on the ratio of top-to-bottom salaries. Many have profit-sharing plans that include all workers, not just top brass, or they are worker-owned. Many make it an explicit goal of their charters to recruit a diverse worker base.

They make products built to last. They educate their customers and raise the issue of consuming less (one of the most radical steps a business can take).

They ensure that their manufacturing and delivery processes are

---

4. Ibid.

environmentally sound. They conserve energy, recycle packaging, and figure out how to minimize transportation.

They make their investments with social and environmental screens.

They examine their relationships with vendors, urging them—even requiring them when they can—to make social and environmental changes like theirs.

They explicitly address what they will do with their profits.

They are involved in their communities.

They work to change the business environment to allow the further development of new vision companies. They also encourage other businesses to embrace the new vision and educate the public about this type of company (see "Building Infrastructure").[5]

When more and more of these characteristics appear in any given company, the look, the feel, the personality, and the policies and the practices of that company all add up to a new way of doing business.

For example, here is how a small clothing manufacturing company in rural Maryland has institutionalized the values in its charter. It buys as much organic cotton as it can, uses nontoxic dyes, and makes clothes for comfort, not fashion, that will wear well season after season—in fact, prides itself on reports from its customers on how long they wear its clothes. It allows people to choose to work at home to be close to their families, staggers the delivery of its catalogs to ensure an even demand all year long—not the dip and dive of seasonal sales that leads to the hiring of temporary workers who get no benefits—and minimizes and reuses its packaging. It invites customer response in many different ways, subcontracts its order service to another local business that hires handicapped workers, and designates a substantial share of its profits to shelters for battered women and children.[6]

New vision companies, like this clothing company, see themselves as playing a role in the transition to a just and sustainable society. Like young trees sprouting on forest floors, these new vision companies are growing up within the current system but are not the same species as the "older-growth" corporations. They are changing the purpose and structure of business. While working with a vision of environmental and social justice for tomorrow, they are creating jobs, community strength, and environmental health today.

---

5. Alisa Gravitz, "Green Business: Truth or Consequence?" *Co-op America Quarterly* 3, no. 3 (Fall 1991): 10–11.

6. Jack Cook, "A Partnership of Consumers and Farmers," *Co-op America Quarterly,* 3, no. 1 (Spring 1991): 11–12.

Indeed, it may be that development banks and new vision businesses are early forms of new structures. In the next section, I discuss some structures that appear to be fairly new but like the banks and businesses could also be familiar structures with visionaries leading them.

Creating New Institutions

As some of the pioneers struggle to see their vision implemented in society, they find they have to create new organizations and institutions to carry them out. The following is a report on some of the new kinds of institutions these pioneers are creating in different parts of the economy—such as food and agriculture (community-supported agriculture), housing (co-housing and community land trusts), land use (conservation easements), and financing (community development loan funds).

What all of these new organizations have in common is that they are creating the new institutions of tomorrow while solving today's problems—for example, the need for affordable housing, job creation in economically disadvantaged communities, and the preservation of family farms.

Community-Supported Agriculture

With growing concern about food safety, the disappearance of the family farm, and the destructiveness of modern agribusiness farming practices, people are banding together to create a new kind of institution called community-supported agriculture (CSA). With variations on the theme, CSA works like this: A group of consumers work with a farmer (or group of farmers). The consumers pay the farmers in advance for the produce they will receive throughout the growing season. The consumers take a stake in the season's production, sharing the risk with the farmers. The farmers, in turn, see a reduction in both their financial risk (they don't have to borrow from the bank to plant this season's crops) and their marketing risk (the consumers are a guaranteed market).

Most CSAs focus on organically grown food, and some include participation by the consumers. Many not only provide healthier and fresher food than consumers can find in their grocery stores, they also offer home delivery, and the total cost to the consumers is often lower than if they had purchased the same quantity through the grocery stores.

One particularly successful CSA in West Virginia provides organic food to several consumer groups in the lucrative Washington, D.C., market and adds an extra dimension to its work. It organizes farmers in

West Virginia to join the CSA both to bring more farmland under sustainable farming practices and to enhance economic development of this relatively impoverished area. This CSA provides regular business to the farmers and keeps the money in the community. This is a tremendous boon to the area—highly preferable to the boom-and-bust cycle it faces through agribusiness contracts that come and go.

Indeed, wherever CSAs are organized, farmers are changing farming practices and consumers are redirecting how their food dollars are spent.[7]

Co-Housing

To counter the increasing expense of housing, the longing for real community, and the stress of balancing the demands of modern life, some people are developing a new institution called co-housing. Pioneered primarily in Denmark and now being adopted in other countries, co-housing reestablishes the advantages of traditional villages within the context of late twentieth-century life.

Co-housing communities are built as neighborhoods and combine the autonomy of private dwellings with the advantages of community living. Each household has a private residence but also shares extensive common facilities with the larger group. Again with variations on the theme, the shared facilities might include a kitchen and dining hall, children's playrooms, guest rooms, laundry facilities, recreation facilities, and maintenance equipment.

Residents often share dinners, child care, and property maintenance, taking turns or hiring people to provide these services. This allows each resident to take time off from these daily activities to spend more time on other pursuits and reduce the stress of juggling so many different roles. One co-housing community describes a typical early evening scene:

> It's five o'clock in the evening, and Anne is glad the work day is over. As she pulls into her driveway, she begins to unwind at last. . . . Instead of frantically trying to put together a nutritious dinner, Anne can spend some time with her children, and then eat in the common house. Walking through the common house on the way home, she stops to chat with the evening's cooks, two of her neighbors, who are busy preparing dinner in the kitchen. After dropping her things off at home, Anne walks through the birch

---

7. Ibid.

trees behind the houses to the childcare center where she picks up her four-year-old son. She will have some time to read him a story before dinner, she thinks to herself.[8]

Residents are involved from the start in designing the community and running it once it is built or retrofitted within existing structures. Co-housing often allows people to have more facilities and services than they could have afforded alone, although it is not in itself an answer to affordable housing needs. And it clearly provides for needs that many people cannot find without turning to this new form of community structure.

As of 1991, over 70 groups have formed in the United States. The co-housing model offers insight into society's needs for home and community. If it takes hold as an institution, it will provide an alternative for people whose needs are not being met by the traditional housing market—and may lead to even broader work on rethinking community, town, and city design.[9]

Community Land Trusts

To deal more directly with the development and permanence of affordable housing, another institution, the Community Land Trust (CLT), is emerging.

The CLT provides permanent housing affordability by removing land from the speculative market. It works like this. The CLT, structured as a nonprofit organization, acquires land and offers low-to-middle-income homeowners lifetime land leases that are transferable to heirs but not salable. Homeowners may own the house, but the CLT retains the option to repurchase the house at a rate that accounts for homeowner improvements. The lessee retains the benefits of homeownership: security, fair equity, and a legacy for heirs and the community benefits from permanent availability of affordable housing for low-to-middle-income people. The flexibility of the CLT model allows a community to meet a variety of housing needs from single-family homes to condominiums to multifamily buildings and co-ops.

As a nonprofit entity owning the land, the CLT not only assures that the housing will remain affordable, it also plays a key role in assembling grants, private capital, and individual donations to provide start-up money for building or renovating the housing for the CLT. Variations on

---

8. Kathryn McCamant and Charles Durret, "Building a Co-housing Community," *Co-op America Quarterly* 3, no. 1 (Spring 1991): 13–15.

9. Ibid.

the theme include sweat equity by the residents as part of the package to create affordable housing. A particularly successful CLT in Hawaii, where average housing prices are three times what the average household income can qualify for, includes a commitment from the prospective buyers to learn how to build the house and provide a total of 30 hours a week of combined labor from the entire family to bring the housing on line.

The CLT model was pioneered by the Institute for Community Economics in the late 1960s. By 1991, there were 90 CLTs in 23 communities. CLTs are operating primarily in smaller towns and cities, although there are two large and successful CLTs in New York City. In larger cities, it often takes a significant partnership between government and the CLT to manage the politics of development and gentrification, along with the magnitude of large cities' problems, to make the CLT work.[10]

Conservation Easements

Conservation easements are a variation on the CLT model that were evolved by people who wished to affect land-use patterns, primarily in rural areas under pressure from suburban development. To create a conservation easement, a landowner or landowners split the rights of ownership into two categories, use rights and development rights. The use rights—which might include the right to live on the land, farm it, or sell it—stay with the owners. The development rights—to subdivide, build, or pave—are eliminated. In some cases, the original owners create the conservation easements. In other cases, a group of individuals, a town, or a nonprofit buys the land and then creates the easements.

The conservation easement is then conveyed to an institution that can maintain it in perpetuity—usually a land trust, a town, or a conservation organization. Since a conservation easement will often depress the market value of the land within the easement while increasing the value of neighboring land, pioneering groups of neighbors may band together to put a larger portion of land under the easement.

One group, in Lyme, New Hampshire, organized to give its conservation easement to a local conservation society and took the loss in market values as a charitable donation deduction. The group also raised the money from other townspeople for those who could not afford to do this.

---

10. Anne Zorc, "Community Land Trusts," *Co-op America Quarterly* 3, no. 1 (Spring 1991): 14.

When challenged about what right the group had to determine land use, one member of the group replied:

> Well, people who develop do the same thing: they dictate the future. They destroy options for farming, forestry, wildlife, peace and quiet. All landowners impose on the future of the land in lots of ways. We've just chosen a way that preserves its beauty and productivity . . . and people should know that we aren't all one kind of person. Some of us own 65 acres, some own 5. Some are retired, some are young couples just starting families. Some are natives, some are newcomers. This isn't just a project for old folks or yuppies.[11]

Some countries institutionalize conservation easements by policy. Norway and Denmark, for example, zone prime agricultural land for agriculture use only. The land is still privately owned. However, since it can only be purchased for farming, agricultural economics determines its price. The land price reflects the return expected from agriculture, not from shopping malls or suburban subdivisions.[12] Here in the United States, people are inventing ways to institutionalize similar values. As more and more people turn to these models, they may show the way to local, state, and federal land policies and even broader institutionalization of these values.

Community Development Loan Funds

Community Development Loan Funds (CDLFs) are new institutions created to raise capital to target specific community development needs. They make loans at low-cost rates to other community development organizations, both nonprofit and for-profit, which develop affordable housing, employment opportunities, and other resources and services for low-income, unemployed, and otherwise economically disadvantaged people. Working together, the CDLFs and their development organization partners provide technical assistance as well as financing to the recipients to help assure the success of both the development and financial goals.

The CDLFs have been tremendously successful, particularly in cre-

---

11. Donella Meadows, "A Neighborhood Plans Its Own Development," in *The Global Citizen* (Washington, D.C.: Island Press, 1991), 162–64.

12. "A Farm Policy That Might Work," *The Global Citizen* (Washington, D.C.: Island Press, 1991), 100–102.

ating affordable housing and self-confident home owners. On the financial front, the National Association of Community Development Loan Funds reports that of the over $88 million loaned by their member funds, only $15,000—or 0.02 percent—has been lost by investors.[13] The National Congress for Community Economic Development reports that more than 320,000 housing units and 90,000 new jobs were created in 2,000 neighborhoods between 1985 and 1990 by community development groups.

The CDLFs were created to provide financing where no other institution was willing to step in. At present, they seem to be focusing primarily on housing and microbusiness development. The technical assistance needs for small business, along with the greater risk of investing in small business, seem for now to be beyond the capacity of most of the funds. However, small business investment might be the next logical step for the funds.

Recently, one of the investment companies involved in socially responsible investing has been exploring the idea of creating a mutual fund to invest in the CDLFs. This would provide an additional institutional structure to ensure their success. It also shows how new institutional structures can help create further new institutions and infrastructure—in this case, a secondary market for the loan funds.

Changing the Rules of the Game: Persuading Existing Institutions to Change

Some of today's pioneers seem to be more focused on trying to pressure existing institutions, particularly private ones, to change. In this section, I discuss several efforts to infuse corporations and the market with social, ethical, and ecological as well as self-interested values. These strategies include creating new standards for corporate behavior, such as the CERES Principles; using shareholder actions as investor-owners to achieve value objectives; and urging new methods of stakeholder accounting and measures of business activity.

The CERES Principles

Interested in motivating corporations to become responsible environmental actors, an unusual coalition of environmental organizations and

---

13. "Alternative Investments: Community Development Loan Funds," *Co-op America's Socially Responsible Financial Planning Handbook* (Washington, D.C.: Co-op America, June 1991), 22.

social investors banded together to create a set of environmental principles to guide corporations. The coalition was formed in 1989 and named itself CERES—from the Coalition for Environmentally Responsible Economies and in honor of the Roman goddess of the harvest. By the early 1990s, coalition members represented over 10 million individuals and $150 billion in assets.

Modeling its strategy on the successful South African divestment movement, CERES created 10 principles for corporate environmental responsibility and set out to get corporations to "sign" on to the principles. The principles not only lay out guidelines for protecting the biosphere—from pollution prevention to waste reduction to energy conservation—they also include "watchdog" provisions. The ninth principle, for example, holds corporate boards accountable for environmental responsibility, calling for each board to specifically assign environmental oversight within the corporation. The tenth principle requires an independent environmental audit with public disclosure. Thus, in signing the principles, a corporation makes a commitment not only to specific environmental behaviors but to reviewing its environmental practices and policies each year, improving any found lacking and disclosing them to the public.

CERES's vision is to create an environmental audit, much like the financial audit, to provide existing and potential shareholders with environmental information critical to their investing decisions. While environmental audits would reveal information important from a purely financial point of view (for example, if a particular corporation has a potential financial liability due to mishandling toxic wastes), the audits would also provide information to those investors interested in creating portfolios of environmentally responsible stocks. As more and more corporations conduct and disclose environmental audits, individual and institutional investors may begin to require CERES signatory status and audit disclosure (see below) as one of their criteria for investing. The criteria may expand into purchasing as well as investing decisions. Several cities and states have even discussed legislation setting up such criteria. Thus, CERES's strategy is a powerful way of incorporating environmental values into investing and purchasing decisions and through those mechanisms into corporate behavior.

In its first two years, its only signers were small, privately held companies. A revision to the principles made it possible for public companies to sign, and several medium-sized, publicly traded companies signed on immediately. Several Fortune 500 companies followed in their footsteps, including Sun Oil, General Motors, and Polaroid. Several more Fortune 500 companies have agreed to follow the disclosure provision. Another twenty or more Fortune 500 and Fortune 1000 companies are presently involved in signatory negotiations and are expected to sign by 1997.

Sun Oil's involvement provides a good example of how the CERES principles can bring about improved environmental health and community well-being today as well as improved corporate responsibility over time. Because of the public commitment Sun Oil made to CERES, Sun Oil adopted new emergency procedures to protect the thousands of families living in neighborhoods near its plants and has agreed to work with the grassroots neighborhood groups on more protection measures.

Most importantly, CERES leaders report that the principles are discussed in every major corporate boardroom in the country. In short, creating a process that requires every corporation to confront how it is going to address issues of environmental responsibility is a major step toward changing the way these businesses and the people in them think and act.

Shareholder Action

As owners of a company, shareholders have the right to influence corporate policy by submitting and/or voting on shareholder resolutions. Many shareholders, both individual and institutional, are increasingly using this right as a tactic to change corporate behavior.

Shareholders are also increasing their influence by filing resolutions in large blocks. For example, the Interfaith Coalition for Corporate Responsibility (ICCR) organizes religious, institutional, and individual investors to file resolutions each year on issues such as apartheid, economic conversion (away from defense-related business), the environment, alcohol, and tobacco. ICCR sponsored over 279 resolutions in 1991, including over 50 requesting corporations to sign the CERES Principles. Thus, the strategy of creating the CERES Principles allowed the tactic of shareholder action to push for greater corporate environmental responsibility.[14]

Individuals and institutions using shareholder actions will be the first to admit that they usually don't win a vote outright. However, they believe deeply that the process of educating corporate management and other shareholders—through the information printed in the proxy statements to all shareholders and the presentation that they are entitled to make at the corporation's annual meeting—is an important pathway toward changing the way America does business.

---

14. "Shareholder Activism: How to Get Involved," *Co-op America's Socially Responsible Financial Planning Handbook,* 10.

The pioneers who use these investor strategies and tactics call corporate attention to social justice and environmental values—even though they usually do not represent a direct economic threat. For example, one executive, who was party to making his board decide to cease business in South Africa, stated that between the political and shareholder actions supporting divestment, they had no option but to pull out of South Africa. He stressed that it wasn't an economic issue. He claimed that the divestment movement hadn't hit the corporate pocketbook, but he explained that he couldn't escape the issue in the comfort of his own country club: even there people were asking him why his company was still in South Africa.

Shareholders also capture media attention through resolutions. A resolution asking Amoco to pull out of Burma—a country ruled by a repressive military regime—resulted in an article in Amoco's hometown paper, the *Chicago Tribune*. Amoco later pulled out. In another action, shareholders used a resolution to catalyze bad publicity for Walmart into a positive outcome. After a television news program showed children in a developing country making shirts for Walmart, Franklin Research and Development, a Boston-based social investment company, introduced a shareholder resolution that led Walmart to adopt the most comprehensive set of social responsibility vendor standards in the retail industry.

In short, these investor strategies and actions make the issues and values that the investors care about very *personal*. Since *people* make corporate decisions, these pioneers can use investor strategies and tactics as outsiders to influence internal corporate decisions.

Shareholder action may become an even stronger pathway to change in the future as employees who own large blocks of stock begin to exercise their rights as owners. Because of the Employee Stock Ownership Plans (ESOPs) put in place over the last decade (in many cases, to resist hostile takeovers), many employees will begin to realize they own the company and look for ways to have their voices heard. Shareholder actions will be particularly useful to them as a tool for change.

Stakeholder Accounting and Changing the Measures of Business Activity

Some of the efforts to pressure corporations to act as if the future matters are geared to changing the accounting and measurement practices of business. The idea behind this work is that many, if not most, people would be willing to play a different business game if the rules were clear and fair and they were rewarded for playing by them.

One way to change the rules would be to broaden accounting practices to measure the impact of a corporation's activity for all the stakeholders—including the workers, the consumers, the local communities, the environment, and society at large—in addition to the stockholders. Called stakeholder or social accounting, this approach would compel corporations to measure their success by other yardsticks besides profitability and would give the stakeholders the information to hold corporations accountable.

Ralph Estes, professor of accounting at American University and one of the leading advocates of stakeholder accounting, makes the case this way:

> Each corporation will have an identified set of objectives. For some, it will be a small set, for others it will be fairly lengthy. General Electric, for example, identifies about ten—one of which [is] profitability to shareholders. The other ones . . . include matters like [being] a good employer, [providing] good products and services at a fair price, [being] a good citizen—there is no accounting for any of these. . . .
>
> Let's take the coal companies. Some 500 coal companies were cited by the Labor Department [in 1991] for doctoring their dust samples. . . . If the managers who made the decisions to falsify these dust samples had known that their annual report wasn't going to show simply revenues and expenses to stockholders, but was also going to show the benefits to workers in salaries and wages . . . and the cost to workers including projected future cost of black lung disease resulting from their actions in tampering with these dust samples, then it is almost certain that their decisions would have been different.[15]

Another way to change the rules of the game is to change the measures of business activity to include social, ethical, and environmental values. The task here is to take inventory of standard business measures and change them to reflect future-oriented values. For example, the definition of productivity could reflect calculations of environmental improvement and decline and favor more labor input. The use of the discount rate, a standard calculation of business that favors the present over the future, needs to be reevaluated and changed or replaced with better ways to quantify the effect of today's decisions on the future. In 1992, then senator Al Gore proposed in his book, *Earth in the Balance,* a

---

15. "Interview with Ralph Estes, Professor of Accounting, American University, Washington, D.C.," *Corporate Crime Reporter* 5, no. 41 (October 1991): 18–19.

global summit of government leaders to agree on changes to economic measures such as these for government decision making and suggested that business do likewise.[16]

The field of corporate social accounting gained momentum in the 1970s, and several of the major accounting organizations and one of the Big Six accounting firms published papers addressing ways to measure social impact. However, the interest fell off during the 1980s. Interestingly, efforts such as the CERES Principles have picked up on the work of social accounting and are pressuring corporations to move in this direction.

Efforts to change the measures of business activity are just beginning. For example, the Society of Logistics Engineers is setting up a project, described below, to incorporate environmental considerations into the life-cycle costing methodology for the engineering profession.

Building Infrastructure

The future-oriented pioneers recognize that their individual actions, while crucial, are not sufficient. They understand that they need to establish an infrastructure to link their efforts, learn from each other, and involve others to allow their vision to flourish across our society. What follows are brief reports on some of their infrastructure-building activities including ensuring that engineers bring environmental considerations into their practices (Society of Logistics Engineers), organizing social investing and business professionals (Social Investment Forum and Social Venture Network), bringing a socially and environmentally responsible business voice to the corporate policy (Businesses for Social Responsibility), organizing the marketplace for consumers and investors who want to see future-minded values incorporated into business practices (Co-op America); and building community (Sustainable Communities Projects).

Engineering and Technology: Society for Logistics Engineers

Pioneers within the Society for Logistics Engineers are setting up in the mid-1990s a project to change the way engineers calculate life-cycle costs, to incorporate pollution prevention goals into project/product design, and to foster the idea of sustainable development through system

---

16. Al Gore, "A Global Marshall Plan," *Earth in the Balance* (Boston: Houghton Mifflin Company, 1991), 337–47.

redesign. The project includes changing design guidelines to incorporate environmental concerns from the initial design of the project/product to taking care of waste generated by the project/product. This visionary project will have far-reaching influence on how engineers access the costs and benefits of building projects. The Society, with 10,000 members, has influence on its own members and works with other professional groups to agree on contemporary engineering practices.[17]

Investing: Social Investment Forum

Incorporated in 1985, the Social Investment Forum's mission is to bring social investing professionals together to learn from each other, bring others into the field, and help the field evolve. The idea behind social investing is to bring social, ethical, and environmental values into investment decisions. By 1994, the Forum, through its members, had seen the number of social investments multiply to over $625 billion. The numbers of social investment professionals, mutual and money market funds, and other socially screened investment products have also seen major growth over the years. Equally important, the Social Investment Forum has played a major role in defining what social investing is and in measuring its performance.

The Forum also plays an important educational role for social investing professionals. Its quarterly meetings are designed to provide continuing education credits for its members from the International Board of Standards and Practices for Certified Financial Planners. Thus, in its many roles, the Forum is bringing credibility, as well as growth, to social investing.

The Social Investment Forum provides infrastructure for the social investing industry. The industry, in turn, is made up of people who are both revitalizing existing investment institutions and creating new ones. Professionals interested in social investing initially started within existing investment companies.

As the work of the social investing pioneers has broadened and deepened, so have the reach and concerns of the industry. Initially focused on investing in the best and screening out the worst of the publicly traded companies from its portfolios, it then began to create both new products (for example, mutual funds and insurance products) and distribution companies (for example, financial planning companies specializing in

---

17. *Soletter: The Newsletter of the Society of Logistics Engineers* 27, no. 5 (May 1991): 1–4.

social investing) devoted entirely to social investing. In the mid-1990s, the industry also began to look at how it can do more direct—what it calls affirmative or proactive—investing in new vision businesses, affordable housing, and other new institutions.

For example, one of Calvert Group's mutual funds has both positive and negative social and environmental screens and channels 1 percent of the money invested in this fund into high impact, affirmative investing. One of the companies that benefits from this program in Industria Electrica Bella Vista, a solar panel distributor in the Dominican Republic that enables low-income rural households to purchase solar units at a rate lower than their monthly costs for kerosene. Another example of how Calvert Group's 1 percent for social change goes to work is the lending it supports through the Cascadia Revolving Loan Fund. One borrower, a Seattle-based women's publishing house, used a loan from Cascadia to help finance the publication of a book on domestic abuse.

A leader in the social investing industry, Calvert Group, based in Bethesda, Maryland, plans to make another social investing innovation in 1995 by offering a new High Impact Fund, 100 percent of which will go to this type of proactive social investment. This is a good sign for the direction of social investing—from screening out the negative to channeling money to high impact investing, where it is most needed, from affordable housing to energy efficiency to microenterprise.

The pioneers in social investing believe that social investing is a powerful way to build an infrastructure that is future-oriented. They believe it will help create a way of thinking and acting that will ultimately guide the financial markets to favor companies that promote a more socially and environmentally responsible society. They are working toward the day when social and environmental values become incorporated into market considerations and destructive companies pay the price with lower stock prices and higher cost of capital. Meanwhile, social investing, especially the proactive investing, helps create jobs and solutions to society's social and environmental problems today.

Business: Social Venture Network

The Social Venture Network brings together the founders and CEOs of businesses who identify themselves by their work to incorporate social and environmental practices into their business activities. The purpose of the Network is to create a support network in which these business leaders can help each other and get together to create new social ventures. The Social Venture Network is less than five years old, yet its members have already birthed many new businesses and organizations, including Businesses for Social Responsibility (see next section).

While the Network has not yet played the kind of role in defining socially responsible business criteria or measuring performance that the Social Investment Forum has for the social investing field, like the Forum, it provides a powerful mechanism for people with similar values and goals to meet, learn from each other, multiply their impact, and involve others.

Public Policy: Businesses for Social Responsibility

As yet another step in building infrastructure and changing the national agenda to incorporate future-oriented values, business leaders who share this vision are forming a new group, Businesses for Social Responsibility (BSR), to play a role in corporate policy. This group helps businesses learn how to incorporate socially and environmentally responsible policies and practices into their everyday work.

BSR takes on both general social issues (for example, the role businesses can play in eliminating child labor practices throughout the world) and issues that are more specific to business (for example, family leave policy). BSR's Eco-Efficiency Initiative, for example, helps both small and large businesses learn how to incorporate energy efficiency from manufacturing to building design to retrofitting. This brings both business benefits (saving money today) and contributes to future-oriented environmental goals (reducing carbon dioxide emissions to help address the threat of global warming).

Marketplace: Co-op America

Co-op America organizes individuals, in their roles as consumers and investors, to get involved in creating a just and sustainable economy. It provides them with information and practical strategies for incorporating social, environmental, and ethical values into the marketplace. Indeed, it provides an "alternative marketplace" where people can learn about, buy from, and invest in the new vision businesses as well as get involved in the new institutions, such as community-supported agriculture and co-housing.

The crucial infrastructure role Co-op America plays is in bringing individuals, businesses, and organizations together through various networks so that they can engage in market activity and thus build a more future-minded economy. Indeed, it is through Co-op America that many people first got involved in social investing, learned about South Shore

Bank and became out-of-state depositors, and bought products or accessed services through a new vision company. Thus, through its "marketing" function—as the "marketing arm" of the emerging responsible economy—Co-op America is providing yet another key part of the infrastructure for a society that incorporates future-oriented values into its thinking and actions.

By reporting on the new vision, ideas, institutions, and strategies of a sustainable ethic, Co-op America also provides an important counter to the "Madison Avenue" consumption ethic. Through its publications and public education campaigns, Co-op America makes information available to the public about the pioneers who are acting as if the future matters and gets more people involved. Through its reports and profiles of the work and satisfaction of other pioneers, Co-op America also shows that people *can* make changes—reduce consumption, invest in new vision businesses, and restructure institutions. Perhaps just as important, Co-op America's networks and publications help affirm and support people as they do the hard work of changing their thinking and actions. Taken together, these kinds of networks and publications show a powerful and appealing picture of people creating change and constructing more meaningful lives—connected to others, enjoying the present, and inventing new ways of thinking and acting that respect the future.

Community: Sustainable Communities Projects

Many of these pioneers are also meeting to discuss how to integrate their efforts and create sustainable communities based on the future-oriented values and practices. Some of these efforts are led by local government: for example, the Sustainable City Project, a tri-city collaboration among Portland, Oregon; San Francisco, California; and San Jose, California. Some are led through nongovernmental organizations such as the Environmental Resource Program at the University of North Carolina. Some, such as Urban Ecology in Berkeley, California, are working in their own communities as well as to build infrastructure for giving information to and exchanging ideas with people worldwide who are trying to create "Eco-Cities."[18]

What all these infrastructure efforts have in common is that they are

---

18. See *The Urban Ecologist* for regular reports on future-oriented efforts to transform communities into eco-cities worldwide. Reports in the summer 1992 issue include efforts in Maine; Ithaca, New York; Los Angeles, California; Greenwich Village, New York City; Portland, Oregon; Maryland; Everett, Washington; New Jersey; Havana, Cuba; the Netherlands; Toronto, Canada; and Zurich, Switzerland.

bringing together diverse groups to ask—and begin to answer—the question of how we can create a just and sustainable society with quality of life for all. Infrastructure efforts like these in engineering, investing, business, public policy, the marketplace, and the community are popping up in many different fields. Pioneers in many arenas—co-housing, for example—are creating their own groups. Many of the pioneers not only work in their own restructured institutions but also spend their time and money to ensure that the infrastructure organizations expand. These infrastructure activities signal that the future-minded pioneers are becoming increasingly sophisticated, recognizing the power of their vision, and identifying that they are numerous enough to make a broader impact and are willing to experiment with many different ways to incorporate their future-oriented values into American practice.

Conclusions

Several themes emerge from this brief field report on people acting as if the future matters:

> With respect to the "whole picture," these pioneers are still a very small group. With respect to context, their new or restructured institutions account for only a tiny part of the activity in our country.
>
> These pioneers seem to be coming together on their own and thinking through what makes sense from the ground up. They seem to be creating—or re-creating—structures because they feel blocked or frustrated by existing institutions. They seem to feel that the dominant public and private structures do not reflect their future-oriented values. They seem to be going around both public and private institutions to create their own and to send the message that both our public and private institutions must change if we are to act as if the future matters.
>
> The ways they are dealing with their frustration—by restructuring existing institutions, creating new institutions, changing the rules of the game, and building infrastructures to nurture and support their new institutions and changes—add up to powerful strategies for social change.
>
> Their new models and future-minded ways of doing business make a real difference today. As they build with a vision of the future and institutionalize future-oriented practices, they help solve immediate social and environmental problems. They create jobs, develop affordable housing, build business opportunities by pro-

tecting the environment, teach skills, and work for human rights from South Africa to Burma to the inner cities here in the United States.

Many of the new institutions they are creating involve community. Indeed, many of the new institutions have "community" in their names. This seems to indicate that the pioneers believe that the changes we need for the future must reflect the fact that we are individuals in community. It may also indicate that, as we learn which strategies and institutions will be successful, we will need to integrate and implement them at the community level. Indeed, to flourish and make an impact on the macroeconomic picture and the future, many of the new institutions will need broader implementation. Happily, many of the models can scale up. For example, the ideas of community land trusts and conservation easements could work in the national policy context, as Norway and Denmark successfully prove in the case of using an easement-like strategy in their agricultural policy.

Many of the new institutions are creating new financing mechanisms in order to get money to other pioneers to use for liberating their energy and ideas.

Many of the new institutions bring together unusual partners— private and nonprofit, business and government—to get the job done. The Shore Bank Corporation, for example, brings together for-profit and nonprofit subsidiaries so it can bring private, foundation, and government funding together to work on neighborhood redevelopment. The question that the pioneers ask is: what will work? They are willing to experiment with new structures and cut across the usual ways of doing business. What is interesting about these experiments is that they can help seed new ideas and values in all of the institutions they cut across—business, government, and nonprofit organizations alike.

Many of the new institutions have value not only as models and experiments but also in the experiential sense. For example, as more people live in co-housing communities and enjoy the benefits of a new way to mix public and private, they will want to create larger communities with the same spirit and values. Indeed, there are a few developers who are trying to redesign neighborhoods with similar concepts.[19] Their tasks will become easier as more people have the experience of enjoying the present within new structures that respect the future. As more people

---

19. See the *Utne Reader,* section on community design, May-June 1992, 93–106.

have experience within new institutions and in using new practices, the values that shape the institutions will also help shape the actions of the individuals.

There are logical next steps for the future development of these new institutions as they gain a stronghold and survive. For example, CDLFs could be expanded to aid in the financing of new vision businesses.

The new structures and practices can help create additional new institutions, infrastructures, and practices. As more people get involved in the new structures and practices, they may pave the way for private as well as local, state, and federal policy and even broader institutionalization of these values.

Additional institutional and legal support needs to evolve for these pioneering efforts to survive. For example, for the new vision businesses to flourish, we will need to evolve different evaluations of investment and risk, access to capital that reflects these new risk assessments, and changes to laws to allow companies to take actions toward goals on behalf of all their stakeholders that may not be specifically designed to maximize shareholder profits. Consumers and markets will need more information, like that of the social and environmental audit, to assess companies' progress on behalf of all their stakeholders and to decide whether or not to purchase from or invest in specific firms.

The work of the pioneers directly addresses the difficult social and environmental problems of our times. And, on another level, the models and empowerment they create as the result of their actions are the focus that will regenerate governments and markets to incorporate healthy social, ethical, and environmental future-oriented values.

Although the pioneers are a small group at present, their vision is large. They are creating an infrastructure, linking their efforts, and reaching out to involve others. Many of the pioneers not only work in their own restructured institutions, they also spend their time and money to ensure that the infrastructure organizations expand. They seem to understand that their individual efforts are essential *and* that they need to establish structures to allow their vision to flourish across our society.

Some of the experiments will succeed, and some will fail. Both the successes and the failures will be valuable for what we will all learn. These pioneers are changing the way we grow and buy food, organize housing, raise our children, structure work, cooperate with each other, and solve conflicts. They are sowing seeds, reweaving the fabric of daily life so that life on this planet can sustain itself and continue with joy. It is vital that we learn from the work of these pioneers as we all struggle to motivate other people, and ourselves, to act as if the future matters.

BIBLIOGRAPHY

Cook, Jack. 1991. "A Partnership of Consumers and Farmers." *Co-op America Quarterly* 3, no. 1 (Spring): 11–12.
Co-op America. 1991. *Co-op America's Socially Responsible Financial Planning Handbook.* Washington, D.C.: Co-op America.
Corporate Crime Reporter. 1991. "Interview with Ralph Estes, Professor of Accounting, American University, Washington, D.C." *Corporate Crime Reporter* 5, no. 41 (October): 18–19.
Gore, Al. 1992. *Earth in the Balance.* Boston: Houghton Mifflin Company.
Gravitz, Alisa. 1991. "Green Business: Truth or Consequence?" *Co-op America Quarterly* 3, no. 3 (Fall): 10–11.
Grzywinski, Ronald. 1991. "The New Old-Fashioned Banking." *Harvard Business Review,* May-June, 87–89.
McCamant, Kathryn, and Charles Durrett. 1989. "Building a Co-housing Community." *Co-op America Quarterly* 3, no. 1 (Spring): 13–15.
Meadows, Donnella. 1991. *The Global Citizen.* Washington, D.C.: Island Press.
Soletter: The Newsletter of the Society of Logistics Engineers 27, no. 5 (1992).
Urban Ecologist, Summer 1992.
Utne Reader, May-June 1992, 93–106.
Zorc, Anne. 1991. "Community Land Trusts." *Co-op America Quarterly* 3, no. 1 (Spring).

9

Energy for Development: Institutions, Incentives, and the Misallocation of Resources

Franklin Tugwell

The most capital-intensive sector in most developing countries is energy, where outlays for the construction of power plants and transmission and distribution lines—so important in facilitating economic growth—are enormously costly. The sector is important, too, because capital commitments tie a country to a set of technical alternatives for many decades. This essay focuses on the set of incentives and disincentives that are critical to shaping these commitments. More specifically, it points to the kinds of incentives that can prevent people from doing things that are irrational in the long term but that go against ingrained habits of thought and the institutional designs that shape everyday decisions. The essay will suggest some of the legal and institutional changes that will be required for countries to move to an economically and environmentally more sensible future.

A new and pervasive energy crisis is quietly overtaking many developing countries, threatening to nullify the hard-won economic advances of recent years. The first of these crises, triggered by the dramatic oil price increases in 1973 and 1978, shook the world economy and forced a major redistribution of income to the oil-rich nations. This time the crisis is caused not by OPEC price increases, but by the crumbling of electricity supply systems in country after country, the result of a decade of neglect and the lack of investment in electrical infrastructure despite continued growth in demand. The symptoms of the crisis are brownouts, blackouts, and a steady deterioration in the quality of power provided. To make matters worse, the enormous financial resources—exceeding $1 trillion over the next decade—needed to expand capacity will not be forthcoming from the traditional sources of these funds, the public and private international lending institutions. The problem is so serious that it will soon take its place as the most crippling single structural obstacle to economic progress in the third world.

Fortunately, renewable energy and energy efficiency technologies, many of which emerged as commercially viable alternatives only in the 1980s, may offer a means for many countries to provide needed energy services without relying on the traditional approach of building more large fossil fuel power plants and extending electricity grids over the countryside to consumers. Equally important, these new technologies, most clearly exemplified by developments in the United States in the 1980s, may also offer a means of providing the same benefits in environmentally more attractive ways.

In order to take full advantage of the opportunity provided by these technologies, however, it will be necessary for developing countries to embrace a new model of service delivery—called here the "developmental utility"—that threatens in important ways the worldview and control of state-run electric power monopolies. Put differently, the new approach will be possible only if governments and utilities prove willing to encourage private initiative in an area that, historically, they have insisted should remain the exclusive domain of the state. A major source of hope for those favoring this transition, however, stems from the crisis itself: turning to smaller-scale, private, renewable energy companies and to opportunities to increase efficiency of energy use has the potential to supply at least 30 percent of the needed power through private channels that will tap into different sources of funding. The alternatives discussed in this essay could, in fact, make up for almost all of the projected shortfall in foreign exchange financing estimated by the World Bank. This may be the only way for many countries to supply the energy needed to continue economic growth.

Background: Power Crisis in LDCs

Although the details differ by country, the common pattern in developing countries since the oil crises of the 1970s has been one of delays in the addition of new generating capacity by governments heavily indebted and strapped for foreign exchange. These delays have occurred despite a steady growth of demand for electricity—averaging nearly 7 percent per year in the last two decades. The result has been a sharp and accelerating decline in the efficiency and financial performance of state-owned public utilities and the onset of brownouts, blackouts, and periods of low-quality service as the gap between supply and demand has tightened in country after country.

The economic impact of this quiet but widespread decomposition of a key part of the economic infrastructure has been extensive. The cost to the economy of a kilowatt-hour shortage is reckoned at more than one dollar, on average, by those who have studied this extensively, while, in contrast, electricity typically costs 7 to 9 cents per kilowatt-hour to produce.[1] Faced with uncertainty in power supply and quality, industries in the most seriously afflicted countries have moved rapidly to self-generation by installing small diesel sets to back up the public grid or to replace it entirely.

In the Dominican Republic, perhaps the most notorious example, electricity for homes and businesses attached to the grid is available less than half the time and private generation capacity almost certainly now exceeds that of the national utility. This capacity, moreover, is nearly all in the form of small diesel systems that are both inefficient and increase the need for imported petroleum.[2] The duplication of an essential element of national infrastructure is not as visible as would be, for example, private roads built parallel to most public roads. But it is nevertheless enormously wasteful and expensive. As is so often the case, the impact has been most dramatic in rural areas, at the end of the distribution line, where power is least available and of the poorest quality.

The decay of national electricity supply systems in many developing countries has created a growing demand for governments to install new capacity, but it is clear that the financial resources for massive new power investments are simply not available. Based on the projections made by assembling the expansion plans of developing country utilities themselves, the World Bank recently estimated that capital investments of approximately $1 trillion, or $100 billion per year, will be needed to meet demand growth in the next decade. Of this, approximately $40 billion would have to be foreign exchange and $60 billion could be comprised of local currency.

Unfortunately, a review of public and private lending practices in the last decade makes it clear that these funds will simply not be available. As World Bank Energy Adviser Günter Schramm has noted, it appears unlikely that official lending institutions will increase their loans beyond the recent average level of approximately $7 billion per year, and private international banks, which have handled the bulk of power sector financing, are unlikely to return to these riskier loans in the near

---

1. A recent study of costs to the economy estimates, for example, that by the early 1980s India and Pakistan were losing between 1.5 percent and 1.8 percent of their entire GNP due to problems of electricity reliability and quality in the industrial sector alone. See D. W. Jones, et al., *The Impacts of Inadequate Electricity Supply in Developing Countries* (Washington, DC: U.S. Department of Energy, Oak Ridge National Laboratory, 1988).

2. This contrasts with private power generation, which is based on cogeneration technology and which is designed to contribute to the national power system as well as supply private energy needs.

future.[3] The World Bank projections thus suggest an annual shortfall of at least $30 billion a year in hard currency in addition to the local currency investments that will themselves be difficult to generate for state-owned public power projects. These facts have not yet resulted in a major reconsideration of utility expansion plans but will almost certainly force such a change in the next half decade.

The Promise of Renewable Energy and Energy Efficiency

At the same time that public power systems in many developing countries have been heading toward crisis, a very different transformation has been taking place in the electric power system of the United States. This transformation has been marked by the sudden growth of grid-connected smaller-scale renewable energy and cogeneration systems and the simultaneous upsurge in private investment in energy efficiency. The forces driving this transformation include: (a) the demise of the nuclear power industry; (b) the opening of the market to private power as a result of the Public Utilities Regulatory Policies Act of 1978 (PURPA); (c) the increased costs of large-scale fossil fuel projects caused by higher petroleum prices, their long lead times, and their need to address environmental problems; and (d) the maturing of a range of renewable energy technologies, most notably biomass cogeneration systems and wind-generating systems, the latter stimulated by early subsidies provided by the State of California (table 9.1).

Renewable energy systems now operate profitably at thousands of locations in the United States. In California alone, generating capacity provided by these technologies, including geothermal plants, wind farms, biomass burners, and solar-thermal troughs, amounts to many thousands of megawatts.[4] Biomass resources now provide more energy than hydroelectricity in the United States and contribute more than 9,000 megawatts to the public electricity supply. Cogeneration has become a profitable business in every state. And major utilities are now setting up programs designed to save hundreds of megawatts, and thus avoid new capacity additions, by purchasing savings from businesses specializing in this work (fig. 9.1).

---

3. Günter Schramm, "Issues and Problems in the Power Sector of Developing Countries," a background paper for the Stockholm Initiative on Energy, Environment and Sustainable Development, November 1991, 1–2.

4. This includes, for example, in the Pacific Gas & Electric service territory: over 1,000 megawatts of biomass, 1,100 megawatts of wind, 1,400 megawatts of geothermal, and 5,000 megawatts of hydro—most of which is smaller scale.

TABLE 9.1.   Renewable Energy Contributions to U.S. Supply in 1988

Source	Quads[a]	MMB Oil Equivalent	% of Total
Biomass	3.27	559.17	4.0
Geothermal	0.23	39.33	0.30
Hydropower	3.14	536.94	3.8
Solar Photovoltaic	0.05	8.55	0.06
Wind	0.02	3.42	0.02

Source: U.S. Export Council for Renewable Energy.
[a]Quadrillion BTUs.

An interesting feature of this transformation is that few Americans are actually aware of what has happened. In the immediate aftermath of the oil crises of the 1970s, renewable energy technologies received a great deal of attention and, during the Carter Administration, public funding to support their development and introduction. When oil prices declined and the Reagan Administration decided to cut public support for solar-based technologies, public attention shifted to other concerns.

Still another feature is the environmental attractiveness of these new technologies. Although no energy technologies are without their environmental impacts—biomass energy, for example, must be adopted with careful attention to the impact on soils and species diversity—there is a broad consensus on the attractiveness of renewable energy systems as part of the solution to our global environmental quandary.[5] Renewable energy systems rely on resources such as sunlight, wind, water, and biomass to generate power. When compared to the nuclear or fossil fuel alternatives they displace, renewable energy systems employ more people, are environmentally more benign, are smaller in scale, are often cheaper when external costs are accounted for, and are often economically more attractive for the country as a whole because they do not require the importation of oil, coal, or uranium-derived fuel. A recent study by the Environmental Protection Agency, to cite but one example, concluded that renewable energy systems—hydro, biomass, wind, and solar technologies—could account for more than 60 percent of the reasonably attainable reductions in carbon dioxide emissions in the next 20 years.

---

5. Most biomass cogeneration power systems utilize wastes that are currently burned in an inefficient manner on fields or in incinerators. The materials involved—such as sawdust or bagasse—are not easily returned to the soil, and their use in high-pressure and high-temperature combustion reduces the particulate emissions that current disposal techniques cause.

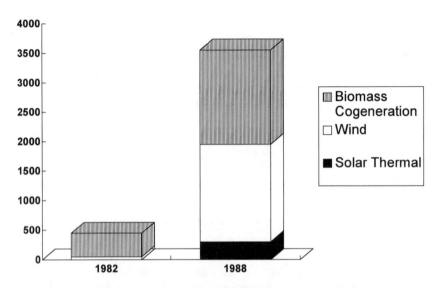

Fig. 9.1. Expansion of utility-connected biomass, wind, and solar thermal power in the United States, 1982–88

The contrast with most of the developing countries is dramatic. Precisely where domestic, environmentally sound, privately financed sources of energy are most needed for the future, they are conspicuously absent. While sugar mills in Hawaii produce 11 percent of the state's electricity, those in Brazil, India, and Indonesia—with sugar industries many times the size—contribute nothing. While Maine's forests generate wood residues sufficient to provide 38 percent of that state's base-load power, developing countries with similar industries in Central America and Southeast Asia burn their residues in open pits, contributing to atmospheric pollution. While utilities plan giant new fossil systems in Pakistan, China, and the Philippines, opportunities for increased efficiency and for small hydro, biomass cogeneration, and wind power go neglected.

The same contrast can be seen in the area of energy efficiency. Since the energy crises of the late 1970s, investments in conservation in the United States have displaced the equivalent of 14 million barrels per day at a savings of some $160 billion per year.[6] Between 1979 and 1986, the intensity of energy use (or the amount of energy needed to produce a

---

6. Michael Phillips, *The Least-Cost Energy Path for Developing Countries* (Washington, DC: International Institute for Energy Conservation, 1991), xii.

unit of GDP) dropped in the Organization for Economic Cooperation and Development (OECD) group an average of 2 to 3 percent per year. In the developing countries, the intensity of energy use remained unchanged during the same period.[7]

The Central-Station Model and Its Problems

It is now becoming quite clear that the quiet growth of smaller-scale renewable energy and energy efficiency technologies, led by private companies, and the institutional changes that have spurred and accompanied this growth, are but a harbinger of a much more comprehensive transformation in energy service systems that will almost certainly occur around the world in the next century. The implications of these changes are particularly profound for developing countries, precisely because so many of them are at a relatively early stage in the development of their national power systems.

Put concisely, the old central-station utility model, in which a few giant facilities, owned by public monopolies, generate power and distribute it over a massive grid to consumers, is technically and institutionally obsolete. So too are the heavily financed rural electrification programs, for decades supported by donor institutions. Both of these will be replaced over time by a new pattern—called here the developmental utility model—in which large numbers of smaller-scale, distributed power systems and grids, carefully optimized by new management systems, provide energy services, including assistance in achieving conservation and efficiency, that are cheaper and more environmentally benign.

The contrast between the central-station and developmental utility models is both physical and operational. The standard image of the growth of energy services is of a grid, extending from a major power plant, that encompasses ever larger portions of a rural population. The technical justification for this model has always been the belief that the very large power plants—now normally as large as 500 to 1000 megawatts of power—are so efficient that they represent the only economically justifiable way to produce electricity. From this belief has grown the centralized public power monopoly and the history of rural electrification programs subsidized heavily by governments and international lending institutions.

---

7. World Bank, Industry and Energy Department, "Energy Efficiency and Conservation in the Developing World," working paper (Washington, DC: World Bank, spring 1992), 8.

This image has been effectively challenged by a number of unheralded advances in (*a*) the efficiency of the smaller-scale generation, cogeneration, and end-use technologies noted earlier; (*b*) our knowledge of the much higher true costs (economic and environmental) of existing energy service delivery systems, and (*c*) our improved understanding of the ways in which privately financed, developed, and managed power systems can contribute to the provision of energy services.

The increases in efficiency of smaller-scale generation systems, such as those used to convert biomass, wind, and sunlight to electricity, has occurred partly as a result of incremental advances in research and development—true in particular for solar photovoltaic systems—and partly due to practical experience and scale-ups that have resulted from the growing market for power created by the U.S. legislation described below. The direct conversion of sunlight to electricity can now be accomplished at a cost (35 to 50 cents per kilowatt-hour) that is one-tenth that of a decade ago, and wind and solar-thermal systems, in the best locations, are now fully competitive (at 7 to 9 cents per kilowatt-hour) with the cheapest "clean" coal-fired systems (those that include equipment to clean up emissions to meet the stricter air quality standards in many parts of the United States) (see figure 9.2). Biomass conversion, while for the most part based on standard steam generation technology, has benefited from the opportunity to cogenerate, allowing those installing these systems to use the energy produced for several purposes at the same time. In addition, experience with handling and converting some of the most difficult biomass fuels, such as abrasive rice hulls, has led to the emergence of reliable equipment where none existed before.

While the central-station model completely dominated the analysis of power service options, analysts paid too little attention to the full costs of energy service delivery. Rough comparisons of the cost of production at the power plant—coal-fired power at 7 cents per kilowatt hour, for , example, versus biomass-fueled power at 12 cents or solar power at 35 cents—dominated discussions of technical alternatives. Missing from these discussions were such things as the costs of service interruptions; poor quality power; transmission and distribution; systems losses, often as much as 15 to 25 percent in developing countries; and environmental damage. Rural electrification programs, in particular, have often required very heavy subsidies since the true costs of delivering four or five hours of low-level power to remote households, over long transmission and distribution systems, often exceeds 35 to 40 cents per kilowatt hour of service delivered. With the household paying a subsidized tariff of 2 or 3 cents for this power, utilities face the prospect of deepening financial difficulty for each new customer added to the system.

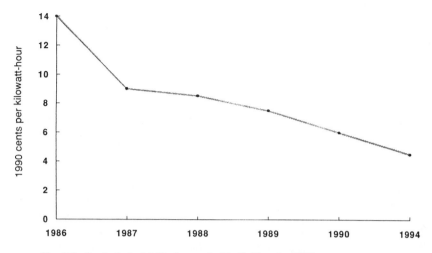

Fig. 9.2. Cost of electricity from wind in California, 1990

    In contrast, distributed, smaller-scale renewable systems such as biomass cogeneration, small hydro, or even home-solar lighting systems, generate power closer to the point of consumption, thus eliminating long transmission and distribution systems. They can also be built by private companies able to mobilize the financing on their own.

    The pattern suggested by the new technologies and our improved understanding of costs is not of a grid extending outward from a central power station located at or near the capital city. It is, rather, of a much more diverse pattern of emerging centers of power production centered on different, distributed resources. Miniutilities based on small hydro projects, sugar or rice mill cogeneration plants, or wind farms near the coast all form centers of energy services, only later to be linked together in regional and then national grids. The new model is of a national energy service system, in effect, growing from the outside in, with the final configuration reliant much more heavily on new distributed centers of generation.

    These new technical and institutional possibilities are an especially important option for developing countries. In the industrialized countries of the world, the transition to distributed power will take half a century or more because infrastructure investments are already so great and new technologies and associated management systems can only be introduced gradually. In developing countries, by contrast, the transformation can move much more rapidly since electric supply systems have yet to be built. In Indonesia, for example, only 6 percent of the people are on the national electric grid. A majority of the country's 7,000 islands have not been bound into the central-station utility system. And, of course, smaller-scale projects can come on line much more quickly, often within 18 months of the decision to go forward.

The Obstacles to Change

Unfortunately, the major institutions that shape the energy future of developing countries—governments, utilities, and international lending institutions—are firmly grounded in the old "central-station plus rural electrification" model and are unlikely to seriously revise their approach for many years unless they are forced to do so. There are simply too many institutional and personal attachments to the old ways. Utility managers and their engineers have been trained in central-station technologies and management concepts, while governments and financing institutions are uncomfortable with the private decision making and control that the new developmental utility model requires.

Among the most important obstacles to the transition to the new model of energy service delivery are the legal and policy barriers that exist in developing countries. The clearest of these is the lack of private power laws. The generation and transmission of electricity in nearly every developing country is a legally established monopoly controlled by a large, centralized state utility company. These companies have been responsible for building power plants and extending the grid to meet the growing demands for power in rural areas. Unfortunately, in many respects they have come to exemplify the worst features of public sector mismanagement, marked in most instances by corruption, inefficiency, and continual political meddling. In this context, a key problem is that, in expanding supply, they have focused almost exclusively on building very large centralized power systems, systems relying mainly on fossil or nuclear fuels and built on a turnkey basis by large foreign contracting companies. They have also consistently opposed efforts to allow private persons and corporations to enter the power market, even where, as in the case of cogeneration, this would allow a much more efficient use of resources and the production of power at a lower cost to the public. In doing this, they have responded to clear organizational and political incentives, seeking centralized control and trying to satisfy the demands of political patrons, usually by extending the grid to important communities or regions of the country.

The experience of the United States is quite relevant here since the innovative U.S. private power law, the Public Utilities Regulatory Policies Act (PURPA) of 1978, was so important in unleashing the heretofore suppressed potential of independent cogeneration and renewable energy facilities. The PURPA required utilities to purchase power from these facilities when that power met the standard of providing electricity at a cost that was below the "avoided cost" of the utility—with avoided cost interpreted to mean, roughly, the cost that the utility would have to pay for increments of power from the next plant the utility would build to meet demand. Put differently, if a private producer, by being more efficient and/or utilizing waste heat effectively (for process heat or air conditioning), could equal or better the utility cost of power, the utility was now required to buy the power offered.

What is critical here, of course, is the change in the incentive structure for this key sector of society. Profits returned to the innovative and efficient replaced centralized control and political efficacy in developing new sources of supply. As a direct result of this law, more than one-third of all the new power capacity added in the United States since the mid-1980s has come from more than 3,000 independent power projects. Utilities suddenly found themselves buying power produced from agricultural and forestry wastes, wind, and hydro facilities, most of them smaller than any power planner would have paid attention to before the passage of private power legislation. Unfortunately, despite compelling arguments, grounded in efficiency, supporting cogeneration and renewable energy, no developing country has adopted and implemented laws truly favoring such power production.[8]

The technical attributes of renewable energy systems make them particularly dependent on the existence of laws and policies favoring private power development: though small, they are rarely amenable to standardization. This means that the development of a particular site requires detailed attention to specific fuel or climatic attributes as well as the design of equipment that fits that fuel and the site quite closely. In addition, in the case of biomass cogeneration, because the uses of steam for cogeneration are likely to be industry specific, the involvement of specialists understanding each industry is critically important. All of this means that the deployment of these small power sources is heavily dependent on the existence of a cadre of entrepreneurial "developers" who identify opportunities, tailor technical systems to specific sites, and work closely with the industries involved. The role of energy "developer," unfortunately, is hardly one suited to utility managers. For smaller-scale

---

8. Private power laws have been passed in a number of countries, notably Costa Rica, Indonesia, Thailand, Pakistan, and the Dominican Republic, but the implementation has been slow and it remains unclear in these cases whether the laws will be matched by the policies needed to make them effective.

renewable energy to become widespread, in other words, private power entrepreneurship is likely to be a necessity—at least at the outset. Unless laws exist to allow private power sales to the grid, these smaller systems will almost never become the focus of utility power planning.

The problems posed by utilities' dislike for smaller-scale, private power development is well enough understood. Utilities in the United States and around the world have been in the business of building and selling power for 70 years. They are unhappy with private power because it implies that utilities are incapable of accomplishing their historical task. At the same time, utilities have been reluctant to develop cogeneration or smaller-scale power opportunities themselves, partly from an engineering commitment to plant (rather than energy system) efficiency and partly from reluctance to cede control over any portion of the electric supply system. Moreover, utility managers in developing countries are often a decade or so behind in terms of their understanding of trends in both technology and policy.

An important corollary to this problem is that, on the one hand, utilities tend to be much more powerful in developing countries, and, on the other, private sector institutions of any kind in the provision of services are less acceptable. Absent crisis conditions and a clear understanding of the lessons—both good and bad—stemming from American experience, governments are unlikely to move quickly to diversified, dispersed energy systems that include smaller-scale private power and cogeneration plants. Clearly, however, a change in utility attitudes is essential if renewable energy is to reach its economic potential around the world. In effect, renewable energy requires that utilities become friendly to smaller-scale, dispersed energy generation for a significant part—perhaps as much as one-third—of the power supply in their system.

Although there has been widespread acknowledgment of the movement toward private power production, what is needed is legislation requiring utilities to offer contracts, on clear and reasonable avoided-cost terms, to those seeking to sell electricity. Vaguely worded statutes, the norm in most developing countries, are often ineffective in changing the rules of the game. Utilities fighting to retain control, for example, often interpret *avoided cost* to mean avoided *average* cost rather than *marginal* cost. This allows them to include the cost of power produced from plants built many years ago when construction costs were lower and currencies had a higher value. Or they insist on very high reliability or dispatchability in power supply, often hard to achieve in small systems (but also of little significance precisely because of the small amount of electricity involved). In sum, private power laws that are not clear and compelling will be easily circumvented by utilities, and the incentives to private entrepreneurship in this sector will not prove powerful enough to change behavior.

Existing policies and practices of financial institutions are also an important barrier. The costs of financial packaging for small-scale power systems is very high in comparison to larger systems, and private and public banks are often unwilling to pay these costs. This problem is particularly acute in the case of international power project development because the costs (and risks) are still higher and because the institutions making energy project or "sector" loans almost always work directly with governments and utilities.

The World Bank and its sister regional development banks, for example, make energy loans to governments in very large sums—typically several hundreds of millions of dollars—and these are then handled by state-run utilities. Dishing these funds out to a wide variety of small-scale power projects is simply not within the institutional capability of these organizations. The same tends to be true of foreign aid institutions. Even the International Finance Corporation (IFC), designated as the mechanism to support private international development projects, sets $10 million (U.S.) as the minimum loan size. This problem is compounded abroad because of the structure of loan and equity markets, which often make it very difficult to quickly assemble financing of the kind needed for smaller energy projects.

The most striking confirmation of the continuing power of the central-station model and the associated institutional and financial obstacles to renewable energy in developing countries is provided by a recent survey by the World Bank of actual capacity expansion plans. Completed in early 1990, the study revealed that developing countries currently plan no small-scale renewable energy systems at all as part of the new 384,000 megawatts of commercial capacity projected for the next decade (fig. 9.3). A review of past lending activities, incidentally, reveals virtually no lending in this area by the World Bank and the Inter-American Development Bank.[9]

Forecasts prepared by Winrock International Institute for Agricultural Development, in contrast, suggest that renewable energy can provide as much as 15 to 20 percent of the total, at a cost that is equal to, or lower than, the giant coal, oil, or nuclear facilities currently planned

---

9. World Bank, "Capital Expenditures for Electric Power in the Developing Countries in the 1990's," Industry and Energy Department Working Paper, Energy Series no. 21 (Washington, DC: World Bank, 1992), 4. See U.S. Export Council for Renewable Energy, "Energy Lending at the World Bank and Inter-American Development Bank" (Washington, DC: World Bank, 1990).

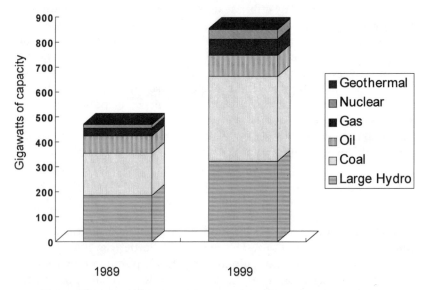

Fig. 9.3. Projected LDC generating capacity additions, 1989–99, without conservation and renewables

(fig. 9.4).[10] If incentive patterns are changed to induce private investors to develop these, it would mean governments could avoid adding at least 57,000 megawatts in capacity and the associated increased public indebtedness of over $156 billion.[11] A study sponsored by U.S. AID estimates that another 15 percent of planned new conventional capacity can be avoided entirely by the introduction of technologies and management techniques designed to improve energy efficiency.[12] Assuming that these

10. These sources can be developed in a quarter of the time it takes to put on line the giant fossil, hydro, or nuclear facilities. For an estimate of the biomass potential in this picture, see Franklin Tugwell, "Prospects and Problems of Biomass Energy Development in the Third World," in *Proceedings from the 1990 Conference on Biomass for Utility Applications,* Electric Power Research Institute, 1991. Note that the recent study of the potential of renewable energy by the U.S. Department of Energy suggests that the goal of 15 percent contribution is plausible even in the United States. See *The Potential of Renewable Energy: An Interlaboratory White Paper* (Washington, DC: U.S. Department of Energy, 1990).

11. Based on the assumption of average capital expenditures of $2,731 per kilowatt capacity, from World Bank, "Capital Expenditures," 94.

12. U.S. AID, "Power Shortages in Developing Countries: Magnitude, Impacts, Solutions and the Role of the Private Sector" (Washington, DC: U.S. AID, March 1988), 13. This study suggests, in fact, that much larger savings could be achieved by the inclusion of improved power production and distribution and demand-side management programs. The estimate here is reduced to reflect an estimate of savings available by the sale, by

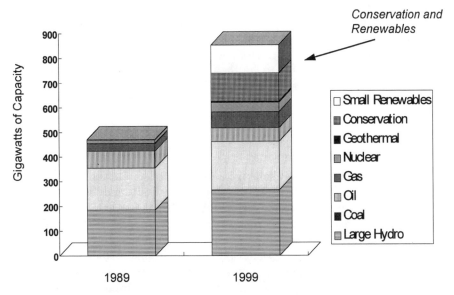

Fig. 9.4. Projected LDC generating capacity additions, 1989–99, with conservation and renewables

renewable energy and energy-efficiency contributions displace coal- or oil-fired capacity, this would result in a reduction in CO_2 emissions of 500 to 600 million tons per year, not to mention a significant reduction in air pollution, acid rain, and land contamination caused by waste disposal.[13]

In practice, there appear to be two conditions under which utility managers will change their views concerning privately produced power and renewable energy. One is when the political elites come to favor such a change, and the second is when they discover that they cannot fulfill their technical mandate without doing so. Fortunately, political elites are increasingly aware that their citizens expect the government to assure the enhancement of life that comes with electric power in homes and workplaces, but they are also aware that they cannot continue to borrow from traditional sources to meet this demand. Similarly, utilities are

---

private companies, of energy efficiency services, excluding such things as improved transmission and distribution systems. Figures here use the World Bank study assumption of capital costs of $2,731 (U.S.) per kilowatt of capacity.

13. Based on a simple calculation of annual CO_2 emissions of 4,244 tons per megawatt for a modern oil-fired facility, and 5.254 tons per megawatt for a modern coal-fired facility. Also assume that the biomass component of the renewable power is sustainable and thus results in no net CO_2 addition.

increasingly concerned about their own institutional future as the quality of the service they can supply—even to existing customers—slowly decays. In this respect, the very crisis in the power sector may force recalcitrant institutions to view private, and privately financed, smaller-scale renewable energy systems to be their only recourse (see fig. 9.5). In short, the crisis may force a change in incentives as those in authority seek solutions to assure their own political and institutional survival.

Conclusion

This, in a nutshell, is the challenge and the opportunity for those who understand the promise of the developmental utility model: to make sure that the future depicted by the World Bank—in which there is virtually no development of renewable energy systems in developing countries—does not come to pass; to help change incentive systems to those favorable to more cost-effective and environmentally responsible technologies in the developing countries; and to do so in such a way as to help developing country leaders and institutions continue this in the future. The savings would be enormous. Just as important, the new energy services would be more environmentally acceptable and rely on fuels produced domestically, thus freeing scarce foreign exchange for more pressing needs. And beyond this first decade the savings would continue.

To recapitulate, it is increasingly clear that renewable energy and energy efficiency represent an important opportunity for developing countries to alleviate the ongoing deterioration of their energy services, services so critical to economic development. But it is equally clear that to take advantage of these alternatives requires a transformation of the institutional and regulatory framework of power production and distribution and, most important, of the incentives that keep the existing framework dominant. More specifically, it requires laws that encourage private power and cogeneration; utilities that are friendly to small-scale, distributed energy systems; and national policies that in some fashion incorporate key external costs of energy production. Fortunately, it appears increasingly likely that the growing crisis in the power sectors of many developing countries is creating conditions that will rapidly alter incentives in favor of these policy and institutional changes. Faced with a growing demand for power-related services but unable to find the financial resources to meet this demand, political leaders and utilities will be increasingly pressured to turn to private power and to favor smaller-scale renewable technologies that do not entail large new commitments to import fossil fuels—thus draining scarce hard currency reserves.

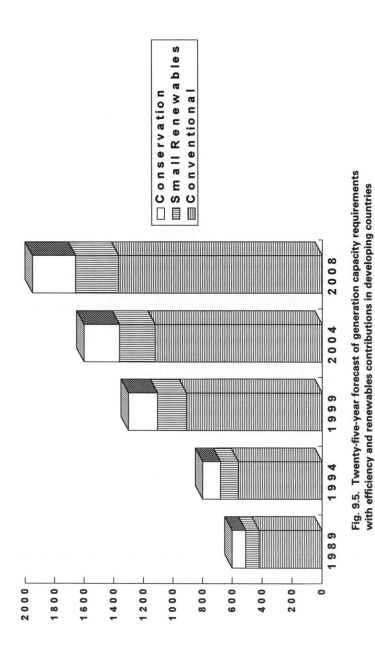

Gigawatts of Capacity

□ Conservation
▤ Small Renewables
▥ Conventional

1989   1994   1999   2004   2008

Fig. 9.5. Twenty-five-year forecast of generation capacity requirements
with efficiency and renewables contributions in developing countries

BIBLIOGRAPHY

Jones, D. W. 1988. *The Impact of Inadequate Electricity Supply in Developing Countries*. Washington, DC: U.S. Department of Energy, Oak Ridge National Laboratory.

Phillips, Michael. 1991. *The Least-Cost Path for Developing Countries*. Washington, DC : International Institute for Energy Conservation.

Schramm, Günter. 1991. *Issues and Problems in the Power Sector of Developing Countries*. A background paper for the Stockholm Initiative on Energy, Environment and Sustainable Development.

Tugwell, Franklin. 1991. "Prospects and Problems of Biomass Energy Development in the Third World." In *Proceedings from the 1990 Conference on Biomass for Utility Application*. Charlotte, NC: Electric Power Research Institute.

U.S. AID. 1988. *Power Shortage in Developing Countries: Magnitude, Impacts, Solutions and the Role of the Private Sector*. Washington, DC: U.S. AID.

U.S. Department of Energy. 1990. *The Potential of Renewable Energy: An Interlaboratory White Paper*. Washington, DC: U.S. Department of Energy.

U.S. Export Council for Renewable Energy. 1991. "Energy Lending at the World Bank and Inter-American Development Bank." Washington, DC: U.S. Export Council for Renewable Energy.

World Bank. 1990. "Capital Expenditure for Electric Power in the Developing Countries in the 1990's." Working Paper No. 21. Washington, DC: World Bank, Industry and Energy Department.

World Bank. 1992. "Energy Efficiency and Conservation in the Developing World." Working Paper. Washington, DC: World Bank, Industry and Energy Department.

10

Leadership for Sustainable Development: Some Reflections on the Central and Eastern European Experience

Zbigniew Bochniarz

Five years after the beginning of the revolution in Eastern Europe that swept like a flood through all the countries in the region, it is time to look back and ask some basic questions. First of all, are these radical changes sustainable? What are the major threats to this revolution? Second, are there new concepts of development emerging from these changes? Is this development path sustainable? Finally, is leadership for sustainable development emerging in the region?

While political backlash from the old totalitarian regime seems to have subsided in most Central and Eastern European (CEE) countries, this does not mean that there is no threat to new democracies in the area. The building and stabilization of new democratic institutions is a long and painful social process. In some cases, the new institutions are less effective than expected, and in some extreme cases they are even less effective than the old institutions. This creates disappointment and an outcry for a "strong" government with a charismatic leader who leans toward the right rather than the left.

CEE societies are astonished, frustrated, and fed up with the scope and intensity of fighting among parties who not long ago had created an anticommunist coalition. In such circumstances, there is declining trust in new democratic institutions such as parliaments, in favor of the army, the police, or particularly strong personalities.[1] These are not good signs for new democracies or for their prospects. They portend that in order to stabilize new democratic institutions, much work remains beyond establishing free elections and freedom of speech.

There is a common perception that CEE societies seem to be preoc-

---

1. See, for example, systematically published Polish opinion surveys linked to the Government daily newspaper *Rzeczpopolita*.

cupied with coping with everyday problems caused by the still serious economic crisis. In such circumstances, however, it is surprising that in a Gallup poll conducted in Hungary, Poland, and Russia and released at the beginning of July 1992, the environment was regarded as "the most important issue in their lives at present."[2] It is also interesting what the survey revealed: "that most people in all three countries believe the protection of the environment is more important than economic development."[3] A couple of months earlier, a survey was conducted in Poland that revealed that poisoning the environment was placed second, just after increasing criminality but before alcoholism, AIDS, and cancer, among the major threats facing current societies.[4]

Despite all the above mentioned political and economic problems, CEE nations understand better than ever that the deteriorated environment in CEE countries due to decades of wasteful economic practices and a totalitarian political system threatens their health and lives. They also understand better than other societies that heavily polluted air, water, and soil, contaminated food, shrinking biodiversity, growing morbidity and mortality caused by a degraded environment, and declining life expectancy create serious barriers to development.

Dependence on high-sulfur coal in several of these countries has created alarming industrial pollution problems. Enterprises were "encouraged" to wastefully consume heavily subsidized natural resources and energy while lack of effective pollution control legislation and technology—especially in heavy industry and in power plants—further worsened the devastating impacts on the environment.

Air pollution is a major environmental problem in several CEE countries, including the Czech Republic, Slovakia, Poland, Hungary, and Bulgaria. The most critical area for air pollution within the region is the "Black Triangle," located in northern Bohemia and northern Moravia (the Czech Republic), Silesia (Poland), and southern Saxony and Lusatia (Germany). This region is often viewed as the most polluted area in the world.

---

2. "Environment a Top Concern, Poll Reveals," *Budapest Week: Hungary's International Weekly:* 2, no. 17 (July 2–8, 1992).

3. Ibid.

4. T. Burger, *Świadomość ekologiczna: Między lękiem a działaniem* (Ecological Awareness: Between Fear and Acting), *Report,* Institute for Sustainable Development, Warsaw, 1/1992. This report based on a national survey conducted on February 6–12, 1992, by the Center of Public Opinion Research (CBOS) is part of a joint research project of the Institute for Sustainable Development and the Humphrey Institute of Public Affairs at the University of Minnesota on "Monitoring of Institutional Changes towards the Implementation of Sustainable Development Policy in Poland."

Water purity is another critical environmental problem in the region. The quality of water has deteriorated continuously for 25 years in most of these countries, resulting in a widespread deficit of potable drinking water. There is also growing evidence of adverse effects on human health in the most polluted areas. For many years, this data was prohibited from publication. Although no one questions the linkage between pollution and human health, the precise changes in metabolism due to environmental contamination in human organisms are, in many cases, not well known. Despite the present limitations of medical research, there are several demonstrable features of the most polluted areas in terms of human health and life expectancy. The average life expectancy at birth for a male in the region is about 65 to 67 years and has been declining or stagnant in CEE countries. Life expectancy for middle-aged males has declined so that it is lower than it was in the 1950s. In contrast, female life expectancy in the region is about 72 to 74 years. In Poland, infant mortality is two times higher in areas of environmental hazards, which cover about 11 percent of the territory and are inhabited by about 35 percent of the population. In addition, children are diagnosed with heavy multidefect syndromes with increased frequency in these areas.[5]

Industrial pollution has caused serious decline in the productivity of natural resources such as soil and forests. About half of all forests in the CEE region are already damaged to different degrees by acid rain, and the productive yield of these forests is shrinking. In the most industrialized countries of CEE, about 35 percent of the arable land is endangered, and in some areas it has already been necessary to prohibit cultivation of lands for food production (e.g., the areas of Legnica-Glogow copper mining in Poland).

In view of these facts, radical political and economic reforms cannot be sustained in the CEE region without radical institutional reform for sustainable development. These are the primary reasons that the concept of sustainable development not only was well received in the region but also has been institutionalized in some cases. For instance, in the roundtable negotiations between the Polish Government and its allies and the Solidarity-led opposition, the idea of sustainable development was incorporated into the final agreement at the Ecological Roundtable in early spring 1989. Among the most outspoken supporters of the concept of sustainable development at the Earth Summit in Rio de Janeiro were the Bulgarian and Czech presidents, Zhelyu Zhelev and Václav

---

5. *National Report of the Czech and Slovak Federal Republic*, 1991, 21–22.

Havel. There are many other examples that demonstrate that the concept of sustainable development is gaining momentum, but there is still a difference between even the most powerful declaration and real commitment and actions.

Current market reforms broke the back of the old central planning system in most of these countries. There is, however, a question about whether the market system is a panacea for all the deficiencies of the previous system. More broadly, is the market itself able to bring these countries along a sustainable path of development?

There is a strong belief among some of the region's leaders, especially among the finance ministers, that the market will solve all deficiencies in the allocation of resources and so put these countries on a path toward sustainable development. Unfortunately, this is not true, despite the crucial role of the market in efficient allocation of resources. In economic theory, as well as in current practices, there are well-known market failures. Consequently, in contemporary society a market has to be institutionally arranged in a particular way to correct its failures. Properly regulated markets are treated as one of the basic preconditions of successful institutional reform for sustainable development, along with a democratic institutional setup and well-developed ecological awareness in the society.[6]

The strong and often naive belief in the omnipotence of the "invisible hand" of the market presents an interesting reaction to the failure of the Soviet-type centrally planned economy. Seventy years of experience indicate that an economy run by central planners by means of numerous plan-targets oriented on maximization of production will always destroy the environment, despite political declarations and even environmental plan-targets. There remains, however, an interesting theoretical question: would an indirect centrally planned economy with democratic political institutions prevent environmental degradation and wasteful allocation of resources? Unfortunately, there is no practical experience to answer this question.

As old institutions disappear, and a vacuum for new ones emerges, the transition period in CEE countries creates a unique opportunity to design and implement radical institutional reform for sustainable development. This is the moment when well-designed foreign assistance programs could help the most.

---

6. Z. Bochniarz, R. Bolan, eds. *Designing Institutions for Sustainable Development: A New Challenge for Poland* (Minneapolis-Białystok: Białystok Technical University Press, 1991), 304.

Background Activities

In 1987, when a small research project on economic mechanisms for environmental protection in CEE was initiated at the Hubert H. Humphrey Institute of Public Affairs (University of Minnesota), its principal investigators did not even dream that it would be the beginning of a long and continuing journey throughout the region. The project not only produced policy recommendations but also resulted in the launching of a new program of institutional design for environmental protection in CEE countries. A team of scholars based in Poland, Hungary, the Czech Republic, Bulgaria, and at the Humphrey Institute has been engaged in a multidisciplinary collaborative effort regarding institutional design in the area of environmental protection and development and, in particular, economic restructuring. Its work focuses on comparative research and design activities for the newly democratized countries in the CEE region. These nations are of particular interest because, since 1989, they have been undergoing rapid and significant changes, moving from totalitarian political systems and centrally planned economies to democracy and free markets. Collectively, they also comprise one of the most heavily polluted regions on earth and have a significantly adverse impact on regional and global ecosystems.

The work plan proceeds in stages, beginning with a study of each of the individual countries and their emerging institutional framework of economic, social, and political organization. After a period of background research and documentation of environmental, social, and economic conditions, an overall "strategic plan" or "blueprint" for institutional reform is prepared as a guide for national strategy. The preparation of the blueprint involves the collaborative effort of leading environmentalists from each country working with the Humphrey Institute team. From this blueprint, a series of follow-up activities are undertaken to help in disseminating the blueprint proposals. A major mechanism of this follow-up work is the creation of a "catalytic institution"—a nongovernmental organization designed to function permanently in each of the four countries both to promote new institutional development and to monitor institutional effectiveness on an ongoing basis. Another feature of the follow-up program is evaluation research, which involves examining the effectiveness of each country's environmental efforts and of the role of the blueprint and the "catalytic institution" in stimulating effective public and private action toward sustainable development.

The above mentioned full cycle of activities—from environmental policy research through institutional design for sustainable development to capacity building for sustainable development—was developed during the last five years in Poland, which was the first country in the region to undertake the project. In collaboration with Polish governmental and nongovernmental experts and organizations, the Blueprint—*The Declaration of Sustainable Development*—was prepared and widely distributed (more than 3,000 copies) and a catalytic institution—the Institute for Sustainable Development in Warsaw—was founded and is currently in operation.

It is worth noting that these efforts have already had a significant impact in Poland. The Polish parliament adopted a policy of sustainable development following many of the principles and recommendations set forth in the *Declaration* in May 1991. The *Declaration* was highly instrumental in shaping the reorganization of the Ministry of Environment, Natural Resources, and Forestry in 1991–92. It has been used actively in drafting new environmental legislation, and principles of sustainable development are being considered by the commission engaged in drafting a new constitution. The *Declaration* served as a basis for consultations with members of parliament and with members of the government, including Prime Minister Bielecki, who succeeded in establishing the ECOFUND—the first debt-for-environment-swap in the CEE region. Follow-up workshops have been held in seven different regions of Poland and have attracted more than 650 local and regional government officials, representatives of nongovernmental organizations, and small environmental entrepreneurs. These are just a few examples of the impact of the recommendations on the Polish transition.

A similar cycle of research, institutional design, and capacity-building activities has also been initiated in three other countries: the Czech Republic and Slovakia, Hungary, and Bulgaria. The respective blueprints were prepared and disseminated and in the mid-1990s follow-up activities with a specific design for each country were progressing.

In the Czech Republic and Slovakia, for instance, the "catalytic" institution—the Institute for Environmental Policy—was established in July 1992 and is now in full operation. Basing its work on the Czecho-Slovak blueprint, the research team succeeded in submitting a draft proposal of two amendments to the federal privatization law addressing environmental liabilities. The federal parliament of the Czech Republic and Slovakia passed those amendments during its session in February 1992 as the first provisions in the whole CEE region requiring environmental auditing as a precondition for privatization.

Finally, it is worth mentioning that the successes of the institutional design resulted in several new projects at the Humphrey Institute: two U.S. AID-sponsored projects—Partnership in Education and Management and the Environmental Training Project for Central and Eastern Europe—and a United Nations Development Program regional assessment report on "capacities and deficiencies for implementing sustainable development in Central and Eastern Europe," which was published and distributed for the UNCED Earth Summit in 1992.[7]

Main Elements of the Blueprints for Institutional Design in Poland, Czecho–Slovakia, Hungary, and Bulgaria

Despite a common name, these "blueprints" differ from one another. They all have, however, one common section that deals with principles for institutional design for sustainable development. They also have some similarities in structure, such as appendixes dealing with existing conditions of a particular country or the division of recommendations among major sectors of a country (government, NGOs, academia). Aside from these elements, the blueprints express the features and needs of the particular country for which they were designed.

In the case of Poland, the distinct feature was the devotion of a significant part of the *Declaration* to the decentralization of power and the establishment of a new administrative structure based on ecological regions (watershed areas). The *Declaration* proposed three stages of establishing regional governments: watershed management centers, environmental management centers, and finally full-fledged regional governments. So far, the first of the three stages of proposed reform—the introduction of watershed management—has been implemented. There is also an advanced discussion in the government and the parliament on a radical administrative reform of the country including the abolition of 49 current districts.

---

7. The Partnership in Education and Management (PEM) is a training program in economics and management started in 1991 through a consortium led by the Humphrey Institute with other units of the University of Minnesota as well as with representatives of the private sector such as Land O'Lakes, Sparks Companies, and the American Trust for Agriculture in Poland.

The Environmental Training Project (ETP) focuses on environmental management for four audiences: business, NGOs, local and regional governments, and academia in six CEE countries: Bulgaria, the Czech Republic, Hungary, Poland, Romania, and Slovakia. It is organized through a consortium headed by the Humphrey Institute and other units of the University of Minnesota and the World Wildlife Fund, the Center for Hazardous Research Materials at the University of Pittsburgh, and the Institute for Sustainable Communities based at the Vermont Law School.

The UNDP Regional Assessment Report was titled *In Our Hands: United Nations Earth Summit '92: Capacities and Deficiencies for Implementing Sustainable Development in Central and Eastern Europe* (United Nations Conference on Environment and Development, Rio de Janeiro, 1992).

Investigators working in the Czech Republic and Slovakia in 1990–91 were aware of a growing tension between the two republics. They were also able to observe the transition process more closely than was possible in Poland in 1989–90. For that very reason, there are two characteristic features of the Czech and Slovak "blueprint"[8]—a federal structure with a strong trend to decentralizing power toward the two republics and a major focus on three main processes of the transition: democratization, privatization, and restructuring. Thanks to those features, the split of Czechoslovakia into the Czech Republic and Slovakia did not depreciate the blueprint. After removing a few short paragraphs dealing with very limited federal structures, the document is still an appealing declaration for institutional change for sustainable development. The most valuable aspect of the Czech and Slovak blueprint, however, is that it addresses very complex environmental aspects of democratization, privatization, and restructuring that are in many cases completely new for its audience. Despite a preliminary reluctance on the part of the indigenous audience of the workshop to internalize these new ideas, some of the innovative solutions have already been implemented and now serve as a model for other countries (e.g., environmental liabilities).

In the case of Hungary, the research indicated the need to launch a national dialog for sustainable development, especially between the government, NGOs, and academia. This is the main focus of the Hungarian blueprint.[9] One of its major recommendations calls for the establishment of a "Sustainable Social Compact." Decentralization of power and the implications of the growing internationalization of the Hungarian economy were emphasized as well. Current development in Hungary indicates that most of the recommendations are still awaiting national dialog.

The most recent of the four, the Bulgarian blueprint,[10] is the most advanced and comprehensive of these documents. Its characteristic feature is that it addresses six major critical challenges facing Bulgarian society: general, institutional, economic, sectoral, regional/local, and social challenges. The blueprint suggests specific recommendations for each of these

---

8. *Sustainable Development in Czechoslovakia: A Blueprint for Transformation* (International Workshop on Institutional Design for Environmental Protection in Czechoslovakia, Lipno, Czechoslovakia, November 4–7, 1991), Hubert H. Humphrey Institute of Public Affairs, University of Minnesota, Minneapolis.

9. *Environment and Development in Hungary: A Blueprint for Transformation* (International Workshop on Institutional Design for Environmental Protection in Hungary, Budapest-Dobogókö, Hungary, March 29–April 2, 1992), Hubert H. Humphrey Institute of Public Affairs, University of Minnesota, Minneapolis.

10. *Environment and Development in Bulgaria: A Blueprint for Transition* (International Workshop on Institutional Design for Environmental Protection in Bulgaria, Shtarkelovo Gnezdo, Bulgaria, September 5–7, 1992), Hubert H. Humphrey Institute of Public Affairs, University of Minnesota, Minneapolis.

kinds of challenges. There is another interesting innovation associated with the Bulgarian case. After the final workshop version of the blueprint was prepared, it was sent to the major actors participating in decision-making processes in the country, with the request that they submit (within a certain period of time) their final comments. This represented another attempt to internalize and socialize the Bulgarian blueprint.

It will be interesting to observe which of these four national blueprints will be implemented most effectively, taking into account differences in the final formulation of the document and its dissemination within a country.

The Need for New Leaders to Implement the Institutional Reforms

Institutions are human inventions. They emerge from people and are based on people. There are many definitions and types of institutions. In the Polish blueprint, institutions are defined as "reproduced social practices. They are patterns of intentional collaborative human actions carried out in repetitive fashion over time."[11] They are either spontaneously developed or consciously designed and introduced by some authority. This latter type of institution is significant in the context of institutional reform for sustainable development.

Imposition of a new institution by an authority requires a certain level of legitimacy. If it is solely based on fear of oppression by this authority, the sustainability of such an institution is closely linked to sustainability of the power. When the communist regimes collapsed, many institutions imposed by them quickly disappeared with them.

In a democratic society, the introduction of institutional reform requires some leaders to attempt to convince the rest of the society about the need for the reform. For that reason, institutional design for sustainable development brings the question of leadership to the fore. This leadership should come from national and local politicians and governments. In the current world, NGOs' leadership is becoming more and more visible, both from nonprofit sectors and from business communities. So far, the nonprofit sector seems be much more advanced in embracing the concept of sustainable development than the business sector. One can, however, observe a new positive trend—a growing number of environmental businesses—in this sector as well.[12]

---

11. *Designing Institutions,* 300.

12. Three unpublished reports prepared by Kenneth Macek for the U.S. AID indicate a quite dynamic development of environmental business, especially in Czechoslovakia and Poland in 1991–92. Recently, the number of exhibitors at the Pozna Ecological Fair "POLECO" passed 400.

There is an old tradition in the CEE-region of intellectual leadership from academia or in general from the intelligentsia. This factor has already been playing a significant role in articulating the concept of sustainable development for individual countries of the region. Currently in CEE countries there is an emerging new actor that could play a leadership role for sustainable development—the judiciary system. Finally, there are always important grassroots leaders.

These leaders interact with a large number of actors in implementing new reforms. Actors could be divided into two groups depending on their attitude toward the concept of sustainable development—positive and negative.

The first group in CEE countries is composed of supporters of the concept of sustainable development. They are academics (from universities and research institutes), teachers, physicians, policymakers and public officials, students, community leaders, well-educated and long-term-oriented businesspeople, farmers and foresters, journalists and artists, retired people, and housewives. The second group possesses a largely negative attitude toward sustainable development in the region. It includes bureaucrats, most financial staff, so-called professional politicians, technocrats, conservative policymakers and public officials, unskilled laborers and farmers, and aggressive and short-term–oriented businesspeople.

It is an interesting fact that, until now, there was no formal training available to shape modern business or community-based leaders. Almost all of the current leaders are self-made amateurs who, based on their own often painful experience, reached a certain level of performance as leaders. This fact indicates an urgent need to provide a professional education for modern CEE leaders who will lead the region in the twenty-first century. It also shows a need for coalition-building on the side of sustainable development. Finally, there is a need to popularize positive examples of leadership.

Is There Any Evidence of Behavioral Change in Favor of Sustainable Development?

The second half of the 1980s could be generally characterized as having witnessed an explosion of environmental activism in the CEE countries, stemming from two causes. One was a reaction to the ever greater and more visible pollution and environmental hazards, especially the Chernobyl disaster. The other cause was the fact that in most of these countries environmental groups were a tolerable form of political protest. Some of these organizations later became the major factor in political revolutions in their countries (e.g., ECOGLASNOST in Bulgaria). Most of these groups have survived the first transition period and are now struggling not only with environmental problems but also with their financial problems in new conditions created by the market.

The new democratic governments are acting more vigorously in the area of the environment. In Poland, in the course of only one year, the government completely or partially closed 117 polluting plants. Some very new policy tools as well as institutional reforms have already been implemented (e.g., market-based instruments or watershed management). There have been attempts to create environmental lobbies in parliaments. Some indicators show a slight improvement in the position of the environmental ministry within governments and the cooperation of the environmental ministry with other ministries. The international conference on "Industry in Service for Sustainable Development" and its "Zaborow Declaration" are good examples of cooperation between environmental and industrial ministers, as well as between NGOs and business, in CEE countries.[13]

There are visible community-based actions in the region that focus on recycling and reuse. Local governments, despite insufficient funds, are undertaking more and more projects oriented toward environmental protection and sustainable development. In addition to the changes within the business community mentioned earlier (closing polluting plants, fast-growing environmental services and manufacturing sectors), there are also examples of the introduction and development of environmentally friendly and energy-efficient technologies, voluntary labeling of products, and modernization and restructuring of polluting plants. These actions have joined with the economic recession in producing a decrease in pollution and an improvement in energy efficiency in the region.

In addition to the above mentioned changes, it is worthwhile to look more carefully at human behavior, especially within top management. Poles witnessed an interesting and unexpected event in 1992 that was very educational for the rest of the region as well as for economists and sociologists worldwide. On October 27 of that year, when the government, under pressure of the industrial lobby, significantly and retroactively reduced rates of pollution charges and fines, a public outcry took place in the mass

---

13. *The Zaborow Declaration: Industrial Policy for Sustainable Development in Central and Eastern Europe,* Zaborow-Warsaw (Central and East European Workshop on Industrial Pollution: Industry in Service for Sustainable Development, Zaborow-Warsaw, Poland, November 12–15, 1991), Hubert H. Humphrey Institute of Public Affairs, University of Minnesota, Minneapolis, 1992.

media. It was almost impossible to find any article legitimizing this poorly motivated decision. The most surprising and unexpected protests came from the business sector, especially from polluting industries. One of the directors of the Hugh Jaworzno power plant in the Silesia region, Janusz Wojcik, wrote a letter to the Polish prime minister protesting that "Our expenditures on environmental protection equipment stopped being economically justified" and the reduced charges and fines are a "guillotine for the pro-ecologically oriented plants."[14] Under strong pressure from environmental and proecological business lobbies, the Polish government canceled the October 1992 decision in January 1993.

This provides an interesting lesson on behavioral change and democracy for the government, business, and general public. It shows that good and ambitious environmental policies designed and implemented by previous governments can be challenged and reversed by a conservative industrial lobby in politically unstable conditions. This is, certainly, bad news. The good news, however, is that modern ecological policy and a strategy of sustainable development is being institutionalized, not only within proecological-oriented segments of society but also within a business community that wants to change old practices while simultaneously taking advantage of the emerging new demand for goods and services regulated by the environmental legislation market.

In rural areas, there are some changes in the behavior of farmers, including a shift toward low-input and organic farming. In Poland, for instance, the most recent public opinion (Center of Public Opinion Research) survey indicates that "41% of farmers are thinking about production of 'healthy food.'"[15] This is a surprisingly high share of farmers interested in a sustainable path of development. However, it is difficult to judge whether this results from environmental education, economic hardships, and searching for market niches or represents instead a declaration or a readiness to restructure their farms. The relative technological and structural backwardness of Polish agriculture could make virtually any restructuring relatively easier than in Hungary or the Czech Republic.

---

14. "Jaworzno protestuje," *Gazeta Wyborcza,* no. 286, December 5–6, 1992, 1. The Jaworzno power plants belong to the largest and most polluting plants in Poland. They were listed among the 80 largest polluters in 1990. However, during the last two years, due to strict regulations and economic incentives, they invested heavily in environmental protection, which resulted in the reduction of dust by about 35 percent and significantly advanced the technology for nitrogen oxides emission.

15. "Rolnicy o swoich gospodarstwach" (Farmers About their Farms), *Donosy* [Warsaw-based electronic daily], February 11, 1993.

How Can People Be Motivated to Change Toward Sustainable Development?

There are many ways to motivate people to act. One of the best ways to motivate people to turn their latent or passive concern about the future into action is environmental education. It helps, first of all, to provide a better understanding of the environmental conditions in CEE countries as well as globally and of the impact of these conditions on human health. This type of education focusing on basic *risk evaluation* should be followed by an analysis of ways (options) to improve environmental quality—*risk management*. Unfortunately, it is a common phenomenon that education starts and ends only with the first step. Such truncated analysis simply scares people without building a better understanding of countermeasures.

These two educational steps should be followed by a third one—*risk communication*—that will explain the personal context of a given environmental problem, including practical steps for dealing with the environmental hazards. These basic steps in environmental education help to create new environmental leaders as well as informed citizens.

In CEE countries, there are many formal and informal educational activities. Unfortunately, most of these activities do not go through the whole cycle of education just mentioned. This leads to further frustration because there is growing knowledge about the quality of the environment and associated risks, but appropriate solutions are missing.

Among the new phenomena in environmental education and interest in the environment are some new and very disparate approaches. On the one hand, there is growing interest and follow-up education in economic aspects of the environment. On the other hand, there are numerous NGO groups popularizing spiritual attitudes toward the environment and a new style of life based on a philosophy of a "deep ecology." There are new audiences grouping behind these trends (e.g., ecological businesspeople, community leaders, municipal officials, farmers, intellectuals, grassroots leaders, students) who should be taken into account when building a coalition for sustainable development.

In most CEE countries, current democratic changes open full access to environmental information and abolish the red tape involved in establishing new organizations. These opportunities should, however, be complemented by organized assistance at the initial stage in order to help people to organize themselves. In addition, it is important to build a broad coalition for solving these problems. One of the most powerful tactics is what I have called risk communication, which is aimed at expanding coalitions to show well-documented consequences and/or costs of inaction. This could also be an important factor in discussions with antagonists of environmental action. A democratic order makes it possible to channel environmental conflicts through the mediation process from an antagonistic to a cooperative relationship. This opportunity is still far from being fully exploited.

It is worth adding that besides the practical steps mentioned above, one of the major ways of awakening environmental awareness is to develop the imagination and sensitivity of the public toward the environment. It is especially difficult to develop an understanding of the threat from a polluted environment for the next generation. Practical experience indicates that using the example of the multigenerational family helps the audience to understand the problem. For that reason, housewives should be invited to participate in environmental activities. This could be a powerful and still untapped resource for sustainable development in the region. At the initial stage, it will require a new way of addressing the issue to reach this audience and to help them to organize themselves. There are already some positive examples in CEE countries that could be replicated throughout the whole region.

What Are the Prospects for the Future and the Barriers That Will Have to Be Overcome to Achieve Sustainable Development?

Despite numerous opinions stressing that the state of technology and lack of capital in CEE countries are the major barriers for sustainable development, I am deeply convinced that the most important is the *psychological* or *attitudinal barrier* based on deep-rooted conservatism or on bad experience with past activities in the old system. There are many examples demonstrating that despite the introduction of new technologies, real changes do not always evolve as expected. During my numerous travels through the CEE region, I often found that even the most high-tech investment (e.g., airline jets, computers, modern hotels) was possible in the "capital-hungry" region, but its economic efficiency was much lower than in the West because of poor management and the old behavior patterns of the labor force. Thus, it is vital for the region to improve environmental awareness by addressing not only ecological issues but also managerial questions. In many cases, the needed scientific knowledge is there, but the management and policy experience is lacking. For that reason, the second most important obstacles to sustainable development are *organizational* and *managerial barriers*. The third type of barriers are *resource barriers: human, capital,* and *know-how.* There is an urgent need to have a strategic plan of capacity building to overcome these barriers during the transition period.

The leadership of CEE countries should incorporate ideas of sustainable development such as democratization, restructuring, privatization, and opening their economies into the major ongoing processes in the transition. The following activities should be implemented:

1. Strengthen the democratization processes by providing full access to environmental information and participation in the decision-making processes;
2. Speed up ecologically sound restructuring by developing environmental firms, production, and services;
3. Facilitate sustainable privatization processes by identifying the environmental liability of firms designated for privatization and carefully monitoring new owners;
4. Support internal and external networking to expand information sources and to develop new knowledge and experience;
5. Strengthen national and local policy-making processes by providing more environmental expertise for policymakers;
6. Enhance capacities of the regional human, institutional, and material resources by better management.

The democratic process must continue to be developed beyond the free election process. The policy-making process could be made environmentally sound by extending public participation. The basic precondition of participation is availability and accessibility of environmental and economic information. The fulfillment of these preconditions should help CEE societies to organize an environmentally conscious coalition to protect their current and future interests.

Ecologically sustainable restructuring will require both the active role of a state in the process (e.g., abolishing old and establishing new institutions) and independent entrepreneurship of private (real or potential) owners. There is a need for national dialog about various options of restructuring, and its financial arrangements and incentives as well as government-backed investment strategies and their local and regional context. Finally, as stated in the Hungarian blueprint, there are "several aspects of restructuring that should be taken into account in an appropriate analysis and pricing of:

all production factors, including the true cost of natural resources, all external costs (pollution, hazardous waste disposal),

risk probability assessments, and
appropriate discounting of future costs.[16]

The positive side of privatization is associated with clarification of the responsibilities of an enterprise, including environmental liabilities related to pollution and damage to the environment. Introducing environmental auditing as a preliminary condition for privatization, which is happening in some of the CEE countries now, will initiate this part of the process. There is, however, a negative side of the privatization process: a potential fragmentation of some of the environmental systems such as forests and underground aquifers. Recent experience with the privatization of forests in CEE countries confirm, unfortunately, that this threat is not only a potential one.

Lifting the previously strict control imposed on the CEE societies opens an opportunity to develop a rich internal and external collaborative network. Since ecosystems do not respect administrative or political borders, such cooperation will be vital to promoting sustainable development in CEE countries. It will also facilitate economic and political collaboration between national, regional, and local governments and NGOs.

The revolutions in CEE countries in 1989 and later brought completely new leaders to power. They have many new and good ideas but lack experience in governing their societies in a democratic manner. This is particularly important in the transition period when these economies have to be put on a path of sustainable development. The region lacks experience not only in environmentally sound policy design but also in basic policy analysis, formulation, and implementation. These economies need to learn, by doing, about national long-term strategy formulation and in particular about assessing issues (e.g., reviewing financial and environmental sustainability of an existing economic base and major barriers for sustainable development), setting goals (e.g., developing alternative scenarios for economic development with preventive and remedial measures), and designing instruments (e.g., finding an appropriate combination of legal and economic tools for environmental protection).[17]

Finally, there is a need to invest in human capacity development through environmental, economic, and managerial education. The human factor is crucial for the other capacities—technological and institutional. In the UNDP-sponsored survey in CEE countries, the highest priority was placed on the capacities oriented toward environmental policy and communication, environmental management, and interdisci-

---

16. *Environment and Development*, 27–28.
17. *Zaborow Declaration*, 30–31.

plinary skills in such areas as the economy, the environment, and ethics and science, application, and evaluation.[18]

The concept of sustainable development presents a chance for the CEE countries, which recently faced not only serious environmental problems but also severe economic and political hardships, to adjust to the new system that is emerging from this painful but so promising transition. This is, however, only a chance because if they lack an "enlightened" leadership with a long-term vision, if they focus on fulfilling only everyday and short-term problems, and if they emphasize differences between themselves and exacerbating old wounds, they will miss this chance. The near future will show which direction they will take. In such circumstances, the question of leadership for sustainable development in CEE countries is the most critical one.

BIBLIOGRAPHY

Bochniarz, Z. and R. Bolan, eds. 1991. *Designing Institutions for Sustainable Development: A New Challenge for Poland.* Minneapolis-Białystok: Białystok Technical University Press.
Bochniarz, Z., R. Bolan, A. Kassenberg, E. Kruzikova, and H. von Witzke, eds. 1991. *Sustainable Development in Czechoslovakia: A Blueprint for Transformation.* Report prepared for the International Workshop on Institutional Design for Environmental Protection in Czechoslovakia, Lipno, November 4–7, 1991. Minneapolis: Hubert H. Humphrey Institute of Public Affairs, University of Minnesota.
Bochniarz, Z., R. Bolan, S. Kerekes, J. Kindler, J. Vargha, H. von Witzke, eds. 1992. *Environment and Development in Hungary: A Blueprint for Transformation.* Report prepared for the International Workshop on Institutional Design for Environmental Protection in Hungary, Budapest-Dobogoko, March 29–April 2, 1992. Minneapolis: Hubert H. Humphrey Institute of Public Affairs, University of Minnesota.
Bochniarz, Z., R. Bolan, T. Fiutak, K. Georgieva, E. Popov, and H. von Witzke, eds. *Environment and Development in Bulgaria: A Blueprint for Transformation.* Report prepared for the International Workshop on Institutional Design for Environmental Protection in Bulgaria, Sgtarkelovo Gnezdo, September 5–7, 1992. Minneapolis: Hubert H. Humphrey Institute of Public Affairs, University of Minnesota.
Budapest Week. 1992. "Environment a Top Concern, Poll Reveals." *Budapest Week: Hungary's International Weekly,* 2, no. 17 (July 2–8).
Burger, T. 1992. *Swiadomosc ekologiczna: Miedzy lekiema dzialaniem.* Warsaw: Institute for Sustainable Development.

---

18. *In Our Hands,* 32–33.

Czechoslovak Academy of Science. 1992. *National Report of the Czech and Slovak Federal Republic*. Prague: Czechoslovak Academy of Science.

Donosy. 1993. "Rolnicy o Swoich gospodarstwach." *Donosy* (Warsaw), (February 11), an electronic periodical.

Gazeta Wyborcza. 1992. "Jaworzno protestuje." *Gazeta Wyborcza*, no. 286 (December 5-6): 1.

United Nations Conference on Environment and Development (UNECD). 1992. "Capacities and Deficiencies for Implementing Sustainable Development in Central and Eastern Europe." *In Our Hands: United Nations Earth Summit '92*, Rio de Janeiro, 1992. New York: United Nations Conference on Environment and Development.

The Zaborow Declaration: Industrial Policy for Sustainable Development in Central and Eastern Europe. 1992. Central and East European Workshop on Industrial Pollution: Industry in Service for Sustainable Development, Zaborow-Warsaw, Poland, November 12-15, 1991. Minneapolis: Hubert H. Humphrey Institute of Public Affairs, University of Minnesota.

11

The Office of the Future Citizen: Commentary on Robert McNamara's "A Vision for Our Nation and the World in the Twenty-first Century"

Neva R. Goodwin

The essay that follows (see chap. 12) was written by Robert McNamara in 1990 and presented in early 1991 at one of the first seminars sponsored by the Program for the Study of Sustainable Change and Development at Tufts University. In terms of historical content, it is dated; events have moved so rapidly that things that were astonishingly new five years ago now feel like fading elements in a continuing, ever less astonishing pattern of change. However, the message of the essay—the part that will not become dated—is an approach to understanding both history and current events that is badly needed in public life.

The paper conveys the author's passion and his sense of urgency as he surveyed the needs of the United States and the world in the coming century. It provides a perfect opportunity to consider—with Mr. McNamara's support and cooperation—how such prescriptions should be analyzed in terms of their potential impact upon the future.

Adam Smith and thinkers of his era called upon the point of view of an imaginary "impartial spectator" to judge proper conduct. John Rawls has made widely known the idea of choosing how to allocate society's resources from behind a "veil of ignorance," creating a mental game wherein the players can design the socioeconomic world they would prefer but without knowing what position they would have in it. As a basis for analyzing material such as that furnished in Robert McNamara's paper, I will propose another position from which to adopt the appropriate point of view. I will imagine that there is such a thing as an "Office of the Future Citizen" and will try to review Mr. McNamara's recommendations as though I were an official representative of such an office.[1]

---

1. The idea of an "Office of the Future Citizen" was first suggested to me by Hank

I believe this office would find much to agree with in Mr. McNamara's approach to reordering national priorities, given his goal of shifting "the balance between private consumption, capital investment, and public expenditures." Starting with the figures given at the end of his paper, where Mr. McNamara lists eight Unmet Needs, with an estimate that meeting them would require a diversion of 8.2 percent of GNP, I'll make here a rough judgment as to how these eight (actually, nine) Unmet Needs might, in turn, be divided among three categories: *growth, maintenance,* and *consumption.* As will quickly become evident, it is not always easy to distinguish between these categories. However, one of the most important tasks of the Office of the Future Citizen should be to do so and to get everyone else thinking about doing so.

There can be little dispute that economic growth and maintenance of our social and economic infrastructure are related to the kind of world we will pass on to our heirs. If all the taxes that had been levied on the future, in the form of borrowing, had been used for purposes of fostering growth and paying for maintenance, the appropriate focus of the Office of the Future Citizen would be upon a second round of issues, especially regarding the *nature* of the growth being encouraged. As things are now, however, its quarrel with the policy of the 1980s would be, by contrast, on the issue of taxing the future to pay for present consumption.

Shortly, I will come back to consider how the consumption category may be supposed to affect the future. First, however, I will take a cut at analyzing the 8.2 percent of GNP that, at the end of his paper, Mr. McNamara proposes to reallocate and will assess how this amount is

---

Patton, who commented that, following the recent era of high government borrowing, the future citizens of this country (or their representatives) could justly complain that they have been victims of something this nation was founded to prevent: the imposition of taxation without representation.

A similar suggestion, for an "Office of Strategic Prevention," was made by Joseph J. Romm in a *New York Times* op-ed article (January 11, 1993) called "Fix Now, Save Later." That argument concludes: "Individual, federal and state agencies cannot devote their resources to finding and financing the best prevention programs. . . . As an agency's budget is cut, it inevitably sacrifices programs with long-term benefits in favor of those with short-term payoffs. A prevention office would help undo this vicious paradox."

Similar ideas for a "guardian" or "proxy" for the future have been suggested from time to time—see, for example, Edith Brown Weiss (cited in Paarlberg and in Goodwin, this volume); or Sidney Holt and Peter Serrachino Inglott in Salvino Busuttil, Emmanuel Agius, Peter Serrachino Inglott, and Tony Macelli (1990), *Our Responsibilities Toward Future Generations* (published by the Foundation for International Studies, Malta, in cooperation with UNESCO, 121). The idea may be found at least as far back as the writing of Edmund Burke.

divided up among the three categories of growth, maintenance, and consumption.

The growth category may be defined to include *savings to support capital investment* (item 1a on Mr. McNamara's list); *primary and secondary education* (as investment in human capital—item 2); and *scientific and technological advances* (3). These combined items, according to Mr. McNamara's estimates, would require a reallocation of 3.5 percent of GNP at the time of his writing—or about 43 percent of that 8.2 percent of GNP that he had proposed reallocating.

The maintenance category includes item 4, *physical infrastructure,* and item 7, *environmental degradation.* Together, these would account for about 16 percent of the proposed total redirection of GNP.

Finally, 41 percent of the proposed reallocations would go to consumption. This includes *financing retirement accounts* (1b), *providing health care for the uninsured* (5), and addressing *poverty, drug abuse, crime, homelessness, and international aid to the needy* (items 6 and 8). However, the category "consumption" needs to be broken down further into the following three elements:

(*a*) *Aid to the most disadvantaged members of society.* This would include most of items 5, 6, and 8.

(*b*) *Consumption activities that build human capital.* This would include most of the rest of items 5, 6, and 8. (Arguably, part of the crime issue might be assigned to "maintenance," while human capital-building could also readily be understood as investment for "growth.")

(*c*) *The satisfaction of wants* (as distinguished, loosely, from needs, which are intended to be represented under my (*a*) above). The financing of retirement accounts would fit partly here and partly under my item (*a*), aid to the disadvantaged.

When we start disaggregating consumption activities, and particularly when we look at aid to disadvantaged members of society and expenditures that may be supposed to increase human capital, we are immediately plunged into troubled waters. *Are* there expenditures that can not only address the immediate needs of the poor but can also help them to get out of poverty? (By and large, political liberals say that there are; conservatives rarely say that there *could not* be any such expenditures, but they tend to deny each liberal claim to have found such instances.) If any expenditure is defined in this way, should it not be defined as an aspect of growth rather than consumption?

For the Office of the Future Citizen, perhaps the most important questions to arise out of the analysis so far are these:

> To what extent will the welfare of the future depend upon progress in improving the lot of the most disadvantaged members of society?
> To what extent can such improvement be counted as real if it is *absolute* but not *relative*? That is, if the resources available to the poorest 20 percent of the population were to double, that would be an absolute gain. If at the same time the much greater amount of resources available to the rest of society were also to double, the relative position of the poor would, in fact, have worsened. (The material progress for both rich and poor in the United States over the whole course of the twentieth century is absolutely very great; however, while the relative position of the poor has fluctuated, over this century it has worsened rather than improved.) Given the high standards of material welfare now experienced by our society, it is increasingly relevant to ask whether it will be relative or absolute improvements in the situation of the poor that will matter more to the well-being of future generations.[2]
> Finally, to what extent will the welfare of the future depend upon investments aimed at creating and maintaining traditionally defined growth in output?

I believe that Mr. McNamara's answers to these questions would be similar to mine, that he would, in fact, prefer to see more funds channeled directly into building and maintaining the human capital that is being destroyed by poverty, drugs, a gravely deficient penal system, and a primary and secondary education system that is inadequate to compensate for these other pressures. I also believe that, in an ideal world, he would choose to increase the emphasis on human capital, even at the expense of some of the physical capital that is used to maintain and increase the output of consumption goods. That is to say, I suppose that

---

2. There are reasons to expect a convergence of the point of view of the Office of the Future Citizen and the Rawlsian point of view (as described, above, in the third paragraph of this commentary). Suppose we start by eschewing an assumption of altruism and proceed from the common neoclassical/sociobiological assumption that the chief reason for caring about the future is because of our evolutionarily programmed concern for our own biological descendents. If we look three or four generations down the road, it will appear almost equally likely that our descendents will marry (and/or produce further descendents with) partners from any socioeconomic group in society. This realization should achieve the same result as Rawls's "veil of ignorance" in giving us equal reason to be concerned with the welfare of all groups in society. Contrary to Rawls's "initial position," we *do* know where we are in the world—but, in reality, we *do not* know where our descendents will be.

his preference would be to divert more money into item 6, the poverty item to which he has assigned 0.5 percent, or one-sixteenth, of his 8.2 percent of the redirected GNP stream and that he might prefer to do so at the expense of item 1a, "capital investment for growth," which in his present scheme receives 2 percent, or nearly a quarter of that 8.2 percent.

This is not, however, an ideal world—one in which all people understand how present actions are likely to affect the people of the future and act responsibly in accordance with this understanding. In a world where, in fact, ignorance, lack of understanding, and lack of altruistic concern play significant roles, Mr. McNamara made the political judgment (a judgment that seems to have been confirmed by subsequent political events) that the middle class will not stand for seeing money diverted to those most in need unless they feel that they, too, are benefiting from the shift in the nation's priorities.

I will not argue with this as a political judgment. What I would like to suggest, however, is that deeply embedded here is an issue more of culture than of economics. It has to do with what is perceived as a "benefit" and what is perceived as a "cost" and with the following questions:

What do people really want? and
What do we mean by growth and progress?

Far more than most of us, including economists, are aware, *what we want* is a cultural artifact—a result of the need for mass markets that were beginning to be required to sop up mass production technologies as early as the eighteenth century. This trend, to define consumers' wants so as to suit producers' needs, had gathered considerable momentum by the late nineteenth century and has continued up to the present to shape our perceptions of what is desirable—what is the good life.[3] All the same, it is not inevitable that we will continue to identify progress with *growth in output* of consumer goods and services. As the notion of sustainable development catches on, it is increasingly being defined as a type of progress wherein there is improvement in the *quality* of goods and services, and indeed—perhaps most importantly—*improvements in our own capabilities for benefiting from these things.*

Sustainable *growth* may be an oxymoron. Sustainable *development* takes the important conceptual leap of imagining that more satisfaction or happiness or virtue (however you want to name your highest value) may be achieved without increasing (perhaps even accompanied by a decrease in) total material throughput. This is especially true for a coun-

---

3. Volume 2 in this series will contain an extended discussion of this point.

try that already possesses as high an average per capita throughput as ours. Mr. McNamara's sources of finance for meeting the Unmet Needs, beginning with a reduction in gasoline consumption per capita and energy consumption per unit of GNP, are a start in this direction.

His solution may, overall, be described as beginning with the directive, "Increase the national output." Then (to paraphrase his prescription) "Allocate a portion of the increased production—the 'growth dividend'—to raise consumption of all groups, particularly the middle class." Politically, this is probably the approach that is most likely to be acceptable. At the same time, in order for such an approach to take us in a direction that is truly sustainable, that truly improves the quality of life for the present *and* for the future, it will be critical to accompany it with efforts (through education and perhaps through media campaigns) to reconsider the values that are served by different approaches to consumption and to the composition of the national output.

There is increasing reason to believe that environmental limits mean that future generations will be seriously harmed by a strategy that focuses upon increasing throughput. Thus, the only agenda that can be accepted simultaneously by advocates of sustainable development and by advocates of overall growth is one in which there is an *increase in the satisfaction derived from total output* (of goods and services) while there is no increase—and perhaps a reduction—in total throughput.

Returning to Mr. McNamara's proposed changes in the way GNP is allocated, I would like, finally, to focus on just one of the particular issues raised there, as an example of the way a representative of the Future Citizen might address the work of that hypothetical office. It seems fairly evident that infrastructure investments should go in the category "maintenance," on the grounds that we should always, in any case, be putting a steady amount of GNP into the infrastructure that provides essential support for our production capacities. However, I now want to consider an argument for thinking about these expenditures differently, at least during the present historical period.

We are now at a critical moment when a new awareness of the present environmental costs of past decisions should make us focus on the consequences to the future of *how* we decide to rebuild, for example, our transportation infrastructure. The full cost to our society of transportation (of both people and materials) has been largely hidden in the total size, the diversity, and the form of subsidies given to that sector. The United States, in part thanks to the deferred maintenance of the 1980s, now faces critically important decisions regarding (*a*) what we will transport (versus what we will produce locally), (*b*) how we will design and anticipate future cities, towns, workplaces, and leisure activities (with what implications for moving people around on a daily basis), and (*c*) what our overall transportation policies should be regarding issues such as the mix of private versus public transportation or a variety of options for technological development—some new, like supermagnetic rail transport, and some old, like bicycles.

Speaking for the Office of the Future Citizen, it is not hard to know where to begin with this subject: the rebuilding of American's infrastructure can and should be done in a manner that turns us away from existing environment-degrading, future-threatening practices and toward a more sustainable development path. Having said that, the hard part is to make it operational. It would be very helpful to any such endeavors if we had a true accounting—beyond anything available today—of as many of the costs and benefits of the existing transportation system and of the proposed alternatives as possible.

In an imperfect world, it is, of course, usually necessary to take action without possessing all of the relevant information. Mr. McNamara proposes some action in the area of rebuilding infrastructure. However, the form that action is to take is still—five years later—not completely settled. It is not only our transportation infrastructure that needs rethinking before rebuilding but also, as suggested earlier, our assumptions about what kind of life we want. The essential question, again, is: how much flexibility do we have in what we will recognize as "progress"? Mr. McNamara's answer to that question is the basis of his (as I have characterized it) political decision to base his framework for change on the dictum, "Increase the national output." There may be a prior task we have to undertake: "Reconceptualize the national output." And even before that, we may have to rethink what it is we mean by the wealth of nations and the welfare of people.

12

A Vision for Our Nation and the World in the Twenty-first Century

Robert S. McNamara

In this essay I want to examine, in what many may consider a provocative and controversial context, whether our nation is following a course consistent with the values that have guided us for over 200 years. The fundamental questions are these: are we maximizing our human and material resources in the interest of all of our people, are we meeting our responsibilities to the rest of the world, and are we taking advantage of the unique opportunities that flow from the end of the Cold War?

We are the most powerful nation in the world—the most powerful economically, politically, and militarily. The most recent example of that power is our response to the Iraqi invasion of Kuwait. Whether or not you agreed with the policy we followed—and I did not—you must accept that no other nation could have provided the political leadership, deployed the military force, or borne the economic costs.

As Lamar Alexander, former governor of Tennessee and Secretary of Education, pointed out recently: "Whose Statue of Liberty did they erect in Tiananmen Square and whose constitution are they debating in Moscow?" And yet at the same time:

Our nation's growth in productivity has slowed, leading to a decline in our competitive position abroad and forecasts of low rates of economic growth at home;

Our society is polarizing: 15 to 20 percent of our people are marginalized, incapable of playing productive roles either politically or economically;

We confront severe racial problems: one in every four young black male citizens today is either facing criminal charges, is in jail, or is on probation;[1] and

---

1. Bill McAllister, "Study: 1 in 4 Young Black Men is in Jail or Court Supervised," *Washington Post*, February 29, 1990, A3.

the country has lost faith in its government's ability to change things for the better: only 36 percent of the nation's eligible voters went to the polls in the 1990 congressional elections.[2]

Is it any wonder that Paul Kennedy's book *The Rise and Fall of Great Powers* was a best-seller for 43 weeks? In it, the British historian, now teaching at Yale University, examines the changing relationships among nations over a period of 500 years. Based on that analysis, he concludes that when the security commitments and economic strength of Great Powers move out of balance they fall into decline. The implication is—and many of those who bought the book believe—that the United States is at such a point today. As I will make clear later, I strongly disagree with that point of view.

Kennedy's book followed by a few months an article in the *Economist* entitled "Has America Lost Its Smile?" The article suggested that the United States, on which the postwar world had depended for leadership in economic and political affairs, had lost its sense of compassion, its optimism, and its self-confidence. As a result, said the *Economist,* we had turned inward, and because of our pessimistic mood we had lost our ability to deal with our domestic problems.

I agree with that appraisal. However, our failure to move toward a solution of our domestic problems is a function, I believe, of our lack of political will—of psychological constraints—and the mismanagement of our economy rather than a lack of resources. As I will seek to demonstrate, we are unwilling to reorder our national priorities—to shift the balance between private consumption, capital investment, and public expenditures—for fear that such action will impinge on our personal freedom and adversely affect our individual welfare.

A primary factor leading to the economic and social problems we face today is that as a nation we have been on an enormous consumption binge. We have been living beyond our means, selling our assets, and borrowing heavily both domestically and abroad in order to finance the unprecedented expansion of domestic spending.

While enjoying our consumption binge, we have permitted severe social problems—some of which I alluded to earlier and more of which I'll comment on later under the heading of "Unmet Needs"—to develop to plague our society.

We have borrowed abroad more than half of the resources required to finance domestic investment. This, in turn, has led to the huge trade

2. Stephen Knack, "Why We Don't Vote—Or Say 'Thank You,'" *Wall Street Journal,* December 31, 1991.

deficit, our comparable current account deficit, and our sharply rising external debt. But the external debt cannot continue to rise indefinitely. Nor can our social problems be allowed to fester much longer without severely weakening the society we will pass on to our children.

Doesn't this litany of problems support the unspoken fears of those who bought Paul Kennedy's book? Absolutely not. My thesis is that we have it entirely within our power to deal with all of these problems. The framework of the solution is simple and clear:

Increase the national output;

Allocate a portion of the increased production—the "growth dividend"—to raise consumption for all groups, particularly the middle class; and

Utilize the remainder of the increase in output, along with a reallocation of both public and private expenditures, to deal with our "Unmet Needs."

We will be assisted in seeing our domestic problems and operations in a new perspective by developments on the international scene that few thought possible as little as six or twelve months ago. Before discussing these, I will expand further on our domestic ills and how we can deal with them.

I want to focus on eight categories of Unmet Needs. Collectively, they are representative, but by no means fully descriptive, of the deep fissures that threaten social and economic stability in our society. The most serious of these Unmet Needs, and one that affects our ability to address the whole range of social problems, is our failure to generate sufficient savings to finance the investment required to maintain economic growth, without unsustainable borrowing from abroad and without borrowing from future generations.

During the 1980s, our net national savings rate fell to about 3.5 percent of GNP, a drop of almost 50 percent from the levels of the previous three decades. In a forthcoming book, Charles Schultze of the Brookings Institution calculates that the savings rate must be raised by at least two percentage points if we are to achieve modest growth in GNP of 2.5 percent per year.[3] In addition, he points out that we must save to build up surpluses in the federal social security and retirement

---

3. Charles L. Schultze, *Memos to the President* (Washington, DC: The Brookings Institution, 1992), 246–54. Throughout this essay, the estimates of the costs of meeting Unmet Needs and the estimates of the sources of funds for such expenditures are approximations only, but they are believed to be sufficiently representative to point to the action our society should initiate.

accounts in order to avoid burdening future generations.[4] This will require approximately two additional percentage points of national savings, raising the required savings rate to the level of the 1950s, 1960s, and 1970s.

The four point increase in savings can come in either the public or the private sector. The government can seek to stimulate an increase in private savings by cutting the tax rate on income from capital or by making consumer borrowing more costly by reducing the tax deductions for interest payments. Both of these approaches have been tried in the past with little success. Therefore, Mr. Schultze concludes, the only realistic way to raise the national savings rate is to increase public savings.

The federal budget is projected to run a deficit—a dissavings—of about $125 billion in 1995. To raise national savings in the public sector by four percentage points would require tax increases, expenditure cuts, or a combination of both. I'll suggest which course to follow in a moment.

The remaining seven Unmet Needs on which I will focus include:

Rebuilding our primary and secondary education systems;
Stimulating scientific and technological advance;
Reversing the deterioration of our physical infrastructure;
Providing adequate health care to the 31 million citizens not now covered by health care;
Lowering the rising levels of poverty—particularly among children—in the richest nation on earth;
Reversing the high rates of environmental degradation; and
Addressing widespread drug abuse, rising crime levels, the problems of the homeless, and disgracefully low levels of assistance to developing countries.

I'll comment briefly on each.

Rebuilding Our Primary and Secondary Education Systems

Mr. Edward Denison, the leading U.S. scholar in the field of productivity changes, has calculated that between 1929 and 1982 savings and

---

4. Medicare is projected to be bankrupt in 20 years, social security now has a long-term deficit that increases from one year to the next, and the Pension Benefit Guarantee Corporation is financially unsound. To balance the flows into and out of these funds, over the long term, will require not only additional national savings but action as well to reduce the disproportionate amount of our resources—one-half of federal domestic expenditures, other than interest on debt—being channeled to the elderly.

investment accounted for about 30 percent of the nation's economic growth, while improvements in the quantity and quality of education and advances in science and technology accounted for 70 percent. Both of these factors affect our international competitiveness, and yet in each we are falling behind not only our competitors but our own past levels of accomplishment.

The effect of education on productivity, in an increasingly technologically oriented world, can be seen by comparing the wage differentials for people with different levels of schooling. In the late 1970s, the average incomes of full-time male workers who attended college exceeded those of high school dropouts by 75 percent. But today, 25 percent of those who start high school fail to graduate with their age group, and in many urban areas the dropout rate exceeds 40 percent; in Japan it is 5 percent.[5]

Not only is the "quantity" of our education deficient, but the quality is low, is falling further, and has become noncompetitive. Thirteen percent of high school students who do graduate do so with the reading skills of sixth graders.[6] College board test scores have been declining since the mid-60s. And the National Science Foundation has reported that, by the twelfth grade, U.S. students in math and science score at or near the bottom of students in advanced countries. By that stage, test scores of U.S. students are four grade equivalents behind those of Japanese students. One reason is that Japanese high school students spend 61 hours per week in class and homework compared with only 30 hours per week for U.S. students.[7]

If we wish to raise the quantity and quality of primary and secondary education, we may not know how to do so. Providing incentives to students for higher performance, in the form of higher wages, after graduation—not now the practice—may help. And incentives to teachers and schools to raise standards, for example, by providing parents with the right of choice among schools, may also contribute. But if we are to find the complete answer, we must devote major attention to the problem over the next decade. Whatever the answer may be, it almost surely will require an increase in educational expenditures both for those now in school and for those functional illiterates—estimated at over 20 percent of all adults—who are now in the workforce. A minimum of 0.5 percent of GNP will probably be required. The addition of that amount

---

5. National Center for Education Statistics, *Digest of Educational Statistics,* 1989, 103.

6. Timothy Saasta, *America's Third Deficit* (Washington, DC: Center for Community Change, 1990), 9.

7. *New York Times,* December 19, 1990, D2.

would bring U.S. expenditures on primary and secondary education to approximately the average of the other 14 industrial nations.[8]

Stimulating Scientific and Technological Advance

In the technological age of the twenty-first century, none of the factors contributing to economic growth will be more important than the advance of scientific knowledge and its translation into new and improved products and methods of production. For decades, the United States has been a leader—and I believe it leads today—in basic research. But we have lagged behind Japan, and we are beginning to lag behind some European nations, in translating that knowledge into better products and lower factory costs. One reason is that Germany and Japan have increased the share of their GNP devoted to commercially oriented research and development (R&D) to 2.8 percent and 2.6 percent, respectively, while for the last two decades, the United States has limited such expenditures to 1.8 percent of GNP.[9]

Clearly, the United States needs to devote more energy and resources to moving scientific and technological discoveries out of the laboratory and onto the production line. The federal government has a role to play in the process. An increase in the current 25 percent tax credit for R&D expenditures would be a desirable step in the right direction, but more federal assistance is likely to be required if total expenditures are to rise to 1 percent of GNP, the German and Japanese levels.

Reversing the Deterioration of Our
Physical Infrastructure

A recent report on America's public works by the National Council on Public Works Improvement, a panel created by Congress to examine the subject, states: "We have worn through the cushion of excess capacity built into earlier investments. In effect, we are drawing down past investments without making commensurate investments of our own."[10] Highways, streets, bridges, and airports as well as public transit, water, and waste disposal systems are all deteriorating.

---

8. Edith Rasell and Lawrence Mishel, *Shortchanging Education: How U.S. Spending on Grades K-12 Lags Behind Other Nations,* Washington, DC: Economic Policy Institute, 1990.

9. Joseph S. Nye, Jr., *Bound to Lead* (New York: Basic Books, 1990), 206.

10. The National Council on Public Works Improvement, *Fragile Foundations: A Report on America's Public Works,* (Washington, DC: National Council on Public Works Improvement, February 1988).

Public works form the skeleton that holds the country together; they are our life-support system. But the life-support system is becoming increasingly inadequate as expenditures decline. The National Council reports that public works spending as a percentage of GNP has dropped from 3.5 percent of GNP in 1960 to 2.6 percent in 1985.[11] The General Accounting Office and Congressional Budget Office estimate that additional expenditures of $23 billion per year are needed to maintain and meet minimum standards for bridges and highways alone.[12] The National Council recommends that annual spending on Infrastructure be increased by approximately 1 percent of GNP, and the Joint Economic Committee estimates that 0.5 percent is required.[13]

Providing Adequate Health Care to the Uninsured

Today more than 31 million Americans, 13 percent of those under 65, have no health insurance or medical coverage.[14] This is a 15 percent increase over the late 1970s, according to the Census Bureau. The number of children receiving immunization declined by 20 percent between 1979 and 1986, and one-fifth of all pregnant women did not receive prenatal care in the 1980s, according to the Children's Defense Fund. The result: our infant mortality rate is the highest in the developed world and twice that of Sweden and Japan.[15] And a black man in Harlem is less likely to reach 65 years of age than a man in Bangladesh.[16]

While our health care system has these immense inadequacies, we are spending more per capita on health and more as a percentage of GNP than any other industrialized country.[17] We should begin by insuring that all Americans have access to health care: the Pepper Commission estimates this would cost $23 billion (0.4 percent of GNP) per year. We must then move to restructure the delivery system in order to begin to reduce our total health care costs toward the levels of the other major industrial countries.

---

11. Ibid.

12. *America's Third Deficit*, 16.

13. *New Directions for the Nation's Public Works* (Washington, DC: Congressional Budget Office, September 1988), 131.

14. Eugene Meyer, "A Revised Look at the Number of Uninsured Americans," *Health Affairs* 8, no. 2 (Summer 1989): 102–11.

15. *World Development Report*, New York: Oxford University Press, 1990, 233.

16. *New York Times*, December 24, 1990, 9.

17. George J. Scheiber and Jean-Pierre Poullier, "Overview of International Comparisons of Health Care Expenditures," *Health Care and Financing Review*, Annual Supplement, 1989, 1–2.

Lowering the Rising Levels of Poverty in the Richest Country on Earth

After seven years of economic growth and relatively low unemployment, poverty levels in the United States remain high in relation to other major industrial powers and higher than they were a decade ago. The distribution of the economic gains of the 1980s was highly skewed:

> The wealthy became wealthier: the after-tax incomes of those in the top 20 percent of the income distribution increased in constant dollars from $73,700 in 1981 to $92,000 in 1990;[18]
> The middle class became poorer—both absolutely and relatively. In 1983, the average American worker in business earned $281 per week, but today, in constant dollars, he or she earns only $267.[19] Ten years ago, the CEOs of the nation's 300-largest companies made on average 29 times what the average manufacturing worker did, while today the ratio is 93 to 1;[20] and
> The number of Americans below the poverty line rose 28 percent, from 24.5 million in 1978 to 32 million in 1988.[21] Worst of all, by 1987, the number of children in poverty rose to a level of almost one in five, more than the ratio in Germany or Canada.

There are many reasons for the disgracefully high poverty levels in the United States, and the problem cannot be solved overnight. A start was made in the budget action of October 1990. Relative tax rates were reduced and expenditures on programs focused on the poor—for example, Head Start—were increased. But, clearly, much more needs to be done. Should we not set as our objective reducing the percentage of children in poverty by half—to Germany's or Canada's level—by the year 2000? Money alone will not accomplish the task, but money is required—perhaps 0.5 percent of GNP per year.

Reducing the High Rate of Environmental Degradation

The United States devotes about 2 percent of GNP to the control of pollution. Much has been accomplished: our air is cleaner and our water is purer, but environmental degradation still continues at unacceptably

---

18. *New York Times,* December 16, 1990, E6.

19. Benjamin M. Friedman, "Reagan Lives," *New York Review of Books,* December 20, 1990, 29.

20. Ibid.

21. *New York Times,* November 25, 1990, 1.

high levels in many areas. Expenditures must be increased on waste control and on the control of pesticides and toxic substances. Moreover, at least a beginning must be made on the reduction of fossil fuel emissions. The total cost: at least 2.8 percent of GNP by the year 2000.[22] Of that amount, approximately 60 percent will be borne by the private sector.

Addressing Drugs, Crime, the Homeless, and Our Disgracefully Low Levels of Foreign Assistance

Our level of assistance to developing countries is disgracefully low (0.2 percent of GNP), the lowest of all industrialized countries.[23] To raise it to the OECD average and begin to attack the problems of drug abuse, crime, and the homeless, all of which interact, will lead to additional expenditures of at least 0.5 percent of GNP.

Items 2 through 8 on my list of Unmet Needs will require the expenditure of $225 to 275 billion per annum, partly by the private sector and the remainder by local, state, and federal governments. When added to the required increase of four percentage points in national savings, there is a need for a shift in expenditures equivalent to approximately eight points of GNP.[24] This is a huge adjustment. Nothing comparable has ever been attempted by any Western nation. But no other Western nation has simultaneously confronted problems as serious as those we face and yet possessed the strengths—economic, institutional, and intellectual—with which we are endowed. I believe the adjustments I propose can be accomplished without a reduction in the standard of living of the average American and with immense benefit to our society. What is needed is a 10-year program, to be carried out in a growing economy, in which there will be shifts in expenditures both within the private and public sectors and between the sectors.

It is commonly supposed that only the public sector wastes resources. But that is an erroneous belief. The private sector is wasteful as well. Let me give you some examples, one inconsequential but illustrative of the point and the other two of greater significance.

Twenty-eight percent of all unleaded gasoline sold in the United States is premium grade. But experts state that no more than 10 percent of all cars can benefit from premium fuel. Hence, there is a waste of at least

---

22. Environmental Protection Agency, as quoted in the *New York Times,* December 1990.

23. *World Development Report,* 214.

24. See the appendix for a breakdown of the 8 percent.

$3 billion per year. Of far greater importance, the average American con-
sumes nearly twice as much motor vehicle fuel per capita as the average
German.[25] There is much evidence to believe that over a decade we could
cut that differential at least in half without adversely affecting our quality
of life. This would lead to a saving of approximately $25 billion per year.

Similarly, excluding motor vehicle fuel, we in the United States
consume roughly twice as much energy per capita, and twice as much
energy per unit of GNP, as do Western Europeans and the Japanese.[26]
By increasing the efficiency with which we utilize energy to Western
European and Japanese levels, we could save over $100 billion per
year.[27] There are many more examples of potential savings that would
not adversely affect our quality of life. These savings could be diverted
to the financing of our Unmet Needs.

There are comparable opportunities for savings in the public sector. As I mentioned earlier, we buy less but spend more on health. We
must increase "efficiency" in that sector. Were we to reduce health care
costs to 10.2 percent of GNP, one-third above the average of Germany,
the United Kingdom, and Canada, we would save 1.8 percent of GNP.
In 1987, Canada and Germany spent 8.6 percent and 8.2 percent,
respectively, versus the 12 percent we would spend after providing for
the uninsured. As I will explain later, it should be possible, within five
or six years, to cut defense expenditures to 3 percent of GNP, 1.2
percentage points below the levels contemplated in the budget compromise of October 1990.

After such changes in both public and private expenditure patterns,
it is probable that a shift from the private sector to the public sector—
that is, an increase of approximately 3.3 points in the percentage of GNP
collected in the form of taxes—will be required. There is room for such
action without weakening the foundations of our economic growth. In
1987, the latest year for which data are available, the United States
devoted 30 percent of its GNP to taxes—local, state, and federal—
compared to 37.5 percent for both Great Britain and Germany (45
percent for France!).[28] In order to finance the restructuring of our soci-

---

25. *Driving Forces* (Washington, DC: World Resources Institute, December 1990),
28.

26. *World Development Report,* 187.

27. The data, relating to energy consumption, are derived from U.S. Energy Information Administration, the Department of Energy's *Annual Review of Energy* (Washington, DC: Department of Energy, 1990) and from the *1990 Statistical Abstract* (Washington,
DC: U.S. Department of Commerce, 1990).

28. *OECD Statistics on Member Countries in Figures,* Supplement to the OECD
Observer No. 164 (Paris, France: OECD, June-July 1990).

ety, we could surely move, if necessary, to cut that difference in half by the end of the century.

It will be said that the public will not support tax increases, that support for such action contributed to Walter Mondale's defeat in 1984 and to Senator Bradley's near loss in 1990, and that proposals to raise taxes were voted down across the land in 1990's state and municipal elections. But consider this: a persuasive program to address Unmet Needs has not yet been presented, and the required tax increases should amount to only a small portion of the growth dividend. That is, they would take effect in an environment of rising personal incomes and increased private consumption. Moreover, we all need to be reminded that in the 1950s, under two great presidents—one Democrat and one Republican—when our real income per capita was no more than one half of what it is today, we spent 2.5 percent of our GNP on a Marshall Plan to restore a war-torn world, including our recent enemies. At that time, at the end of the Eisenhower Administration, incremental federal tax rates on earned income were 91 percent—I paid that rate—compared to 31 percent today. Why should we not consider a Marshall Plan today, not for our enemies but for our own people—a plan shaped to realize our dreams and recapture the values and traditions that have made this nation the envy of the world.

As I mentioned earlier, we may be assisted in making the psychological transition—the required shift in mind-set—that will be necessary to initiate such fundamental changes in the management of our public and private affairs by changes in the international scene that would have seemed wildly impossible only a few months ago. It is to those to that I now turn.

Mikhail Gorbachev has initiated actions that have brought the Cold War to an end. He has emphasized on numerous occasions that modern military technologies make war between the superpowers no longer an acceptable instrument of political change. He says, "today's problems between East and West must be resolved through political means." By his actions, he has removed the very foundations on which we in the West constructed our foreign policies and defense programs for nearly half a century. Since the end of World War II, we have faced—or at least we believed we faced—the threat of communist aggression across the world. It has shaped our behavior in such disparate places as the Middle East, the Caribbean, and Vietnam. We have spent more energy, and more political and financial capital, trying to deal with Noriega, the Shah, and the contras than we have on drugs, poverty, and the decline of our schools.

Although the Cold War has ended, we in the West have hardly

begun to revise our foreign or defense policies, or our domestic economic and social programs, to reflect that proposition.

In the United States, for example, in the fiscal year ending September 30, 1990, defense expenditures totaled approximately $300 billion. In constant dollars, that is 35 percent more than a decade ago, only 6 percent less than at the height of the Vietnam War, and only 10 percent below the peak of Korean War expenditures. Moreover, many security experts, at least until recently, have forecast superpower rivalry and global conflict throughout the 1990s. In conformity with such views, the Bush Administration's five-year defense program, after incorporating the reductions of October 1990's budget compromise, projects that expenditures will decline only gradually from present levels. On that basis, defense outlays in 1995, in constant dollars, are currently projected to be at least 10 percent higher than 20 years earlier, under Richard Nixon in the midst of the Cold War.

Such a defense program is not consistent with my view of the post–cold war world.

For over 40 years, the foreign policy and defense programs of Western nations have been shaped largely by one major force: fear of, and opposition to, the spread of Soviet-sponsored communism. It will require a leap of the imagination for us to conceive of our national goals—our role—in a world not dominated by the struggle between East and West.

Before we can respond to Russia—and before we can deter and, if deterrence fails, respond properly to further Iraqi-type aggressions—we need a vision of a world that would not be dominated by that rivalry. As the Iraqi action demonstrates, it would not be a world without conflict, either conflict between disparate groups within nations or conflict extending across national borders. Racial and ethnic differences will remain. Political revolutions will erupt as societies advance. Historical disputes over political boundaries will continue. Economic differentials among nations, as the technological revolution of the twenty-first century spreads unevenly across the globe, will increase.

In the past 45 years, 125 wars, leading to 22 million deaths, have taken place in the third world. Third-world military expenditures, now approximating $220 billion per year, quintupled in constant dollars between 1960 and 1987, increasing at a rate of 7.5 percent annually compared with 2.8 percent per year in the industrialized countries.[29]

It is often suggested that the third world has been turned into an

---

29. These data are drawn from: Ruth Leger Sevard, *World Military and Social Expenditure: 1989* (Washington, DC, World Priorities, 1989).

ideological battleground by the Cold War and the rivalries of the Great Powers. That rivalry has been a contributing factor, but the underlying causes of third-world conflict existed before the origin of the Cold War and will almost certainly continue even if it ends. In those respects, therefore, the world of the future will not be different from the world of the past—conflicts within and between nations will not disappear. But despite the conflicts, I believe we should strive to move toward a world in which relations among nations will be based on the rule of law, supported by a system of collective security, with conflict resolution and peacekeeping functions performed by multilateral institutions such as the United Nations and regional organizations.

That is my vision of the post-Cold War world. It is, I believe, consistent with Roosevelt's and Churchill's conception of the post-World War II world. In contrast to my vision, many political theorists today predict a return to the power politics of the nineteenth century. They claim that as ideological competition between East and West is reduced, there will be a reversion to more traditional relationships. They say that major powers will be guided by basic territorial and economic imperatives: that the United States, former USSR, China, Japan, and Eastern Europe will seek to assert themselves in their own regions while competing for dominance in other areas of the world where conditions are fluid.

This view has been expressed by Michael J. Sandel, a political theorist at Harvard, who was quoted in the *New York Times* of December 31, 1989 as stating, "The end of the Cold War does not mean an end of global competition between the Superpowers. Once the ideological dimension fades, what you are left with is not peace and harmony, but old-fashioned global politics based on dominant powers competing for influence and pursuing their internal interests."[30]

Professor Sandel's conception of relations among nations in the post–Cold War world is historically well founded, but I would argue that it is not consistent with the increasingly interdependent world— interdependent economically, environmentally, and in terms of security—into which we are now moving. In that interdependent world, I do not believe any nation will be able to stand alone. The UN Charter offers a far more appropriate framework for relations among nations in such a world than does the doctrine of power politics.

In contrast to Professor Sandel, Carl Kaysen, former director of the Institute of Advanced Studies at Princeton, wrote in a recent edition of *International Security* that

---

30. M. J. Sandel, *New York Times,* December 31, 1989.

The international system that relies on the national use of military force as the ultimate guarantor of security, and the threat of its use as the basis of order, is not the only possible one. To seek a different system . . . is no longer the pursuit of an illusion, but a necessary effort toward a necessary goal.[31]

This is exactly what I propose we undertake.

Gorbachev's initiatives present us with an opportunity to move toward just such a conception of the post–Cold War world, a world in which order would be maintained through international cooperation and support for a system of collective security.

Had we made clear that was our objective, and that the Great Powers would not only pursue their own political interests through diplomacy without the use of military force but would seek to protect third-world nations against attack by other nations, the Iraqi invasion of Kuwait might well have been deterred.

While steps are being taken to reduce the danger to Great Powers of political conflict and to establish a worldwide system of collective security, the arms control negotiations now underway should be expanded rapidly in scope and accelerated in time. Both short-term and long-term objectives should be set for the process.

The short-term agenda should be obvious: early completion of the START talks, which I will label START I; further progress in the restructuring and balancing of conventional forces in Europe, which I will designate as CFE I; and, in association with the conventional force adjustments, large reductions in tactical nuclear forces.

START I and CFE I should be followed very quickly by what I will call START II and III and CFE II and III. We should now begin to set goals for those follow-on treaties.

START I will result in reductions of 10 to 20 percent in each side's strategic nuclear war heads, say from 12,000 to something on the order of 8 to 10,000. START II could well cut those totals to 5,000. A reduction in NATO's strategic nuclear forces to 5,000 warheads, when matched by the Soviets, would still permit—irrational as it may appear—approximately the same coverage as we have today of Soviet military targets.

CFE I calls for balancing Warsaw Pact and NATO forces at levels 10 to 15 percent below NATO's 1989 conventional force levels. I would favor levels for CFE II and III as low as those proposed by the former

---

31. Carl Kaysen, "Is War Obsolete? A Review Essay." *International Security* 14, no. 4: 42–64.

Supreme Allied Commander in Europe, General Goodpaster, who recommended cuts in conventional forces to 50 percent of NATO's 1989 strength.

Such a short-term program will greatly improve crisis stability. However, after it is completed, NATO and the Warsaw Pact nations will retain thousands of nuclear warheads. The danger of nuclear war—the risk of destruction of our societies—will have been reduced but not eliminated. Can we go further? Surely the answer must be "yes."

With existing nuclear forces totaling in excess of 50,000 warheads, with the Cold War ended, and with the danger of proliferation of weapons of mass destruction increasing with every passing day, should we not begin immediately to debate the merits of alternative long-term objectives for the nuclear forces of existing nuclear powers, choosing, for example, from the following?:

A continuation of the present "counterforce strategy" but with each side limited to approximately 3,000 warheads instead of 12,000; or

A minimum deterrent force for each side of perhaps 500 warheads; or

As I myself would urge, a return, insofar as practicable, to a nonnuclear world.

And should we not debate as well how best to deal with the proliferation of weapons of mass destruction—with Saddam after Kuwait? If we truly wish to stop proliferation, I see no alternative to some form of collective, coercive force by order of the Security Council.

As we move to limit nuclear forces and as we complete Gorbachev's plan for restructuring and reducing conventional forces, Western defense budgets, while providing for collective action against military aggression wherever it may occur, can be reduced substantially. In the case of the United States, as I have indicated, I believe it should be possible, within five or six years, to cut military expenditures in half in relation to GNP; that is, from 6 percent in 1989 to 3 percent. That would make available, in 1989 dollars and in relation to 1989 GNP, $150 billion per year.[32]

The actions I have proposed give the people of the United States

---

32. A collective security regime, of the type I propose, should permit the third world as well to make substantial reductions in military expenditures. It should be able to save at least $100 billion a year, a sum twice as large as its annual receipts of development assistance from the OECD countries.

high confidence that we can move down a path that provides for terminating the Cold War, for establishing a system of collective security, and for addressing our pressing domestic economic and social problems. With such a shift in foreign and domestic policy, the long-term outlook for the United States will be brighter than at any time in the past half century.

As a nation, we are in the forefront of the technological revolution. We have the largest common market in the world. We possess a flexible, skilled labor force (albeit one that requires large investments in continuing education and training), strong capital markets, adventuresome entrepreneurs, and stable political institutions. With these strengths, the United States is uniquely situated to move into the twenty-first century as the strongest of the nations in a multipolar world in which there will be a far lower risk of war between the Great Powers.

It is true, as Paul Kennedy says, that in the twenty-first century the relative power of the United States will be less. But no nation will have greater power. And in absolute terms, we can be far stronger than today, economically, politically, and psychologically. There need then be no divergence, as there has been in recent years, between our ideals—our belief in representative government, individual liberty, and economic and social advance for all peoples—and our behavior both at home and abroad.

If together we in the West are bold—if we dare to break out of the mind-sets of the last four decades—we can help reshape our own societies, as well as other nations, in ways that will lead to a far more peaceful and a far more prosperous world for the peoples of East and West as well as North and South.

It is the first time in my adult life that we have had such an opportunity. Pray God that we seize it.

APPENDIX: A PROGRAM OF NATIONAL REVIVAL, UNMET NEEDS AND HOW TO FINANCE THEM

Note: The estimates of the costs of meeting Unmet Needs and the estimates of the sources of funds for such expenditures are approximations only, but they are believed to be sufficiently representative to point to the action our society should initiate. (R.M.)

Unmet Needs	*% of GNP*
1a. Increase savings to support capital investment for growth.	2.0

1b.	Increase savings to finance retirement accounts.	2.0
2.	Strengthen primary and secondary education.	0.5
3.	Strengthen scientific and technological advance.	1.0
4.	Rebuild the physical infrastructure.	0.5
5.	Provide health care for 31 million uninsured.	0.4
6.	Lower the number of citizens—particularly children—living in poverty.	0.5
7.	Reduce the rate of environmental deterioration.	0.8
8.	Address: widespread drug abuse, rising crime levels, the problems of the homeless, and disgracefully low levels of assistance to developing countries.	0.5
	Total	8.2

Sources of Finance		*% of GNP*
1.	Reduce gasoline consumption per capita to a level 50 percent greater than Germany's level.	0.4
2.	Reduce energy consumption (excluding motor fuel) per unit of GNP to Western European and Japanese levels.	1.5
3.	Reduce health expenditures, as a percentage of GNP, to 10.2 percent—50 percent above the average of Germany, the United Kingdom, and Canada.	1.8
4.	Reduce defense expenditures, as a percentage of GNP, 30 percent below the current level planned by the Bush Administration.	1.2
5.	Raise tax revenues as a percentage of GNP from 30 percent to 33.3 percent compared to Germany's and Britain's 37.5 percent, by allocating a small portion of the growth dividend to tax increases.	3.3
	Total	8.2

BIBLIOGRAPHY

Congressional Budget Office. 1988. *New Directions for the Nation's Public Works*. Washington, DC: Congressional Budget Office.
Driving Forces. 1990. Washington DC: World Resources Institute (December).
Friedman, Benjamin M. 1990. "Reagan Lives." *New York Review of Books* (December 20).
Kaysen, Carl. 1990. "Is War Obsolete? A Review Essay." *International Security* 14, no. 4: 42–64.

Knack, Stephen. 1990. "Why We Don't Vote Or Say 'Thank You'." *Wall Street Journal* (December 31).

McAllister, Bill. 1990. "Study: 1 in 4 Young Black Men is in Jail or Court Supervised." *Washington Post* February 29, A3.

Moyer, Eugene. 1989. "A Revised Look at the Number of Uninsured Americans." *Health Affairs,* 8, no. 2 (Summer): 102–11 .

National Center for Education Statistics. 1989. *Digest of Educational Statistics* Washington, DC: U.S. Department of Health Education and Welfare.

National Council on Public Works Improvement. 1988. *Fragile Foundations: A Report on America's Public Works,* Washington, DC: National Council on Public Works Improvement.

New York Times, December 16, 1990, E6.

New York Times, December 19, 1990.

New York Times, December 19, 1990.

New York Times, November 25, 1990, 1.

1990 Statistical Abstract. 1990. Washington, DC: United States Department of Commerce.

Nye, Joseph S., Jr. 1990. *Bound to Lead.* New York: Basic Books.

Organization for Economic Development and Cooperation (OECD). 1990. *Statistics on Member Countries in Figures.* Paris, France: OECD.

Rasell, Edith, and Lawrence Mishel. 1990. *Shortchanging Education: How U.S. Spending on Grades K-12 Lags Behind Other Nations,* Washington, DC: Economic Policy Institute.

Saasta, Timothy. 1990. *America's Third Deficit,* Washington, DC: Center for Community Change.

Sandel, M. J. 1989. *New York Times,* December 31.

Scheiber, George J., and Jean-Pierre Poullier. 1989. "Overview of International Comparisons of Health Care Expenditures." *Health Care and Financing Review,* Annual Supplement. Baltimore, MD: U.S. Department of Health and Human Services.

Schultze, Charles L. 1992. *Memos to the President,* Washington, DC: The Brookings Institution.

Sevard, Ruth Leger. 1989. *World Military and Social Expenditure: 1989.* Washington, DC: World Priorities.

United States Energy Information Administration. 1990. *Annual Energy Review.* Washington, DC: Department of Energy.

World Development Report. 1990. New York: Oxford University Press.

Conclusion: A Moral/Economic Regime That Could Act as if the Future Matters

Neva R. Goodwin

This concluding chapter will consist of three parts, dealing with (1) the particular assumptions about rationality that shape neoclassical social science, (2) the relationship between market capitalism and the modern rise of humanitarianism, contrasting the record of history with the implications of neoclassical theory, and (3) the possibility of a broad shift in the economic/moral regime that might permit and encourage an increase in the kind of future-regardingness that has been discussed in various forms in the earlier chapters of this book. The concept that will emerge as central to the possibility of such a regime shift is familiar, but its essentially radical possibilities may not have been fully recognized. I refer to the economic concept of "internalizing externalities."

Rationality in Neoclassical Social Science

As a modern economist, I have a problem with morality: the mainstream, neoclassical paradigm in economics is built upon premises that, if followed to their logical conclusions, suggest that morality does not exist.

In most traditional views of morality, altruism and egoism are opposed. Altruism has to do with acting for the sake of others, whether or not such actions will redound to one's own interest.[1] Egoism has to do with serving one's own interests, regardless of whether one's actions will

---

1. Altruism includes "an element of conceptual generality, that is, a concern for others not based only on some limited factual relationship such as kinship but on general conceptual features which puts the 'other' on a similar footing with the agent and allows the others' interests to be weighed similarly with the agent's" (Griffin and Goldfarb 1989, 23).

help or hurt others.[2] The sets of altruistic and egoistic behavior intersect, but they are distinct sets, and each also possesses areas that do not overlap the other.

The rationality postulate of neoclassical economics—"rational economic man acts so as to maximize his perceived self-interest"—by definition excludes the possibility of nonegoistic acts. All behavior is either rationally egoistic or else it is irrational. Irrational behavior is considered to be so rare as to be almost nonexistent and is of little or no economic interest.

It is felt to be a little embarrassing to give much attention to something that does not exist—unless it is something, such as an individual or social utility function, that possesses such methodological convenience that the profession has agreed to lay aside embarrassment. By contrast to "utility," morality has practical usefulness in the world, but it has no obvious methodological advantages. Indeed, its inclusion in economic theory could even prove disruptive to elegant techniques of neoclassical economics.

However, there is now a growing awareness that our economic as well as our social well-being depends upon such elements of morality as future-regardingness, cooperation, self-restraint, responsibility, trust, trustworthiness, fairness, and the like. If we accept this as true, we then must ask: *can a social science that deduces all its understanding of human behavior from rational pursuit of self-interest adequately represent, analyze, and give policy advice on issues where morality matters?*

I believe the correct answer to that question is a negative one, which will lead to a requirement to rethink some basic aspects of economic theory. Such a rethinking is, in fact, being pursued by a number of groups within a growing movement to devise systems of economic theory that can serve, in place of Marxism, as an alternative to neoclassical economics. As a participant in this movement, I will use the remainder of this section to outline the debate on the place of morality in *economic theory*. Then, in the next section, I will come back to the place of morality in *economic behavior*. The argument of this essay will hinge critically on the gap between the two: economic theory and economic behavior.

Concern for the future—for people and events that are distant from us in time—has much in common with a more general topic of moral

---

2. "The price system can . . . be attacked on the grounds that it harnesses motives which our ethical systems frequently condemn. . . . We are always disturbed by a system which relies completely on selfish motives. These motives are selfish in the strict, literal sense of the word. They pertain only to the individual; he, by definition, can ignore the rest of the world" (Arrow 1974, 21).

thought and feeling: the concern for other people who are separated from us in space. This symmetry was expressed by the nineteenth-century utilitarian philosopher-economist Henry Sidgwick:

> If the Utilitarian has to answer the question, "Why should I sacrifice my own happiness for the greater happiness of another?" it must surely be admissible to ask the Egoist, "Why should I sacrifice a present pleasure for one in the future? Why should I concern myself about my own future feelings any more than about the feelings of other persons?" . . . Grant that the Ego is merely a system of coherent phenomena, that the permanent identical "I" is not a fact but a fiction, as Hume and his followers maintain; why, then, should one part of the series of feelings into which the Ego is resolved be concerned with another part of the same series, any more than with any other series?[3]

Why, indeed, should any one person, or any one "series of feelings," be concerned with another, whether that other is separated only by the boundary of the skin, is distant in space, or is distant in time? This question arises out of a confrontation with what Charles Sabel calls liberalism (a position to which I will generally refer as neoclassical rationalism), with its "paralyzing belief that present preferences inevitably rule."[4] Referring to mutual dependence as "the precondition of both individuality and sociability," Sabel states:

> What precise bearing this mutual dependence has for economic exchanges is another open question, to which one might expect a wide range of answers, depending on circumstances. The answer one would *not* expect is precisely the one liberalism, in the sense intended here, has taught us to count on: that by our nature we cannot discuss the question as though the discussion could be consequential.[5]

Michael McPherson is a leading spokesperson for the minority view, that economics must take account of moral behavior.[6] He notes that

---

3. Henry Sidgwick, quoted in Sen 1977, 343.
4. Charles Sabel, quoted in Sengenberger and Pyke 1990, 223.
5. Ibid., 223.
6. This view is held by only a minority of economists, but those that do hold it are well represented in the bibliographies for this author's contributions to this book, including this concluding essay, the introduction, and "Economic Meanings of Trust and Responsibility" (chap. 2). Especially prominent representatives of this "minority view" include Arrow, Etzioni, Frank, Hirschman, McPherson, and Sen.

the moral ideas of the participants in the economy *themselves*—their willingness to restrain their pursuit of self-interest within morally prescribed limits—is essential to normal economic functioning. Thus morality is an important part of the reality economists try to understand. Even market economies (to reduce a central theme of this literature to a slogan) are built not only in mutual interest but also on mutual trust.[7]

Such observations are not new. Adam Smith was well aware of how society is built upon accepted standards such as justice:

> Society cannot subsist among those who are at all times ready to hurt and injure one another. . . . Society may subsist, though not in the most comfortable state, without beneficence; but the prevalence of injustice must utterly destroy it. . . . Justice is the main pillar that upholds the whole edifice. If it is removed, the great, the immense fabric of human society . . . must in a moment crumble into atoms.[8]

Modern theories of rationality often emphasize such game-theoretic matters as the "prisoner's dilemma" wherein each person chooses a suboptimal outcome because of his or her reluctance to be the "sucker" who trusts inappropriately. By contrast, we find in a collection of essays from King's College, Cambridge, called *Trust: Making and Breaking Cooperative Relations,* such comments as this by John Dunn: "A purposeful determination to avoid being a sucker . . . if generalized to the human race, would subvert human sociality more or less in its entirety."[9] The authors and editor of this volume evidently found that much of what is true of trust is also true of that thing (trustworthiness or responsibility) on which trust depends, as well as of the further possibilities, such as cooperation or social cohesion, which, in turn, depend on trust.

The neoclassical focus upon self-interest has been fruitful in many ways, but it is a beam of light that leaves some important things outside of its illumination. Here is Kenneth Arrow's description of some of the important material that lies beyond the neoclassical flashlight:

> there are two types of situations in which the simple rule of maximizing profits is socially inefficient: the case in which costs are not paid

---

7. See McPherson 1984, 71.
8. See Smith 1982, 86.
9. In Gambetta 1988, 85. See also Streeten's list in the introduction to this volume.

for, as in pollution, and the case in which the seller has considerably more knowledge about his product than the buyer, particularly with regard to safety. In these situations it is clearly desirable to have some idea of social responsibility, that is, to experience an obligation, whether ethical, moral, or legal.[10]

In *The Limits of Organization,* Arrow expands upon the way uncertainty shapes the requirements for trust and responsibility in a market economy. Of more interest to our present discussion is the first set of exceptions, regarding externalities, public goods, and related issues. The study of these has too often been limited by the rather narrow definitions of rationality that emerge in such game-theoretic concepts as the tragedy of the commons or the prisoner's dilemma. James Coleman states:

> It is when there are consequences of action for actors who have no control over it that neoclassical economic theory bogs down. The action in such a case has externalities (positive and negative), or is a public good (or bad), with consequences that cannot be arbitrarily restricted. The central problem that arises for rational choice theory in such situations is that these consequences of the action, experienced by actors other than the actor or actors in control of the action, do not enter the latter's utility function.[11]

In the last section of this essay, I will return to the critically important issue of externalities that was just raised. Here, however, I will continue to pursue what I see as the neoclassical paradox of morality. It may be stated as follows: elements of morality such as trust, justice, cooperation, future-regardingness, and the like, are evidently necessary for the organization of an economic and social life that is neither collapsed into chaos nor paralyzed by bureaucracy. Yet there is insufficient space for their existence in a world described by the neoclassical view of rationality; however, we do not all live under conditions of collapse or paralysis—so we know these elements of morality must exist.

What is one to conclude? Ernest Gellner, in an article called "Trust, Cohesion, and the Social Order," wryly remarks on how to explain morality: "in the absence of a designer and creator, the favorite logical substitutes are our old friends, natural selection and logical foresight."[12]

---

10. Arrow 1973, 309.
11. James Coleman, in Radin and Bernholz 1987, 138–39.
12. Ernest Gellner, in Gambetta 1988, 145.

Patrick Bateson, in the same volume, takes on natural selection to explain the three ways in which cooperation could arise:

> The first explanation is that, at least in the past, the aided individuals were relatives; cooperation is like parental care and has evolved for similar reasons. The second is that the cooperative behavior generated characteristics in a collection of individuals that, under special conditions, favored such groups over those that did not cooperate so effectively. Finally, cooperating individuals jointly benefited even though they were not related; the cooperative behavior has evolved because those who did it were more likely to survive as individuals and reproduce than those who did not. The three evolutionary explanations are not mutually exclusive.[13]

The danger of the evolutionary approach is that it may be used to explain too much. It contains what at some times becomes a naive assumption, that everything that happens (from the simplest choice, between red or blue thread, to the most momentous one, of whether to send an army, a multinational corporation, or a team of doctors into a neighboring state) is programmed, down to the smallest details, in our genes. (If it is not in our genetic makeup, it is not subject to biological evolutionary explanations.)

Without taking on, here, the thorny issue of free will, I would note that the natural sciences have, in this century, found the world to be far less deterministic than had been expected. Physics does not have much to say about choice, but it is eloquent on the large role of chance and has achieved a comfortable modus vivendi with chaos. Like rational choice theory, modern forms of social Darwinism, such as sociobiology, fail to recognize the possibly large area of human (and other animal) behavior that occurs within the context of characteristics and capabilities selected by the evolutionary process but that, itself, occurs neither *because of* nor *in spite of* any direct evolutionary significance.[14]

As for logical foresight (Gellner's other option), McPherson puts that in the context of the three dominant approaches used by economists

---

13. Patrick Bateson, in Gambetta 1988, 14–15.

14. For an exceptionally incisive analysis of the weaknesses of sociobiological attempts to explain either why altruism exists, or that it could not exist, see Mary Midgley, *Beast and Man: The Roots of Human Nature* (New York: Cornell University Press, 1979). I have also dealt with this issue in *Social Economics: An Alternative Theory* (Goodwin 1991, London: Macmillan; New York: St. Martin's Press), chapter 11; it may be expected to return again, also, in vol. 3 of this series.

to account for the surprising fact that morality manages to exist at all. One of these is reductionism, which "attempts to show that all apparently moral behavior is actually rooted in self-interest" (McPherson, 76). The second approach, functionalism, "assumes that the fact that morality is economically beneficial, or 'functional,' for society is enough to explain its presence" (78). The third, instrumentalism, "is similar to functionalism in assuming that moral conduct exists because of the social benefits it produces, but it differs in assuming that the 'rulers' of society consciously aim to produce those benefits" (79).

These explanations, taken together, go a good part of the way toward indicating why, if not how, societies might evolve mechanisms to reinforce moral behavior on the part of individuals and groups (such as firms). Evolutionary theory can give some hints as to why human nature might have evolved so that, for example, "trust at a basic personal level is psychologically rewarding."[15] Neoclassical theory reluctantly discovers that morality may at least *appear* to exist and that that appearance *might* be encouraged if it is useful to society. Neither of these intellectual arenas offers much answer to the questions posed by McPherson: "Where does all this wonderful moral stuff come from? And how can we get some more?"[16] However, I believe that part of the answer to this question, provoked by the neoclassical theory of capitalist economy, can be found in an examination of capitalism itself.

Market Capitalism and the Modern Rise of Humanitarianism

The discussion of the previous section was intended to indicate the scope of the problems we encounter if, as social scientists, we attempt to grapple with issues of morality. *As* issues of morality, they are apt simply to be explained out of existence by the neoclassical version of rationalism that is dominant not only in economics but also in sociology and which is spreading to other branches of the social sciences as well. This is a problem because it is difficult to think and write about something after it has been explained away.

Some would suggest that the reason for the tension between neoclassical theory and the reality of moral motives is that capitalism is antithetical to morality. The paradox is that one of the strengths of a market system is its use of an impersonal system for making many societal decisions, while the growing complexity and ever increasing interdependency of

---

15. David Good, in Gambetta 1988, 32.
16. Ibid., 76.

individuals in modern market economies results in an increasing, not a lessening, need for moral behavior on a personal level.

The neoclassical social sciences have come down predominantly on one side of this paradox. In fact, I will argue that it is not capitalism—an economic *system*—that is antithetical to morality. It is neoclassical *theory* that asserts, for example, "that firms ought to maximize profits: not merely that they like to do so but there is practically a social obligation to do so."[17]

The author of this statement apologized for the possible effect of such theory, saying "[p]rofit maximization has yet another effect on society. It tends to point away from the expression of altruistic motives."[18] The two-way interaction between economic theory and economic reality includes the danger I have emphasized, of an undesirable feedback from theory to reality. It also includes the expectation that reality will be reflected in theory. In section 2 of my earlier essay in this volume (see chap. 2), I criticized the inadequate fulfillment of that expectation, suggesting that there are strong forces (including some of those studied in the field of sociology of science) that weaken the tropism that economic theory might be expected to have toward reality. In the remainder of this essay, I will express a relatively optimistic view of the actual effects of capitalism—the economic system that is supposed to be described by neoclassical economic theory. I will suggest that capitalism, which depends so strongly upon trust and responsibility, still finds these qualities reasonably current, in spite of the possibly negative effects of the economic theory that is used to describe capitalism.

In particular it appears that, unlike its theoretical reflection, and in spite of all the many criticisms that can justly be leveled against this system of economic organization, nevertheless capitalism may actually have a positive effect upon public and private morality. In making this point, I will refer especially to historian Thomas Haskell's essay on "Capitalism and the Origins of the Humanitarian Sensibility," which contains a wealth of intriguing historical and philosophical insights.[19] It is worth quoting at some length Haskell's description of the character of capitalism:

> [B]oth friends and foes of capitalism often read into technical analyses of wage and price movements a very simple message: since the laws of supply and demand automatically transmute each individ-

---

17. Arrow 1973, 304.
18. Ibid., 306.
19. See Haskell, Part I, 1985a; and Haskell, Part II, 1985b.

ual's self-interest into the greater good of the greater number, no one need be concerned with the public interest. Once this lesson with its time bomb of antitraditional implications was incorporated into common sense, the very possibility of moral obligation was put in doubt; the burden of proof henceforth rested on those who wished to deny that "everything is permitted." If we couple this familiar line of argument with the rich nineteenth-century folklore about avaricious landlords and piratical factory owners, and then add to that combination the metahistorical imagery of a class of me-first bourgeois individualists displacing a feudal aristocracy still enmeshed in a traditional web of clientage and patronage relations, we will indeed scarcely see how the coming of capitalism could have expanded the conventional boundaries of moral responsibility. And yet it did. . . . [C]ontrary to romantic folklore, the marketplace is not a Hobbesian war of all against all. Many holds are barred. Success ordinarily requires not only pugnacity and shrewdness but also restraint.

The market presents another face—perhaps equally unsmiling but suggesting quite different conclusions—as soon as we think of it as the abolitionists and their generation often did: *as an agency of social discipline or of education and character modification.* Adam Smith's "invisible hand" was, after all, not merely an economic mechanism but also a sweeping new mode of social discipline that displaced older, more overt forms of control precisely because of its welcome impersonality and the efficiency with which it allocated goods and resources. The spread of competitive relationships not only channeled behavior directly, encouraging people through shifting wage and price levels to engage in some activities and disengage from others, but also provided an immensely powerful educational force, capable of reaching into the depths of personal psychology. The market altered character by heaping tangible rewards on people who displayed a certain calculating, moderately assertive style of conduct, while humbling others whose manner was more unbuttoned or who pitched their affairs at a level of aggressiveness either higher or lower than the prevailing standard. (Haskell, Part II, 1985b, 549–50; emphasis added.)

Haskell's essay is motivated by the questions: Why was slavery, a practice that had been accepted through most of human history, finally found to be unacceptable and abolished in the nineteenth century? What, if any, was the relationship between this dramatic fact and the development of capitalism?

I will broaden Haskell's questions; where his paper focuses on the abolition of slavery, I will consider the wider list of reforms, not only those that occurred in the period he discusses, but others that have occurred since.[20] Haskell's closely reasoned analysis (of which some examples will be given below) of the relationship between the socioeconomic system of market capitalism and the abolitionist movement can be extended to shed light upon most, perhaps all, of the other reforms I will cite. I will not attempt (though the subject deserves such attention) a detailed consideration of the different ways in which Haskell's analysis would apply to the other reforms but will go on to discuss how this history provides the backdrop for an optimistic projection for further rapprochements between capitalism and some of the better impulses of the human character, including concern for the future. For reasons that will become clear later, I will emphasize that all the examples to be given are of situations in which the strong have, to some important extent *voluntarily,* made transfers of power to the weak.

Beyond the primary example emphasized by Haskell—the fact that slavery is now everywhere illegal (even if not everywhere extinct)— other instances of voluntary transfers of power and/or resources from the strong to the weak include:

The treatment of convicted criminals. There has been wide progress in acceptance of laws against brutal treatment of prisoners (although one must also note the less-than-universal existence of such laws, and frequent violations even where they do exist).
A progressive alteration in the way political leaders view the relationship they have with their people. This change has become especially (but not uniquely) noticeable in the recent wave of democratization. Its earlier form (which some parts of the world are still awaiting) was the shift from regarding political leadership

---

20. Haskell notes that

An unprecedented wave of humanitarian reform sentiment swept through societies of Western Europe, England and North America in the hundred years following 1750. Among the movements spawned by this new sensibility, the most spectacular was that to abolish slavery. Although its morality was often questioned before 1750, slavery was routinely defended and hardly ever condemned outright, even by the most scrupulous moralists. About the time that slavery was being transformed from a problematical but readily defensible institution into a self-evidently evil and abominable one, new attitudes began to appear on how to deter criminals, relieve the poor, cure the insane, school the young, and deal with primitive peoples. The resulting reforms were, by almost any reasonable standard, an improvement over old practices that were often barbarous. (Haskell, Part I, 1985a, 339)

simply as an opportunity for personal and family enrichment and power to the growing belief and expectation that the leader represents the led and must identify with their interests.[21]

Improvements in the treatment of the mentally ill. Such persons have been treated miserably throughout much of human history. In Europe, in the nineteenth and early twentieth centuries, there began to be a significant change related to science and medicine, on the one side, and to growing humanitarian sensibilities, on the other.

The enfranchisement of women, with continuing progress toward equal treatment of the sexes in various parts of society, in spite of the power disadvantage that women have because of (on average) less physical strength and a greater willingness to accept disadvantageous personal bargains for the sake of male support in child rearing.

Progress in the treatment of the indigent: the idea that one of the obligations of government is to organize society to provide some sort of "safety net" for those who are destitute, and rejection of the belief that poverty is divinely ordained and not a subject for human intervention.

The end of the colonial era. Gathering momentum at the end of the end of the Second World War, and continuing through the breakup of the Soviet empire, we see a remarkable movement, motivated by many forces, to begin to undo at least the most overt forms of the tragedy of colonialism.

Recognition of the rights of many kinds of minorities (including groups that stand out by reason of ethnicity, religion, or sexual preference) and of the necessity to make special arrangements for their protection and advancement when they dwell in a hostile social environment.

Acceptance of the obligation to make special efforts to integrate the physically handicapped into society and to give them the means for a full and satisfying life.

Recognition that the values and interest of every member of a

---

21. For an excellent discussion, see Lindblom 1977, chap. 9. A summary comment is this: "The contemporary common rule that authority be specific—that A exercise authority over B only in specified circumstances for a specified category of responses—man can claim as one of his greatest inventions" (27).

Michel Foucault has "deconstructed" these reforms to expose them as being, in his view, motivated by sadism and a craving for power no less marked than the situations they replaced. Whatever one may think of this analysis of motive, I find it hard to see the results as inferior or equal to the preexisting situations.

family group are not necessarily well represented by its dominant member. This leads to attempts to reduce spouse and child abuse as well as to a growing consensus that societies at large must accept a basic level of responsibility for children's protection and welfare.

An animal rights movement that has grown slowly but persistently.

Most recently, going beyond the animal rights movement, there is a growing effort to inject into the spreading context of Western impositions of control over nature a respect for "rights" or values that are seen to be inherent in nature. (In many places, this trend is new only because Western rationalism is new, creating problems that must be undone by new or rediscovered values and attitudes.)

Several caveats can be made about this list. For one thing, it is most relevant to Europe and North America; the items listed in it have different meanings in different parts of the world. Nor is progress in each case simple or unidirectional; there are enough examples of slippages in any one of the categories to prevent complacency. Nor would I dare to say that this record shows an overall improvement in the moral character of humanity: this century's purges, tortures, and mass murders have set gruesome historical records.

How is one to balance progress in some areas against atrocities in others? I do not believe there is a meaningful "bottom line" to be drawn for this ledger. We must be sobered by what the twentieth century has shown about how horrible our species can be, even while we survey a list of changes and trends that are, I believe, relevant and true for enough of humanity so as to offer a basis for some hope. Pessimists would say that the best that can be said of this list is that it represents progress in public espousals of morality. There are uncountable instances of deviation from such a morality, but perhaps it is too much to expect that a few decades, or even a century or two, of a new public sensibility could yet be translated with any consistency into improved behavior. The optimism expressed in this essay depends rather heavily upon taking a long historical view.

In spite of these caveats, we may note some important generalizations about the list offered above. Every instance concerns groups that generally lack the political, physical, or other strength to claim for themselves power, resources, or protection: slaves; convicts; colonial subjects; the mentally or physically handicapped; children; unpopular religious, ethnic, or other minorities; women; the indigent; and, generally, the proletariat, or *hoc genus omne*; animals, and, more generally, the natural world (whose power is often not felt in the short run, even though it may dwarf human power in the long run). Improvements in the treatment of these groups have been based upon largely voluntary acts, wherein people (who felt they had some choice in whether to give or to withhold) relinquished some of their own claims upon power or resources.

Relating these changes to the effect of the spread of capitalism, I will begin with Haskell's thesis, that

> Whatever influence the rise of capitalism may have had generally on ideas and values through the medium of class interest, it had a more telling influence on the origins of humanitarianism through changes the market wrought in *perception* and *cognitive style*. And it was primarily a change in cognitive style—specifically a change in the perception of causal connection and consequently a shift in the conventions of moral responsibility—that underlay the new constellation of attitudes and activities that we call humanitarianism. (Haskell, Part I, 1985a, 342.)

Noting that "new techniques, or ways of intervening in the course of events, can change the conventional limits within which we feel responsible enough to act" (Part I, 1985a, 356; see also Haskell 1993), Haskell suggests that the character of a market economy empowers individuals by making them aware of causal connections between individual acts (or failures to act) and the sufferings of others. He stresses the interplay of a new form of economic life with a moral sensibility: "the very possibility of feeling obliged to go to the aid of a suffering stranger . . . was enormously heightened by the emergence of a form of life that makes attention to the remote consequences of one's life (or omissions) an emblem of civilization itself" (Part II, 1985b, 562). Haskell cites "two 'lessons' taught (and simultaneously presupposed) by the market . . . the first taught people to keep their promises; the second taught them to attend to the remote consequences of their action" (Part II, 1985b, 551). With regard to the second of these lessons, he stresses the close interrelationship between future-regardingness and the idea of "principle," so ascendent during the early entrepreneurial phase of capitalism:

> The defining characteristic of the "man of principle," the moral paragon of a promise-keeping, market-centered form of life, was his willingness to act on principle no matter how inconvenient it might be. Comparatively speaking, he cared little for the short-term consequences of his actions and was firmly convinced that in the long run adherence to the highly generalized maxims of conduct

that he called principles would produce the most desirable out-comes. (560)

In sum, the whole socioeconomic system of beliefs, technologies, knowledge, institutions, and modes of behavior which Haskell refers to as capitalism contains within it two opposing forces. One, which has been codified in neoclassical social science, especially economics, empha-sizes a concern for self-interest that can be, and most often is, inter-preted as short-term selfishness. The other, more often found in practice than in theory, provides the self-confidence, restraint, and understand-ing that, when united with feelings of sympathy and empathy, was strong enough to persuade modern societies to set aside increasing portions of their wealth and power for the protection and support of groups who could not, on their own, effectively command such support.

Though the record of changed standards and (to a somewhat lesser extent) changed behavior is impressive, one cannot help but respond to it with a sharpened awareness of how much remains to be done—the prisons that are still ineffective with respect to their objectives and inhu-mane with respect to their conditions; the inability of modern societies to treat all groups fairly while still ensuring attention to the caretaking tasks on which the well-being of the old, the ill, and the children depend; the number of children who die from malnourishment and, of those who live, the number who suffer a stunted adulthood; and so on.

Among the areas that still cry out for reform, one of the most widely recognized is the area of relationship between humans and nature—which translates, often, to a relationship between humans who are getting rich *here* and others who are getting ill *there,* or between humans who are making money *now* and others who will have to pay for the cleanup *in the future.* Environmentalists are increasingly insisting that the strong (including the wealthy) must relinquish some of their privileges, especially with respect to production and consumption, if the biosphere is to survive as a system capable of supporting anything we would call civilization. This altered balance of power must be made voluntarily; if the weak were able to effect such a change by compulsion, they would, almost by definition, not be weak.

But why might the rich people and nations of the world be willing to make sacrifices to move the human race toward shared sufficiency and sustainable development? The neoclassical answer to such a question can only refer to the self-interest that might, for example, motivate the industrial nations to make grants to cover technology transfer to im-prove the efficiency with which the poorer nations produce what they need. However, there is a problem in referring to self-interest as if it were the only relevant motivating force.

Self-interest is most forcefully felt in the local and short-term framework that has led to the rational choice school's prediction that the ideal achievement is to be a free rider while public goods are provided by others. The kind of long-run self-interest that is involved in preserving the global commons, alleviating poverty in distant parts of the earth, and planning for the future, often in fact conflicts with narrow, short-term selfishness. Those who appeal to self-interest to motivate generous acts may lose their way in the thickets of short-termism before they manage to make contact with the broader self-interest that identifies the self and its interests with a community stretching out to encompass our whole species or even the whole biosphere.

If we are going to find reasons to expect any continuation of the trend of voluntary transfer of power from the strong to the weak, we must not forget or ignore self-interest. Neither, however, should we expect that the principle of self-interest can, alone, take on this burden, in addition to all the other tasks allotted to it under the neoliberal understanding of capitalism. Fortunately, when we revisit early misinterpretations both of evolutionary theory and of sociobiology, we will find that these sciences do not oblige us to understand the whole of human nature as summed up in the neoclassical rationality postulate.

Interlinked Forces for Change

We have seen how the rationality postulate of neoclassical thought has percolated through the deductive system of modern economics, ultimately throwing out of bounds serious consideration of moral behavior. In order to escape this limitation and to illuminate important areas of human (including economic) concern that lie beyond the light shed by neoclassical economics, it is necessary to propose an alternative view of human nature, as being something more than the condition described in the statement: "rational economic man only acts so as to maximize his perceived self-interest."

A reasonable alternative is to consider human nature as a set of options, or potentialities: for empathy, sympathy, concern, honesty, cooperation, future-regardingness—or for selfishness, shortsightedness, brutality, sadism, and the like.[22] Any of these characteristics can be real,

---

22. We can easily find examples of brutality and sadism that are neither more nor less "rational" than a collection of examples of altruism and disinterested honesty. One interpretation of the rationality postulate, which by definition obliges it to be true, says

even "normal," for a given person who has had life experiences that enhanced them. A particular characteristic may, of course, exist more strongly in one newborn infant than in another, so that it might be nearly impossible to turn *this* individual into a sadist or *that* one into an altruist. With all these points accepted (and assuming they are not in direct conflict with what we know of evolution), we have no a priori reason to be *surprised* at the appearance of one or another of these characteristics. Our job is not to explain the "unexpected" appearance of either altruism of selfishness—neither is unexpected—but rather, given the diverse potentialities of human nature, to ask what the social sciences should do about it.

In attempting to answer that question, we may turn to the recent focus upon the broad effects of economic activities, especially those effects (called externalities) whose costs or benefits are not borne or captured by the actors responsible for the economic behavior that generated those costs or benefits. (Air or water polluted by industrial or farming activities are examples of negative externalities. As suggested in earlier essays in this volume, businesses can create positive externalities, for example, by raising the skill level of the society through worker-training programs.)

One of the forces urging our attention to externalities is environmentalism, bearing with it a growing recognition of the essential truth of ecology—"everything is connected with everything else"—and the application of this awareness to the interconnections between economic behavior and social and environmental health. Another impetus comes from the widespread economic ideology of the 1980s. The prescription to "get the prices right" implied a scrutiny of the true costs and benefits of economic activity. This dovetailed nicely (if unexpectedly) with the environmental interest in tracing impacts of industrial activity to their source.

The result of these two convergent forces is a powerful growing movement to *internalize externalities* (at least, the negative ones): to ensure, that is, that *the economic entity that creates a cost will have to bear it.* (A somewhat weaker movement to internalize positive externalities would urge that the entity that creates a broader good is encouraged to go on doing so by receiving at least part of the benefit of that good.)[23]

---

that the sadistic act of the sadist and the altruistic act of the altruist are equally self-interested in that these individuals' utility functions are defined by their natures, and each is at all times—by definition—maximizing this or her utility. So tautological a postulate seems too vacuous to be of interest, or of use.

23. This tendency has been generalized as "the increasing replacement of danger by

In order to assess the likelihood that externalities will in future be internalized to a much greater extent than hitherto, we must ask, first, why have they been allowed to remain external up to now and, second, what has changed so that we can expect the future to be different in this respect?

The principal answer to the first question is power. The economic actor, X, who can avoid the costs of his or her economic activities by leaving them to be borne by a, b, and c, very often has some or all of the following characteristics:

> X is either a single actor or else a small group and is able to organize in pursuit of clearly perceived goals.
> X possesses knowledge, in particular of what is in his or her interest; he or she also knows what he or she is doing (and may deliberately conceal certain actions from a, b, and c).
> X possesses economic power.
> X possesses political power.

By contrast, a, b, and c are apt to be relatively small actors, diffuse, unorganized, ignorant of how they are being affected by X, possessing fewer financial resources, and (largely because of these characteristics) lacking in political power.

What has happened that might change this? As suggested above, environmentalism is altering the balance of power. It does so, first by increasing the knowledge possessed by a, b, and c—informing those affected by negative externalities about the ways in which individual economic actors may be off-loading some costs of their activity in the form of environmental degradation and threats to the health and safety of workers, neighbors, consumers, and other stakeholders. Environmental groups and movements, as they overcome the ignorance of a, b and c, are also taking advantage of the communications revolution to overcome the disadvantages of diffuseness (consider the growth, and the present and potential uses, of such a recent innovation as eco-net). They are also assisting the organization of those adversely affected by economic externalities. All of these changes together have a significant potential to shift power from the creators of negative externalities to those who have suffered from them.

We should note, however, that this description of the environmental movement ignores the extraordinary and growing economic and political

---

risk, that is by the possibility of future damages which we will have to consider a consequence of our own action or omission" (Luhmann, in Gambetta 1988, 105).

power of what could well be a countervailing force. The reality and the perception of globalization is enlarging the context for environmentalism. Another major force unleashed by globalization is the influence of the multinational corporations. As of 1988, there were 105 multinational corporations with annual gross revenues in the range of $10 to $119 billion. Only 14 of the world's nations had higher GNPs than that; 52 of the nations were smaller. These 105 multinational corporations ranked with the 43 medium-sized national economies.[24]

If environmentalism were all we had on which to base a hope for a shift into a new moral/economic regime that would accept and enforce the internalization of externalities, we could be looking to a massive competition in power between the publics of various nations who have become energized, informed, and empowered by environmentalist solidarity and the multinational behemoths. That is not a promising scenario: in a contest of raw power, the environmentalists and their friends are still some distance away from winning. At least it would take many more Chernobyls, Bhopals, Exxon Valdezes, and the like (occurring especially in industrialized countries) to give enough force to the environmentalist side that it would be viable in such a contest.

Fortunately, the trend toward environmentalism is backed up by something that may be able to alter the terms of the moral/economic regime so that a regime shift need not take the form (at least not solely or perhaps even principally) of a raw contest of power. What Haskell described as a rise in humanitarianism has, as we have seen, flowered into an extraordinary set of human accomplishments. Whether or not his analysis—as sweeping in its explanation of the consequences of capitalism as Weber's was for its causes—is sufficient to explain the list of reforms, the evidence stands that it *is possible* for the relatively strong voluntarily to cede power and resources to the relatively weak. It is within the realm of possibility that this trend will continue to broaden in the form of a growing (though still very vague) reduction in general willingness to allow might to make right. An additional factor may be globalism itself—the expanded transboundary relationships, communications, and consciousness which are both cause and effect of the growth of multinationals as well as of the environmental movement. Looking back, one can also discern the effects of globalization upon the growth of humanitarianism as our species has progressed, with many a faltering and backward step, toward a recognition of common humanity among a community of nations that increasingly respond to the world's opinion and the most broadly accepted global norms.

---

24. See Morss 1991, 61.

The rise of humanitarianism (in the context of capitalism or perhaps in some other context) may thus be a *necessary* precondition to permit the internalization of externalities. It is just conceivable that the addition of the other forces cited above—the unusual convergence of the environmentalist movement with economic ideology, along with a globalized recognition of common humanity—may prove *sufficient* to make an effective norm of the concept that each economic actor should pay all costs for which he or she is responsible.

It should be noted that, while the "polluter pays principle" (e.g., the requirement to internalize negative externalities) has been perceived as an environmental issue, within the new subfields that are emerging to respond to modern requirements of social science, this is as much a matter of social economics as of ecological economics.

It should also be emphasized that while the idea under discussion may appear simple, it represents a potentially enormous change. If you think, in the context of the history of colonialism and the industrial revolution, of the freedom with which industrialists have polluted, disrupted communities, and absorbed and destroyed resources—even more, if you think back to the plundering of the colonies by the nineteenth- and twentieth-century colonial empires—you will recognize what a radical proposal is "internalizing externalities."

Can it happen? In this section, we have seen the coming together of several interlinked forces: the historical trajectory of humanitarianism provides a context for the environmental movement, while the latter interacts with and supports the combination of intellectual, legal, and economic beliefs that are converging on the prescription to "internalize externalities." However, the reality of economic actors absorbing all the costs they generate will result in short-term losses that will fall in many places—not only on the rich and powerful, although probably most heavily on them. There are many situations in which those with political and economic power can arrange it so that the costs of important changes fall relatively (and sometimes absolutely) more heavily on other members of society. Will the strong use their strength to shift the burden of internalizing externalities? This question emphasizes the fact that the externalities issue is a special one whose very definition excludes such a distortion: if the wrong economic actor bears the brunt, then the externalities have *not* been internalized. This is why the movement to internalize externalities may be seen as a climactic effort in the historical picture of cumulative transfers of power from the strong (including the people of the present) to the weak (including the people of the future).

Voluntary acts (as contrasted to those imposed by law) are the most important ones in most social settings, for they are the most numerous. I have suggested that we can and should work toward social science theories that go beyond the narrow neoclassical definition of rationality to a larger view of the diverse potentialities of human nature. Such a view, including the moral basis for future-regardingness, is necessary if we are to be able to perceive, let alone understand, what is happening when people voluntarily cede present, selfish advantage for some larger good. It is even more necessary if the understanding afforded by the social sciences is to play a role in encouraging such behavior.

BIBLIOGRAPHY

Arrow, Kenneth J. 1973. "Social Responsibility and Economic Efficiency." *Public Policy* 21, no. 3, 303–17.
———. 1974. *The Limits of Organization*. New York: W.W. Norton and Company.
Ausubel, Jesse H. 1992. "Industrial Ecology: Reflections on a Colloquium." *Proceedings of the National Academy of Sciences, U.S.A.* 89 (February): 879–84.
Bateson, Patrick. 1988. "The Biological Evolution of Cooperation and Trust." In *Trust: Making and Breaking Cooperative Relations*, ed. Diego Gambetta. New York: Basil Blackwell, Ltd.
Coleman, James S. 1987. "Norms as Social Capital." In *Economic Imperialism*, ed. Gerald Radin and Peter Bernholz. New York: Paragon Press.
Dunn, John. 1988. "Trust and Political Agency." In *Trust: Making and Breaking Cooperative Relations*, ed. Diego Gambetta. New York: Basil Blackwell, Ltd.
Durkheim, Emile. 1833. *The Division of Labor in Society*. Trans. George Simpson. New York: The Free Press.
Etzioni, Amitai. 1988. *The Moral Dimension: Towards a New Economics*. New York: The Free Press.
Gambetta, Diego, ed. 1988. *Trust: Making and Breaking Cooperative Relations*. New York: Basil Blackwell, Ltd.
Gellner, Ernest. 1988. "Trust, Cohesion, and the Social Order." In *Trust: Making and Breaking Cooperative Relations*, ed. Diego Gambetta. New York: Basil Blackwell, Ltd.
Good, David. 1988. "Individuals, Interpersonal Relations, and Trust." In *Trust: Making and Breaking Cooperative Relations*, ed. Diego Gambetta. New York: Basil Blackwell, Ltd.
Goodwin, Neva R. 1991. *Social Economics: An Alternative Theory*. Vol. I, *Building Anew on Marshall's Principles*. London: MacMillan; New York: St. Martin's Press.
Griffin, William B., and Robert S. Goldfarb. 1989. "Amending the Economist's 'Rational Egoist' Model to Include Norms." Manuscript.

Haskell, Thomas L. 1985a. "Capitalism and the Origins of the Humanitarian Sensibility, Part I." *American Historical Review* 90, no. 2 (April).

————. 1985b. "Capitalism and the Origins of the Humanitarian Sensibility, Part II." *American Historical Review* 90, no. 3 (June).

Haskell, Thomas L., and R. F. Teichgraeber. 1993. "Persons as Uncaused Causes: John Stuart Mill, The Spirit of Capitalism, and the 'Invention' of Formalism." In *The Culture of the Market: Historical Essays.* Cambridge, England, and New York: Cambridge University Press.

Hirschman, Albert O. 1984. "Against Parsimony: Three Easy Ways of Complicating Some Categories of Economic Discourse." *American Economic Review,* Proceedings, no. 74, 88–96.

Lindblom, Charles. 1977. *Politics and Markets: The World's Political Economic Systems.* New York: Basic Books.

Luhmann, Niklass. 1988. "Familiarity, Confidence, Trust: Problems and Alternatives." In *Trust: Making and Breaking Cooperative Relations,* ed. Diego Gambetta. New York: Basil Blackwell, Ltd.

Marwell, Gerald, and Ruth E. Ames. 1981. "Economists Ride Free. Does Anyone Else?" *Journal of Public Economics,* no. 15.

McPherson, Michael. 1984. "Limits on Self-Seeking: The Role of Morality in Economic Life." In *Neoclassical Political Economy,* ed. David Colander. Cambridge, MA: Ballinger Publishing Company.

Midgley, Mary. 1979. *Beast and Man: The Roots of Human Nature.* Ithaca, NY: Cornell University Press.

Morss, Elliott. 1991. "The New Global Players: How They Compete and Collaborate." *World Development,* no. 1: 55–64.

Sen, Amartya K. 1977. "Rational Fools: A Critique of the Behavioral Foundations of Economic Theory." *Philosophy and Public Affairs* 6:317–44.

Sengenberger, Werner, and Frank Pyke. 1990. *Industrial Districts and Local Economic Regeneration.* Geneva: Institute for Labour Studies.

Smith, Adam. 1982. *The Theory of Moral Sentiments,* ed. D. D. Raphael and A. L. Macfie. Indianapolis: Liberty Classics.